Haifa: Transformation of a Palestinian Arab Society 1918–1939

HAIFA

Transformation of a Palestinian
Arab Society 1918–1939

MAY SEIKALY

I.B. Tauris Publishers
LONDON · NEW YORK

Published in 1995 by
I.B.Tauris & Co Ltd
45 Bloomsbury Square
London WC1A 2HY

175 Fifth Avenue
New York NY 10010

In the United States of America
and in Canada distributed by
St Martin's Press
175 Fifth Avenue
New York NY 10010

A full CIP record for this book is available from the British
Library

A full CIP record for this book is available from the Library of
Congress

ISBN 1 85043 958 3

Library of Congress catalog card number: available

Set in Monotype Baskerville by Ewan Smith, London

Printed and bound in Great Britain by
WBC Ltd, Bridgend, Mid Glamorgan

Contents

To the memory of my parents, Evelyn and Ibrahim Seikaly
And my teacher Albert Habib Hourani

Explanatory Notes

Transliteration

Arabic   Arabic terms, names of people and places which are used in British official documents have been transliterated according to the most common form appearing there. Some family names have been written in the form which the family itself normally uses. Other Arabic terms, names of people and places have been rendered according to the system of transliteration adopted by the *International Journal of Middle East Studies* (*IJMES*).

Hebrew   The form in which Hebrew names have appeared in official correspondence or in English print has been used.

Currency

Until 1927, the monetary unit in Palestine was the Egyptian pound (£E), which equalled 100 piastres (P.T.). The pound sterling was worth 97.5 Egyptian piastres. In 1927, the Palestinian pound was introduced (£P), which equalled 1,000 mils. Although there was no intermediate unit between the pound and the mil, in practice the term 'piastre' was adopted as the equivalent of ten mils. The Palestinian pound was valued at par with the pound sterling. Because of the almost negligible difference in value of these respective pounds, British officials were not always careful to distinguish among them.

Square measures (land)

Land in Palestine was measured in dunums. The old Turkish dunum was equivalent to 919.3 square metres, but the British Administration adopted a metric dunum of 1,000 square metres (about one quarter of an acre). In general, no distinction was made between the two measures despite the 8-per-cent variation.

Notes

First references to any publication in the notes to each chapter have been given in full, but subsequent references have been given in truncated form. References to archival material are notated according to the list of acronyms that follows. Unless there is a special significance attached, no differentiation is made between despatches and telegrams or official and semi-official communications. Israeli State Archives documents are numbered by record groups in accordance with the listing in the bibliography unless they were not yet classified; in this case, the full notation appearing on the file cover has been reproduced.

Acronyms

ACS	Assistant Chief Secretary
ADPS	Assistant District Police Superintendent
AE	Arab Executive
AHC	Arab Higher Committee
CA	Chief Administrator
CID	Criminal Investigation Department
CO	Colonial Office
CS	Chief Secretary
CZA	Central Zionist Archives
DC	District Commissioner
DG	District Governor
FO	Foreign Office
GFJL	General Federation of Jewish Labour
HC	High Commissioner
HMG	His Majesty's Government
IPC	Iraq Petroleum Company
ISA	Israeli State Archives
JA	Jewish Agency
JNH	Jewish National Home
ND	Northern District
OAG	Officer Administering the Government
OETA	Occupied Enemy Territory Administration
PICA	Palestine Jewish Colonization Association
PLDC	Palestine Land Development Company
PRO	Public Records Office
PWD	Public Works Department
S of S	Secretary of State
SMC	Supreme Muslim Council
YMMA	Young Men's Muslim Association
ZE	Zionist Executive
ZO	Zionist Organization

Acknowledgements

The basic research for this book was undertaken for my D.Phil. thesis at Oxford University over ten years ago. While the basic data of that research still form the nucleus of this altered study, the focus and time-span in this book have been reformulated and extended. My thesis adviser and my mentor, the late Albert Hourani, was the main moving spirit encouraging and prodding me to complete the work and publish it. It was his belief, and that of a number of Middle East historians and intellectuals, that the thesis should be published in order to fill a need in the field of Palestinian urban and socio-economic history. It is in appreciation of his insight and tremendous help in preparing the manuscript, until his passing away in 1993, that I dedicate this book to his memory. Without his intellectual help, and the emotional support of both he and Odile, this book would not have been published.

A number of institutions and a large number of people have helped and supported my efforts in the completion of this work, both during the initial period of collecting the data and the more recent work on the book manuscript; I wish to thank them collectively, although their contributions are valued and remembered separately. St. Anthony's College, its staff, and especially its Middle East Centre, the Lebanese Studies Centre, Oxford, as well as the University of California Los Angeles and its Middle East Librarian: all should be particularly thanked for the assistance rendered to me, whether by providing a congenial working atmosphere, library assistance or expert help and advice. Here I would like to single out the friendship and interest extended by Nadim Shehadi, who provided me with valuable insights and with the photographs from his extensive collection which have been used for the jacket of the book. Special gratitude goes to a number of Middle East specialists who have been generous with their time by reading all or parts of the early and later drafts of the manuscript, suggesting changes and giving invaluable advice. Among these are Walid Khalidi, Derek Hopwood, Peter Sluglett, Barbara Smith, Sarah Graham Brown, Nels Johnson, John Ruedy, Rosemarie Said Zahlan, Nancy

Gallagher, Leila Fawaz, Usama Khalidi, Pamela Smith, Sonia El-Nimr, Antoine Zahlan and Nahid Osseiran. The views and suggestions of these scholars have helped me reach my own interpretations and conclusions, for which I am solely responsible.

Particular thanks go to the late Yosef Washitz of Lehavot Habashan, Israel, whose innate scholarship and moral commitment superseded all differences between us. He made available to me his personal un-published manuscript and data of the Haifa Municipal reports and history, whose existence had been denied by the Municipality. In Israel and Haifa, my work was smoothed by the support of Butrus Abu Manneh, Alex Carmel and Moshe Maoz of the Universities of Haifa and Jerusalem respectively. Bernard Wasserstein was helpful in un-tangling the mysteries of the Israel State Archives and their selectively restrictive policies.

My unbound gratitude goes to the people of Haifa: the old men who walked with me through its streets reconstructing maps from their memories, the families who generously offered me their information, nostalgic memories and private documents, and the incredible en-thusiasm of its communities in the diaspora from Amman to London to San Diego who have enriched my work and my personal life. My own extended and spread-out family – particularly my uncles and aunts – have been a constant source of information, support and contact. However, it was my mother who remained the beacon that pushed me to persist in the project and to commemorate her memories of the city of her birth and youth.

Anna Enayat, in addition to being a supportive friend, has led me gently through the maze of publishing a book and all its intricacies. I am grateful for her continued consideration and support. The staff at I.B.Tauris, and particularly those in charge of my manuscript, have done a great job with understanding and indulgence. Margaret Cornell has been patience itself in performing the complicated editorial job of helping me transform my thesis into a book over long distances and an extended period of time. My deepest gratitude goes to her for her tolerance, cheerful disposition and professionalism. Special thanks also go to Abier Ziyadeh Shamma, who proof-read the final draft of the manuscript and drew my attention to significant last-minute corrections. The central source of my well-being and strength has been my im-mediate family, my brothers and sisters as well as my huge repertoire of close friends. My sister Maha and her children, Rania, Kareem, Ameen and Waleed, have provided me with constant stability, joy and affection.

Foreword

May Seikaly's work is an original and important contribution to the scholarship of mandatory Palestine. As a multi-dimensional profile of the growth of Haifa into one of the major cities of the eastern Mediterranean, it is perhaps unique in the field of Middle East urban studies. Its principal theme is the impact on its indigenous Arab population, both Christian and Muslim, of global British imperial policy and the implementation of the Zionist programme in Palestine in the wake of the Balfour Declaration and Britain's assumption of the Mandate for the country. At the start of the period covered by this work, Jews constituted one-eighth of Haifa's population; by the period's end, they had grown to more than 50 per cent, largely through immigration under British protection. Haifa was one of the three major locations of Jewish demographic concentration, which comprised between them almost 80 per cent of the total population of the Yishuv on the eve of the establishment of Israel.

Long before the First World War, London had identified Haifa's harbour as the 'most suitable landing site' for its troops to take in the rear an Ottoman army advancing upon the Suez Canal. Also well before the First World War, Arthur Ruppin, the master architect of Zionist colonization, had pinpointed Haifa as the fulcrum for the two major axes of Jewish settlement he envisaged: one extending southwards along the coast towards Tel Aviv (which he was instrumental in founding) and the other cutting across Palestine along the Marj Ibn Amr towards Lake Tiberias and then extending northwards towards the upper reaches of the River Jordan.

The author thoroughly covers the demographic, spatial, economic, industrial, strategic, institutional (municipal and other) and ethnic evolution of the city in the two decades between the end of the First World War and the eve of the Second World War. She marshals her data from an extraordinary range of sources, official and unofficial, British and Zionist. She supplements these with interviews stretching back to the mid-1970s with former Arab residents of Haifa in various countries of their diaspora. While she is entirely at home discussing the minutiae of British politics on town planning or municipal taxes, and the wranglings between London and the Zionist Organization on the specific site of the proposed Haifa port or the location of the Iraq Petroleum Company's terminal in Haifa bay, the trees never blur her view of the Haifa wood.

It is against the background of the convergence between British and Zionist interests in the development of Haifa, tempered to some extent in the case of the former by attempts, mostly ineffectual, to soften its impact on Haifa's Arab population, that the author develops the underlying theme of her work. This is the steady change in the balance of power within the city between its Jewish and Arab communities in favour of the former. The author analyses the emergence of a new mercantile and entrepreneurial Arab class whose characteristics were defined by the Zionist monopoly, because of superior organization and financial resources, of the city's industrial sector.

She traces the relations within the Arab community between, on the one hand, its political and mercantile elite and, on the other, the growing underclass of Palestinian villagers attracted to the city by employment opportunities afforded by its economic development. Even in the early 1920s, a senior British official remarks on the feeling of 'claustrophobia' experienced by Haifa's Arab population as a result of its encirclement by Jewish residential quarters and rural colonies. The author investigates the intra-Arab tensions as well as those between the haves and have-nots, the Christians and the Muslims, and examines the mounting sense of frustration and despair among the alienated and proletarianized Arab village immigrants from the hinterland of Galilee.

She explains how these feelings were drawn upon by the charismatic and puritanical Syrian cleric Sheikh Ez eddin al-Qassam, himself a resident of Haifa, who preached a powerful mixture of Islamic reformism and national resistance to British and Zionist policies, which crystallized in an open call to armed struggle in defence of Palestinian rights. It was this call to arms by Qassam in 1934-35, and his death in an encounter with British security forces, that forced the hands of the more moderate and conservative Palestinian Jerusalem leadership and ushered in the 1936 country-wide strike, the prelude to the Palestinian 1936-39 rebellion. The disciples of Qassam were to bear the brunt of the armed rebellion against the British, which reached its zenith in northern Palestine, where the overwhelming majority was Arab, particularly in the wake of the Peel partition proposals to incorporate the entire region in the proposed Jewish state. The author does not flinch from describing and analysing the adverse impact of this rebellion on the coherence of Haifa's Arab population and the deterioration of the revolt, as its leadership slipped into the hands of rural elements after the flight or imprisonment of the more sophisticated middle-class leadership.

The author's analysis of the socio-economic and psycho-political milieu that gave rise to the radicalization of Haifa's underclass has almost prophetic contemporary resonance. This work goes a long way to explaining why Haifa, after the sudden withdrawal of the British army, fell virtually overnight to the Haganah battalions on that fateful day, 23 April 1948. With Haifa militarily in its hands, the Zionist leadership was able to use the city's Jewish manpower for the conquest of the rest of Galilee. Indeed this work is paradigmatic in throwing light on the plight of Eastern Jerusalem today.

The text is accompanied by useful maps and statistical tables, and a poignant appendix containing the names of members of the principal families of Haifa, Christian and Muslim, now dead or scattered with their descendants to the four winds.

Walid Khalidi
Cambridge, Massachusetts

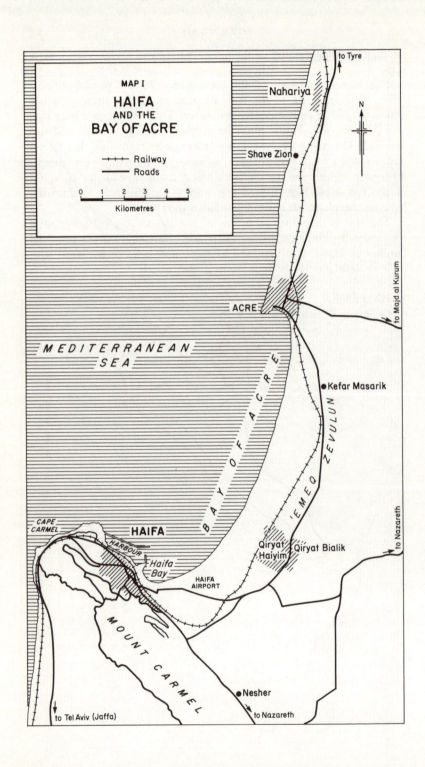

MAP I

HAIFA
AND THE
BAY OF ACRE

Railway
Roads

0 1 2 3 4 5
Kilometres

N

to Tyre

Nahariya

Shave Zion

ACRE

to Majd al Kurum

MEDITERRANEAN
SEA

Kefar Masarik

B A Y   O F   A C R E

'E M E Q   Z E V U L U N

to Nazareth

CAPE
CARMEL

HAIFA

HARBOUR

Haifa
Bay

HAIFA
AIRPORT

Qiryat
Haiyim

Qiryat Bialik

M O U N T   C A R M E L

Nesher

to Tel Aviv (Jaffa)

to Nazareth

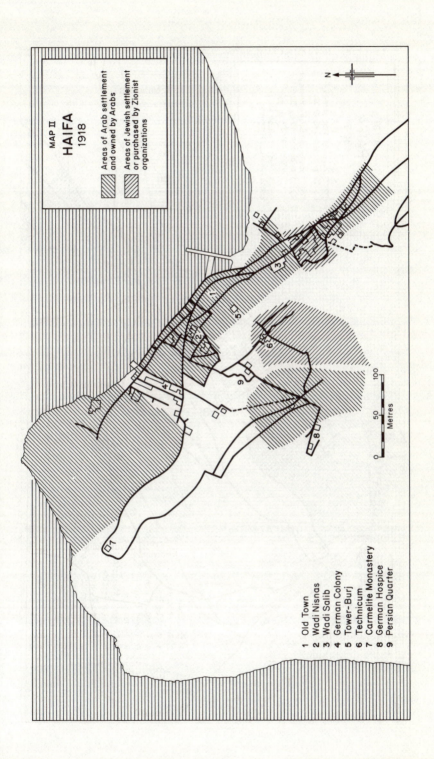

MAP II

HAIFA
1918

▨ Areas of Arab settlement
and owned by Arabs

▨ Areas of Jewish settlement
or purchased by Zionist
organizations

N

1 Old Town
2 Wadi Nisnas
3 Wadi Salib
4 German Colony
5 Tower–Burj
6 Technicum
7 Carmelite Monastery
8 German Hospice
9 Persian Quarter

0   50   100
Metres

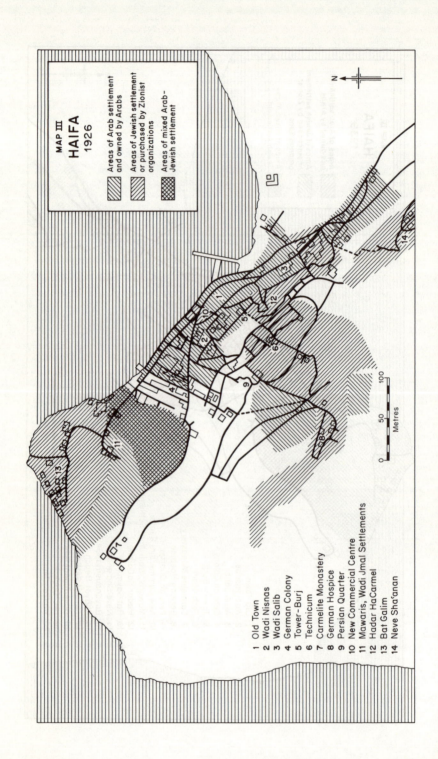

MAP Ⅲ
HAIFA
1926

N

Areas of Arab settlement and owned by Arabs

Areas of Jewish settlement or purchased by Zionist organizations

Areas of mixed Arab–Jewish settlement

1 Old Town
2 Wadi Nisnas
3 Wadi Salib
4 German Colony
5 Tower–Burj
6 Technicum
7 Carmelite Monastery
8 German Hospice
9 Persian Quarter
10 New Commercial Centre
11 Mawaris, Wadi Jmal Settlements
12 Hadar HaCarmel
13 Bat Galim
14 Neve Sha'anan

0   50   100
Metres

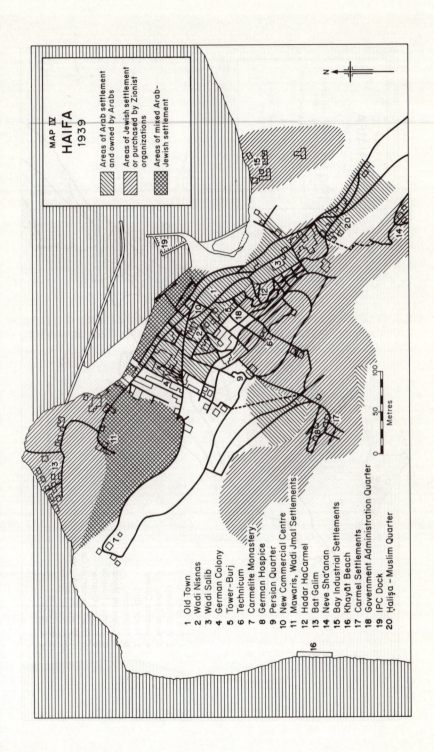

MAP IV
HAIFA
1939

Areas of Arab settlement and owned by Arabs

Areas of Jewish settlement or purchased by Zionist organizations

Areas of mixed Arab–Jewish settlement

N

1 Old Town
2 Wadi Nisnas
3 Wadi Salib
4 German Colony
5 Tower–Burj
6 Technicum
7 Carmelite Monastery
8 German Hospice
9 Persian Quarter
10 New Commercial Centre
11 Mawaris, Wadi Jmal Settlements
12 Hadar HaCarmel
13 Bat Galim
14 Neve Sha'anan
15 Bay Industrial Settlements
16 Khayāt Beach
17 Carmel Settlements
18 Government Administration Quarter
19 IPC Dock
20 Ḥalişa – Muslim Quarter

Metres
0   50   100

Introduction

Scholarly work on the British Mandate in Palestine has mostly been concerned with British policies or Zionist activities, and it is only recently that proper attention has begun to be given to the development of the Palestinians. While a certain interest in and concern with Palestinian studies has picked up in the last decade, its main focus has been the political and the contemporary. There has been an obvious gap in the research on the evolution of the Palestinian national community in its social, cultural, economic and political aspects.[1] The political development of the Palestinians has been a field of great interest to scholars, especially in view of the timely significance of the subject.[2] More recently there has been more concern with particular features of Palestinian history such as the revolt of 1936–9 and the Intifadah as well as concentrated studies on particular towns, villages and cities.[3] Other features of the community's life have been touched upon incidentally in studies on Jewish Zionist settlement and the development of the Jewish National Home (JNH).[4] They reflect only the reaction of the Arabs to these developments, which was on the whole negative, and so transmit a distorted picture of Arab social behaviour in toto. The latest attempts to fill this gap by studying the dynamics and experience of the Arab community in a socio-political framework,[5] while initiating the path towards a more thorough study of the community, have concentrated on such factors as demography, social stratification and education, and have not provided a comprehensive study of all aspects of community life. Such studies have laid most emphasis on the Palestinian communities after 1948, leaving a gap that needs to be filled by further research on the Mandate period.

This book is an attempt to meet part of the demand for Arab community studies, by highlighting the transformation of one Arab urban community in conditions of extreme mobility and change during the Mandate period. The Arab community that resided in Haifa between 1918 and 1939, and was influenced by the socio-economic changes that were particular to the city and to northern Palestine, was made up of a core group of Arabs who had resided there for generations and of a continuous flow of Arabs from other areas of Palestine, as well as neighbouring Lebanon and Syria. This Arab amalgam was united not only by its common cultural heritage but by a sense of a common destiny formed largely by the course of events after the First World War. During the nineteenth century the majority of this community had been Christian, but the Muslims had outnumbered the Christians since the early 1900s. The minority of Jews was originally minute, and most of them were Arabic-speaking; the Jewish population grew significantly only with the influx of the European Jews who came in fulfilment of the Zionist dream, thus changing the overall character of that minority.

Another significant feature of this community was its non-conformist character, in the sense that it differed from what scholars have come to accept as the particular social and political Palestinian culture. The intense concentration of such studies on Central Palestine for the patterns of social and political behaviour has left the field without a full, dynamic and comprehensive picture of Palestinian national development. This book highlights the socio-political atmosphere specific to northern Palestine and to the Opposition front, and the contribution of these particulars to the many facets of Palestinian national history.

Both the town and its community were drastically transformed during the period under study. Haifa changed from a small roadstead with a promising commercial centre into a congested modern harbour city with major industrial projects and sophisticated trading activities. This transformation reflected many features of the development of European industrial and commercial cities. In Haifa, however, the process was not the result of a natural development of the economic structure of the country or the social consciousness of the people; it was a transplanted phenomenon, in which the financial and human components were alien to the inhabitants. The demographic transformation of the Arab community, both in size and character, was shaped by these factors. While the total population of Haifa was approximately 18,000 in 1918, it had grown to over 100,000 in 1939. Foreign elements had been a small proportion of the community at the end of the First World War, but in the mid-1930s the Jewish population, which was overwhelmingly foreign (Polish, Russian and German), made up a little less than 50 per cent of the total inhabitants of the town. The Arab community, because of improved health conditions and immigration, had practically doubled in number, but it had lost the social and psychological power of its previous majority status; more significantly, the fundamental nature of that community had been recast under the impact of the new political and economic realities, depriving it of a normal, progressive national evolution.

Having stated the focus of this book, it is also important to specify what the study will omit in its treatment of the subject. While all factors that contribute to the understanding of Arab development in Haifa are thoroughly investigated, it is not the intention to consider the evolution of other communities in the city unless they bear directly upon the subject. The Jewish community, in particular, which was the largest and the most rapidly growing minority, is treated only in terms of its economic, political and social impact on Arab development and on the transformation of the city; the dynamics of Haifa's development and its gradual Zionization are touched upon from that angle only. Intercommunal relationships are given the same degree of emphasis and consideration. Because this book concentrates on economic, social and political changes, details about the overall history of Palestine will be omitted except for a brief general framework to facilitate understanding of particulars relevant to Haifa. These will be recorded and referred to in due time. Similarly, while the imperialist nature of the British Mandate and the implications of its support for Zionist policy have a direct bearing on the subject of this research, a thorough analysis of that topic is beyond its scope, and it will be touched upon only indirectly.

A main assumption on which this research builds its approach to both the British Administration and the Zionist experiment in Palestine is that the political and economic practices of the Mandate reflected an imperialist policy.[6] This is so important a precondition for the understanding of the framework in which Arab communities developed that something must be said at the very beginning about the tortuous history of Arab-British-Jewish relations.

Whatever altruistic motives Britain may have had in relation to the Mandate, it also had concrete political aspirations which frequently overrode Jewish and Arab needs. The traditional British concern about securing easy and complete access to Britain's eastern domains was still of paramount interest. This was even more pressing at a time when new territories could be opened up for British trade, territories which were also potential sources of natural resources. Palestine had long been important for the defence of the eastern bank of the Suez Canal, and it became more so after the discovery of oil in Iraq and the laying of the pipelines through northern Palestine. At the economic level, Palestine was made dependent on Britain in its trade relations, financial guarantees and methods of collection and allocation of public funds. The Colonial Office (CO) and the Treasury showed an unswerving imperialist spirit in their economic policy. Although Palestine did not promise material gains, it was essential that the country should achieve a viable economy in order not to become a financial liability to Britain.

It was only in relation to its political commitment to the Zionists and the establishment of the JNH that British economic policy faltered.

Theoretically, the Administration saw the aims of the incipient Zionist movement as compatible with and complementary to its own. It also perceived its own role to be that of a catalyst in the Palestinian economic future. The Zionist Organization (ZO), after 1927 the Jewish Agency (JA), was accepted as the main institution for channelling Jewish economic development in Palestine, which, in addition to serving the Jewish community, would depend on and bolster the Administration. As such, the function of this organization was to be an extension of British policy. Its aim was to pool and monopolize Jewish investment and expertise, thus developing the whole country, strengthening the government and helping to establish the JNH. Development on these lines was sought, but with time the situation grew more complex. Initially Zionist plans were much more accommodating to British demands than later on, when the JA had evolved into a stronger, more independent organization. Irrespective of the limitations, Zionist insistence often imposed its demands on British policy, while the Administration continued to hope for compromise and stabilization of the status quo, a situation that would make full use of Zionist co-operation while tempering Arab unrest. Nevertheless, when the Zionist experiment was facing financial problems, the Administration, uncharacteristically, bailed it out by providing extraordinary funds to employ Jewish workers in 1927–8, and covered the debts of the bankrupt Tel-Aviv municipality. But the largest expense went on defence needed to enforce the application of the policy of the JNH.

Support for Zionism was interpreted as meaning help towards the establishment of the movement's economic infrastructure, by invoking colonial power to give legislative form to the special advantages awarded to the Zionists. This in turn reinforced the movement's political and economic separatism, which had emerged in concrete shape by the end of the 1920s. An influx of Zionist immigrants entered Palestine as a result of this support. British commitment to minimal economic involvement permitted the Jewish minority a heavy stake in the economic growth of the country, especially in its larger cities. Zionist adherence to a political platform guided the economic development of the Jewish sector. Arab economic and social needs and political aspirations had to contend with these factors imposed from outside that contributed towards the form that the Arab struggle for self-expression took.

The mentality prevalent in the administrative apparatus compounded an already complex situation; the attempt to reconcile conflicting Arab and Jewish interests and to minimize animosity between Arabs and Jews was frustrated by an ambiguous British policy towards the two communities. For a long time, the government in London refused to acknowledge any disparity between its overall policy and the aspirations of these communities, and their conflict was recognized only when it resulted in violence, especially after British money and lives had been lost. The Arabs and Jews, however, maintained a more consistent approach in their attitude towards the government of the country and their demands for the future. The Administration rarely had the support of the local population. While the policy of the National Home was vehemently opposed by the Arabs, its method of application often failed to satisfy the Jews. At no time did the three parties co-operate harmoniously, and more often than not the Administration faced the hostility of both Arabs and Jews. It was only in 1936 that the British government faced up to the irreconcilable conditions of the Palestinian dilemma. Even then it remained adamant about maintaining its control in the area:

> The British government could not consider the abandonment of Palestine in this period without shuddering at the thought of a foreign power (even a relatively friendly power such as France) acquiring a base from which it might threaten the imperial lifeline at Suez.[7]

Even though the Partition Plan of 1936 was put aside, no alternative changes were introduced in Palestine by way of a British initiative. By the late 1930s the Administration had lost its political credibility in the eyes of the local population, especially the Arabs, and it meandered on to its distressing demise in 1948.

Haifa ranked quite high in British and Zionist plans. It was to be the starting point of alternative routes, by land, by sea and by air, to India. Its geographic position and topography had great potential for its development into a major transport centre. It became the headquarters of the Palestine Railways, the location of a harbour for ocean-going ships, the terminus of the pipeline for oil from Iraq and the place of storage and refinery for the oil. For the Zionists too, Haifa held great attraction as the urban centre closest to the multiplying number of settlements in the newly acquired agricultural plains of Marj Ibn 'Amir. In addition to being the potential distributing centre for the agricultural produce of these settlements, it was also perceived as the location for the major heavy industries from which products could be easily distributed in the Near East and to the West. In fact, the largest Zionist industrial projects, the Shemen and Nesher factories, the Grands Moulins and the Rutenberg electrification project, were concentrated in the town; Jewish labour settlements were a direct corollary to these enterprises. Haifa offered an opportunity to fulfil three main aims of Zionism: the conquest of the labour market, the acquisition of land for eternal Jewish ownership and settlement, and the creation of economic openings in order to attract Jewish immigrants.

These large-scale plans created a feverish economic atmosphere in Haifa, and made it a point of attraction for those seeking employment and prosperity. Even before this, another process of development had been taking place in Haifa from before the First World War, similar to that which had been at work in the main Palestinian cities and especially the coastal towns of the eastern Mediterranean. Members of the Arab community had been the main participants in this process of change, which involved all aspects of their life – social, political, economic and intellectual. Under the Mandate, this process did not continue in a vacuum but became entangled with the process initiated by British mandatory policy and Zionist aims; the way in which they affected its evolution is the main subject of this book.

Among the Palestinian towns subjected to the impact of British and Zionist policies, Haifa provides the best example for the study of the Arab community's transformation. Haifa acquired all the specific features of the other main towns, while not one of them combined all of Haifa's characteristics. Like Jerusalem, Haifa became a centre for administrative activities and personnel, especially for the railways and the port; like Tel-Aviv, it became a centre of industry, and, like all the other Palestinian towns, a centre of commerce. Unlike the other large towns with mixed populations, however, Haifa was relatively new, and was unhampered by long tradition and history. For this reason, in Haifa both the setting and the people were more receptive to change. It was partly because of this, too, that Haifa was chosen by the Mandatory government and by the Zionist planners as the location for their major projects. The British intended to bestow on Haifa certain characteristics that were bound to turn it into a cosmopolitan city, while the Zionists were anxious lest it become too cosmopolitan, preventing it from becoming a predominantly Jewish city. Unlike Tel-Aviv, which had become an insular Jewish town, Haifa offered to the Zionists the opportunity to control a wider part of the country and an area of economic influence beyond Palestinian frontiers. Haifa presented a challenge to the wider Zionist aspirations, both for Palestine and the region. The implementation of Zionist plans in the town, in their physical, economic and political aspects, provides an excellent example of that policy's subtle and gradual development. The fact that the transformation of the city and its Arab community was more rapid and sudden than in any of the other towns is a further reason to study the phenomenon of change in Haifa, where the results were relatively clear.

The heterogeneous character of the population is, perhaps, the most significant reason for the choice of Haifa as a model of study. In addition to a mixed Arab population, Haifa had foreign residents, who had begun to make an impact on local society even before 1900. The strongest influence was that of the French missionary and educational institutions; other influences were those of the German Templar settlement and the large number of European consulates. By the early 1920s, the influx of Russian and Eastern European Jews, and in the early 1930s the immigration of a noticeably large number of German Jews, added to the cosmopolitan atmosphere of the town. The British Administration also brought to Haifa a residential British community of officials, businessmen and their families. These changes in the composition of the population influenced the socio-economic development of the Arab community, which in its turn was also undergoing change in its social and religious composition. By the mid-1930s Haifa had a mixed population, with more or less equal numbers of Arabs and Jews, many of whom had been recently attracted by the economic potentialities of the town. The struggle of the Arab sector of the population to survive and to maintain its socio-national identity, under highly competitive and adverse conditions, is a main focus of this study.

At the turn of the century, the composition of Haifa's Arab population was very similar to that of Beirut.[8] Compared with the other Palestinian towns, Haifa had a proportionately larger number of Christian merchants, mainly Arabs, who had been educated in the European missionary institutions and were qualified to carry on business both with European firms and with Arabs in the towns and villages. Even when the Muslim population had overtaken the Christians in number, the Christian community still had the larger number of wealthy landowners, merchants and entrepreneurs. From the mid-1920s this stratum was enlarged by wealthy Muslims from Beirut and Damascus as well as the Palestinian towns. However, economic and political developments were such as to limit the opportunities open to this class. While the entrepreneurial merchant class in Beirut was able to develop its potential and diversify its investment, building a network of financial connections, in Haifa investment in fields other than the traditional mercantile activities was rendered practically impossible, except in a very few cases. The industrial field was monopolized by the Jewish sector, which financed it as part of a national Zionist economy. It became impossible for the Arab entrepreneurial class to compete in the new economic fields conquered by Jewish and Zionist capital. Many ambitious Arabs with limited capital had to seek opportunities to develop untapped lines of business outside Haifa, in the less advanced Arab towns such as Ludd, Ramlah and even Jaffa.[9] Only a few Arabs, the very wealthy ones, were able to consolidate their economic base and initiate a few industrial projects or accumulate real estate. It is significant that those Arabs remained in Haifa after 1948, while most of the merchants and small entrepreneurs, whose wealth was engaged in small individual businesses and whose assets were more mobile, left Palestine at the outbreak of hostilities.

In addition to the expanding Arab mercantile class, other elements in Haifa's Arab population, especially the mainly Muslim working class, grew noticeably during the 1920s and 1930s. Government employment provided a living for a substantial number of Arabs in the civil service and in the more menial jobs of the municipality, the harbour and government building projects. It was mainly the building boom, both in the private and the public sector, that attracted the large number of labourers, mostly from the economically distressed peasantry of the northern districts.[10] The concentration of such a proletariat in Haifa was unprecedented; the town was unprepared and the Administration unwilling to deal with the problems resulting from congestion. For the Arab community, this influx altered the social structure of the society and intensified the gaps between the social classes.

The political transformation, in turn, was strongly affected by the socio-economic changes experienced by the community. Immediately after the British occupation, Haifa's political community was similar to those of other towns in the Arab East, touched by the same mood of nationalism and aspirations for a changed polity and reform. The intensity of the external threats drew all sectors of the community together and strengthened their political stand. However, when these threats diminished, whether in reality or imagination, differences between religious communities and between social classes emerged. Such differences were aggravated by the lopsided economic growth of some sectors of the community and by the entrenchment of the individualistic ethos which prevented the emergence of an Arab economy that could be geared towards Arab needs. This, in turn, led the different sections of society, the 'haves' and the 'have-nots', to acquire widely differing political aspirations and visions. It was the 'have-nots' who felt the political and economic deprivations most keenly and who retaliated in the mid-1930s by militant activities; but other classes as well were not unaware of the political dangers. The political experience of the Arab community in Haifa also provides an interesting study of the opposition movement in Palestinian politics. The main nationalist movement, as represented in the Jerusalem leadership which controlled the Arab Executive (AE) of the Palestinian Congresses and later on in the religious leadership of the Supreme Muslim Council (SMC), has been thoroughly investigated, but the opposition movement, especially that of northern Palestine, has not been given the same importance.

Even though this study attempts to investigate the community's development in the main aspects where change showed itself, it cannot claim to have exhausted the subject. The timespan has been confined to the years 1918–39, a significant period both in its initial and final stages. It ushered in a new form of government, the British Mandate, which brought in and legalized the application of the Zionist policy. The Palestinian revolt of 1936–9 was a landmark in the long process of Arab Palestinian struggle for self-determination and was to remain the first stage in that long struggle. The main features of change had completely taken shape by 1939, but the way in which the community dealt with the altered circumstances in the city after the 1936–9 revolt still needs investigation. Haifa played a significant role during the period of the revolt since it was the breeding ground for the first fighters, who were recruited from among its poorer class. Those years have remained a unique era in the town's history.

Other limitations that should be recorded are those imposed by the difficulties and restrictions met when collecting the source material. The official documentation on the period was easily accessible in the British and Israeli archives; however, some restrictions were placed on certain records in the latter. But the main difficulty lay in collecting data from the Arab community, which has not traditionally kept written records; moreover, most of the informants, whether living in Israel or outside, asked that only restricted use should be made of their material, in view of the still turbulent political conditions in the region. My close connection, however, with a large number of people who lived through the experience of the period and who have for a long time unconsciously imparted to me various facets of that period of their lives, has provided me with a more discerning perception of the subject; in a way, it has helped me to determine the significance and value of the oral source material.

The approach used in dealing with the subject is to examine four main aspects of the Arab community's transformation. In Part One, the physical and demographic character of Haifa in 1918 is discussed; this section deals with the community's composition, the town's size and the distribution of quarters. Part Two analyses the demographic transformation of Haifa's population and the movement of the various sectors of the community from certain areas to others. Gradual Zionist control of areas encircling the town, and the growth of new Jewish quarters encircling the old traditional Arab quarters, are shown here. This part investigates British policy in matters relating to town development in general and its application to Haifa and its municipality; here emphasis is placed on British ambitions to make Haifa a showpiece of spectacular British projects, thus accelerating the urban process as well as strengthening the causes of population expansion, mobility and gradual Zionist control of the urban scene.

Part Three concentrates on the economic aspects of change. Haifa had two distinct economies, of industry and of commerce. Industry, which gradually became a Jewish monopoly, is discussed in relation to the role played by the Administration in helping the Jewish sector to achieve industrial control through legislation. The basis of the Arabs' commercial role is also investigated, and their gradual loss of supremacy in this line is discussed. The human factor of these two economies, labour, is placed within the context of the two and of British policy towards both Jewish and Arab labour. Part Four deals with the Arab community's political transformation in three consecutive stages punctuated by drastic local occurrences. The first ends in 1923, the second in the disturbances of 1929, and the third in the last stages of the Arab revolt in 1939.

The uniqueness of Haifa rests in the fact that it was the earliest and the best suited model for the application of the dual British/Zionist policy to its physical, economic and human components. The special feature of Haifa in 1918 as a youthful, forward-looking and economically viable town was a reason for this attraction. Another appealing characteristic was the type of population it attracted and their acceptance of change. The mechanics applied to bring about these changes are traced here historically to show the way in which the tactics of fragmentation, dependence and co-option were used in differing forms and with different degrees of success. At the same time, and while one level of this process was taking place, another process of change was going on within the Arab community itself, affecting its development and reaction to outside influences. Because and in spite of the highly charged political situation, the Arab community nevertheless developed economically, socially and politically within these restricted peripheries which led, inevitably, to armed struggle. Since then this pattern, in which the town was physically encircled, economically segmented, and its Arab community diminished, politically suppressed and socially fragmented, has been repeated in many Palestinian towns.

Notes

1. The need to study the evolution of the Palestinian Arab community and the dearth of such research has been emphasized by scholars in the field such as I. Abu-Lughod in 'The Pitfalls of Palestiniology', *Arab Studies Quarterly* 3 (Fall 1981), p. 404. It is also becoming a focus for social historians in the classroom but has still to show its accomplishments in publications.

2. For a few books on the subject, see: A. M. Lesch, *Arab Politics in Palestine, 1917–1939* (London, 1979); Y. Porath, *The Emergence of the Palestinian Arab National Movement, 1918–1929* (London, 1974); Y. Porath, *The Palestinian Arab National Movement, 1929–1939* (London, 1977); E. Tuma, *Sittun 'Aman 'ala al-Haraka al-Qawmiyya al-'Arabiyya al-Filastiniyya* (The Last Sixty Years of the Palestinian Arab National Movement) (Beirut, 1978); N. 'Allush, *Al-Muqawama al-'Arabiyya fi Filastin 1917–1948* (The Arab National Struggle in Palestine 1917–1948) (Beirut, 1970); P. A. Smith, *Palestine and the Palestinians 1876–1983* (New York, 1984).

3. See: S. F. El-Nimr, 'The Arab Revolt in Palestine: A Study based on Oral Sources', unpublished Ph.D. thesis, University of Exeter, 1990; T. R. Swedenberg, 'Memories of Revolt: the 1936–39 Rebellion and the Struggle for a Palestinian National Past', unpublished Ph.D. thesis, University of Texas, Austin, Texas,

1988; K. W. Stein, 'The Intifadah and the 1936–1939 Uprising', The Carter Center of Emory University, Occasional Paper Series, Vol. 1, No. 1, March 1990; N. K. Al-Agha, *Mada' in Filastin* (The Cities of Palestine) (Amman, 1993); I. F. Al-Durr, *Shefa 'Amr* (Beirut, 1988).

4. To name only a few in a field that is tremendously rich: N. Caplan, *Palestine Jewry and the Arab Question, 1917–1925* (London, 1978); S. Schama, *Two Rothschilds and the Land of Israel* (London,1978); F. H. Kisch, *Palestine Diary* (London, 1938).

5. See J. S. Migdal, *Palestinian Society and Politics* (Princeton, NJ, 1980); K. Nakhleh and E. Zureik (eds), *The Sociology of the Palestinians* (London, 1980); N. A. Badran, *Al-Ta'lim wal-Tahdith fil-Mujtama' al-'Arabi 'al-Filastini* (Education and Modernization in Arab Palestinian Society) (Beirut, 1969); R. S. Sayigh, *Palestinians: from Peasants to Revolutionaries* (London, 1988).

6. For a study of Britain's economic policy during the first decade of the Mandate and the contribution of that policy towards the establishment of Zionist settlement, see B. J. Smith, *The Roots of Separatism in Palestine* (Syracuse, NY, 1993).

7. B. Wasserstein, *The British in Palestine: the Mandatory Government and the Arab–Jewish Conflict 1917–1929* (London, 1978), p. 157.

8. L. T. Fawaz, *Merchants and Migrants in Nineteenth Century Beirut* (Cambridge, 1983).

9. This was especially the situation of ambitious entrepreneurs, with limited capital, who wished to start new businesses such as cinemas and theatres, the import of novelties and Western-style services such as dry cleaning. (Oral information, family members as well as many of the interviewees, 1974–94.)

10. For a study of emigration into Haifa during the Mandate period see: M. Yazbek, *Al-Hijra al-'Arabiyya ila Haifa* (Arab Migration into Haifa) (Nazareth, 1988).

PART ONE

Haifa: the Town
in 1918

1

Physical Characteristics of Haifa in 1918

The city of Haifa is situated on the southern shore of the Bay of Acre in the lee of Mount Carmel. Its geographical position gives it the advantage of easy natural access to the hinterland. To the south, the coastal plain leads to Jaffa, the south of Palestine and Egypt, and to the north it connects with Acre and on to Lebanon. To the east, the plain lying between the Carmel coastal range and the hills of Galilee gives access to the Marj Ibn 'Amir, the most fertile agricultural region in Palestine, and further east, by way of the Jordan valley, to the wheat-growing areas of Hauran in Syria. Haifa's prime geographical position is further enhanced by its fine natural harbour, the best on the Palestine coast.

Compared with other major Palestinian towns – Jerusalem, Jaffa, Nablus and neighbouring Acre – Haifa is a relatively new city. In its present location, its existence began in the mid-eighteenth century when, in 1764–5, the governor of Acre, Dhahir al-'Umar, laid waste the older hamlet of Haifa al-'Atiqa, located some one and a half miles to the west of the modern site, and transferred the population, around 250 people, to a new site, which he had surrounded by a protective wall. He also built a citadel overlooking the settlement to the south, the remains of which were still in use at the time of the British occupation in 1918.[1]

Apart, however, from the damage caused by the violence of war and the wear and tear of four years of poverty, the town which the British occupied on 23 September 1918 had altered little physically from its description by Tamimi and Halabi, two Ottoman officials, in 1914 – one of the most accurate of the period. Their overall assessment was appreciative and optimistic. They compared Haifa to Beirut with its similar large buildings and glass-windowed shops. In their view, Haifa was 'like a bride' with its red-tiled and broad-windowed houses and its

15

active life as well as beautiful natural surroundings. The paths and alleys were clean and the people well behaved and educated. Here, they felt, a proper urban life could be lived. They had no doubt that Haifa was the most advanced town on the eastern Mediterranean coast after Beirut and Jaffa.[2]

The oldest and most densely populated part of modern Haifa at this date was the agglomeration of residences and public buildings clustered between the narrow central stretch of seashore and mountain west of the bay and east of the Carmel promontory. Residences in this area were almost entirely confined to the centre and flanks of the narrow valleys, Wadi al-Nisnas and Wadi al-Salib, though a few isolated buildings had sprung up outside these valleys.

As was traditional in Middle Eastern towns, economic and religious institutions were located in the centre of the city and, in the case of Haifa, also along the northern seashore. Jaffa Road, the town's principal artery, which originally connected the eastern and western gates, was also the main market street, divided into sections, each housing a different branch of trade.[3] This market had been cleaned, its roof discarded and its paths tiled a few years before 1914. Almost all the public institutions could be found in this central area and spreading along the coast in both directions. The area functioned as the dividing point between the two residential sectors of the town – the eastern and western quarters.

On the flanks of Mount Carmel stood the citadel (Burj) commanding a bird's-eye view of the central town. Directly below it lay the religious centres of the communities. To one side spread the Quarter of Churches (Harat al-Kana'is), where the Maronite, Greek Catholic, Greek Orthodox and Latin churches were congregated. The Great Mosque with its clock tower was situated to the east of this area. The three centres of public assembly were also nearby: Jraineh Square in front of the Great Mosque; Sahat al-'Arabat (the transport centre); and al-Khamra Square, named after a large landowning family. Further east along the seashore were to be found the oldest public buildings: the Post Office, Government House (Saray), the Small Mosque, a public slaughterhouse and the prison which had been built from the remains of a Crusader castle.

The two residential quarters, Christian and Muslim, fanned out west and east from the central, common areas. Distribution of socio-religious and educational institutions followed no set pattern in either quarter, but residential distribution was dictated mainly by religious affiliation.

The whole eastern section of Haifa (al-Hara al-Sharqiyya), covering the floor and slopes of Wadi al-Salib and stretching from the shoreline public buildings to the slopes of Mount Carmel and limited to the east by the marshy banks of the Muqata' River, was inhabited by the Muslim community. As pictured by Tamimi, its living conditions were those of wretched poverty and unhygienic squalor.[4] The more well-to-do Muslims tended to move towards the eastern boundary of the quarter or further south to the more elevated areas. This section of Haifa originally included an area populated by Sephardic Jews, mostly from North Africa, who had taken refuge in the town in 1829, and was known as Harat al-Yahud. Later, in 1881, the Oriental Jewish community also founded a new quarter in the extreme east of the town, which, despite its official name of Hadar HaCarmel, generally came to be known to the Arabs as Ard al-Yahud.

The Christian western quarter (al-Hara al-Gharbiyya), stretching from the marketplace in the east to the German colony in the west, also spread out parallel to the seashore. Many religious and educational institutions were scattered throughout the quarter, practically all of them foreign and exerting a strong influence on the communities they served. Convents of the Sisters of Nazareth, the German Catholic sisters of St Charles Borromeo, and the barefoot Carmelite nuns as well as cemeteries for the different congregations lined the shore from east to west.

Like the Muslim quarter, the Christian residential quarter was built in the heart and on the slopes of Wadi al-Nisnas. A very small Armenian community attached itself to the south-western part of the wadi, and many of the Ashkenazi and well-off Sephardic Jews resided either in the western quarter or in the German colony at the western extremity of the town. In 1909 a new Jewish neighbourhood (Herzelia) sprang up on the mountainside above Wadi al-Nisnas. It was made up of twelve building plots owned by a group composed of Sephardic and, for the first time, Ashkenazi Jews. Although the area to the south and east of this quarter was purchased in 1912 by private Jewish individuals and organizations, very few buildings were erected there before the First World War. The main points around which new quarters were destined to grow were a technical college (the Technion) and the Reali School, as well as the School of the Sisters of Nazareth. The nucleus of a Persian quarter was established to the west of what was to become Herzelia by Bahai immigrants in 1908 (see also Chapter 2, p. 20 and Map II).[5]

Living conditions in the Muslim and Christian communities were generally similar, though those of the Christians were slightly more affluent and had better sanitary conditions. The houses of both communities were of masoned and often decorated stone extracted from quarries either on the eastern periphery of Haifa for the Muslims or from the Carmel quarries for the Christians. Each household attempted to build the outer rampart of the house around an enclosed inner courtyard where the family well was usually located. This was a carefully guarded possession since it was the main source of fresh water, along with the few public wells in the north-west of the town. Both residential quarters had the same features of narrow, tortuous and uneven roads, flanked on either side by high houses, haphazardly built with extensions added at different periods and often on two or more split levels. This was due to the rocky nature of the terrain and the desire of the inhabitants to live in close proximity to each other. The overall impression was of a labyrinth of intricately linked dwellings which, though highly picturesque, lacked most modern conveniences.

Thus in 1918 Haifa, now freed from the confines of its old eighteenth-century walls, remained sequestered into religious quarters, though these were becoming less and less exclusive. Economic stratification was not a significant index of population distribution between quarters, though it certainly had some significance for the distribution of the richer and poorer elements within each. The native residential areas, squeezed between mountains and sea, converged on a common socio-economic centre. It was the Europeans, mostly Jews, who purchased land on the outskirts of the town before and during the First World War; those Arabs who did own land outside the town were still reluctant to abandon the security of their traditional quarters (see Map II).[6]

Notes

1. For the eighteenth-century history of Haifa see A. Cohen, *Palestine in the 18th Century* (Jerusalem, 1973), pp. 137-44; A. Carmel, *Tarikh Haifa fi 'Ahd al-Atrak al-'Uthmaniyyin* (History of Haifa in the Ottoman Period) (Haifa, 1979), pp. 77-96.

2. M. R. Tamimi and M. B. Halabi, *Wilayat Beirut* (Beirut, 1335H/1914), p. 230.

3. Ibid., p. 230; Y. Washitz, 'Jewish-Arab Relations in Haifa during the Mandate' (unpublished manuscript), Ch. 1, p. 12.

4. Tamimi and Halabi, *Wilayat Beirut*, p. 247.

5. Carmel, *Tarikh Haifa*, p. 280.

6. The maps of Haifa in 1918, 1926 and 1939 have been reconstructed from a number of official maps used by the Administration for town planning purposes, the building of the Port and the IPC terminal; also from Zionist records as used in planning Jewish quarters and land-purchasing activities. These were corroborated and endorsed by information collected orally from eight old Arab residents of Haifa, communicated in April-May 1975.

2

Demography and Distribution of Haifa's Communities

Demography

The population of Haifa grew from the original tiny community transplanted from Haifa al-'Atiqa by Dhahir al-'Umar in the mid-1760s. There is conflicting and contradictory evidence on the exact numbers of inhabitants in Palestinian towns during the nineteenth and early twentieth centuries, and indeed until the first British census of 1922. These discrepancies were caused by a number of factors, including inaccurate methods of counting and reporting as well as the ideological prejudices and personal idiosyncrasies of those who gathered the figures.

The statistics which are available for the nineteenth century were provided mostly by travellers, pilgrims, monks or government agents. Each of these groups had its own biases, so that an objective assessment is hard to achieve. Religious zeal often led clerics to exaggerate the numbers of their own communities while underestimating the figures for others. This type of bias was also to be found in the reporting of local residents.[1] When the Ottoman Government sponsored a census in 1868 with the aim of assessing manpower for labour on the roads there was an obvious reason for local people to conceal their true numbers. Again, Jewish organizations and spokesmen had their own reasons for inflating the numbers of the Jewish community and exaggerating its development.

Political events in the nineteenth century explain the growth of Haifa. Syria, including Palestine, was under Egyptian occupation between 1832 and 1840. Acre fell to Egyptian siege in 1832 and was badly damaged in the process, leading many of its merchant families and foreign residents to move to Haifa. A further blow came in 1840 with the bombardment of Acre by the British fleet, causing more inhabitants to flee the violence and take up residence in Haifa. Furthermore, the earthquake which hit parts of Palestine in 1837 caused a significant shift

19

in the distribution of population in northern Palestine, again to the benefit of Haifa.[2]

These events had particular effects on the demography of Haifa and by mid-century the population was estimated to have reached between 2,000 and 3,000. More dependable informants then began to turn their attention to Haifa – namely, members of the newly formed German colony and its consulate in the town, and the participants in the Palestine Exploration Fund's Survey of Western Palestine, which conducted its investigations in the 1870s and 1880s.[3] Both sources depended on experienced researchers who viewed the population in an objective, scientific fashion. Their estimates appeared to take into consideration the local Arab, Muslim and Christian inhabitants and to exclude the few Europeans, and both seemed to agree on the approximate size of that population between 1868 and 1875. Hoffman, the founder of the German colony, estimated the number as 4,000 in 1868, and the surveyors of the Palestine Exploration Fund, Conder and Kitchener, estimated it to be the same in 1875.[4] Furthermore, in 1886 the German engineer G. Schumacher made a population count on behalf of the Ottoman authorities which put the total population at 7,165,[5] while a semi-official census of 1891 estimated it at 8,140.[6] By the end of the century, Haifa's population probably numbered between 8,000 and 9,000. Cuinet, writing in 1895, estimated it at 9,908.[7]

The period 1900–1914 witnessed even faster growth which was checked only by the outbreak of the First World War. One of the main reasons for this growth was the increase in the town's economic activity and particularly the new developments in construction, both public and private, such as the branch line of the Hijaz Railway from Damascus to Haifa, completed in 1905, as well as large building projects for both Jewish and Christian religious organizations. Many workers from Acre, Nazareth, Nablus, and the Carmel and Marj Ibn 'Amir villages came to Haifa during this period. The German Vice Consul, Keller, reported as early as 1903 that employment on the railroad had brought new elements into the town not only from Palestine but from neighbouring countries as well.[8] The immigration of non-Arabs also contributed to the growth in Haifa's population. In addition to Oriental Jews from Turkey and Morocco, some Ashkenazi Jews were also settling in the town. One community that settled in Haifa at this time was the Bahai.[9] Resident in Acre since the second half of the nineteenth century, some of this community led by Abbas Effendi, congregated in a quarter on the flanks of Mount Carmel.

Thus, by the outbreak of the First World War, Haifa's inhabitants probably numbered up to 20,000. During the war their ranks were depleted by epidemics and deportations as well as by fighting, though there are no statistics measuring this loss with any precision. Carmel estimates that Haifa may have lost up to one-third of its 1914 population,[10] but other sources put the loss at a lower figure; the consensus seems to be that at the end of the war the population was between 16,000 and 18,000. Counting is made doubly difficult by the fact that at the end of the war deportees as well as soldiers would have gradually returned home, thus reflating the figures.

Growth and distribution of Haifa's communities

Apart from the rapid growth of the city's total population, the weight within it of various communities was also changing. The Ottoman system of government operated in accordance with the *millet* system; that is, it treated communities separately according to their religious affiliations, thus relieving the Ottoman authorities of certain administrative functions and ensuring the loyalty of the communities as a whole.[11] As a result, the census figures available are given in terms of religious communities. In the mid-nineteenth century the breakdown was reported as follows: Muslims, 51 per cent; Christians, 36 per cent; and Jews, 13 per cent.[12] However, it should be noted that in comparison with the other Palestinian towns, Haifa had a very small Jewish community of Ottoman citizenship. While Safad had 1,197 households, Jerusalem 630 and Tiberias 400 in 1871/72, Haifa had only 8.[13] Thereafter, both official and unofficial figures, taken as a whole, seem to indicate that the Muslim population lost its numerical supremacy, but was growing faster than the Christians from the turn of the century onward, and that the Jewish community was growing fairly steadily.

It is probably safe to assume that an unusually large proportion of the increase in all communities was due to migration, both internal and external. For instance, Haifa's Christian community, which made up over 20 per cent of the total population in the 1830s, grew to 40 per cent in the 1870s and to 45 per cent by the end of the century; it had decreased, however, to less than 40 per cent by 1915.[14] Similarly, the Jewish population increased from 3 per cent in the 1830s to 10 per cent by the end of the century, and made up 15 per cent of the total population in 1915.[15] As for the Muslim population, it experienced an equivalent decrease in numbers from approximately 80 per cent in the 1830s to around 45 per cent by the end of the century; however, it began to increase again during the early 1900s.[16] At the turn of the century, the influx of villagers, the majority of them probably Muslims, who came to Haifa to seek work may have combined with a higher average rate of natural increase to boost the growth rate of the Muslim community, compared with the Christians.

Despite rapid population growth Haifa remained, in comparison

with other Palestinian cities, a small and unimportant town until the
second decade of the twentieth century. Compared with Jaffa, Jerusalem and even Acre, it held a minor position both politically and
economically. However, change and innovation did occur in the last
days of the Ottoman Empire, emanating from three main sources: the
Christian educational institutions, the German urban settlement and
the extension of the Hijaz Railway.

Christian educational influence, predominantly French, was first
introduced to Haifa by the Roman Catholics (Latins[17]), who had re-
established their religious influence by building an imposing monastery
on Mount Carmel in the 1830s. In spite of the very small number of
Latins among the local population, this congregation had the largest
number of schools and convents and an impressive amount of real
estate. The first Christian school was built by them and was open to
children of all communities, especially those of the uniate churches, the
Greek Catholics and the Maronites. These uniate denominations also
established schools attached to their churches; but the increasing number
of European institutions, run by Catholic orders which specialized in
education, were more attractive to all Christian groups, including the
Greek Orthodox. The most famous of these institutions was the Carmelite School, where the order of Frères des Ecoles Chrétiennes had taught
in French since 1882. Various other schools for boys and girls – the
School of St Joseph, run by the Carmelite nuns since 1910, the School
of the Italian Carmelite nuns, opened in 1907,[18] and at least eight other
French-oriented schools – were operating before 1914.[19]

The Greek Orthodox community also had a school attached to the
church, which taught Greek in addition to Arabic. Towards the turn of
the century, the Russian Orthodox church tried to upstage it by providing Russian education, but neither was as successful as the French
education, which attracted members of the Orthodox community in
addition to Catholics. By 1914, about 80 per cent of Haifa's Catholics
knew French.[20] English was introduced as a medium of education for
the Protestant community by the Christian Missionary Society, which
opened two schools in the 1880s, one for girls and the other for boys;
these were soon followed by three more schools.[21] The German Templar
community also had their own religious schools, but these were not
opened to the local Arab community and their influence on the life of
the town was limited. During the first decade of the twentieth century,
further German influence over the educated generation came through
the Jewish Technical Institute, which was sponsored by Ezra, a German
Jewish organization, and taught in German.[22] Jewish educational institutes had grown in number since the 1880s and the influx of Ashkenazi
Jews. In addition to Hebrew, many of these schools – such as the
Alliance Israélite Universelle School – taught in French. The Muslim

community was the least affected by these institutions, and was less fortunate in the ineffective education provided in the three government schools.[23]

The second influence for change came from the establishment of the German colony on the western frontiers of the town. This colony was founded in 1869 by the Templar Association, a German pietistic movement of puritanical social persuasion.[24] It began as an agricultural settlement but grew into an urban centre, planned and developed on European lines and quite unlike any other to be seen in Haifa. By 1914 it had 750 residents, most of them German, with some Austrians and Americans. The land owned and used by the Germans extended from their residential quarter up to the Carmel promontory at Ras al-Kurum, beyond old Haifa, where the colony's vineyards and fields lay in the sloping plain. In the residential sector, the spacious, red-roofed houses flanked both sides of a wide tree-lined avenue running at right angles to the seashore, an unusual feature for Middle Eastern towns of the time. Building on the central part of the Carmel was first undertaken in the 1880s by the Germans. They also built a road to connect the colony with the mountainside settlement. By 1918 the community was completely detached from the town, but its presence had been influential in that it had provided an example of a new and different style of urban living, and had also extended the borders of Haifa beyond those of the traditional town.

The third factor of importance to Haifa's development at this time was the building of the railway branch line from Haifa to Dera'a, which was completed in late 1905 as an addition to the main Hijaz pilgrim railway running from Damascus to Dera'a (completed in 1903) and then on to Medina and Mecca. However, plans to connect Haifa by rail to the interior go back further than this. In 1890 a British company, Fifling, had acquired a concession to construct a line from Haifa to Damascus, and work started (at the Haifa end) in 1892. Progress was very slow, however, and by 1903 only 8 kilometres of track had been laid. This was bought by the Hijaz Railway authority and the connecting line was laid to the Hijaz Railway at Dera'a. In the meantime, a French company had received a concession in the 1890s to run a line from Damascus to Beirut. This was completed in 1898 and deprived Haifa of some of the Hauran cereal traffic. Thus the policy behind the purchase of the Damascus–Haifa line and its incorporation into the Hijaz Railway was designed to divert economic benefits to the southern shores of the eastern Mediterranean. In addition, it was a way of playing down the importance of Beirut, with its growing local nationalist aspirations and its blatant domination by European powers, and of giving further economic importance to a project proclaimed for its pan-Islamic character.[25]

Haifa thereby regained its importance as a port for the export of wheat and barley from the Syrian interior, and a large new central railway station was built to handle this traffic. At the same time, the old pier in the harbour, built by the Russians in the 1850s, was extended. Both projects, the pier and the railway, had important repercussions on the town's development. In particular, the employment they created attracted a large labour force, mostly Muslim Arabs from the rest of Palestine, Syria and Egypt. The eastern entrance of the town where the yards and workshops were located came to be known as Tel al-'Amal or Umm al-'Amal (Hill of Work or Mother of Work). Many of these labourers settled in the town, to become a major factor in the Muslim character Haifa assumed from the early twentieth century onwards.

Clearly, then, by 1918 the physical and demographic growth of Haifa had begun to spread upwards on to the slopes of Mount Carmel. Modernity could be measured by the altitude of settlements and their distance from the seashore. In earlier times the traditional quarters had been squeezed between the mountain and the sea and had converged on the socio-economic centre on the shore line. New buildings spread southwards to the flanks of Mount Carmel and even to the mountain top. Although it was the European, urban immigrant community who initially bought land and built on the mountain outskirts, the local population had begun to follow suit, though on a much smaller scale.

Notes

1. J. Bahri, *Tarikh Haifa* (History of Haifa) (Haifa, 1922), p. 17.

2. Y. Ben-Arieh, 'The Population of the Large Towns of Palestine during the First Eighty Years of the Nineteenth Century According to Western Sources', in M. Ma'oz (ed.), *Studies on Palestine during the Ottoman Period* (Jerusalem, 1975), p. 56.

3. C. R. Conder and H. H. Kitchener, *The Survey of Western Palestine*, Vol. 1, sheets I–VI (London, 1881), p. 283.

4. A. Carmel, *Tarikh Haifa fi 'Ahd al-Atrak al-'Uthmaniyyin* (History of Haifa in the Ottoman Period) (Haifa, 1979), p. 261; Conder and Kitchener, *The Survey*.

5. Carmel, *Tarikh Haifa*, p. 262. According to Carmel, who studied Schumacher's census, the total population would have come to about 6,400 natives and 765 Europeans. Of the local population, the Muslims accounted for 3,025, the Christians 3,200, and the Jews 185.

6. N. Qub'ain, *Taqrir Tarikhi lil-ta'ifa al-Injiliyya al-Usqufyya al-'Arabiyya bi-Haifa* (Historical Report on the Arab Evangelical Episcopalian Community of Haifa) (Haifa, 1940), p. 4. This semi-official census, as reported by Qub'ain, was carried out by the Ottoman authorities.

7. V. Cuinet, *Syrie et Palestine: géographie administrative, statistique, descriptive et raisonnée* (Paris, 1896), p. 106.

8. Carmel, *Tarikh Haifa*, p. 227.

9. E. Esselmont, *Baha'ullah and the New Era* (London, 1923), p. 5. The Bahai religion developed out of the Babi movement, which was an offshoot of Shiism started in Iran by Mirza 'Ali Mohammad in 1844. After his execution, his

followers moved first to Iraq and later to Acre with the new exiled leader, entitled Baha'ullah, under whom the Bahai movement began to develop into a separate religion. His son 'Abbas ('Abdul-Baha) moved the Bahai quarters to Haifa.

10. Carmel, *Tarikh Haifa*, p. 265. For a thorough study of Haifa's demographic changes between 1800 and 1918 see M. Seikaly, 'The Arab Community of Haifa 1918–1936: A Study in Transformation', D.Phil. thesis, Oxford, 1983, pp. 16–23.

11. See A. H. Hourani, *Minorities in the Arab World* (London, 1947), pp. 20–22. See also CO to S of S, 10 June 1924, on the Organisation of the Jewish Community in Palestine (PRO CO 733/67).

12. Mary Rogers, sister of the British Vice Consul, Edward Rogers, lived in Haifa between 1855 and 1857, and was in close touch with all sectors of Haifa society during that period. See M. E. Rogers, *Domestic Life in Palestine* (London, 1863), p. 85.

13. Justin McCarthy, *The Population of Palestine: Population, History and Statistics of the Late Ottoman Period and the Mandate* (New York, 1990), p. 13.

14. Carmel, *Tarikh Haifa*, p. 147; M. R. Tamimi and M. B. Halabi, *Wilayat Beirut* (Beirut, 1335H/1914), p. 232; Qub'ain, *Taqrir Tarikhi*, p. 5.

15. Z. Vilnay, *Khaifa Be'avar Ve Bahoveh* (Haifa in the Past and the Future) (Tel-Aviv, 1936), p. 110; Carmel, *Tarikh Haifa*, pp. 147, 209–10.

16. Carmel, *Tarikh Haifa*, p. 147; Qub'ain, *Taqrir Tarikhi*, p. 5.

17. 'Latin' is the common name used for the Roman Catholic church in the Middle East, to differentiate it from the uniate churches.

18. History of 'Scuola Femminile Italiana Dell'ANMI', Diretta delle Suore Carmelitane (Haifa, May 1975).

19. Carmel, *Tarikh Haifa*, pp. 267–71; Vilnay, *Khaifa*, pp. 146–50.

20. Tamimi and Halabi, *Wilayat Beirut*, p. 251.

21. Qub'ain, *Taqrir Tarikhi*, pp. 6–7.

22. Carmel, *Tarikh Haifa*, p. 272.

23. Ibid., p. 267, and Tamimi and Halabi, *Wilayat Beirut*, p. 237.

24. A. Carmel, 'The German Settlers in Palestine and Their Relations with the Local Arab Population and the Jewish Community 1868–1918', in M. Ma'oz (ed.), *Studies on Palestine during the Ottoman Period* (Jerusalem, 1975), pp. 442–65. See also A. Schölch, 'European Penetration and the Economic Development of Palestine, 1856–82', in R. Owen (ed.), *Studies in the Economic and Social History of Palestine in the Nineteenth and Twentieth Centuries* (Oxford, 1982; London, 1987), pp. 42–5.

25. Carmel, *Tarikh Haifa*, pp. 222–4; Vilnay, *Khaifa*, p. 89. The Hijaz Railway was instrumental in securing the Ottoman Sultan a strong political and religious position and ensuring the allegiance of his Arab provinces and Indian co-religionists. The project was started by 'Abdul-Hamid II in 1900 and was initially financed by Muslim donations for the purpose of facilitating the pilgrimage to Mecca.

3

The Economic, Social and Political Structure of Haifa's Society in 1918

At the time of the British occupation of Haifa in late 1918, the mood of the Arab population reflected the diverse political ideas which had been circulating in the Fertile Crescent for at least fifty years. Since the early 1850s, both the rural and urban populations in the region had been introduced to a process that irrevocably changed their social and political realities and perceptions. The policy of administrative and legal modernization, known as the Tanzimat, was applied throughout the Ottoman Empire, including the Syrian provinces, during the nineteenth century. However, it was only during the second half of the century that any significant results could be felt. Under this policy, Western-influenced reforms were to be applied, in order to produce a centralized government machinery that would be capable of generating economic and financial growth and consequently would transform the political and social structures of the Empire. For this purpose many radical changes were imposed which affected the established structures of the state and its communities, including new laws governing land tenure and commercial activities which transformed the burden of taxation.

In addition to government efforts to implement a centralizing policy in the Empire, the application of the Tanzimat modernizing measures was influenced by the intensification of Western religious, economic and imperialist interests and rivalries.[1] Encouraged by the revolution in maritime transport, European industrial expansion now moved towards Ottoman markets. Gradually these contacts forged commercial agreements and concessions between the European exporters and their governments and the Ottoman state. By the second half of the century these contacts had developed to the point where, in addition to importing goods into the Empire, Europeans and the interests of their

26

countries determined the articles to be produced and exported. The Ottoman Empire was being integrated into the world capitalist system controlled, at that time, by Europe. Simultaneously European Christian missionary and pietistic groups grew alongside and often in co-operation with the European trading communities. This development took the form of a gradual infiltration of European personnel, economic concerns, and institutions and their protection by formal concessions and regulations.[2] The growing power of Europeans within the Empire extended to the protection of certain communities of the Ottoman population; this was bound to cause social upheavals and invariably happened in the cities.

Thus, at the dawn of the twentieth century, the whole region was in a process of change, although this differed in its manifestations from one province, or even town, to another. While the effects of the Tanzimat were gradual, it definitely shifted government focus from the countryside to the cities.[3] It was in these socio-economic centres that a more effective centralizing policy could be achieved and a more modern Westernized community could survive.

The coastal cities of Syria were acquiring a special importance as ports for European import and export trade. For northern Palestine, this development was also significant in relation to the hinterland. The fertile coastal plains had been minimally cultivated because of lack of security and had consequently remained unhealthy marshy lands. The immediate vicinity of the walled cities of Haifa, Acre and Jaffa was cultivated by city dwellers, but it was only by the 1860s, with improved security, that the settled urban communities were able to extend their area of cultivation and with it an agricultural trade that was moved through the northern ports of Acre and Haifa. Until then, for example, Haifa remained subject to vandalizing attacks by the Tirah villagers from Mount Carmel.[4]

The application of the Tanzimat reforms caused serious changes in urban social structures and determined the formation of new socio-political forces. By the application of the new land laws (1850s–1870s), which were meant to yield better financial returns to the central treasury, the government created a new stratum of wealthy landowners, confirmed and legalized the financial power of some of the traditional notables, and permitted foreigners to own land.[5] A new class of notables emerged in the cities, including those of Palestine, with political and social influence.

New patterns of political alliance by Ottoman rulers with town notables (ac‘an) and local mukhtars resulted in subtle but critical changes in stratification patterns in Palestine. These changes included the predominance of a single, more cohesive leadership group (urban notables displacing rural shaykhs); more inter dependence among different elements of the society; and greater social gaps between the layers of society. Most obvious was the accrual of broad autonomous powers throughout the countryside by the rising tax-farming townsmen.[6]

While these measures added new elements to the stratum of privileged urban notables, some of whom were Christian, the social and, to a limited extent, economic power of the traditional rural shaykhs continued to be felt. The rural notable families of the Triangle, Nablus, Jenin and Tulkarem, even though weakened economically, were able to retain some rural control and sometimes to transfer their influence to the towns. For example, in 1856–8, the 'Abdul Hadi family had one member as governor of Haifa, another controlling 'Arraba, and a third governing Nablus.[7] Even when this official status was withheld from rural families, their social influence did not disappear. Of course the religious and secular notables, whose power and composition had changed in the course of the century, were still significant in urban politics as intermediaries between the people and the government. Turkish administrative and military officials and the families they established in the Arab towns maintained a prominent role in this newly emerging and enlarged urban notable class.

By the end of the century the effects of the Tanzimat reforms had clearly altered and intensified the burden on the countryside and the peasantry. In order to meet tax increases and the changes in tax laws,[8] the peasant population became more dependent on urban moneylenders of all faiths. The urban merchants and landlords also benefited from the system by controlling the local councils and administrative offices, the finances of the countryside and often the prices of wheat and other staples in the towns. In this way the social and economic gap between the upper and lower classes of the Muslim population further widened during the era of modernization.[9] It is paradoxical that while Palestinian peasants were increasingly working for capital as part of the country's shift into the cycle of Western capitalism, they remained in the realm of pre-capitalist productive relations. The new notable class, mostly urban-based, made up of rural and urban landowners and the emerging commercial bourgeoisie, perpetrated these relations and defined the socio-economic differentiations.

It was mostly in the cities, too, that Western influence found fertile soil, although in varying degrees. This influence, on the whole, benefited the Christian communities at the expense of the Muslim inhabitants.[10] Official acceptance of the European governments' special privileges in the Ottoman provinces diminished the power of the central government over its non-Muslim subjects. The presence of Western consuls and merchants stimulated the economies of the coastal towns, but the increased imports of foreign goods contributed to a decline in local crafts and consequently to the impoverishment of the urban middle class of artisans and small traders, both Muslim and Christian. Furthermore, the protection and assistance afforded by these foreign agents to the Christians of the towns exacerbated the hostility of the Muslim inhabitants, who were already antagonized by the changing socio-economic status of non-Muslims.

Haifa's communities: origins and composition

The Tanzimat period witnessed the rapid growth of the western coastal towns of Palestine, where, in addition to the influx of local Arab populations, Greek, Italian and other European commercial agents congregated. Improved security and a deliberately more egalitarian official policy towards the religious communities were the main reasons for the changed conditions. The make-up of Haifa's population in the mid-nineteenth century is highly illuminating. In addition to the Muslim, Christian and Jewish communities living in their respective quarters, which were rigidly adhered to, a European community of consuls for England, France and Austria also resided there, many of them natives of Scio and the Dalmatian islands who had married into native Syrian and Greek families. Other resident Europeans engaged in commerce were of French and Maltese extraction. As noted earlier, French influence was the oldest and most effective because of the large number of French educational institutions. Despite Russian attempts in the 1860s to attract the Greek Orthodox community, their influence could not detract from the francophone trend.

These resident foreign communities played a significant part in the politics of the town up to the outbreak of the First World War, both overtly and covertly.[11] The Arab community of Haifa had been subjected to the varying political and cultural influences of competing European interests, coming in by way of educational missions, the Templar settlement and the trading opportunities provided by European consulates. These consulates had specifically chosen Haifa for their activities as opposed to Acre, the seat of the *mutasarrifiyya* (administrative district) and the base of Ottoman authority.[12] In Haifa, European merchants and their local agents were more free to trade and to organize their export business from the fast-growing port, the main items being the Hauran and northern Palestine grains and olive oil.

An emerging merchant class which included a large number of Christians contributed new members to the notable stratum. This new class was closely connected with the growing trade with Europe, and many of its members acquired socio-economic privileges through the patronage of foreign agents. France, Austria, England and Russia protected members of this emerging class in Alexandria, Beirut, Jaffa and somewhat belatedly in Haifa.[13]

As in Beirut, membership of this class in Haifa came from the local, mostly Christian, entrepreneurs. In Beirut, by the end of the nineteenth century, this merchant class had developed and mastered a complex and sophisticated system of socio-commercial relations utilizing both the advantages of its cultural heritage and the new Western consular protection.[14] In addition to the old-established Christian and Muslim Beiruti families, members of the less privileged classes could move up this new social ladder, and members of mountain communities found channels for development. This phenomenon was virtually reproduced in Haifa, though a few decades later than in Beirut and in a much narrower and less sophisticated fashion.

In the general structure and composition of its population in 1918, Haifa resembled Beirut more than Jerusalem, Palestine's main administrative centre, or Jaffa, its foremost port. In Haifa, the Muslim and Christian communities had maintained parity for a fairly long time, and while the religious groups lived in their respective quarters, they shared the same marketplace and public facilities (see Chapter 1). Although the other Palestinian towns also had various and large Christian minorities, their numerical strength always lagged behind that of the Muslim inhabitants. In these towns, this feature tended to create a picture of social cohesion, while in Haifa heterogeneity was a more pronounced characteristic. The large number of Christian denominations living in Haifa – Greek Orthodox, Greek and Latin Catholics, Maronites and Protestants – helped create a more tolerant atmosphere and encouraged the settlement of other peripheral communities. By the early 1900s, a Bahai, an Armenian and a small Druze community had been added to the growing and diversifying Christian denominations and Jewish communities.

By 1918, however, Haifa's Muslims made up the largest single community in the town. A number of official families of Turkish origin, the Sadiqs, the Khalils[15] and the Shukris, had been established in the region and had intermarried with local notable families. Their prominence emanated from their background and their acquired status as landowners, along with a handful of local Muslims such as the Khamra, the Taha, the Miqati, the Muhammadi, the Hajj Ibrahim and the Shaikh Hasan families. The latter two families also held religious posts as guardians of the Mar Ilias grotto on Mount Carmel,[16] the only religious site to which Haifa's Muslims laid claim – a fact which explains the lack of outstanding notable religious elements in the town. The Muslims of Haifa looked more towards Acre, a centre of Islamic historical-religious foundations, and families such as the Shuqairs, for guidance and leadership. Another indication of the relatively modest status of the Haifa Muslim community was the paucity and small size of the religious and educational endowments in the town, mostly established by the Khalil and Khamra families. Until 1936, the Khalil family was the *waqf* administrator, first Muhammad, then Ibrahim al-Khalil.[17] However, the religious leadership was to become a significant element in the political life of the town in the 1920s, directly after the Jerusalem religious leadership had established its ascendancy and a Palestinian political movement had begun to crystallize (see Chapters 13 and 14).

In addition to the above-mentioned notable Muslim families who traced their roots to the inception of Haifa itself, the town attracted, in the early twentieth century, various members of Palestinian families with agricultural bases. Among these were the Madis from Ijzim, the Sa'ds from Umm al-Fahm, the Tamimis, the Karamans and the 'Abdul-Hadis from the Nablus region, while some came, as officials or merchants, from other Palestinian towns or, like the Baiduns, from Beirut.

However, before the advent of large numbers of relatively sophisticated and wealthy Damascene and Beiruti families during the British occupation, the class of Muslim notables in Haifa was very small. This was in glaring contrast to the uneducated Muslim masses, particularly when compared with the emerging bourgeoisie among the various Christian denominations in the town. Socially and politically, a deep gap existed between the rich and poor of the Muslim community. There are also indications of feuds and competition separating its families – though not as intense as the conflicts between the Jerusalem Muslim families.[18] On the whole, the notable stratum identified itself with the Ottoman administration, whose presence in Haifa had grown perceptibly after 1900. Both the social and economic power of these families was linked with this presence and the application of Ottoman policy. Their members held administrative positions in the town, they were awarded easier opportunities for the acquisition of land in Haifa and the countryside, and they profited from the more secure conditions and the building of the Hijaz Railway to develop their inland trade. It should be noted, however, that the younger generation who were educated in the Ottoman schools[19] produced political figures calling for pan-Arabism, such as Rashid al-Hajj Ibrahim and Mu'in al-Madi.

The Greek Orthodox community, the oldest and originally the largest religious minority in Haifa, and the Greek Catholic community, which had achieved numerical superiority over all other denominations by the end of the century, were both indigenous communities with their roots in northern Palestine, Syria and Lebanon – a fact which was significant in explaining the role played by members of both communities in the social and political life of the town. The ethos of both confessions was based on their close attachment to the region and to the land as well as on an openness and malleability that allowed them to survive among different and often exclusivist socio-religious ideologies.

However, their religious affiliations gave each of them particular predispositions. The Greek Orthodox, with the help of the Russian church and government, vociferously rebelled against the domination of the Greek clergy and searched for more secular means of fulfilling their national identification.[20] Unlike the churches affiliated to Rome, the Orthodox church in the East did not provide a unifying leadership with which the laity could identify, nor did it supply its adherents with adequate material, social, educational or spiritual services. For this reason, European and American missionary activities won the majority of their converts from this church and provided them with an education which was attractive by promoting the Arabic language and culture. A substantial number of Greek Orthodox and Protestants educated in these institutions joined the professional class of lawyers, doctors and pharmacists in Haifa.[21] This also explains the Arab-oriented outlook of this congregation. Some of its members were active in the various cultural clubs and committees organized in Haifa before 1914, which were the only channels for social and political expression. At this date too, some of them – especially the literate ones – expressed definite political aspirations for a democratic system with equal representation, whether pan-Ottoman or pan-Arab.[22] Similarly, the Greek Catholics were inclined towards a national identification, even while religious foreign education tended to give the community francophile leanings.

The politicization of the Christian religious structure dates back to the Tanzimat period. Through the concession to the *millets* of freedom to organize and control their secular affairs, the Christian leadership, both lay and religious, was allowed to emerge and take part in the overall affairs of the society. A strong identification on the part of the lay members of this class with the clergy, although to a lesser degree among the Greek Orthodox, gave these communities cohesive social and political orientations. Cultural and political needs were now to be seriously considered by this wealthy and better-educated class, which was often directed by the spiritual head of the community. The absence or weakness of religious guidance in the Orthodox community allowed the expression of more radical opinion, while in the Greek Catholic community these same tendencies were very early on channelled and directed by church leadership; Bishop Hajjar was identified with the national movement and represented his congregation's political viewpoints even before the First World War.[23]

Various literary and cultural committees were sponsored by the churches on behalf of the youth of their communities, and several newspapers were published in Haifa by Christians.[24] The Greek Catholic community, even more than the other religious groups in the town, had cultural clubs before the war. Various news publications were circulated among the reading public and some were even donated to the schools for pupils to read. As early as 1908, *al-Nafa'is* and *Jirab al-kurdi*, owned by Khalil Baidas and Tawfiq Jana respectively, were established. *Al-Karmil*, which survived until the 1940s, was started by the Greek Orthodox Najib Nassar in 1909, and *al-Nafir*, owned by the Greek Orthodox Elia Zakka, in 1911.

Another differentiating feature of the Haifa communities was their origin. From early times there were inhabitants belonging to all three religious groups – Muslims, Christians (Greek Orthodox, Greek Catholics, Roman Catholics) and Jews. These communities were constantly enlarged from the 1870s onwards by the influx of Muslim workers from other Palestinian towns and the northern countryside and from Hauran; by a Maronite community focused around the Khuri family from Bkaisin in Mount Lebanon;[25] by Greek Catholic merchants from the north Galilee villages and towns as well as from Beirut and the Lebanese mountain villages;[26] by Greek Orthodox, often turned Protestant, from the villages around Acre and Nazareth, from Nablus and from the Shuf villages of Mount Lebanon;[27] and by Ashkenazi Jews from Europe and the Sephardic communities of Shefa 'Amr and Acre.[28] In the early 1900s, the nucleus of a Persian community of the Bahai faith came from Acre, and a few Druze families from the villages on Mount Carmel were also settling in the town. The foreign communities – consuls, merchants and the German colony – added to this colourful array of diverse origins and contributed a motley of customs and lifestyles as well as a spirit of tolerance and innovation.

Socio-economic stratification of Haifa's communities

In addition to wealth, education was becoming an important index of social differentiation between the religious communities and among members of the same community in the early twentieth century. Haifa boasted a large number of schools attached to the diverse Christian denominations, where the majority of the Christian inhabitants sent their children. The proximity of higher-level institutes of education affiliated to these religious communities in Jerusalem and Beirut led some of the better-off Haifa families to send their sons there. These educational opportunities were more available to the Christian communities in the town and explain the growth of a generation of educated Christians who were versed in foreign languages and had acquired professional training. However, the uniate Christian denominations were luckier in this respect than the Greek Orthodox community, which had a less educated younger generation. The least fortunate group were the

Muslims, who had to depend on the inadequate *Kuttab* (rudimentary school attached to the mosque) and the three small government elementary schools. For this reason, wealthy Muslims sent their sons either to local Christian schools, especially the Ecoles des Frères Chrétiens, or to Christian and Ottoman schools in the larger cities of the Empire. While some of these families, taking advantage of the Ottoman educational system, sent their sons as far afield as Istanbul, others sent them to the Christian mission schools in Jerusalem, 'Ain Tura and Beirut, where they met the sons of the wealthier Christian communities. In the Muslim community, education remained limited to a small stratum of wealthy families.

The wealth of the Haifa population, which had always been linked to landownership in the town and the agricultural hinterland, was gradually becoming associated with education as a means of economic betterment. On the whole, this worked to the advantage of the Christian section of the population, who found employment opportunities as interpreters and secretaries in the European consulates and as tourist guides and money-changers, as well as in the new reformed government departments and as commercial entrepreneurs.

The emerging merchant class included both Muslim and Christian landowners and/or grain merchants, with a preponderance of Christians at varying levels of wealth. It should be noted that a substantial section of this notable and middle-class wealth was new. In fact, it was associated with the laws commercializing land tenure and leading to capitalist investment in agricultural production. Ownership of agricultural land in northern Palestine and participation in the export trade of Hauran and Palestinian grain were the main indices of this wealth. Consequently economic control determined the socio-political status of the group; while the notable stratum was made up of wealthy landowners and capitalists, the middle-class merchants controlled the trade outlets in the town.

Among the Christians, Greek Catholic merchants were the most successful in exploiting their community assets and the new opportunities provided by the reforms, as well as their contacts with the West and their education in Western institutions. Such names as Sa'd, Khayyat, Sahyoun, Sanbar and Swaidan are examples of prominent Greek Catholic families whose educational background and commercial relations placed them among the wealthy of the town. Similarly, but to a lesser degree, the Kassab, Rayyis, Tuma and Abu Fadil families enjoyed prestige among the Greek Orthodox.[29] The two outstanding Maronite families were the Khuris and the Bustanis. The Khuris were, in fact, the wealthiest family in the whole of Haifa. Salim al-Khuri, a partner and agent of the Lebanese Sursuk family, owned various villages in the Marj and land in Haifa. Wadi' al-Bustani was prominent as a lawyer and vocal antagonist of Zionist activities in Haifa. The Maronite religious *waqf* consisting of a church and school was donated by the Khuris, and the whole community, which was generally poor, sought a livelihood through work provided by this family.[30] The richest Protestant family, whose wealth was greatly enhanced by British influence, was the Boutagy family,[31] while the Zahlans were the notable Roman Catholic family.

This picture of the socio-economic stratification of the Arab communities of Haifa can be further corroborated through a study of their marriage registers for the period before and during the First World War,[32] which give some indication of the occupational distribution among males of working age. The Muslim community, by far the largest of the communities, had the smallest number of landowners, merchants and professionals (i.e. doctors, pharmacists and lawyers); next in this scale came the Roman Catholics, followed by the Greek Orthodox. The Protestants and the Greek Catholics had the largest number of wealthy and professional people. It is also clear from the registers that the Muslim community had a high percentage of simple labourers, indicating the wide social gap between the well-off and the poorer class in that community. Among the Christians, a large number of tradesmen, builders, carpenters, teachers, fishermen and coachmen were registered, along with a smaller number of simple labourers, which, in turn, indicated that the social gap between the very rich and the very poor was narrower among the Christian denominations.

The stratification of Arab society in Haifa was affected by the same factors as in the other coastal cities of Palestine during the latter half of the nineteenth century. Since Haifa was less prosperous and less developed than Jaffa and Beirut, this process produced less clearly defined social classes than it did in the other towns. Nevertheless, by 1918, conscious social differences indicated by religion, wealth and education had taken root.

At this stage, the population of Haifa was roughly distributed into three social classes.[33] The class of notables had achieved its prestige either through its Muslim-Turkish origin and its traditional control of official positions and landholdings[34] or through Muslim commercial power, especially through trade with inland Syria.[35] Added to this class were the Christian landowning and commercial strata which had acquired wealth through the changes in the Ottoman system and Western assistance.[36] A middle class was also emerging during this period, whose financial wealth was a result of the growing importance of the towns, and the increase in the price of land and in the number and variety of work opportunities. The upper stratum of this class included Muslim and Christian merchants and landowners in the town[37] and families holding official and professional positions.[38] The lower stratum, the petit bourgeoisie, was partly made up of Muslims in the lower echelons of government employment, but came mostly from the Christian communities who, though educated, lacked financial strength and filled the newly created jobs in the commercial and administrative sectors. Most members of this class came from the less fortunate branches of families in the upper stratum. The large class of labourers was made up mostly of Muslim manual labourers in the railways, the roads, and the building and commercial sectors, as well as small craftsmen.

During the war years 1914–18 all the social classes of Haifa experienced economic and personal hardship. Credit for local merchants and businessmen was curtailed and the few industrial enterprises started up during the previous decade, such as alcohol, soap and metal factories, came to a standstill, due both to the lack of financial liquidity and therefore of local purchasing power and to the deportation of enemy aliens, some of whom had played an important role in these enterprises. The British and French schools were closed and all building activities were suspended. The male population between the ages of seventeen and fifty was conscripted, thus depriving the town of most of its breadwinners. Conditions were further worsened by the recurrence of locust attacks, which in 1915 destroyed an already poor harvest and added hunger and disease to the sufferings of the population. These conditions led many of Haifa's old-established families to sell their land in the town and on the mountain at depressed prices.[39] Starvation and typhus were the cause of many deaths; hundreds and possibly thousands perished.[40] The inhabitants, especially the non-Muslims, were often subjected to maltreatment, imprisonment and exile on real or trumped-up allegations of spying for and sympathizing with the enemy. In short, the end of the war found Haifa's population diminished, impoverished, sick and dispirited.

Political orientations

As early as mid-century some among the literate class in Haifa had already reached an understanding of the political and economic factors which influenced the fate of the local populations. Among this class, there was also a sense of identification as Arabs, as distinct from the Turkish civilians and military officers who administered the system and who were regarded as foreigners.[41] There are also indications that these opinions were not confined to the Christians among the inhabitants. When the British Vice Consul, Edward Thomas Rogers, formed a society for 'the acquisition and diffusion of useful knowledge' in 1859, he invited 'the best-informed of the Arabs' in Haifa to lectures on the past history of the East, its grandeur, its scientific attainments, and its intellectual and moral influence over the world at large.[42] It was through the growth of such discussion circles, whether intercommunal or under the auspices of the more influential religious institutions, that a sense of cultural and historical self-awareness was nurtured among the Arab inhabitants.

By the turn of the century, a new generation of better-educated and more confident Arabs had grown up or settled in the town, sometimes bringing with them more developed social and political ideas. Among the notable and literate classes, these ideas differed according to social and economic interests. The notable class, and, more specifically, the Muslims among them, identified with the ruling system; but nationalist tendencies, whether demanding equal rights with the Turks or de-centralization or even Arab independence, were apparent among the younger generation, and were also expressed among the merchant and professional classes of the Christian communities. The Muslim notables were naturally, by virtue of their vested interest, pro-Ottoman and supported Islamic overtones to that orientation. Some of the more educated Muslims and Christians had been introduced to the political currents and secret national societies active from Istanbul to Cairo, to Beirut, and to Nablus. The two main currents were Ottomanism and Arabism and their variants. Before the First World War the only vocal opposition was that supporting the Ottoman Decentralization Party, established in Cairo in 1912,[43] and the Islah (Reform) Societies of Beirut,[44] which called for the reform of Arab provinces within the Ottoman Empire. These activities and perhaps those of the more radical organizations were known among the young Muslims and Christians of Haifa, particularly those who had active contacts with co-religionists and relatives and trading connections in Beirut and Damascus, the strongholds of Arab nationalist activities.

Despite the economic impact of the German colony in Haifa, German influence was very limited.[45] The influence of the large number of francophone educational institutions showed clearly in the orientation of the Catholic denominations and even among some members of the Orthodox church whose education was French. Similarly, British, Russian, Italian and Austrian influences had their adherents. These orientations were so significant that during the war many Catholics, including the Greek Catholic Bishop, were accused – and convicted – of spying for the French.[46] There are also indications that a ring of Haifa residents worked for British Intelligence.[47]

These tendencies to ally with the Western powers whose cultural and financial influence had been imbibed by the local inhabitants did not contradict the tendency towards identification with the general trend of Arab nationalism and some form of independence from Otto-man control. The local press played a crucial part in publicizing these ideas and forming public opinion among the literate class. The pioneers of this method of political activism were members of the Eastern churches: Najib Nassar, Iliya Zakka and Jamil Bahri, who were also instrumental in organizing political committees before the First World War. Members of all denominations were involved in this movement, which emphasized the secular unity of the Arab elements of the Otto-man peoples. Another factor which increased this feeling of unity among both Muslims and Christians was the opposition to Zionism.

As early as the 1890s, peasants in the north of Palestine had been displaced by Jewish land purchases and had often reacted by attacking the settlements. The north had little spare arable land, and any pur-chases were instantly felt by the agricultural community. In the cities, the protest against Jewish land purchases and immigration came from the class of tradesmen and professional people, who were mostly Chris-tian. Initially, their apprehensions were based on economic competition, but by 1909 a certain opposition to Zionist plans was being expressed on the basis of national ideology.

The anti-Zionist campaign mounted by the press in Haifa was more intense than in other Palestinian cities, due, of course, to the direct effect of Zionist land purchases and immigration in northern Palestine.[48] The message of Nassar's articles in his newspaper *al-Karmil* was that the Syrian provinces, in particular the Palestinian region, were Arab, and that foreign – i.e. Zionist – designs to buy land and settle there should be stopped.[49] Nassar's purpose was not only to incite public opinion against Zionism, but to alert it to instances of collusion on the part of the authorities to facilitate Jewish land purchases. In Haifa, Nassar was vigilant in keeping track of all activities undertaken by the Jewish immigrants and publicizing every new change in their condition and status. The public was kept informed of the numerical and economic growth of the Haifa Jewish community, of the sales of land to them and of their large-scale projects, such as the establishment of the Technion (Technical Institute) in the town.[50] Nevertheless, a competing Haifa paper, *al-Nafir*, supported the Zionists, and elements among the Haifa notable landowning class, both Muslim and Christian, favoured its line. But Nassar's message was in tune with a growing mood in the other Palestinian towns, and his articles were reported and reprinted even outside Palestine.[51]

At this stage, these national feelings and local discontents were neither clearly articulated nor structurally channelled. Socio-political leadership was confined to the traditional notables and religious leaders, a situation which was perpetuated during the Mandate period. While both public and secret societies had been set up in Istanbul, Beirut, Jerusalem, Nablus, and Jaffa to express these national demands in one form or another, in Haifa the press was the only public channel of expression. However, religious leaders soon joined political committees whenever these were set up. A branch of al-Muntada al-Adabi[52] was opened in Haifa on 12 September 1911. This political club had been started in Istanbul in 1909 by a number of Arab students, three of them from Palestine, with the aim of reviving Arab culture, irrespective of religious belief, under the banner of Ottomanism. When this club opened in Haifa under the auspices of 'Arfan Bek, the Qa'im-maqam (deputy mayor) of the Qada, an executive committee consisting of all the religious leaders was set up in support of programmes for reform in the Arab provinces, especially in the field of elementary education. Not much was mentioned of its activities or achievements thereafter, however.[53] No doubt the reason for the cessation of such activities was the policy of the new ruling party in Istanbul, the Committee of Union and Progress (CUP), which had become less tolerant of Arab particularist activities and aspirations and aimed at consolidating Ottoman political and ideological control over the Syrian provinces – a policy which alienated the majority of the population and drove them towards a more Arab nationalist orientation. Nevertheless, a substantial number of educated Haifa residents were clearly aware of the political implications of the reforms and the necessity for a united front to achieve them.

On the other subject of local concern, Zionism, political activities continued after the change of government in Istanbul in April 1909, especially through the press. An association founded by Nassar in Haifa in 1910 had as its sole purpose to struggle against Zionism by persuading the government to prohibit land sales and Jewish immigration.[54] A combination of the two objectives, reform of the Arab provinces and containment of the Zionist threat, lay behind Haifa's strong expression of support for the 1913 Arab Congress in Paris.[55] Of 139 signatories of support from Palestine, 50 came from Haifa. Considering the French influence behind the convening of this Congress, the high number of Christian signatories – 43, of whom 27 were Catholic – as against 7 Muslims is readily explained.[56] It is noteworthy that not one of the notable landowning families, Muslim or Christian, lent its support to a movement which threatened separation from the Ottoman Empire and was disapproved of by the government. However, when it became clear that the main concern of the Palestinians, namely, the Zionist threat, was not even discussed at the Congress, anti-Zionists from Haifa and Jaffa tried to convene a conference in Nablus with the purpose of organizing the struggle against Zionism.[57] In Haifa, where the emerging merchant and educated classes were of significant size, and had a large proportion of Christian members, Arab nationalism and anti-Zionism went hand in hand.

During the war, political activities were subjected to the centralizing policy of the Ottoman state and all expressions of Arab national feeling or sympathy with the Allied powers were harshly dealt with. Najib Nassar had to go into hiding because of his pan-Arab activities and his support of al-Muntada al-Adabi, whose members were associated with the Arab separatist movement in 1915–16,[58] and various Catholic residents were accused of complicity with the French and were exiled from Palestine.[59] The harsh physical conditions in Haifa during the war years diverted the attention of the politically conscious strata to the problems of survival.

Thus a political consciousness was clearly developing among the educated classes of Haifa in 1918. Whether it was to support affiliation to an Ottoman entity – pan-Ottomanism; or to seek some form of independence from Ottoman control – decentralization; or to aspire to all-out independent rule for the Arab-speaking provinces – pan-Arabism; or even to search for solutions under the religious banner of Islam – pan-Islam: all these ideas could find adherents among the communities of Haifa. However, at this early date, these ideas and political orientations were amorphous and not clearly enough articulated to be defined as an identification. The communities, at varying levels, were exposed to a diversity of external cultural and political influences which were sometimes contradictory and certainly difficult to reconcile. While, on one level, ideas imported through the Western educational institutions and trading contacts encouraged an alliance with foreign policies, on another level this period saw a stronger pride in the Arab culture and heritage and a sharper sense of the threat from some of these Western policies. This was not unlike what was happening in Beirut, Damascus and Jerusalem, to which the Haifa merchants often travelled and from which some Haifa families originated. In spite of the social diversity of Haifa, a more cohesive political orientation was emerging which coalesced around the issue of the slow encroachment of Zionist plans and against the heavy-handed policy of the CUP to stifle Arab cultural and political expression.

Notes

1. S. Shamir, 'The Modernization of Syria: Problems and Solutions in the Early Period of 'Abdul-Hamid', and D. Chevalier, 'Western Development and Eastern Crisis in the Mid-Nineteenth Century: Syria Confronted with the European Economy', in Polk and Chambers (eds), *Beginnings of Modernization in the Middle East* (Chicago, IL, 1968); A. Schölch, 'European Penetration and the Economic Development of Palestine, 1856–82', in R. Owen (ed.), *Studies in the Economic and Social History of Palestine in the Nineteenth and Twentieth Centuries* (Oxford, 1982).

2. A. H. Hourani, 'Ottoman Reform and the Politics of Notables', in his *The Emergence of the Modern Middle East* (London, 1981), pp. 62–4.

3. M. Ma'oz, 'The Impact of Modernization on Syrian Politics and Society during the Early Tanzimat Period', in Polk and Chambers, *Beginnings of Modernization*, p. 333.

4. For a perceptive account of the threat to settled life in Haifa and to the livelihood of the peasants in northern Palestine, see M. E. Rogers, *Domestic Life in Palestine* (London, 1863), pp. 86–90 and pp. 178–9.

5. Schölch, 'European Penetration', pp. 21–2; J. S. Migdal, *Palestinian Society and Politics* (Princeton, NJ, 1980), pp. 12–13.

6. Ibid., p. 11. See also Hourani, 'Ottoman Reform'.

7. Rogers, *Domestic Life*, pp. 216–17. Saleh Bek 'Abdul Hadi was governor of Haifa in 1858.

8. Migdal, *Palestinian Society*, pp. 12–14; Hourani, *The Emergence*, p. 66.

9. Ma'oz, 'The Impact', p. 347.

10. Beirut is an excellent model of Western influence on the population during the nineteenth century. The socio-economic effect of this influence led to sharp sectarian strife and animosities. See L. T. Fawaz, *Merchants and Migrants in Nineteenth Century Beirut* (Cambridge, 1983).

11. A. Carmel, *Tarikh Haifa fi 'Ahd al-Atrak al-'Uthmaniyyin* (History of Haifa in the Ottoman Period) (Haifa, 1979), pp. 171–250; Hourani, *The Emergence*, p. 65; for the earlier period see Rogers, *Domestic Life*.

12. Schölch, 'European Penetration', p. 47.

13. Rogers, *Domestic Life*, pp. 86, 376, 380, and 391–2.

14. Fawaz, *Merchants*, pp. 85–9.

15. The Khalil family was the most prominent Muslim family of Haifa and had intermarried with the Shukri family. Mustafa Pasha al-Khalil (died 1919) was the patriarch of the family and owned lands in the eastern part of Haifa, where the only public bath, Hammam al-Basha, was built by him. He also endowed 40 dunums of land from the grotto of Mar Ilias on Mount Carmel to the sea in the Mawares area to the west of Haifa (oral information, Suhail Shukri, Haifa, May 1975). Mustafa al-Khalil acted as agent for the Sursuks for a while (oral information, Iskandar Majdalani, Haifa, May 1975).

16. The Khamra family was an old landowning Muslim family after whom a square in the centre of town was named. The Hajj Ibrahims, a lay family, held the guardianship of the grotto of the prophet Ilias, a site of religious pilgrimage for the three faiths (Z. Vilnay, *Khaifa Be'avar Ve Bahoveh* (Haifa in the Past and the Future) (Tel-Aviv, 1936), p. 145). Members of this family were prominent grain merchants handling the produce of the interior and the Hauran. The Shaikh Hasans, who can trace their background in Haifa to the fifth grandfather, also held, at different periods, hereditary responsibility at the grotto (oral information, Khalid al-Hasan, London, March 1982). Another section of this family was engaged in trade.

17. Oral information, Suhail Shukri and Fawwaz al-Sa'd, Haifa, May 1975.

18. For relations between Haifa families see: Carmel, *Tarikh Haifa*, p. 267; also confirmed by oral information, Iskandar Majdalani, Haifa, May 1975. For feuds and animosity between Jerusalem Muslim families see: K. Sakakini, *Kadha Ana Ya Dunya* (Such I am, O World) (Jerusalem, 1955), pp. 165–6.

19. Families of Turkish origin and many of the wealthier Muslim families sent their sons to be educated in the government schools in Beirut and Damascus

and even to Istanbul. Oral information, Suhail Shukri, Tannus Salama, Iskandar Majdalani and Fawwaz al-Sa'd, Haifa, May 1975.

20. The struggle of the Arab Orthodox community against the stultifying control of the Greek clergy started in the last two decades of the nineteenth century, aided and abetted by the Russian Archimandrite in Jerusalem and the various educational institutes set up in Palestine by the Russian church. D. Hopwood, *The Russian Presence in Syria and Palestine 1843–1914* (Oxford, 1969). See Sakakini, *Kadha Ana*, pp. 39–40, and E. Kedourie, 'Religion and Politics: The Diaries of Khalil Sakakini', in *Middle Eastern Affairs*, 1 (*St Antony's Papers No. 4*, London, 1958), pp. 92–5.

21. A few names as examples of these professionals are from the families of Nassar, Abu Rahma, Saba, Dumian, Zu'rub (oral information, family members and Wadi' Jabbur, Haifa, March/April 1975).

22. 'Issa al-'Issa, editor and owner of the Palestinian newspaper *Falastin*, was a Greek Orthodox who supported the pan-Ottoman trend and Najib Nassar, owner of *al-Karmil* from Haifa, was for the pan-Arab orientation. See Y. Porath, *The Emergence of the Palestinian Arab National Movement, 1918–1929* (London, 1974), pp. 26–8.

23. J. 'Asfour, *Palestine: My Land, My Country, My Home* (Beirut, 1967), p. 52.

24. J. Bahri, *Tarikh Haifa* (History of Haifa) (Haifa, 1922), pp. 29–34. See also A. K. al-'Aqqad, *Tarikh al-Sahafa al-'Arabiyya fi Filastin* (History of the Arabic Press in Palestine) (Damascus, 1967).

25. Q. Khuri, *Al-Dhikrayyat* (Memories) (Jerusalem, 1945), p. 35.

26. Examples were the Sahyoun family, which had originally, in the mid-1880s, come from 'Iblin in western Galilee, the Khayyat family, which had come from Tyre, and the Swaidan family from Mount Lebanon. Oral information, Dr Maurice Sahyoun, Beirut, June 1977 and Wadi' Jabbur, Haifa, April 1975.

27. Examples of Greek Orthodox families, some of whose members had joined the Protestant church and had come to settle in Haifa, were the Habibis from Shefa 'Amr, the Itayyims from Kufr Yasif, the Abu Fadils and the Nassars from 'Ain 'Anoub in the Lebanese Shuf region. Oral information, E. Seikaly and F. Abu Fadil, Los Angeles, 1977.

28. Vilnay, *Khaifa*, pp. 100–110.

29. Oral information, Iskandar Majdalani, Haifa, May 1975. Iskandar Kassab was an agent for the Sursuk family and thereby acquired fruit gardens to the east of Haifa on the banks of the Muqata' River. He also owned built-up areas in the west of the town.

30. Khuri, *Al-Dhikrayyat*, pp. 34–5 and p. 215. Salim al-Khuri started a silk production project in Yajur, the land he had acquired from the Sursuk brothers. For this purpose he brought many Lebanese farmers to work in silk cultivation and production, and he had a branch of the factory on Jaffa Street in Haifa. The project failed mainly because the farmers could not survive the hardship of malaria in Yajur (oral information, Tannus Salama, Haifa, April 1975).

31. The Boutagy family was of Maltese origin; its ancestor had accompanied the Napoleonic expedition to Palestine and settled in Acre. Teofil Boutagy (1870–1944) was educated at the Syrian Protestant school in Beirut and was a pioneer of British trade and appointed honorary consul for the United States and Finland. E. Boutagy, 'My Life Story' (unpublished document, n.d.).

32. This study was compiled from the church marriage registers of the Roman Catholic church, Haifa, 1975; the Greek Orthodox church, Haifa, 1975; the Protestant, St Luke's church, Haifa, 1975; and the Istiqlal Mosque, Haifa, 1975. It should be borne in mind that in the years 1890–1920 the Muslim community was the largest, followed by the Greek Catholic and then the Greek Orthodox, the Roman Catholic, the Maronite and – smallest of all – the Protestant community.

33. For a detailed stratification of the Palestine Arab society prior to the British Mandate, see: N. A. Badran, *Al-Ta'lim wal-Tahdith fil-Mujtama' al-'Arabi al-Filastini* (Education and Modernization in Arab Palestinian Society) (Beirut, 1969), pp. 17–94.

34. Such as the Khalil and Sadiq families.

35. Such as the Hajj Ibrahim, Taha, Khamra, Muwaqa' and Miqati families.

36. Such as the Khuri, Sa'd, Khayyat and Kassab families.

37. Such as the Shaikh Hasan, Tamimi, Murad, Tuma, Rayyis, Sahyoun, Sanbar, Zahlan and Boutagy families.

38. Such as the Mukhlis, Madi, Nassar, Zakka, Bustani, Saba and Dumit families.

39. Carmel, *Tarikh Haifa*, p. 290; oral information, Tannus Salama, Haifa, May 1975, also confirmed by oral information from many family members.

40. Carmel, *Tarikh Haifa*, p. 290; J. Rothschild, *History of Haifa and Mount Carmel* (Haifa, 1934), p. 5; Bahri, *Haifa*, p. 41.

41. In conversation with Mary Rogers, the Vice Consul's sister in Haifa, Elias Sekhali, a thoughtful Greek Orthodox man, gave vent to his despondency about the corruption of Turkish rule in Syria. Irregular and heavy taxation, he said, prohibited the Arabs from cultivating the land and the rapacity of Turkish governors and officials hampered the development of all wealth or commerce. Other complaints concerned the lack of security, justice and educational opportunities. Rogers, *Domestic Life*, pp. 161–3.

42. Ibid., p. 376.

43. C. E. Dawn, *From Ottomanism to Arabism* (London, 1973), p. 149.

44. Porath, *The Emergence*, pp. 23–4.

45. Carmel, *Tarikh Haifa*, p. 276; Schölch, 'European Penetration', p. 44.

46. Bahri, *Haifa*, pp. 36–40; Carmel, *Tarikh Haifa*, p. 290; and A. Mansur, *Tarikh al-Nasira: Min Awwal 'Usuriha wa-hatta Ayyamina al-Hadira* (History of Nazareth from its Early Period until the Present) (Cairo, 1924), pp. 106–9.

47. Teofil Boutagy and 'Abbas Effendi were among those said to have been involved in spying for the British. There seems to have been some truth in these rumours as reported in P. Knightley and C. Simpson, *The Secret Lives of Lawrence of Arabia* (London, 1969), pp. 42–4. Oral information, Iskandar Majdalani, Haifa, May 1975, and Suhail Shukri, Haifa, May 1975. Suhail Shukri was told by his father, Hasan Shukri, the mayor of Haifa in 1918, that when General King entered the town, he asked him about 'Abbas Bahai (Effendi) and Hajj Za'lan, with whom he had previous contacts.

48. N. Mandel, 'Turks, Arabs and Jewish Immigration into Palestine, 1882–1914', in A. Hourani (ed.), *St Antony's Papers No. 17* (Oxford, 1965), pp. 85–95.

49. For Nassar's career as a journalist dedicated to opposition to the Zionist movement and the attempts by Zionist organizations and authorities to vilify

him, cause his arrest and suspend his paper between 1909 and 1915, see Mandel, 'Turks, Arabs', pp. 94–5; Carmel, *Tarikh Haifa*, pp. 272–4; and K. Qasimiyya, 'Mawaqif 'Arabiyya min al-Tafahum ma'al-Sahyuniyya 1913–1914' (Arab Approaches for Understanding Zionism 1913–1914), *Shu'un Falastiniyya*, Vol. 31 (March 1974), p. 137; N. Mandel, *The Arabs and Zionism before World War I* (London, 1976), pp. 85–6, 123–4, 219–28; Porath, *The Emergence*, pp. 25–30.

50. *Al-Karmil*, 4 June 1930, reprinted an excerpt taken from the newspaper of 14 May 1910, on the sale of land by Ilyas Sursuk. See also *al-Karmil*, 26 September 1931, with a reprint of information on the Technion and its policies from *al-Karmil*, 26 July 1911.

51. Porath, *The Emergence*, p. 27.

52. M. I. Darwaza, *Nash'at al-Haraka al-'Arabiyya al-Haditha* (Development of the Modern Arab Movement), 2nd edition (Sidon, 1971), pp. 353–60.

53. *Al-Karmil*, 11 November 1931, reprinted this excerpt from its issue of 12 September 1911.

54. Porath, *The Emergence*, p. 28. Mandel, *The Arabs and Zionism*, pp. 123–4.

55. Qasimiyya, 'Mawaqif 'Arabiyya', pp. 135–6.

56. W. Kawtharani, *Watha'iq al-Mu'tamar al-'Arabi al-Awwal, 1913* (Documents of the First Arab Congress, 1913) (Beirut, 1980), pp. 197–8. Najib Nassar was among the Haifa signatories.

57. Porath, *The Emergence*, p. 29.

58. Saif ad-Din al-Khatib, a magistrate from Haifa, was among the Arab nationalists hanged in Damascus in May 1915. See G. Antonius, *The Arab Awakening* (London, 1955), p. 189.

59. Bahri, *Haifa*, pp. 36–8.

PART TWO

British Policy and the Development of Haifa

4

The Demographic Transformation of Haifa 1918–39

Haifa's physical character changed quite dramatically between 1918 and 1939. The population grew from 24,634 in 1922 to an estimated 105,900 in 1939,[1] so that what had been a relatively small town became one of the four largest cities in Palestine in the course of twenty years. The city also acquired distinctive features as a result of the changing balance of communities. As we have seen, this process had already begun: as far as the sketchy figures for the nineteenth century indicate, the Jewish population had grown slowly but steadily up until the First World War, while the Muslim population had gradually overtaken the Christian one, probably through a combination of higher birth rates and immigration from the countryside. The most phenomenal change during the Mandate period was in the Jewish community. While Jews made up approximately an eighth of the population in 1918, their number grew to a quarter in 1922, then to a third in 1931 and to slightly over a half of the total inhabitants of Haifa in 1939.[2] This drastic increase can only be explained by the number of Jewish immigrants that flooded the country, in successive waves, and the large numbers that settled in the urban centres. In Haifa, the Jewish community was continuously expanded by the addition of new arrivals; these additions came in two major waves, a smaller one between 1920 and 1926 and a larger one in the early 1930s.

The two censuses carried out by the Administration in October 1922 and November 1931 are the only two official sources of statistical information on population growth for the Mandate period, and only the 1931 census provides a thorough survey of socio-economic statistics and a wealth of information on the composition of the population. Soon after the start of the occupation, government officials began reporting estimates for the population in their districts, but this was done neither regularly nor scientifically. For example, the population of Haifa was estimated at 34,100 in January 1922, ten months before the official census was undertaken, at which time the population was computed at 24,634.[3]

By the late 1940s, the Administration released vital statistics on births and deaths as recorded by the Health Department; these statistics supply the means for assessing the natural increase of the population, setting aside the increase through immigration, for the years when no censuses were held. Using these sources, Table 4.1 shows the hypothetical growth of the population of Haifa, taking into account only the natural increase for the intercensal period 1922-31, and Table 4.2, using the statistics of the 1931 census, shows the hypothetical increase up to 1939.[4] This exercise is important in order to estimate the population growth in each community through immigration, since such figures are recorded only for the whole of Palestine.

The intercensal increase of 25,769 shows that Haifa's population had doubled. Only 7,998 of this increase was due to an excess of births over deaths, and 17,771 came through immigration in all religious communities. The improved health conditions for all communities and the higher standard of living among the Jews and Christians explain the relatively high natural population growth. The difference between the estimated figures for population increase in 1931 in Table 4.1 and the actual figures for 1931 in Table 4.2 (as provided by the 1931 census) indicates that both the Muslim and the Jewish communities had grown very sharply in the interval through immigration, the Muslims by 8,469 and the Jews by 6,232, while the Christians grew by only 2,900 immigrants. The ratio of this increase to the total population in each religious group gives the Jews the highest rate of immigration, though not much higher than that of the Muslims. It is clear, however, that while 56 per cent of Haifa's Jewish inhabitants, in 1931, claimed Europe as their birthplace, 90 per cent of the Muslims came from inside Palestine.[5] Similarly, the Christians had a high percentage of Palestinian-born residents and about 10 per cent who came from adjoining Arab regions such as Syria and Lebanon.

Another significant characteristic of Haifa's immigrant population was its division among age groups. In 1931, 27.6 per cent of the Jewish population were between the ages of twenty-five and thirty-five, while only 18.5 per cent of the Arabs, both Muslim and Christian, fell into this age group.[6] This shows that while Haifa, like other coastal towns in the eastern Mediterranean at this period, attracted local immigrants from the inland towns and the economically depressed countryside, it also attracted Zionist Jewish immigrants, mostly from Europe, at the peak of their working and child-bearing life.

By 1939 the population of Haifa had more than doubled its size in

Table 4.1 Hypothetical growth of Haifa's population 1922–31

Year	Total	Muslims	% of total	Christians	% of total	Jews	% of total
1922	24,634	9,377	38.3	8,863	36.2	6,230	25.4
1923	24,951	9,386	37.6	9,016	36.1	6,385	25.5
1924	25,656	9,587	37.3	9,260	36.0	6,645	25.9
1925	26,304	9,797	37.2	9,438	35.8	6,905	26.2
1926	27,307	10,065	36.8	9,659	35.3	7,419	27.1
1927	28,269	10,372	36.7	9,896	35.0	7,837	27.7
1928	29,159	10,612	36.4	10,104	34.6	8,279	28.4
1929	30,086	10,919	36.3	10,298	34.2	8,705	28.9
1930	31,349	11,374	36.3	10,598	33.8	9,213	29.3
1931	32,632	11,853	36.3	10,924	33.5	9,691	29.7

Table 4.2 Hypothetical growth of Haifa's population 1931–39

Year	Total	Muslims	% of total	Christians	% of total	Jews	% of total
1931	50,403	20,324	40.6	13,824	27.6	15,923	31.8
1932	51,607	20,792	40.3	14,146	27.4	16,337	31.6
1933	52,939	21,279	40.2	14,506	27.4	16,822	31.8
1934	54,143	21,541	39.8	14,797	27.3	17,473	32.3
1935	56,284	22,112	39.3	15,194	27.0	18,646	33.1
1936	58,805	22,868	38.9	15,687	26.7	19,918	33.9
1937	60,935	23,327	38.2	16,086	26.3	21,189	34.7
1938	63,292	24,357	38.4	16,612	26.2	21,990	34.7
1939	65,350	25,184	38.5	17,131	26.2	22,707	34.7

Sources: Census of Palestine, 1922 (Jerusalem, 1923), p. 6; *Census of Palestine, 1931* (Alexandria, 1933), II, p. 16; *Vital Statistics, 1922–1945*, Dept of Statistics (Jerusalem, 1947).

1931, through natural increase. However, the official estimates, taking into account the increase through immigration, raised the population by a further 40 per cent to 105,900 inhabitants,[7] competing in size with Jerusalem and Tel-Aviv. Clearly the population explosion in Haifa occurred after the last official census in 1931 and was largely caused by increased immigration.

Because of the lack of specific data on legal and illegal immigration, it is possible to give only rough estimates for this increase. Table 4.2 makes it clear that the rate of growth of the Jewish community was overtaking that of both the Muslim and the Christian communities.

The immigration wave starting in 1932 doubled the Jewish population of Palestine, and by the end of the 1930s Jews constituted some 30.5 per cent of the total population.[8] The official registry of immigrants into Palestine shows the sharp increase of these waves and their overriding Jewish membership.[9] How many of these filtered into Haifa and swelled its Jewish communities is impossible to assess with accuracy. But there was already a high concentration of Jews in the city, and British and Jewish economic development projects proved a great attraction to the influx of immigrants, especially of German Jews. Official Zionist sources in the city computed Jewish population increase between 1931 and 1938 at 239 per cent, which inflated the Jewish population of the city from 15,923 to 54,118.[10] This was due mainly to immigration, both legal and illegal. There has been confirmed information of illegal Jewish immigration through Haifa during the 1920s and particularly in the 1930s, which would suggest that a certain percentage of those immigrants could have remained in the city.[11]

An increase of approximately 40 per cent has been computed between the natural and the estimated actual population of Haifa since the mid-1930s. Taking into consideration the fact that over 90 per cent of the total immigration was Jewish,[12] a large proportion of this increase would be due to Jewish newcomers into the city. This inevitably transformed the composition of the population and goes a long way towards explaining the roots of the popular uprising of 1936 which started in Haifa.

However, it would be erroneous to assume that the tremendous population explosion in the city leading to the Arab revolt was made up mostly of Jewish immigrants. The Arab population had also grown tremendously during the 1930s as a result of natural increase and immigration. Both the British Administration and the Zionists initiated a number of projects that attracted Arab workers, both skilled and unskilled. Haifa had become a haven of employment for Palestinians as well as for opportunity seekers from the neighbouring Arab regions. A study of the Shari'a Court records (Sijil) indicated that 75 per cent of Arab immigrants into Haifa during the Mandate period were of Palestinian origin, of whom only 32 per cent came from towns and cities.[13] While there is a rough estimate of Jewish population growth by 1939, it is much more difficult to calculate for the Arab sector. However, the events of 1936-9 in Haifa implied the concentration of very large numbers of Arabs in the city, of Palestinian origin, many of them from peasant backgrounds and economically depressed.

Notes

1. For the 1922 demographic statistics see *Census of Palestine, 1922* (Jerusalem, 1923), compiled by J. B. Barron. For the 1939 estimate of population see Government of Palestine, *Statistical Abstract of Palestine* (Jerusalem, 1940), p. 10.

2. During the war, the Jewish community decreased because of deportation and hardships, but it increased very rapidly between 1918 and 1922, doubling its number. It more than doubled again by the 1931 census; see E. Mills, *Census of Palestine, 1931* (Alexandria, 1933). By 1936, five years after the census, the Jewish population of Haifa was assessed at close to 50,000, which means that it had more than tripled. Even though this assessment is supplied only by Jewish scholars (Y. Washitz, 'Jewish-Arab Relations in Haifa during the Mandate' (unpublished manuscript), Chapter II, p. 1) and Zionist literature (Report by Hadar Ha-Carmel and other Jewish co-operatives, 6 October 1937, CZA J16/104), it is probably basically true, even if somewhat exaggerated, since Jewish immigrants had come to Palestine in great numbers in the early 1930s, and inflated the numbers of urban Jewry.

By late 1938, the official estimate of Jewish population in Haifa was reported at 52,000, topping the combined Muslim and Christian total population by 1,000. See: Government of Palestine, *Palestine Blue Book, 1938*, p. 332.

3. Approximate figures for the population of Palestine as of 1 January 1922 in Government of Palestine, Department of Commerce and Industry, *Commercial Bulletin*, Vol. I, 1922.

4. Tables 4.1 and 4.2 are computed by using as base the population statistics for Haifa of the two censuses of 1922 and 1931. The figures for births and deaths, as supplied by the Department of Statistics' *Vital Statistics, 1922–1945* (Jerusalem, 1947), are then used to show the annual natural increase. In addition to the three main religious communities, Haifa had a fourth category (entitled 'Other'), which accounted for 0.6 per cent of the total inhabitants for the period studied. This category has been left out of the computation, which makes the results fractionally less accurate.

5. *Census of Palestine, 1931*, II, p. 184.

6. Ibid., p. 106.

7. *Statistical Abstract of Palestine, 1939–1941*, Jerusalem, 1942, p. 10.

8. J. L. Abu-Lughod, 'The Demographic Transformation of Palestine', in I. Abu-Lughod (ed.), *The Transformation of Palestine* (Evanston, IL, 1971), p. 151. Also see: *Statistical Abstract of Palestine*, Jerusalem, 1940, p. 21.

9. See: Department of Statistics, Palestine Government, *Vital Statistics Tables 1922–1945*, p. 84.

10. This is referred to in M. Yazbek, *Al-Hijra al-'Arabiyya ila Haifa* (Arab Migration into Haifa) (Nazareth, 1988), p. 37, as quoted from Aba Khoshi, Histadrut archives.

11. A. Khalifa (trans.), *Al-Thawra al-'Arabiyya al-Kubra fi Filastin, 1936–1939: Al-Riwaya al-Israeliyya al-Rasmiyya* (The Great Arab Revolt in Palestine 1936–1939: An Official Israeli Account) translated from Hebrew: Books of the Haganah, Vol. 2, Books 5, 6 (Beirut, 1989), p. 435, pp. 479-501; D. HaCohen, *Time to Tell* (New York, London, 1984), p. 85.

12. This has been computed from tables showing registered immigrants into Palestine and their religious affiliation since 1932. Department of Statistics, Palestine Government, *Vital Statistics Tables 1922–1945*, p. 84, and *Statistical Abstract of Palestine*, p. 31.

13. Yazbek, *Al-Hijra al-'Arabiyya*, pp. 13, 75, 119.

5

The Administrative Set-up: the Municipality and its Functions

Haifa's physical development was formally under the control of the British Administration in Jerusalem, with some powers devolved to local bodies, including the Municipality. In this chapter the development of Haifa's finances within the overall British administrative policy for the towns of Palestine traces the capabilities and constraints imposed upon these local institutions. Developing Haifa's infrastructural requirements was the primary task facing the new British Civil Administration. The more pressing tasks were performed either directly by the Administration or through the local government departments, while responsibility for more routine work was relegated to the Municipal Council. Until 1927, this Council was appointed by the High Commissioner and its activities were controlled by his representative, the District Commissioner, who received his instructions from Jerusalem.

The history of municipal revenues under the Mandate was similar to that of the central administration. The erratic changes in the system reflected the lack of an initial comprehensive financial programme, and at the same time demonstrated the Administration's adherence to the principle of balanced budgets, an attitude in line with a major aim of the British government, to create a financially self-supporting country with the minimum of embarrassment and cost. At the time of the British occupation, municipal revenues were governed by the Ottoman Municipal Tax Law of 1915, the main sources being customs fees (Kantar, Octroi and Gate Tax[1]), taxes on immovable property (Werko and Musaqqafat), various levies on building sites (commercial and industrial premises), vehicles and ships, as well as a large number of miscellaneous local fees. There was also a small element of government subsidy. Some of these taxes were applied uniformly throughout Palestine, while others differed from one town to another. In particular, a new form of property (or roof) tax, the Musaqqafat, introduced in 1910, was gradually replacing the older Werko.

At the outset of the British occupation the Military Administration found Haifa Municipality completely bankrupt. To meet this situation, in 1919 it levied extraordinary taxes on petrol, carriages, slaughter-houses, entertainment, alcoholic beverages and buildings.[2] Gradually a more regular system of raising local revenue was introduced. The collection of customs dues on goods brought into the town was abolished in 1924, and thereafter customs duties accrued to the central revenues.[3] Property taxes therefore became increasingly important. Under the Municipal Corporation Ordinance of 1934, the revenue system and its application were finally formulated along lines very similar to those of the British colonial system. With a devolution of responsibility, the Municipality was authorized to levy, in addition to the rate on im-movable property (maximum 10 per cent) paid by owners and assessed on the rateable value of buildings, two rates on occupiers: one a general rate (maximum 15 per cent of the rateable value of the property) and the other an education rate (maximum 7.5 per cent of the rateable value of the property),[4] together with sewerage and water rates where applicable. Since by 1934 owners were also paying an urban property tax of 12.5 per cent of the net annual value, this raised the tax on their property to approximately 25 per cent. Naturally, landlords made up their loss by raising rents, which explains the abnormally high rents and the rising cost of living during this period.

Taxes, especially on immovable property, generated approximately 45 per cent of municipal income, with an equivalent amount from fees and services. The rest was provided by government subsidies. Palestinian towns had been partially supported by the central government during the Ottoman era, and early in the Mandate period the Administration became aware of the need to support municipal expenses from central revenues. Initially, these 'grants-in-aid' were justified as a substitute for the loss of revenue from the altered, and later rescinded, customs dues. They were subject to the Administration's conditions and were con-tinuously cut back in the hope of making the municipalities self-sufficient.

These subventions gave rise to serious Colonial Office concern early in the 1920s. The Secretary of State, Winston Churchill, was insistent that this aid should be considered as a temporary relief pending changes in the revenue system. In a letter of 16 January 1922 to the High Commissioner, he said:

> These grants-in-aid should be regarded as something quite exceptional and intended to meet exceptional circumstances, and their amount should be reviewed annually with a view to discovering whether their reduction or abolition is possible.[5]

The view that the amount of financial support was related to the hypothetical loss of revenue from customs duties was strongly objected to by the Colonial Office. Using the Octroi and Kantar tax of 1920-21 as a basis, Haifa, where customs revenue amounted to 56 per cent of total municipal income, was given only 13.53 and 26.90 per cent respectively in 1921-2.[6] The towns, and in particular Haifa, which depended heavily on the customs tax, were being dealt a severe blow through these fiscal changes.

In the early years, however, this form of apportionment was the most expedient method for the day-to-day administration of municipal affairs. Only in 1925 was the system altered. The then Secretary of State for the Colonies, W. Ormsby-Gore, set out the future policy for assessment of government grants-in-aid to municipalities in a letter of 23 April:

> I consider that the time has now come to discontinue the grant to munici-palities of any subvention from the funds of the Government, which cannot be adequately defended on the ground that the individual municipality to which the grant is made can be shown by its own estimates of revenue and expenditure to be definitely in need of support from outside sources to enable it to carry out its essential functions.[7]

He stressed the difference between the obligation of the Administration to supply public services and municipal duties: the municipalities had to depend on their own income for their needs. From this policy came the Municipal Councils Validation Ordinance of 1925, which required each council to submit an annual budget to the District Commissioner for approval. Earlier, in 1921, the Municipal Loans Ordinance had been formulated to help cover municipal needs and support future development programmes; loans were permitted to use estimated local income, excluding government grants, as collateral.

Even with regard to these loans, however, the Administration was sensitive to the effect they could have on its long-range policy. In 1925, Sir Herbert Samuel was approached by a group of solicitors for Ruten-berg (Herbert, Oppenheimer, Nathan and Vandyke), who proposed the grouping together of local authorities in order to facilitate raising loans and carrying out projects for a number of combined municipalities. (For details on Rutenberg see Chapters 8 and 13.) Under Samuel's successor, Lord Plumer, the suggestion was presented to the Colonial Office. In 1926 the then Secretary of State for the Colonies, L. S. Amery, replied:

> You will, I feel confident, agree with me that it is important to guard against the possibility that a measure which is intended to provide increased facilities for the legitimate purpose of local Government and for the construction by

two or more municipalities jointly of such useful public works as a water supply and drainage system might be used as a cloak for the organization of the Jewish community in Palestine for political purposes.[8]

At that specific juncture, the British were concerned with safe-guarding Arab goodwill and did not wish to antagonize the Arabs with further evidence of their sympathy for the development of the Jewish National Home; another concern was to use this opportunity to demon-strate their intention to centralize financial activities. The previous year, a similar loan had been suggested by E. Mills, Assistant to the Chief Secretary, to be extended to the Haifa Municipality in order to assuage Arab fears and ensure municipal support for the Adminis-tration's policy. In his political report of September 1924, Mills wrote:

> There is in Haifa claustrophobia. The town is ringed round by Jewish enter-prises and Jewish-owned lands. A concession to local feeling would be made if the municipality were to participate with cash in the Kishon drainage scheme on the condition of endowment with state lands in that area. The proposal now is, however, to leave these lands to the *P.L.D.C.*, the rentals being devoted to the fund required for the execution of the work. As it seems to me the Haifa municipality is bound by circumstances in the long run to become the most progressive organ of local government in the country and it will be an infinite pity if opportunity is lost to strengthen its young life by binding it to the central organ in policy.[9]

The Kishon scheme was finally executed by the Palestine Land Development Company (PLDC) without the participation of the Haifa Municipality. Such projects were directly connected with the Adminis-tration's commitment to the principle of Zionist colonization of the land for settlement. An earlier project emphasizing even more sharply the Administration's attitude towards this policy was that concerning the electrification of Jaffa and Haifa. When the High Commissioner tried to persuade the Colonial Office to extend a special loan to the municipalities for this purpose, his concern was to make the most of circumstances in which the Arab municipalities would be willing to join the scheme, if the loan was extended. In his memo to Sir J. Masterton Smith and Mr Ormsby-Gore, Sir Herbert Samuel wrote in April 1923:

> There is the further consideration that it is very desirable on political grounds to interest the Arab municipalities in the Rutenberg scheme. This would certainly be achieved if the present project goes through, whereas if it breaks down it is possible that the opportunity of bringing the municipalities into the scheme may not recur.

He further elaborated the government's stand concerning the broader political question:

The grant of the Rutenberg concession was part and parcel of our Zionist policy. The assumption underlying it was that Jewish enthusiasm for Zionism was such as to exclude all difficulty in financing Zionist projects, even when (as in the case of Rutenberg) undertaken by the concessionaire on disadvantageous terms.[10]

The loans were finally granted through the Anglo-Egyptian Bank at the request of the Colonial Office.

The control and manipulation of all sources of revenue, central as well as municipal, were an underlying policy of the British Mandate. Only in respect of the Jewish municipality of Tel-Aviv did this policy lapse for a short while; between 1921, when the town acquired municipal status, and 1927, Tel-Aviv had become indebted to the Administration and the Zionist Executive; it also had a loan from Jewish organizations in America.[11] By 1928 it had to be bailed out by the Administration with public funds. The Financial Control and Default Ordinance of that year was intended to empower the High Commissioner to institute a series of rigorous controls over the financial dealings of all municipal and local councils. He was authorized to appoint an outside authority to control municipal finances and could remove a council from office in the event of its failure to carry out its statutory functions satisfactorily.[12]

By 1934 the imposition of full central control over the municipal system was a calculated step at a time when political events threatened the administrative fabric. Even though policy towards this end differed between London and Jerusalem, both saw the advantage of an effective structure for British short-term economic and long-term political policy. The attitude of the Colonial Office in London was somewhat highhanded and impatient. It was concerned only with the transformation of the Palestine system into a 'rational' one modelled on the British colonial pattern. The municipalities were treated like recalcitrant minors who had to be constantly scolded. The authorities in Palestine, on the other hand, being fully aware of local economic realities, took a more understanding view. It was the High Commissioner who – year after year – pleaded the cause of the grants-in-aid and tried to lower the tax rating proposed by the Colonial Office.[13] At the same time, the Administration saw the tremendous growth in the responsibilities of the local councils and thus the growing need for revenue. In practice, its management of the revenue system was shaped by the circumstances of its application and by its own amateurish efforts.

An interesting feature of Haifa is the fact that the Municipality was practically never in debt. In accordance with the Administration's conservative financial policy it was never allowed to extend its capacities without ensuring that they were covered. There was a surplus in its accounts every year; in 1935 it amounted to £P18,220.[14] But while income was sufficient for the maintenance of existing services, it did not allow for any expansion or for new services. The application for substantial loans for the development of the drainage system in conjunction with the harbour development was continually postponed. As late as 1931, the then Colonial Secretary, Cunliffe-Lister, opposed these loans, on the ground of lack of secure returns, and advised the Municipality to wait for more prosperous times.[15] However, after the harbour started operations, in 1933, the Administration had to be more forthcoming.

Grants-in-aid maintained an average of 15 to 18 per cent of total revenue and were clearly on the decrease by 1934. A drastic drop occurred after the promulgation of the urban property tax in 1932 and the sudden increase in municipal income, partly from the tax on immovable property, but also from building permits and the supply of municipal services. Of course, the main reason for the increase in revenue from the building tax was the rising immigration and building activity in the city between 1931 and 1935, but it was also due to the new, efficient method of rating under the supervision of the best tax administrator of the Mandate, E. Keith-Roach, in his capacity as District Commissioner.[16] As soon as he took over in September 1931, he worked towards collecting all arrears of the Musaqqafat.[17] It was mostly wealthy landlords who were in debt to the Municipality, and he pursued them mercilessly. His powers were reinforced by the Municipal Corporation Ordinance of 1934, which authorized him to replace or dismiss municipal councils or members, and also gave him control over the financial activities of the Municipality. These measures were strongly resented by the Council and the local inhabitants.[18]

Municipal expenditure increased in tandem with the increase in revenue.[19] Projects were undertaken and services provided from fees that did not necessarily cover the cost. The sanitation programme necessitated extraordinary loans that had to be provided by the Administration, since these improvements were deemed essential in conjunction with the harbour project. The future economic benefits to be derived from the harbour were inducement enough. Similar loans had to be raised to cover the expense of new roads. Even though landowners often met a large percentage of these expenses by paying an improvement tax, the Municipality – particularly after 1930 – had to carry out the plans and subsidize the balance. The bulk of these improvements benefited the new quarters and the modern sectors of the town where more Jews congregated to take advantage of the reforms. These measures were bitterly criticized by the Arabs, who felt that necessary improvements to their quarters were deliberately ignored, and that loans were made available only for construction in the Jewish quarters.[20] The rapidly growing new quarters on the Carmel had to be connected to the town by roads.[21] For security reasons following the events of 1921, 1929 and 1931, the inhabitants of these Jewish quarters insisted on routes connecting them to the various Jewish areas – Ahuza, Herzelia, Carmel and the new Commercial Centre – which by-passed the Arab quarters. For instance, Rushmiya Bridge was one expensive project designed to ensure a direct link between Hadar HaCarmel and Neve Sha'anan, thus connecting the Jewish eastern and western parts of Haifa.

Other expenditures in which the Municipality had to share, if not fully support, were those of the town's school system, health facilities and police force. Expenditure for the administration of the public education system, including maintenance of premises and teachers' salaries, was met from central funds. The Education Ordinance of 1927–8 'recognizes education as falling partly within the functions of municipalities or other local authorities of existing types and legalizes the imposition of an education rate. The general principle of the Bill is that local authorities should provide teaching staff'.[22] Up to 1939, however, the Haifa Municipal Council contributed only by providing supervisory and advisory committees for both the national (Arab) and the Jewish educational systems. No rate specifically for local educational purposes, even though provided for in the Municipal Corporation Ordinance of 1934, was ever imposed.

While most of the expenses of the Health Department were met from public funds and supervised by the department in conjunction with the Municipality, the Council had to meet all expenditures prescribed by the department, such as providing the hospital building and non-technical services, and sanitary maintenance.[23] From 1924 onwards, a British sanitary officer was appointed by the Medical Department and his salary was paid by the Municipality. The subsequent dispute when his contract was terminated by the Council was symptomatic of the ambiguity characterizing financial relations between the central and local authorities:

> The Senior Medical Officer at Haifa writing on Feb. 13, 1929 to the Director of Health, explaining Mr. Oakey's case: 'The attitude of the Municipality towards the whole situation appears to be characterized by non-understanding of the significance of the post, lack of concern as to the necessity for a competent officer, alleged inability or unwillingness to pay the necessary salary.'[24]

A letter from the Sanitary Inspectors Association to the Secretary of State on 18 March 1929 expressed deep anger that a British Administration employing the service of a British professional should 'place him with a native council' and subsequently allow that council to dismiss him!'[25] Despite the limited revenue of the Municipality, subtle pressure was exerted and the officer was finally reappointed.

The police force was initially maintained by the towns. Following a general reorganization in 1932, the municipal forces were amalgamated with the state police and their maintenance was fully borne by the state. A corresponding deduction was made in the municipal grants-in-aid.[26]

While the demands on a growing Haifa pressurized the Municipality to meet its needs, the Central Administration kept a tight rein on its independent functioning and financial support. A conservative colonial approach to local government guided the Administration's policy towards Haifa's municipal finances on the one hand, but this policy disintegrated when it came to issues related to Jewish concerns in the city. In order to meet the Mandate demand for the JNH, this conservative policy could be overlooked or bent, as was demonstrated in the functioning of the Haifa Municipality.

Notes

1. *Octroi and gate tax*: local fees of 1 per cent ad valorem upon imported articles, whether of foreign or Palestinian origin. *Kantar*: a tax levied on goods calculated by weight and measurement, usually applied to domestic produce only (Sir Herbert Samuel to Earl Curzon, 1 January 1921; PRO CO 733/9). They were replaced by an additional duty of 1 per cent ad valorem on all imported and dutiable articles in 1920, and were finally abandoned when the Administration abolished the local customs duties in 1924.

2. *Palestine News*, 30 January 1919, Vol. I, No. 43.

3. Sir Herbert Samuel to Earl Curzon, 1 January 1921 (PRO CO 733/9); A. Granovsky, *The Fiscal System of Palestine* (Jerusalem, 1935), p. 255.

4. HC to S of S, 27 June 1931 (PRO CO 733/207).

5. S of S to HC, 16 January 1922 (PRO CO 733/8).

6. CO to HC, 2 January 1925 (PRO CO 733/87); Sir H. Samuel to Earl Curzon, 1 January 1921 (PRO CO 733/9).

7. CO to HC, 23 April 1925 (PRO CO 733/90).

8. CO to HC, 12 March 1926 (PRO CO 733/112).

9. E. Mills, Assistant to CS, Political Report, September 1924 (PRO CO 733/74). The Palestine Land Development Company (PLDC) had been registered in London in 1909 with a capital of £50,000, and was registered locally in Palestine in 1920 as the first 'Company of Public Utility'. Department of Commerce and Industry, *Commercial Bulletin*, Vol. II, December 1922, and Esco Foundation for Palestine, *Palestine: A Study of Jewish, Arab and British Policies*, Vol. I (New York, 1970), p. 342. It was the main land-purchasing arm of the Zionist Organization, meant to centralize land acquisition both for the Jewish National Fund and for private colonization companies and individuals.

10. HC to CO, April 1923 (PRO CO 733/44).

11. B. J. Smith, *The Roots of Separatism in Palestine* (Syracuse, NY, 1993), pp. 154–5.

12. Lloyd's minute, 22 December 1928 (PRO CO 733/162).

13. HC to S of S, 13 May 1933 (PRO CO 733/244), and HC to S of S, 27 June 1931 (PRO CO 733/207).

14. Government of Palestine, *Palestine Blue Book, 1936*, p. 117.

15. CO to HC, 24 November 1931 (PRO CO 733/196).

16. HC to S of S, 14 June 1934 (PRO CO 733/263).

17. E. Keith-Roach, 'Pasha of Jerusalem', Vol. 2, Chapter IX (Private Papers Collection, St Antony's College, Oxford). In a despatch to CS, 8 August 1932, he even suggested legal methods to penalize municipal members who were remiss in paying the Musaqqafat tax (Keith-Roach to CS, ISA 2G/99/33).

18. *Al-Karmil*, 22 June and 26 October 1932.

19. For details see M. Seikaly, 'The Arab Community of Haifa 1918–1936', D.Phil. thesis, Oxford University, 1983, Table IV.

20. *Al-Karmil*, 22 June 1932; see also Chapter 14.

21. Treasurer to CS, 14 May 1934 (ISA 2 G/159/34); Treasurer to CS, 14 May 1935 (ISA 2 G/112/32); HC to CO, 20 February 1936 (PRO CO 733/286).

22. Education Department, *Annual Report*, 1927–8.

23. Department of Health, *Annual Report*, 1928, p. 7.

24. HC to S of S and enclosures, 8 August 1929 (PRO CO 733/168).

25. Ibid.

26. CO memo on Municipal Police, 16 October 1932 (PRO CO 733/227); HC to S of S, 30 June 1934 (PRO CO 733/268).

6

Town Planning: Policies and the New Quarters

As with the Municipality, policies governing the physical development of the town, its residential quarters and infrastructures were controlled from Jerusalem. Up to 1930, however, much was left to local initiative, which meant that the best-organized sections of the community – particularly the Jews, with the encouragement of the Zionist Organization – enjoyed a good deal of autonomy in developing residential quarters and services which were not necessarily integrated into the city's overall infrastructure. Thus by the time a more coherent town plan was drawn up in 1930, much of the geography of the city had already been determined.

From the beginning of the occupation, the British were well aware of Haifa's value both as a deep-water port and as a strategic asset. During the Military Administration, attention was mostly focused on meeting the basic needs of a population which had suffered serious economic and social disruption during the First World War. But after 1922, with the establishment of the Civil Administration, several government departments, including Customs and Communications, were moved to Haifa, providing one of the first new opportunities for employment, especially for the few English-speaking local people. The consolidated Railway Authority was also based in Haifa, but brought in its personnel from Egypt and Lebanon.

The position of the Municipal Council, active during the later Ottoman period (since 1882), was confirmed and amended by the Municipal Councils Validation Ordinance, 1925.[1] Basically, it was to perform minor regulatory and service functions: to supervise and license building, oversee street cleaning, repair lighting, control markets and public places, register births and deaths, uphold standards of morality, supervise public health and control weights and measures. With the rapid growth of the town, however, these functions became increasingly extensive and other local Departments of Health, Public Works and

Education were established by the Administration to assist in implementing these duties, and to carry out central government policy in the city. Thus, the Municipality's powers were encroached upon gradually by central government agencies (see Chapter 5).

Another body designed to regulate and control the development of Haifa, along with that of other cities in Palestine, was the Central Town Planning Commission, first established in February 1921 by the High Commissioner, Sir Herbert Samuel, with ultimate authority over town planning schemes and control of building within approved town planning areas. Local planning commissions were established with the approval of the Central Commission and the High Commissioner, and were vested with all municipal powers as specified under the Ottoman Law of Ramadan 27, 1294 (1875).[2] In other words, they were responsible for implementing urban building schemes, with authority to expropriate property and levy fees and taxes as stipulated in municipal regulations. Since, however, they were finally responsible not to the municipalities but to the Central Commission, this was a means of securing municipal co-operation while implementing policies which the Municipality could not control.

At least in the case of Haifa, however, the enlightened principles specified in the Ordinance of 1921 were slow to be transformed from theory into practice. The first official reference to a local commission in Haifa came only in 1929, from which it may be concluded that until the late 1920s the city's development was supervised by the Central Commission in Jerusalem and not locally.[3] The Central Commission itself worked under various disadvantages, not the least of which was a lack of funds and expert help. Only in 1936 was there the permanent appointment of a specialized town planner for consultation and advice.

This situation could explain why town planning regulations were not seriously applied in Haifa during the first decade of the British Administration. The attitude towards residential areas in particular was that, where quarters catered for their own needs within broad planning regulations, they were left to do so without official interference. This naturally benefited the most dynamic and well-organized sections of the community, one of the best-documented instances in the Jewish community being the Co-operative Committee of the Hadar HaCarmel residential quarter, whose building regulations were accepted by the Municipality and the Town Planning Commission for many years.[4]

The second phase in the case of Haifa was the result of the 1930 Master Plan for the city. The Outline Scheme was drawn up under the direction of the senior planner in the Central Commission, Mr C. Holliday, a member of the Town Planning Institute of Great Britain. Thereafter a more coherent approach was implemented and more autonomy for local authorities was encouraged by the establishment of a local Planning Commission. By 1930, the whole area, from the bulge of the promontory in the west to beyond the Muqata' River in the east (a boundary hard to define because of the marshy nature of the river banks), and from the waterfront in the north to the mountain crest in the south, comprising the old town, the new residential quarters and the waterfront with the railway and commercial centres, was included in the plan. The built-up areas were to receive a major facelift, while the unbuilt areas in the east and south were designated as 'undetermined', a definition meant to keep certain undeveloped areas adjacent to the built-up areas for future use. In fact, however, this ruling had the opposite effect. As a result of demographic and economic pressures, and the drift of migrant workers to the city from the late 1920s onwards, these areas became squatter settlements, and buildings mushroomed in them without any municipal control.

Official pressure to adhere to the plan and the regulations of the local Planning Commission was motivated mainly by concern to ensure the success of two major government-sponsored economic development projects designed to have an impact on the wider Palestine economy and on British strategic concerns: the new harbour, which was started in 1929 and completed in 1933, and the IPC pipeline and the refinery, which was completed in 1939 (the pipeline carrying crude oil from Iraq was completed in 1934)[5] but was in the planning stage from the mid-1920s.

The manner in which the plan was drawn up illustrates the significantly different official attitudes towards the rapidly growing Jewish community and the indigenous Palestinian inhabitants. The Arab sector in general was unfamiliar with the new concepts of development as embodied in the Master Plan and therefore not in a good position to lobby for its own interests. Furthermore, when dealing with the Arab sector, the Administration tended to consider benefits to the community, however minimal, as concessions which ought to be appreciated. In contrast, the Jewish sector was consulted about decisions on the development of Jewish areas, although sometimes grudgingly and only in response to pressure.

This was especially true as regards the drawing up and implementation of the Master Plan: the input of the Zionist Organization had a definitive influence on the final shape of the scheme as it related to the Bay area, the Jewish quarter and the IPC plant. The scope of the Outline Scheme was also subsequently amended in response to pressures from local Jewish interests, as was particularly evident in the case of the eastern edge of the city, where the IPC terminal was to be sited. Government plans for such major projects had initiated a wave of commercial and industrial real-estate speculation. Those most directly affected were the owners of the land directly adjacent to the project area in the marshy Muqata' Valley.

This large area was owned principally by Jewish organizations: the Jewish National Fund (Keren Kayemeth LeIsrael), the Bayside Land Corporation Ltd and the Haifa Bay Development Company.[6] At their insistence the government arranged meetings of the Local Planning Commission with their representatives on 29 December 1931 and 8 January 1932, which the British town planning expert Professor P. Abercrombie was invited to attend.[7] Thereafter, the Outline Scheme, approved in 1930, was extended to include the Bay area, a site intended for industrial zones and workers' settlements. In fact, architects and entrepreneurs from these Jewish organizations had been negotiating since 1926 for the inclusion of their holdings in the Master Plan. Their most serious concern related to the location of the harbour. Throughout 1927 and 1928, the town planner of the Haifa Bay Development Co., R. Kaufmann, tried to persuade the Administration to build the harbour, not in the south-western corner of the town, but in the Bay area, directly open to the lands owned by the Jewish organizations.[8] He also tried to enlist the support of the other companies, the Zionist Executive (ZE) and the General Federation of Jewish Labour (GFJL).[9] However, his arguments proved unconvincing, especially since his proposed scheme would have been more costly.

Nevertheless, it had become clear to all the Zionist institutions concerned that Haifa held tremendous potential for Jewish economic development in Palestine, with benefits from oil returns and trade with the eastern frontiers.[10] In the final event, the harbour was not placed adjacent to the Jewish-owned lands in the Bay, but the IPC plant was, and this involved the Jewish companies directly in the negotiations for land transfers, zoning and development. Many of their suggestions were considered by the Central Planning Commission and incorporated in the final Master Plan. They also fought for various concessions to safeguard the future of their holdings. For example, a road to connect the Jewish quarters in the Bay and at Neve Sha'anan was to be built at IPC's expense within the area designed for the IPC plant.[11]

A major concern of the Administration in its application of the Master Plan was the preservation of the city's aesthetic setting, in particular the panoramic view of Mount Carmel.[12] Roads in the heart of the town and along the coast were enlarged and new, wide thoroughfares (Kingsway) were built and connected by squares (Plumer Square) in 1934–5. Even built-up areas such as sections of the old town were included in detailed improvement schemes. Limitations were imposed on the height of buildings and houses in certain areas of Hadar HaCarmel, and buildings on the southern side of Kingsway in the commercial zone were restricted to two storeys. The Outline Scheme also provided for the preservation of natural valleys and forests and the planting of trees, and an area on the Carmel was set aside as a future park site.

The traditional residential quarters of Haifa were supposedly subject to the new planning regulations when these were put into effect, but in practice they were applied fully and comprehensively only to the new quarters which grew up after 1930, mainly those inhabited by the new Jewish immigrants. Before that date extensions to the old quarters and the new residential areas on the Carmel slopes to the west and south were the result of individual or sometimes community endeavours and tastes.

Most of the new residential quarters fanned out from the nucleus of the old town. To the west spread the better-off and more aesthetically pleasing residential neighbourhoods based on religion and/or origin as people migrated from the inland towns and from the countryside. Such were the areas where the villagers from 'Arraba (near Jenin), Burin (near Nablus), Shefa 'Amr, Kufr Yasif and Tarshiha (in Upper Galilee) congregated, and also the Tayarneh quarter, where people from Tirah lived. In the eastern commercial and industrial sector similar residential pockets emerged, for instance the area where people from Nablus and Gaza lived, and the Syrian sector of the market (Suq al-Shawam).[13]

Among the new residential quarters in the west and south, Hadar HaCarmel (established in 1920), Ahuza on Mount Carmel (1923) and Bat Galim on the seashore (1923) were almost exclusively Jewish quarters.[14] Arab, mostly Christian, quarters also spread in the same direction. Zawara, also known as Tel al-Semak or Haifa al-'Atiqa, owned by the Latin Convent and stretching westward to the area known as Mawaress (later called Wadi Jmal), was sold cheaply to the Catholic congregation in the early 1920s.[15] Two quarters grew up here which did not remain exclusively Christian but were nonetheless almost totally Arab. Some Christian residential pockets were also to be found in the midst of the Jewish quarters, for instance the Mifhara area in the heart of Herzelia and the Shawafneh neighbourhood (people from Shuwaifat in Lebanon) in the heart of Hadar HaCarmel.

The new Jewish residential quarters in the east were either an extension of Neve Sha'anan, established in 1922, or the new labour settlements (*kiryot*) established in the Bay industrial zone starting in 1934. By the mid-1930s, new Jewish quarters encircled the town from the extreme east in the Bay residential quarters to the top of Mount Carmel, where the better-off European immigrant settlements were established, and finally to the west at Bat Galim. The only new quarter inhabited by Muslim Arabs was Halissa to the east of the traditional Muslim quarter.

In the old quarter itself there was no physical expansion: old buildings were either extended or replaced by high-rise apartment buildings. The biggest problem in this area was the large influx of migrant labourers who, when the houses of kinsmen overflowed, set up their

huts in any open space available. An additional attraction of this quarter
was its proximity to sources of employment – on the railways, roads
and in the port. The expansion of employment opportunities as Haifa
grew, combined with the difficulties experienced by Palestinian agriculture from the late 1920s onwards, brought an ever-increasing number
of rural people into the city, so that overcrowding and poor housing
became a serious problem (see also Chapter 14).[16] As a result, the
shanty town known as Ard al-Raml (sandy land) – or more revealingly
as al-Mantanah (the rotten-smelling place) – had sprung up to the east
of the city and housed a few thousand poor Arabs by 1932.

Generally speaking, most of the new residential quarters functioned
as separate nuclei, at first utilizing the city's commercial centre and
services, but gradually becoming more self-sufficient, often catering for
their own commercial and financial needs. The increasingly hostile
political atmosphere in the country as a whole in the 1930s, with
growing tension between Jews and Arabs, reinforced this trend (see
Maps III and IV).

The semi-residential zones, as defined in the Master Plan, covered
parts of the old town, the heart of socio-commercial activities, as well
as the residential quarters adjacent to it. The marketplace continued to
be as active as in the pre-war period and new commercial centres
sprang up both to east and west. In the west, a modern business centre
was built in 1926 with Jewish capital, while to the east markets on
traditional lines were established by Palestinian and Arab immigrants,
such as the Syrian market mentioned earlier. All these centres were
initiated by private enterprise but came under the jurisdiction of the
local Planning Commission. Even though by the mid-1930s this area
had grown to include very active and cosmopolitan commercial centres,
it remained the heart of the traditional Arab town. In this district also
were located the two major government projects which certainly contributed to quickening the pace of economic activity – the central
railway station and the harbour. In addition, the commercial area had
the largest concentration of public facilities such as government buildings, parks, hospitals and the like, though they were also distributed all
over the city.

In fact, the Administration's contribution to the city's public buildings
was minimal in the 1920s when compared with the upsurge of private
building activity. The Public Works Department concentrated on the
construction and improvement of roads, the renovation of existing,
mostly rented, buildings, and the erection of a few small buildings for
government use. Initially, all government offices, and even the government hospital, were established in rented premises. It was only in the
early 1930s that the Administration began to build facilities for specific
services, one of the first to be constructed being the district magistrate's

court, built in the Burj district in 1929. This whole area was soon
transformed into a district of official buildings. A slaughterhouse and
government hospital were completed only in 1937-8, even though the
obvious need for both had been acknowledged since the early 1930s
(see Maps III and IV).[17]

The provision of water, sanitation and drainage became the responsibility of the Health and Public Works Departments in co-operation
with the Municipality. The Health Department initially carried out
most of these public service activities and remained in an advisory
capacity to the Municipal Council in all matters pertaining to water
supplies, sanitation and drainage.[18] Piecemeal developments were effected, which proved inadequate to meet the demands of a fast-growing
population.

At the time of the British occupation, Haifa's water supply came
mainly from private wells and was often polluted, brackish and in-
sufficient. From 1928 onwards, the need for a better supply was more
urgently stressed by the Health Department; the search for new sources
continued and water was found in 1930 at 'Ayn Sa'adah and in 1934
in the south of the city. In the new quarters, especially Hadar
HaCarmel, piped water had been provided since 1922; in 1930 new
wells were added to that of the Technion, and the Hadar HaCarmel
committee supplied water to many of the newly developed mountainside
quarters on a commercial basis. It was only in the mid-1930s that the
Municipality attempted to incorporate all the private sources of water
into the public system.[19]

The drainage system also depended on private cesspits, which perpetuated insanitary conditions, and temporary and partial remedies
were totally inadequate. With the construction of the harbour from
1929 onwards it became necessary to divert the existing drains from the
harbour area. By the mid-1930s, Haifa still lacked a main drainage
system, even though subsidiary sewage lines were laid out and connected
to the main drains in some areas.

The most significant achievement of the Public Works Department
(PWD) in Haifa, and in the country generally, was in the road networks
built. Under the terms of the Town Planning Ordinance, roads in the
city could be constructed, diverted or widened, and land expropriated
whenever necessary without compensation when such land comprised
no more than a quarter of the total plot. The PWD concentrated on
building an impressive road network in and around the downtown
business centres, especially after the construction of the harbour, thus
facilitating traffic around it and the central railway station. This network
was also connected by first-class, all-weather roads, and bridges where
necessary, to the residential quarters, the Carmel, the industrial zone
and the approaches to the town. Within the residential districts, road

building depended again on the initiative and wealth of the local
community. In quarters like Hadar HaCarmel, the local committee
collected the funds for the cost of construction and undertook the work
itself.[20] Subsequently, by the mid-1930s and after the implementation of
the Outline Scheme, the Municipality had to share in the cost and
planning. In the case of the less organized and poorer sectors, the PWD
undertook the business of construction whenever it was deemed essential, and special fees were imposed on the owners of the land through
which the road passed.

The Town Planning Ordinance also stipulated schemes for roads to
and from the city. During the 1920s, the Administration had maintained
an active road policy, and by 1926 an Advisory Road Board was set up
to construct a comprehensive programme of (mainly cross-country) road
building. Despite this programme, Haifa suffered considerably from the
lack of good road communications with the rest of Palestine. In 1920,
there was only one good external trunk road, leading to Jerusalem via
Nablus. The other main roads, to Nazareth, Beirut and Damascus,
were in urgent need of repair; the road to Damascus was unmetalled
and even dangerous. By 1936, no new roads had been built, though the
old ones had slowly been put into working order; for instance, the
Haifa–Acre coastal road was repaired only in 1933.

The most crucial lack, however, given the new geopolitical situation
under the British and the growing agricultural and industrial importance
of the coastal plain, was of a connecting coast road from Haifa to Jaffa.
The key to this omission lies in the Administration's attitude towards
the railways. In an effort to safeguard the interests of the railways,
which were state-owned, against the steadily growing competition of
motor traffic, the Palestine Administration unduly hampered road construction and maintenance.[21] The Haifa–Jaffa road was finally built
only in 1937.

This was one example of the way in which the British Administration's policies were dictated by interests which diverged from local
interests. In this case, the policy of favouring railway development
hampered the growth of other modes of transport at a time when the
railway service was both inefficient and inadequate. Further examples
of this divergence will be found in the case histories of the harbour and
the IPC terminal (see Chapter 7).

The manner in which the city's planning authorities carried out
their task, whether consciously or not, prepared the way for Jewish
predominance in its economic life. Early on in British rule, formulas for
its development on European lines were drawn up and bodies devised
to carry them out, but the application of these principles was another
matter. A strategy for the administration of Palestine's major cities
gradually emerged, but the slowness of this process meant that many

new 'facts' had already been created by local interests, and it was often too late to do anything but take account of them. Although the Administration promoted principles of development derived from the British experience at home and in the colonies, it volunteered a minimum of aid for their execution, except when such measures would yield immediate benefit to its own policies.

The sectors of the community which benefited most from the new planned developments, when they were finally implemented, were mainly the newcomers settling in the new residential quarters and sections of the business community. And even they had to depend for a long time on group organizational initiatives to maintain and apply government stipulations. Willing independent bodies such as the Zionist Organization and its subsidiaries were often given a free hand in the implementation of these principles. By attracting new immigrants, and with them capital, projects were speedily developed – such as the new commercial centre adjacent to the port and the Jewish residential and industrial quarters. However, this laissez-faire period in the 1920s and even in the early 1930s did not have the same beneficial effect for most of the local Arab population, which, with no independent organizations comparable to those of the Zionists, relied for city improvements on the Municipality and, through it, the Administration. Thus as a group it was unable to meet and take full advantage of the changing conditions. As a result, its overall development was generally ignored, particularly where the poorer strata of the population were concerned.

Failure of the Administration to improve conditions for these strata was usually blamed on lack of funds:

> Lack of credit for expropriation by local authorities to bring about open spaced areas for public facilities caused towns to be overcrowded with buildings, especially there was no credit for building workmen dwellings.[22]

However, on further scrutiny this shortage of funds usually turns out to be the result either of the generally tight spending policies favoured by the Administration or of its priorities, with defence, internal security and strategic infrastructural projects such as the harbour and the IPC terminal taking the lion's share of the funds, while basic amenities like sewage and water were still inadequate by the 1930s. In addition, the contribution of local administrative bodies to the planned growth of the city was slight. Policy was decided far from Haifa, either in Jerusalem or London, and it was the planning and development priorities set in these centres of power which were crucial in determining the path of Haifa's physical and economic development.

Notes

1. Government of Palestine, *Palestine Blue Book, 1927* (Revenues, Expenses, Municipalities), p. 63. Also, for the first legal confirmation of local councils after the British occupation, see HC to CO and FO, February 1921 (FO 371 E2345/2345/88) and HC to FO, 14 February 1921 and July 1921 (FO 371 E2354/2345/88). See also Chapter 13.

2. Town Planning Ordinance, 1921, originally published in *Official Gazette*, No. 36 of 1 February 1921, pp. 1–9 (Government of Palestine, *The Town Planning Handbook of Palestine*, Jerusalem, 1930), p. 6.

3. Membership of Town Planning Commission, 1929. Shabatai Levy files (CZA J15/3683).

4. Hadar HaCarmel Co-operative Committee, *History of Hadar HaCarmel*, 1931 (CZA J16/95).

5. S. H. Longrigg, *Oil in the Middle East* (London, 1954), pp. 77, 89.

6. *The Jewish National Fund* (JNF) (Keren Kayemeth LeIsrael) was established by the Zionist Congress in 1901, and incorporated as an English company in 1907. The original plan was that it should use two-thirds of its capital on land acquisition and the remaining third on conservation and cultivation. (Esco Foundation for Palestine, *Palestine: A Study of Jewish, Arab and British Policies*, Vol. I (New York, 1970), pp. 338–41.) Land acquisition was a fundamental principle of the Zionist movement in Palestine; by this means land becomes the inalienable property of the Jewish people.

The Bayside Land Corporation Ltd was formed in 1928 in conjunction with the JNF and acquired a large area of waste and marshy land in the Haifa Bay district. It aimed at minimizing real-estate speculation in an area planned as an industrial suburb to Haifa proper (ibid., p. 346).

The Haifa Bay Development Company was a private real-estate company that acted as a broker for private Jewish purchases in the Bay area.

7. Minutes of meetings at District Commissioner's office, Haifa, on 29 December 1931 and 8 December 1932 (CZA J15/4205).

8. Interview between Kaufmann and Henriquez from the Haifa Bay Development Co. and Abramson and Keith-Roach from the Administration on 27 May 1926 (CZA A175/149). Also see Kaufmann to H. Sacher, 22 January 1929, Kaufmann to ZE, January 1929, Kaufmann to Lord Melchett, 30 October 1928 (CZA A175/136). On the same subject, also see R. Kaufmann, 'Fundamental Problems of Haifa's Future Development', *Palestine and Near East Economic Magazine*, Vol. 3, No. 19, October 1928, pp. 433–6.

9. The General Federation of Jewish Labour (GFJL), generally referred to as *Histadrut* from its Hebrew title, is the organized official mouthpiece of the Jewish labour movement. It was formed in 1920 as an amalgamation of labour organizations that had developed in Palestine prior to the First World War (Esco, *Palestine*, Vol. I, pp. 359–66).

10. The Zionist Labour Office in Haifa in a letter to Dr Vanshtein of the Zionist Tourist Office expressed Zionist optimism in regard to the development of Jewish land in the Haifa Bay. Secretary of the Zionist Labour Office to Dr Vanshtein, 1 August 1926 (CZA A58/1216).

11. Minutes of the local Town Planning Commission, 21 June 1929 (CZA J15/3683).

12. For the local Town Planning Commission's decisions on these matters, see meetings for March 1929 (CZA A175/136), July 1933, January 1934 and February 1934 (CZA J15/2577).

13. M. Yazbek, *Al-Hijra al-'Arabiyya ila Haifa* (Arab Migration into Haifa) (Nazareth, 1988), pp. 75, 95–8; oral information, Tannus Salama, Haifa, May 1975, and Ilyas Mazzawi, Haifa, May 1975.

14. Chamber of Commerce and Industry (Jewish), *Haifa – City of the Future* (Haifa, 1932), and Hadar HaCarmel Co-operative Committee, *History*.

15. Oral information from Father Cyril Borg, Administrator of the Latin Church in Haifa, May 1975.

16. Government of Palestine, Health Department, *Annual Report*, 1932 (Jerusalem), p. 10.

17. Government of Palestine, Health Department, *Annual Report*, 1937 (Jerusalem), p. 46.

18. Government of Palestine, Health Department, *Annual Report*, 1935 (Jerusalem), p. 91.

19. Government of Palestine, Health Department, *Annual Report*, 1934 (Jerusalem), p. 74; Government of Palestine, Department of Public Works, *Annual Report*, 1935–6 (Jerusalem), p. 21.

20. Hadar HaCarmel Co-operative Committee, *History*, p. 14.

21. H. Sawwaf, 'Transportation and Communication', in S. B. Himadeh (ed.), *Economic Organization of Palestine* (Beirut, 1938), p. 307.

22. Government of Palestine, Health Department, *Annual Report*, 1933 (Jerusalem), p. 9. See also: Yazbek, *Al-Hijra al-'Arabiyya*, pp. 31, 132–43.

7

British Plans and Projects

The strategic importance of Haifa had always been a significant factor in British plans for the area. From 1906, the War Office had included Haifa in its schemes as the 'most suitable landing site in Syria' if Egypt should need military protection against a Turkish threat.[1] In addition to being on the eastern flank of the Suez Canal, it provided convenient access to the Syrian interior and its railway network.

By the time the Civil Administration was established in 1922, the role of Haifa as a future centre of communications had become a serious objective of the British government. A positive step in this direction was taken at an interdepartmental conference on 11 May 1922 about the development of the port. In 1927, the proposal for an oil pipeline from Iraq to the Mediterranean led to combined efforts by the Air Ministry, the Colonial Office, and the Board of Trade to ensure that it passed through Transjordan and Palestine rather than Syria. By 1929, a new project to reserve a site for the building of an aerodrome and seaplane base was being considered. Though the Air Council never regarded Haifa as important in connection with the strategic air route to the East, it advised the establishment of a civil base, which would increase the mobility of the Air Force in Palestine, in addition to civil air communications.[2] Thus the Administration hoped to transform Haifa into a centre of transport and communications by land, sea and air.[3]

The government's decision to make Haifa its strategic centre in Palestine had other economic effects. The resulting influx of labour and capital enhanced the level of economic activity but also placed strains on the city's infrastructure. The Administration was therefore obliged to carry out additional public works, despite its overall policy of minimal involvement and expenditure.

The economic policy of the Palestine Mandate was governed by three main agencies in London: the Treasury, the Colonial Office and the Crown Agents. The Administration's budget estimates were carefully considered in London before projects could be authorized. In view of Palestine's lack of natural resources, revenue was almost invariably earmarked for maintenance of the infrastructure, with little scope for large-scale development projects, for which Jewish finance was expected to be used. This expectation did not materialize, however, and the Mandatory power was obliged to provide financial support, with inevitable political implications.

> The need for a public loan was well understood by all Palestinian administrators; the Administration's ability to carry out a development programme of its own was an important element in encouraging the confidence of the Arab population in British rule, and also a means of restricting the Zionists' attempts to manipulate development patterns by use of the supposed capital resources of the Zionist Organization.[4]

The controversy between the Treasury and the Colonial Office over the raising of this loan was indicative of the ambivalent nature of the Mandate system as a whole and of Palestine's ambiguous status. It was not until 1926 that the Palestine and East Africa Loan Act was approved and the sum of £4,500,000 extended to the Palestine Administration with an imperial guarantee through the Crown Agents.

The three major government projects in Haifa – the railways, the harbour and the oil terminal – were the main practical achievements of British policy, in all its aspects, in Palestine. The potential economic prosperity to be derived from Iraqi oil would be secured when channelled to the storage site adjacent to the Haifa harbour, facilitated through the railway and improved road networks and exported through the harbour. A corollary to this interest was the traditional importance of the area as a buffer and a link to imperial trade and military routes. The development of Haifa *per se* was an incidental result of this policy. Thus the economic prosperity of the city became dependent on financial support sponsored and guaranteed by the British government.

When Britain occupied Palestine, the main junction for the country's railway system was located in Haifa. The Palestine Railways provided direct communication to Egypt and the Hijaz Railway[5] to Syria. The railways, a purely government project, were officially considered the backbone of the Palestine system of communications, with roads acting as feeders, subordinated to rail extensions in such a way as to exclude competition between them.[6] Initially the Administration proposed grandiose imperial projects to connect Egypt with Iraq and Europe through the Palestine railway system. In 1925, Sir Herbert Samuel was attacked by the Colonial Office for grossly extravagant expenses, especially on the railways. Following that date, modest rail development was sanctioned only within Palestinian boundaries, the most significant being the extensions to Haifa harbour and to some of the remote Jewish settlements. Beyond these measures, the Administration's efforts halted in the face of the great strides in the private sector and its promotion of motor vehicles.

The most impressive government achievement during the Mandate period was the construction of the Haifa harbour. In 1934, six months after its completion, a committee was set up to develop the reclaimed area[7] and handle the auctioning of business and storage leases as well as ensuring development in accordance with the Town Plan scheme approved for the area. Movement of cargo and passengers was increased immensely by these modern facilities. By 1933 almost 68 per cent of all immigrants entering Palestine came through Haifa.[8] Imports and exports shifted away from Acre and Jaffa to Haifa, transforming the city into the focal centre of the north. The impact of these developments was not confined to the city of Haifa alone, but also affected the wider Bay area to the east.

This whole complex had been incorporated in the Town Planning Commission's comprehensive scheme of 1932 as a zone of light and heavy industrial enterprises plus their housing. A drainage scheme on the Muqata' River to clear government land nearest to the town had been completed in 1931. Higher up, the Jewish National Fund had also channelled the river bed with a view to colonization. By 1936, an active start in the process of building up labour settlements and industrial projects had been made in the Bay area. These activities were primarily the concerns of Jewish organizations.

The IPC oil terminal lent an industrial character to the whole Bay area. The laying of a pipeline from Iraq to the Mediterranean had been proposed in 1927. As noted earlier, the British wanted to ensure that the pipeline should pass to a Palestinian and not a Syrian port. The case for Haifa had to be made to the IPC entirely on economic grounds, though additional arguments were based on the security of the area through which it would pass.[9] There was little to be said from the point of view of distance, the nature of the terrain to be traversed and the supplies of water when compared with the two other proposed routes – to Tripoli or Alexandretta. The final decision came in June 1930, when the Iraqi government insisted that its interests demanded that the pipeline should be laid by the southern route through Palestine. Along with a secure route the Iraqi government was also promised a railway connecting Baghdad to Haifa in the near future.

The pipeline was started in 1932 and pumping of oil through it began in 1934.[10] The Central Town Planning Commission in 1930 approved a scheme already drawn up for the oil storage area. The oil tanks were built on government land in the eastern reclaimed area, and a special dock on the lee breakwater was added to facilitate shipping.

The company also set up a modern automobile repair shop. In the late 1930s the petroleum refinery was built in the same complex.

The site of the project aroused the fears and hopes of the owners of the adjacent land plots, the Jewish National Fund and the PEC (Palestine Economic Corporation). As a concession to them the central and local Planning Commissions recommended that a road be built by the oil company running from west to east through the oil area, thus giving easier accessibility from the Bay to the town.

A proviso of the 1931 concession agreement with the IPC was that at least 50 per cent of the company's whole production should pass through Haifa harbour. A flat tonnage charge was made on all oil loaded, subject to a guaranteed minimum of £P25,000 per annum to be paid to the Palestine government. In return the company was accorded privileges unprecedented except for those extended to the Zionist Organization. The most interesting concession related to labour: the IPC works were exempted from the fair wages clauses by which the construction of the Haifa harbour was bound, and the company was even allowed to import labour, if it could not find the necessary skills locally. Another significant concession was the company's right to transport its goods, i.e. oil, through Palestine free of charge.[11] These exceptionally lenient measures illustrate how British local policy could be manipulated to serve its overall regional interests.

These projects reflected clearly the Mandate's colonial philosophy, when Britain's imperial interest was still the imperative behind these operations. It was fortuitous that, because of time and circumstance, Haifa was the chosen location for them. For the same reasons, all other developments in the city linked to immediate administrative policy reflected Britain's dual obligations: its colonial vested interest and its commitment to the establishment of the JNH. In Haifa during this period, central and local finances took these commitments into priority consideration, balancing their policy, affecting the demographic changes in the city as a by-product of employment opportunities, and in the final analysis having very deep and far-reaching consequences on the Arabs of Haifa – the community that elicited the least British concern at this stage.

Notes

1. R. Khalidi, *British Policy Towards Syria and Palestine 1906–1914*, St Antony's Middle East Monograph No. 11 (London, 1980), pp. 62–6.

2. Air Ministry to S of S, 30 October 1929 (PRO CO 733 168/67146).

3. The deep-water port was a handy alternative port for transshipment to Port Said, especially in view of the existence of the railway link to the Suez Canal. From the early stages of military preparations in 1936–7, the Suez Canal base and smaller ports to its east and west were given special attention. The

eastern Mediterranean ports became even more important after 1938, when the danger of Italy's belligerence precluded British dependence on its harbours. Haifa was well-linked to Qantara on the Suez Canal by rail and had adequate fuel storage, though not yet a refinery, for the Iraq Petroleum Company (IPC). During the Second World War, Haifa served the British war effort by acting as a station for oil storage and replenishing tankers for the Navy; its repair facilities also relieved the congestion at Alexandria. I. S. O. Playfair, G. M. S. Stitt, C. J. C. Molony and S. E. Toomer, *The Mediterranean and Middle East* (London, 1954), Vol. II, pp. 27, 74, 79, 164 and 214.

4. B. J. Smith, *The Roots of Separatism in Palestine* (Syracuse, NY, 1993), p. 32. See also Chapter 6 for a discussion of the loan issue.

5. The status of the Hijaz Railway occupied the attention of the FO early in 1921 prior to the Lausanne Treaty. Its inquiry into the legal position of the railway was carried out confidentially among British officers stationed in Transjordan and Palestine, lest French ambitions to assume a predominant role in controlling the pilgrim traffic on the railway were raised. FO to Under S of S, 19 October 1923 (PRO CO 733/56). Both Col. Lawrence and Major Young were convinced that the railway was legal *waqf*, and its documents were to be found in Damascus. 'Memo on the History and Ownership of the Hijaz Railway with Recommendations for its Disposal' by A. F. Kirby (General Manager, Palestine Railways), 28 October 1947 (Private Papers, A. F. Kirby, St Antony's College, Oxford). Also HC to S of S, 10 December 1921 (ISA 2/181 2057 POL). Sherif Hussein, through the agency of General Haddad, informed the FO that in fact the railway was a *waqf* documented through an imperial firman that could be consulted at the Ministry of Awqaf in Constantinople. FO to Major Marshall, 19 July 1921, and FO to Under S of S, 15 August 1921 (ISA 2/181 2057 POL). This firman was confirmed by the Transjordan government; the railway had been attached to the Ministry of Awqaf on 19 July 1914 but was not a declared *waqf*. Even though no conclusive evidence could be produced to prove its legal status, none could be produced to prove the opposite. Thus the Bompard Declaration following a joint Anglo-French agreement on 27 January 1923 reflected the admission by the two governments of the religious status of the line (Kirby, 'Memo on the Hijaz Railway').

6. Sir Herbert Samuel, Administrative Report, January 1923, and A. Anthony, Railways Report, 15 October 1925 (PRO CO 733/42).

7. Since houses and buildings lined the sea front from east to west, an additional piece of land was reclaimed from the sea on which the main harbour activities could be carried out. A 670-metre-long wall was built parallel to the seashore from the German colony in the west to the railway station in the east. An area of 108.7 acres (approximately 34 dunums) was reclaimed as the enclosed space was filled with sand dug up in the deepening of the bay. Opposite this area were the two breakwaters, converging to form a gateway 183 metres wide.

8. Report, Jewish Chamber of Commerce, 13th Annual Meeting, 1935 (ISA 128 Cust 296/34).

9. CO to HC, 21 December 1927 (PRO FO371 E1412/2543/General). Simultaneously a CO memorandum (FO 371 E5268/1412/65) provisionally suggested various measures to pressure the IPC into laying the line along the southern route, the most drastic being to tell the company that it must comply if it wished

to have any future proposals put to the Iraqi government accepted and not thwarted through the influence of HMG. 'It might even be added that, in such event [the laying of a pipeline through the northern route] the company could not, as in the past, necessarily count upon the whole-hearted support of HMG in any future transactions with the Iraq Government.' The Acting High Commissioner for Iraq thought that such a line could be detrimental to the interests of Iraq and by extension to British interests. He suggested the positive approach of promising the company a railway from Baghdad to Haifa.

10. S. H. Longrigg, *Oil in the Middle East* (London, 1954), p. 77.

11. A. Bonné, 'The Concessions for the Mosul-Haifa Pipe Line', in Viteles and Totah (eds), 'Palestine, a Decade of Development', *The Annals of the American Academy of Political and Social Science*, Vol. 164 (November 1932), p. 125.

PART THREE

The Evolution of
the Economic Sectors

The Evolution of the Economic Sectors

8

Industry: a Jewish Monopoly

Although industry played only a minor part in the economy of Haifa before the First World War, industrialization became important in the programmes for national development and independence to which Arabs aspired in the immediate post-war period.[1] Clearly, however, these hopes depended on the attitude of the British Administration. But instead of providing protective tariffs and financial support, the Mandatory power rested on its traditional view of dependencies as suppliers of raw materials and importers of British manufactures. This left the door open for Western Jewish immigrants to take the industrial initiative in Palestine, initially by means of private Jewish enterprise and capital, but from the 1920s onwards as part of the Zionist programme. The large-scale immigration of people with industrial experience and capital, first in the mid-1920s from Poland and then later in the mid-1930s the more industrially sophisticated German immigrants, convinced the Zionist Organization of the importance of urban and industrial development. Official Zionist support for Jewish industrial efforts was a tactical step calculated to uphold the Zionist ideological programme.

A return to the land and agricultural work was a main tenet of the Zionist philosophy for Jewish revival, and initial efforts and funds were invested mostly in land purchase and the establishment of agricultural settlements. But by the early 1920s it was clear that these efforts were neither economically successful nor able to attract the largely untapped middle-class Jewry of Eastern Europe who were engaged in industrial and commercial activities. The ZO attached an advisory committee to its Department of Urban Colonization to express official Zionist industrial policy and to put pressure on the Administration to adopt favourable measures towards that policy.[2] Thereafter, the government was inexorably, if reluctantly, drawn into support and protection of Jewish industry in a pattern typical of British-Zionist relations throughout the Mandate period.

Development of the industrial sector

A lack of compatibility in statistics prevents a full and exact description of the development of industry in Haifa, or in Palestine as a whole, during the 1920–39 period. Nevertheless, censuses of Jewish industries carried out in 1930, 1934 and 1937 have been used by researchers to detail Jewish industrial development in terms of its effect on the Jewish sector.[3] Government surveys of all Palestinian industries were also made during the Mandate period, the first in 1928. From these two sources, the general trend of industrial progress in both communities can be described. Industrialization, in the Western sense of production for a market economy, grew rapidly in terms of the number of new enterprises and the amount of capital invested in them. Using data on imports and industrial utilization of electric power as indices for overall development between 1925 and 1937, Himadeh attempts to simplify the statistical problem by providing a relatively co-ordinated and comprehensive view of general progress. While industry used 1,427,475 KWH of electricity in 1926 and imported raw materials to the value of £506,281, it used 20,314,114 KWH and imported £1,607,885 worth in 1937.[4]

More specific aspects of this progress are well documented for the Jewish sector. Jewish industries experienced a tremendously rapid growth in their number, variety and investment of capital between 1921 and 1937, by which date they outdistanced Arab industry by a large margin. Jewish enterprises grew from 1,850 with a capital of £600,000 in 1921, to 5,606 and an investment of £11,637,300 in 1936.[5] Of the total of 3,505 Palestinian industrial establishments (with £3,514,886 capital investment) registered in 1927, the Arab share was roughly estimated at 65 per cent.[6] But while Arab industrial firms outnumbered those of the Jewish sector at this date, new Jewish projects invested a larger amount of capital, with a threefold numerical increase over pre-war conditions, made possible by the introduction of electricity.[7] For the period 1931–7, even though Arab development is reported to have been significant and diversified, with 529 new projects, Arab industries constituted only 20 per cent of all industries in Palestine; no statistics can be provided on Arab invested capital.[8] This growth, however, hid a factor which was significant for the development of the Arab economy. The new enterprises were small in size and capital, and the large, already established, industries, notably in oil processing and soap making, declined.[9]

This survey of the qualitative progress of Palestinian industry becomes more significant when the conditions of its growth are brought to light. The contribution of Jewish industry was the introduction of a wide range of new enterprises, backed by private and institutional capital and manned by a Western industrialized proletariat. The fact that this industry was transplanted along with European capital, imported machinery, raw and semi-manufactured materials, as well as with a labour force that maintained a Western standard of living, contributed to the difficulties it created for the whole Palestine population. Its production was directed towards domestic consumption within the Jewish community and thus the type and the number of new industries were linked to the flow of immigration. Expansion was experienced in two periods, 1924–5, following the Polish immigration wave, and 1934–5, following the wave of even wealthier German immigrants. A slump followed in 1936, due in large measure to the political disturbances.[10] On the one hand, expansion had naturally slowed after the upsurge of 1934-5, and on the other hand, the political troubles had a deleterious effect on all aspects of industry and construction. Lack of confidence in the political stability of the country led to a much reduced volume of immigration and new investments. A distinct curtailment in demand for Jewish products was felt, because of the Arab boycott, and even wages were adversely affected. This period of hardship was short-lived, and was felt in varying degrees by the various industries. A direct result was stronger dependence on Jewish labour and the Jewish market, and a more introverted ideological stance. Though the creation of an exporting industry had been the principal aim of all the large enterprises, it was to be fulfilled only during the Second World War.[11]

The best example of Jewish industrial development was in Tel-Aviv, a purely Jewish town where industrial plants were set up by immigrants who brought to Palestine their previous expertise and catered to the tastes of the newly created market. The inevitable duplication of projects and resultant bankruptcies encouraged more official involvement of the ZO in the co-ordination and promotion of industrial development in the Jewish sector. This process coincided with a more precise definition of the ideological stance of Zionist industry, which in turn dictated the range of variety in manufactures:

> Industries dependent on cheaper or specially skilled labor were precluded by the policy opposing employment of Arab labor, by the restricted employment of women, and by the absence of readily applicable skills among the mass of the Jewish labor force.[12]

Because of this special functional relationship, the sector exhibited a character that was nationalistic and exclusive, a feature which became progressively clearer in the major industries – electricity, oil, cement and chemicals – which accounted for approximately 60 per cent of all Jewish industrial capital and employed about 75 per cent of the entire labour force.[13]

The pattern of Arab industrial development was rather different, resulting from the demand of the British occupation and of the local community, and concentrating on the production of traditional foodstuffs and basic commodities, plus venturing into new areas of food products demanded by the Western communities. After 1925, larger volumes of capital were raised by means of partnerships, companies and co-operatives for more ambitious projects such as cigarette manufacture, rice milling and ceramic plants, whose products even filtered into the Jewish market. Other Arab industries, on the other hand, were challenged by new Jewish enterprises. Competition was felt most strongly in the field of oil manufacture, dairy products, flour milling and brick making. The Nablus oil presses were in decline, while the supply of oil and soap exports produced from the large modern Jewish factories was on the increase. Olive-oil soap suffered most, replaced by soap manufactured with acid oil. Similarly the Zionist dairy co-operative, Tnuvah, began to replace conventional Arab methods. A few new Arab enterprises, in products such as confectionery and macaroni and rice milling, were established in direct response to the needs of the immigrant population, but they experienced stiff competition.

In general, Arab industry was characterized by the large number of small individually owned enterprises with low capital and low yield. A common feature of Arab business was its conservative personalized financial dealings. The Arabs maintained an advantage in labour-intensive industries, such as quarrying, partly because the Zionists eschewed such ventures.

The introduction of protectionism

Although it was not surprising that Jewish immigrants with industrial backgrounds should try to resurrect these industrial interests once they arrived in Palestine, it is also clear that, without the Zionist Organization's efforts to rationalize the Jewish industrial effort and to put pressure on the Administration for assistance, many more would-be industrialists would have ended up in bankruptcy. Conditions in Palestine in the 1920s by no means assured the success of a Western-oriented industrial sector. As early as 1921, however, the Administration evinced its support for the embryonic industrial sector, not only because it reflected Jewish efforts, but also because the Administration felt it provided scope to impress upon the Arab population the benefits that the sudden influx of Jewish immigrants could bring in terms of the modernization and improvement of the whole economy.[14] Sir Herbert Samuel was obstructed in even his mild attempts to bolster local industry by the Colonial Office, which saw in local import-substitution ventures a threat to customs tariffs, which provided the Administration's main revenues. The colonial policy of tariffs for revenue was reinforced in 1923 by the need for retrenchment in administrative expenditure, and it was not until the mid-1920s that the local customs system began to be amended.

The Zionist Organization then began to receive more positive responses from the Administration to its campaign for support of the growing Jewish industrial sector – a campaign which was forged by maintaining constant contacts between the industries and the ZO's Department of Trade and Industry, later expanded into the Department for Urban Colonization. Its pressure for tariff protection was clearly based on a deeply introverted viewpoint; the higher cost of living which such a policy would engender was regarded as tolerable because it would ultimately result in higher national income, certainly for those engaged in the process. By 1925, tentative measures to protect the nascent industries by tariff exemptions opened the gates to a flood of further demands and the emergence of a fully fledged policy of protection.[15] The demands of industry were strongly upheld by the Director of Customs, who recommended major concessions to the new sector. His arguments demonstrated the overriding concern with one angle of the Mandate policy, that of the Jewish National Home. Loss of revenue to the state would be compensated by employment and consumption by new immigrants. Support of Jewish firms was also seen as necessary to counter Zionist attacks to the contrary, especially when reporting to the League of Nations – a position considered important by the Colonial Office.[16] A whole range of customs exemptions was authorized by the Customs Duties Exemption Ordinance of 1926, covering, in addition to prime movers, machinery and components, a large list of raw materials used by industry. By implication, these measures protected projects that could inject a large capital investment. Indirectly, they had a deleterious effect on the cost of living, especially on prices for basic commodities such as cement, salt, oil and wheat. Jewish industry nevertheless intensified its campaign for more concessions, which were generally granted, as shown by the Customs Tariff Ordinance of 1927 and the series of amendments to it.

Until the Arab outbreak against the Mandate policy and the JNH in 1929, the Administration seemed oblivious to the repercussions of its policy on the Arab sector. Together with the Colonial Office, it regarded industrial questions as a purely Jewish affair, a view reinforced in large measure by impressive Zionist influence and Arab ineffectiveness on that score. Arab criticism and protests against what the Arab population considered a discriminatory policy[17] were taken seriously only when they degenerated into violence and unbalanced the 'contented stability' of the political system.

Arab grievances found reflection in the Hope Simpson Report:[18]

In fact, large industry in Palestine appears to depend on manipulation of the tariff. The rest of the population is taxed in order that the proprietors of these industrial concerns may be in the position to pay the wages of the labourers and to make a profit for themselves.

After the 1929 events, Arab protests seemed better informed and more precise. A conference of Arab Chambers of Commerce, held on 23 December 1929, submitted a memorandum to the High Commissioner criticizing the government's policy of protecting the industries of a few Jewish capitalists 'at the expense of a higher cost of living to the majority of the inhabitants'.[19] Specifically, the policy of protecting the Nesher cement factory, which was a particular concern of the Arab Executive, was seen as 'an attempt by the authorities to direct the economy of the Arabs into channels not in keeping with their economic interests and political aspirations' and also as a danger to Syrian industries, by encouraging the introduction of dumped cement from Palestine. Arab voices continued to argue that Arab manufactures were unprotected, both because of the import of the same articles free of duty and because of the imposition of tariffs on the raw materials for their production. These grievances were vividly expressed in the Arab press; al-Karmil and al-Yarmuk, both Haifa newspapers, explored the issue of tariffs and their effect on the Arab economy and society.[20]

The pattern of Jewish industrial development was essentially Western, urban and formulated within a capitalist economic framework. As was natural with an urban industry-oriented population, enterprises clustered in Tel-Aviv, Haifa and – to a lesser extent – Jerusalem. While only a third of all Jewish immigrants had settled in the cities by 1931, this proportion was reversed and two-thirds established themselves in the towns between 1932 and 1935. A similar concentration of Arabs in the towns was observed for the same period.[21] Tel-Aviv had the largest number of small and medium-sized enterprises, while Haifa was deliberately chosen by the Zionists as the future centre of large Jewish industry. A statistical survey of industries registered at the Jewish Agency in 1922 recorded six major projects already established, specializing in such products as furniture, metal and small machinery, only one of which had started in Haifa.[22] All were connected in one way or another with the Zionist Organization, but at this stage they were all experiencing difficulties in finances, management, and marketing. By 1936, however, heavy industry was concentrated in Haifa. Though the number of factories and employees was similar to that in Tel-Aviv, more than double the capital was invested in Haifa's industries. As noted in Chapter 6, Haifa Bay[23] was the area suggested in the Master Plan formulated by the Central Planning Commission for a concentration of spectacular British projects and a multitude of smaller, mostly Jewish, factories, together with residential quarters for the workers.

The history of the large Jewish industries which by 1936 had achieved some prominence in Haifa – the electrification plant, the Shemen oil industry, the Grands Moulins flour mills and the Nesher cement factory[24] – underlines the development of both British and Zionist industrial policy. These enterprises were founded in the first decade of the Administration, supported by heavy capital investment and managed by corporate structures which adhered, in varying degrees, to Zionist principles; they produced commodities essential for establishing a national entity and were reared under protective laws. Within the Jewish sector, there were differing philosophies and attitudes towards the achievement of Jewish revival in Palestine. The main Zionist current with an articulate ideology was the labour movement: for this group, development was to be achieved on a national basis where Zionist ethics and ideals often superseded economic wisdom. Other Zionist organizations, such as the Rothschilds' enterprises, saw themselves as independent but equal partners in this process, but were guided by economic principles of return on investment and were instrumental in supplementing Zionist efforts by creating private capital.

The Administration had some say only concerning the employment policies of the electrification plant, which was part of the Rutenberg electrification project and a government concession (see Chapter 13). This explains the number of Arabs employed in the building of the power station and also the small number of Arabs among the personnel later on. Nevertheless, the granting of this concession was a deliberate act providing the Zionist movement and representatives of Jewish national capital with vital monopolies, notwithstanding the Administration's assumption, later proved to be mistaken, that such enterprises would benefit the entire population. The electrification project was continually upheld as a symbol of the Jewish contribution to the modernization and Westernization of the country. Furthermore, the existence of the whole Jewish industrial venture depended on the economic success of electricity production.

The three other large factories in Haifa were initiated by private enterprise. Shemen was the earliest project, registered in London in October 1919, with a capital of £250,000, most of which came from Jewish capitalists in Berlin. Before embarking on their project, the Shemen directors sought the approval and support of Zionist leaders and the advice of the Zionist Organization in London.[25] These contacts resulted in an agreement between the ZO and the company which was to be used as a model for further co-operation between Zionist work in Palestine and private projects. The company pledged itself to abide by principles set by the ZO; namely, that all land should be purchased through the agency of the ZO and that the undertaking would comply with ZO conditions of labour control,[26] a main condition being the employment of Jewish labour to the largest degree possible.

Similarly, but to a lesser degree, Nesher and the Grands Moulins accepted these principles and tried to reconcile the aim of creating a Jewish Palestine with the running of viable industrial concerns. Nesher was privately initiated by a Jewish capitalist, Michael Polak, previously a Baku oil magnate, who aligned himself with the Rothschilds and their business methods. He founded the Nesher Cement Company in 1923, and it was floated as a public company in 1925 on £E250,000, with the support and encouragement of PICA (the Palestine Jewish Colonization Association), the organ of the Rothschilds' projects in Palestine. By the mid-1930s, with a further capital investment of £350,000, it employed about 700 workers, both Arab and Jewish. The Grands Moulins flour mill was the largest Rothschild project in Haifa financed by PICA.[27] Founded in 1923 with an initial investment of £200,000, it also employed both Arabs and Jews.

The difference between Shemen and the Nesher and Grands Moulins ventures in their adherence to Zionist ideals is clear from their employment policy. Practical financial considerations were the guiding principle for hiring Arabs in the mills and in Nesher, where hard-working, cheap labour was sought. This signified no lack of commitment to Zionist ideology but denoted these ventures' more practical approach and their exploitation of cheap Arab labour when necessary. Nevertheless, the growing influence of the labour organization (GFJL) among their Jewish employees, coupled with the changing political atmosphere, led to stricter compliance with orthodox Zionist doctrine.[28]

Jewish industry owed its success and economic viability to such tactics. Nesher was awarded the first customs exemptions as a result of a purposeful political campaign involving the ZO, the Administration and the Colonial Office, despite the fact that Shemen had demanded customs concessions as soon as it started operations in December 1924. The political significance of customs exemptions to assist Zionist undertakings was not lost on the colonial officials, who felt that, however much out of tradition this policy was, it had to be followed.[29] This action heralded an onslaught of demands that were progressively more exacting and insistent. Nesher is an excellent example. Between 1925 and 1928, the import duty on cement was raised from 7 per cent to 40 per cent ad valorem – achieved by constant insistence on the part of Nesher and its supporters on substantial protection tariffs, which were finally extracted from the Administration.[30] In addition, various raw materials needed for the oil industry, as demanded by Shemen, were exempted from import duty by August 1925. Salt needed by the cement and oil industries was also exempted, and requests by the major industries for exemptions on machinery, and on raw and semi-manufactured imports, as well as for the taxing of manufactured items, were accepted. In brief, Jewish industry during its infancy was provided with hot-house conditions.

The detrimental effects on other aspects of Palestinian economic life need some elaboration. At one level, the revenue system and public

expenditure were negatively affected; at another, expensive local production and imports meant a higher cost of living. For political reasons,
the Administration and the Colonial Office refused to reverse the
protectionist policy even in 1926, when £E350,000 in revenue was
sacrificed in order to encourage industrial enterprises. This deviation
from traditional colonial practice could be explained only in terms of
the British government's policy commitment to the Jewish National
Home. The items exempted from duty in the interests of the major
industrial concerns were also items crucial to the livelihood of the local
communities, both agricultural and urban. Wheat and flour, oil and oil
seeds, building machinery and cement made up the major portion of
the exemption schedules. By 1930, when a Jewish modern industrial
nucleus had taken shape, its corollary was a deteriorating Arab agricultural sector. Following the Hope Simpson Report and that of the
Committee appointed to inquire into the economic conditions of the
Arab peasantry, the connection between Jewish industrial activities and
Arab agricultural difficulties was officially recognized. Both the Administration and the Colonial Office admitted, even if obscurely and
reluctantly, that Arab grievances, especially in the field of agriculture,
had their roots in the official policy of supporting Jewish industries and
in the latter's practices.[31]

The protectionist policy was not totally reversed, however; exceptions
were made in a few cases to prevent further impoverishment of the
Arab sector. The 1929 riots came as a rude reminder of these deteriorating conditions, but only in 1930 did the Colonial Office concede the
need to protect local production of wheat, olive oil and sesame by
reimposing an import tax on these items. By then the price of locally
produced wheat and olive oil had halved, while imports had risen. A
further cause of concern to the Administration was the suspicion of a
deliberate ploy by Jewish industrialists to boycott Arab produce; it was
noted that in 1930 the same volume of sesame seed was imported as
exported, at a higher price but for a lower quality. The attitude of
Jewish industrialists to this particular issue often confirmed these suspicions; Shemen adopted a belligerent attitude, linking its willingness to
buy local produce to concessions awarded by the Administration.[32]

As early as 1926, the Director of Agriculture complained that customs
concessions were undermining the efforts of his department to encourage the production of olives and sesame. The fall in their price on
the local market, because of imports, impoverished the fallahin and, in
addition to the loss of land, was instrumental in creating the influx of
seasonal labour into the cities. The plight of sesame farmers in the
areas around Haifa was highlighted by the Arab Economic Congress,
held in Haifa on 11 November 1929; demands for protective tariffs to
aid these farmers were put to the Administration.

It should also be noted that the changes in the Administration's policy did not stem from a sympathetic or knowledgeable understanding of the dynamics of Arab objections but were purely a palliative and an expedient to maintain political stability. Even the High Commissioner recognized the seriousness of the situation and, in view of the deteriorating conditions of the fallahin because of tax exemptions on agricultural imports, strenuously demanded these changes.[33] From the early 1930s on, new requests for customs exemptions to benefit Jewish industry were to be examined with an eye to the effect on intercommunal relations and the cost of living. But this revision of policy came a decade too late from the Arab point of view. By then, a Zionist industrial sector with an inherently exclusivist ideology had been protectively nurtured into adulthood at the expense of Arab development.

Arab industry: tobacco and other industries

The main Arab industry in Haifa was the cultivation and manufacture of tobacco. Three-quarters of Palestine's crop came from the Acre villages in the Northern District, and three-fifths of the manufactured product came from the Haifa factories. The repeal of the Ottoman tobacco monopoly, the Régie, in February 1921 awoke the interest of the private sector, as well as of the Administration. Outside interests immediately set up cigarette factories, but it was the Karaman, Dik and Salti factory, established at that time in Haifa, which was to become the largest in Palestine. Like all smaller Arab workshops in the city, these factories depended on the Arab market.[34] In fact, cigarettes were promoted as an Arab product and consumption was either encouraged in order to promote the Arab economy, and consequently Arab political status, or discouraged in order to boycott Jewish interests in the industry.

The Administration paid particular attention to tobacco and implemented unusual measures to promote its success. During the early period, an expert from the Department of Agriculture toured the country instructing growers in the best methods of cultivation. Minimum taxation was also imposed on local production in contrast to a higher import tax – a side-effect of which was the active business in tobacco and cigarette smuggling on the northern frontiers. Attempts were made to compensate for the loss of revenue to the Treasury by adding an excise to the land tax and reinforcing measures to control contraband, but these new regulations were amended in 1925, in such a manner as to continue helping the local industry to compete with manufactured imports.[35]

The Administration was clearly ready to go far to help create an exporting resource, but in its attempt to protect the Arab grower from foreign competition, it overlooked his need for protection from local

exploitation. Jewish growers had, very early on, set up Tobacco Cultivators Associations to supply the Jewish market. The Arab cultivators,
who were the majority of tobacco growers, lacked this organization and
left the major manufacturing concerns a free hand to decide local
selling prices. Gradually, they acquired a monopoly of the local market.
The Palestine crop never achieved a sufficiently competitive quality for
export, nor was the volume it produced large enough.[36] Thus, despite
the legislation, it was the grower and the consumer who ultimately paid
the taxes and enriched the capitalist monopoly.

The example of tobacco illustrates the problems of all Arab industries
during this period. There was a generally conservative attitude towards
industrial investment which stemmed from the scarcity of large amounts
of capital and the novelty of the industrial field. Moreover, the government did nothing to change this; on the contrary, it promoted an anti-
industrial bias among Arabs by deliberately refraining from encouraging
industrial training or modernizing existing enterprises in the Arab
sector.[37] In fact, Arab resentment at the inefficiency of the government
education system, especially in the fields of agriculture and technical
training, became progressively more virulent with the deterioration of
political conditions. Arab nationalists regarded the education system as
totally inadequate to raise Arab standards to a level equal to those in
the Jewish sector in professional and technical training. The approach
of the education syllabus was towards the creation of a static conservative society. Even though an industrial technical school was opened
in Haifa in response to persistent demands following the events of
1929–30, it was only a palliative, with no genuine programme of
substantive changes. In short, the Arab sector saw the government
educational curriculum as yet another instrument to reduce future
generations of Arab Palestinians to conditions of dependence and to
facilitate the application of the British-Zionist programme.[38] Thus, it
was natural that, following the period of prosperity in the cities, more
capital was invested in citriculture and in trade. For this reason, too, we
can find a few names of industrialists engaged in more than one line,
an example being Karaman, who extended his business from tobacco
to quarrying, packaging and nail production.

The large Arab industrial concerns in Haifa, such as the rice mill
and the cigarette factory, were meant mainly to service the Arab
public.[39] The wholesalers Wardi, Tawil and Saraqibi established the
rice mill late in 1935, as a project dependent on the combined financial
support of merchants in trades that were traditionally Arab.

It should be added here that the protection awarded to Jewish
industries and the tobacco industry did not extend to small Arab
projects. The decade after 1925 saw numerous attempts at industrial
projects in Haifa ranging from ice, oil and liquor to shoes, nightwear

and bed factories; these were short-lived and often ended in financial loss. Small entrepreneurs recognized the help which a protectionist policy would give their projects, and voiced their requests through the Arabic press. The Jabbour and Karkabi cardboard factory appealed to the Administration to facilitate its business in a similar way to the policy applied to Jewish factories, by permitting the import of Egyptian master artisans.[40] Another case was the small spirits factory which considered many of the official regulations to ensure strict safety measures and the payment of increased fees as shortsighted, inconsiderate and in the interests of large industries and monopolies.[41]

With the expansion in urban construction, especially after 1933, many small Arab investors dabbled in industries allied to building, such as ceramics, pipes, nails and wire factories. But these projects served local needs only, and remained peripheral to the major industries. The raison d'être of the most important Arab concerns was the traditional one of supplying the community with its immediate consumer goods, especially foodstuffs. Thus, modern flour mills and bakeries, and furniture and clothing plants appeared in the Arab quarters and around the old shopping centres, and cardboard and paper-bag factories were established to serve the cigarette and citrus industries. By the mid-1930s, however, a change in the attitude towards production for a market economy was indicated by the number of new workshops to supplement and service both the industrial and commercial fields.

Aspects of segregation

Intercommunal co-operation in industry was minimal and must be considered from the perspective of the overall development and ideological stance of the two sectors. Among the few joint endeavours were the lime pits on the Carmel, owned jointly by Solel Boneh (Histadrut) and Karaman,[42] and the ice factory of Albina (an Arab family from Jerusalem), Dunia and Katinka. The Silverberg cardboard-box industry mainly supplied the Arab tobacco manufacturers in the city. Karaman, Dik and Salti bought two paper-bag factories from Jewish owners in 1931; later, a controlling share in their cigarette factory was sold to Maspero Frères.[43] (Interestingly the name of the factory remained the same, presumably to maintain its popularity among the Arab clientele.)

Promotion of Arab industries should be seen in the context of the Zionist ideology of 'the conquest of land and labour' and campaigns to further Jewish products. At no time did Arab industries pose a threat to Jewish production, while the latter's infiltration into the Arab market was seen by Arab nationalists as a deterrent to Arab development. Nevertheless, the campaign against Arab labour in industry spread to Arab products, too, and became more articulate in purely Jewish and mixed towns, particularly during periods of economic depression among the Jewish community and acceleration of sectoral political strife. The boycott weapon was inherent in the nationalist character of both parties, and was activated by both communities for the same basic reason, though the immediate cause might have been different. Arab calls for a boycott during the 1929 events were strong in the cities, and Jewish industries serving the needs of the local population suffered a severe blow as a result. The ZO blamed the Christian Arabs who competed with Jewish businesses,[44] while overlooking the politico-economic roots of the movement and similar activities in the Jewish sector. In Haifa, these events increased the tendency of the two communities to draw apart. At this stage, the Arab nationalist front, through the Arab press, preached boycott and economic solidarity in the Arab community.

However limited in variety and circulation, the fact that Arab products filtered through to the Jewish market was systematically resisted by the Zionists, especially in the period after 1933 when prosperity and competition in Haifa bred stronger sentiments of introversion. The exclusivist character of Zionist industries took concrete shape during this period. A committee representing Jewish producers and public organizations, the Association for Produce of the Country (Haigud Letotseret Ha'aretz), was set up to discourage the buying of Arab products. Its campaign took the form of canvassing homes and shops, and having these principles taught in schools.[45] Washitz's study of the debates in the Jewish Chamber of Commerce sheds light on the conflicting interests within the Haifa Jewish community on this issue. In a mixed city like Haifa, direct and indirect economic contacts had been going on for at least a decade, and interdependence in certain fields had become a fact. Arab produce, especially agricultural produce, and Arab labour were cheap and for that reason were purchased by the Jewish sector. The Jewish working class found it especially profitable to buy Arab produce instead of the more expensive Jewish dairy and other food products as well as some building materials. Representatives of the trading community in the Chamber opposed any boycott of Arab products, while the industrialists supported the policy of 'Buy Jewish'. Zionist ideologues endorsed the view that Arab produce should be resorted to only as a supplement to Jewish produce during this stage in the development of the Jewish economy. David HaCohen is quoted as having said:

> We have not declared a boycott on Arab products and we will be careful to avoid it in future too; it is alright to eat Arab melons if we do not grow melons; it is alright to use Khayat Beach.[46]

By 1936, however, a militant policy of boycott was adopted by both sectors; Jewish industrial products had flooded the Arab market and competed with traditional produce. Shemen manufactured an edible oil to be used instead of samna, the traditional Arab cooking fat, and dyed its soap the colour of Nabulsi soap. Western-style clothes, shoes, furniture and confectionery were bought by Arabs. To counter this, propaganda pamphlets were distributed by Arab nationalist groups to the Arab community in Haifa and the other cities, urging them to boycott Jewish industries.

While the Arabs lacked the capital and expertise to initiate vital heavy industries, nevertheless certain labour-intensive branches of production were still within their particular domain to meet the specific requirements of the Arab market. The Arab community in Haifa in the 1920s and early 1930s had established its apparent hegemony over one industry, tobacco, and founded new projects which were peripheral – although complementary – to heavy industry. But the Zionists came to control electricity generation as well as large-scale oil extraction, cement and flour plants; and in pressing the government to introduce measures that would ensure the economic viability of these projects, they effectively impoverished the urban Arab population and squeezed out many traditional Arab manufacturers. In general, the refusal of the Administration to encourage industrial training or modernization of existing enterprises in the Arab sector left the Arab population painfully exposed to the influences of imported industrial development and an inflated economy. The nature of Jewish industrial interests and the operational framework providing for its growth cancelled the chances for similar attempts in the Arab sector. Irrespective of the attitudes of both Jews and Arabs towards industrialization, conditions for the success of Jewish industry could never be duplicated in the Arabs' case. Furthermore, the violent events of 1936–9, and their aftermath, entrenched the separation of the two economic sectors in the city, weakened the financial capacities of the Arab economy and precluded the potential for its recovery.

Notes

1. Z. Y. Hershlag, *Introduction to the Modern Economic History of the Middle East* (London, 1964), p. 166.

2. For a detailed discussion see B. J. Smith, *The Roots of Separatism in Palestine* (Syracuse, NY, 1993), pp. 162–7, and K. Grunwald and J. O. Ronall, *Industrialization in the Middle East* (New York, 1960), p. 258.

3. For references, see D. Horowitz and R. Hinden, *Economic Survey of Palestine* (Tel-Aviv, 1938), and R. Nathan, O. Gass and D. Creamer, *Palestine: Problem and Promise* (Washington, DC, 1946).

4. S. B. Himadeh, 'Industry', in S. B. Himadeh (ed.), *Economic Organization of Palestine* (Beirut, 1938), p. 251, Table IX.

5. Ibid., p. 244, Table VII, and Nathan, Gass and Creamer, *Palestine*, p. 222.

6. Himadeh, 'Industry', p. 234, and Esco Foundation for Palestine, *Palestine: A Study of Jewish, Arab and British Policies* (New York, 1970), p. 381.

7. Himadeh, 'Industry', p. 231, Table II.

8. Ibid., p. 245, and Horowitz and Hinden, *Economic Survey*, p. 208.

9. S. Essaleh, *L'Etat actuel de l'économie syrienne* (Paris, 1944), p. 173.

10. Horowitz and Hinden, *Economic Survey*, pp. 86–103.

11. Nathan, Gass and Creamer, *Palestine*, pp. 231–41.

12. Ibid., p. 222.

13. Ibid., p. 223, and Himadeh, 'Industry', pp. 249 and 250, Table VIII. For more detail on Jewish industry see: M. Seikaly, 'The Arab Community of Haifa 1918–1936: A Study in Transformation', D.Phil. thesis, Oxford University, 1983, pp. 104–5.

14. See B. Wasserstein, *The British in Palestine: the Mandatory Government and the Arab-Jewish Conflict 1917–1929* (London, 1978), for a discussion of Sir Herbert Samuel's attitude towards Zionist policy and his persistent attempts at reconciling the Arab population to the Mandate policy. The Zionist Executive in Palestine also believed that reconciliation could be achieved by interesting the Arabs in Jewish industrial and commercial undertakings. See F. H. Kisch, *Palestine Diary* (London, 1938), pp. 75 and 118.

15. A. Michaelis, 'The Industrial Development of Palestine', *Palnews* (Tel-Aviv, 1936), p. 62.

16. Grindle's minute of 9 April 1929, Shuckburgh's minute of 25 April 1929, and Williams' minute of 8 June 1929 (PRO CO 733/166). See also Smith, *The Roots*, pp. 167–76.

17. 'Report by the Palestine Arab Congress on the State of Palestine', 6 October 1924 (PRO CO 733/74); the Arab Executive to the Acting CS, 13 February 1930 (ISA 65 61/1 AHC/01943).

18. Sir John Hope Simpson, *Palestine: Report on Immigration, Land Settlement and Development* (London, 1930), p. 144.

19. Memo by Conference of the Arab Chambers of Commerce to the HC, December 1929 (ISA 65/1 AHC/00560).

20. *Al-Karmil*, 9 October 1929, 26 March 1930, and 23 March 1932.

21. D. Dusterwald, 'The City in the Economic Life of Palestine', *Palnews* (Tel-Aviv, 1936).

22. Index of Industries as registered on 14 March 1922 by N. J. T. (CZA A226/15).

23. In 1921, an area of 17,000 dunums between Haifa and Acre was purchased by the Jewish National Fund from Joseph Khuri for £110,000. Economic Resume since the Appointment of Sir Herbert Samuel, 13 August 1921 (PRO CO 733/14).

24. S. Schama, *Two Rothschilds and the Land of Israel* (London, 1978), pp. 247–51, and Esco, *Palestine*, pp. 383–4.

25 Exposé by M. W. Willbushevich, sent with Dr A. Ruppin, Zurich, 29 July 1919, to Mr Snowman of Palestine Zionist Office; and Willbushevich to Mr Goldberg, ZO London, 15 August 1919; also, Secretary of Trade and Industry to Mr Aaronson, 27 February 1920 (CZA S8/1152).

26. Statement on 'Shemen', London, 21 October 1919 (CZA S8/1152); Department of Trade and Industry to Justice Brandeis, 5 November 1919 (CZA Z4/1331); Secretary of Trade and Industry to Mr Aaronson, 27 February 1920 (CZA S8/1152); and Herbert Samuel to Laudman, 8 September 1920 (CZA Z4/1804).

27. *PICA*: The Palestine Jewish Colonization Association (1924) was the successor of the JCA-Palestine Colonization Association, the administrative organ of the Rothschild projects in Palestine. It acted as a merchant bank to attract commercial and industrial investment as well as to acquire land for such purposes. Its ideological stance gradually converged with the mainstream Zionist movement and away from the individualistic independent views of Baron Edmond de Rothschild.

28. *Davar*, 28 June and 18 and 19 October 1933.

29. Stead's memo to CS, 10 May 1925 (PRO CO 733/26); HC to CO, 3 July 1925, and Clauson's minute, 16 July 1925 (PRO CO 733/95).

30. Pollak to CS, 6 March 1925 (ISA 128 Cust/1795/26), and OAG to CO, 23 November 1928 (PRO CO 733/157).

31. Director of Agriculture to CS, 1 April 1926 (ISA 128 Cust/956/26); HC to CO, 21 June 1930 (PRO CO 733/189); and Campbell's minute of 9 August 1930 (PRO CO 733/189).

32. Shemen to the Director of Customs, 29 and 30 January 1930 (ISA 128 Cust/956/26), and HC to CO, 15 February 1930 (PRO CO 733/189).

33. See Smith, *The Roots*, p. 174; Director of Agriculture to CS, 1 April 1926 (ISA 128 Cust/956/26); HC to CO, 21 June 1930 (PRO CO 733/189).

34. For a more thorough study of the tobacco industry of Palestine and Arab attempts to promote it see: Seikaly, 'The Arab Community', pp. 120–27.

35. HC to CO, 23 May 1924, Tobacco Ordinance (PRO CO 733/68); HC to CO, 20 February 1925, Tobacco Excise (PRO CO 733/89); HC to S of S, 8 June 1925, Tobacco Import Duty (PRO CO 733/94); HC to CO, 19 February 1926 (PRO CO 733/112); CS to Director of Customs, Excise and Trade, 26 July 1926 (ISA 128 Cust/691/27); Stead to CS, 27 June 1927, ibid., and Director of Customs, Excise and Trade to CS, 24 March 1927 (ISA 128 Cust/475/27).

36. M. Brown, 'Agriculture', in S. B. Himadeh (ed.), *Economic Organization of Palestine* (Beirut, 1938), p. 164.

37. R. Taqqu, 'Arab Labor in Mandatory Palestine, 1920–1948' (unpublished Ph.D. thesis, Columbia University, 1977), p. 61. A similar view, although in less vehement terms, was expressed by A. L. Tibawi, *Arab Education in Mandatory Palestine* (London, 1956), pp. 79–80 and 284, when assessing the overall Mandatory attitude towards education. 'The Palestine syllabus was no more than a transition from the purely academic to the academic that admits the practical.' Also see N. A. Badran, *Al-Ta'lim wal-Tahdith fil-Mujtama' al-'Arabi al-Filastini* (Education and Modernization in Arab Palestinian Society) (Beirut, 1969), pp. 138–45.

38. *Al-Karmil*, 11 May 1929; 13 February, 25 March, and 26 September 1931; 26 July 1933.

39. For listing of Arab industrial projects see: Seikaly, 'The Arab Community', pp. 120–29; M. Yazbek, *Al-Hijra al-'Arabiyya ila Haifa* (Arab Migration into Haifa) (Nazareth, 1988), pp. 24–5.

40. *Al-Karmil*, 25 February 1930.

41. *Al-Karmil*, 22 March 1928.

42. D. HaCohen, *Time to Tell* (New York, London, 1984), p. 79. Solel Boneh (Levelling and Building) was the co-operative contracting agency of the Histadrut, established in March 1925 for road-building and public works projects. Until 1927, when it went bankrupt, it carried out various building activities, providing openings for new immigrants. Esco, *Palestine*, p. 363.

43. *Ha'aretz*, 19 July 1936, and *al-Karmil*, 20 February 1927, 23 September 1928, and 2 May 1931. Even though the Anglo-American nationality of Maspero was common knowledge in Palestine, it was the fact that a high percentage of its shareholders were Jewish that elicited the concern of the Arab press.

44. Report of Department of Trade and Industry to General Council of ZO, 23 August 1929 – 28 February 1931 (CZA Z10 264/II).

45. Y. Washitz, 'Jewish-Arab Relations in Haifa during the Mandate' (unpublished manuscript, n.d.), Chapter V, pp. 49–50.

46. David HaCohen was Chairman of Solel Boneh and later a member of Haifa's Municipal Council. Ibid., Chapter V, pp. 51–2.

9

Banking and Commerce

As noted in Part One, commercial activity in Haifa expanded rapidly in the early part of the twentieth century in conjunction with the development of Palestine's export-oriented agricultural economy. Although the prime movers were the resident European agents and officials, the native Arab commercial population responded to the modernizing influences, and by the outbreak of the First World War were active participants in transforming the town's economy. The greater economic prosperity also attracted a considerable Arab immigration from other Palestinian towns and villages, from Hauran and from Lebanon, and this influx ensured that real-estate, construction and retail marketing activities developed along with external trade and trade-related finance.

After the war, which paralysed Haifa's development, commercial activity revived but under markedly changed circumstances that frequently exposed the Arab commercial community to threatening challenges. Under the newly created Palestine Administration, the foreign trade balance of surplus agricultural produce for other necessary consumer items was replaced by a deficit trading account in which the value of agricultural exports was dwarfed by a new range of luxury and capital goods imports, whose volume fluctuated with the availability of Jewish and British Administration capital transfers. This chapter examines the general trading and investment climate for Arab merchants in Haifa during the 1920–39 period, and their gradual eclipse by Jewish immigrants.

Banking

Chapter 8 clearly demonstrated that one of the essential elements lacking in any Arab attempt at industrial development was financial backing. Certain sectors of the Arab community understood the need for saving funds, and from the early 1920s the press called for communal savings to be directed towards the specific task of saving Arab land from purchase by the Zionists. Unfortunately, these sectors of the community were generally not the owners of capital, who were described in 1919 by the General Manager of the Anglo-Palestine Bank as, in large part, adhering to 'the tradition of keeping their ready cash in their own hands'.[1] The lower echelons of Arab society were on the whole probably even more wary of banks and paper money; in 1931, when Britain abandoned the gold standard and the Palestine pound depreciated accordingly on the international exchange market, a mass hoarding of brass and silver coins by the entire Arab community was stopped only when articles in the press explained the futility of such action.

Although the British Administration, innately conservative as it was with respect to monetary matters, imposed certain operating restrictions on banks in Palestine and would countenance no form of government-financed cheap credit scheme for Zionist or Arab, its general attitude to banking was one of laissez-faire.[2] The Banking Ordinance of 1921, for instance, merely provided that banking business should be transacted only by registered companies, and contained no rules concerning minimum capital or liquidity ratios.[3] Local Zionist banks flourished, led by the Anglo-Palestine Bank (which was in fact incorporated in London), and by 1936 there were seventy local and seven foreign banks,[4] the largest growth occurring between 1932 and 1936 as a result of the large and wealthy immigration of those years. The foreign banks were on the whole interested only in financing trade and exporting capital back to their metropolitan bases; even the local banks, until at least the 1930s, concentrated on short-term credit secured by the collateral of immovable property or established business accounts. The scope for lending was limited both by the shortage of investment opportunities and by the short-term nature of deposits; in 1936, current accounts represented 80 per cent of all bank deposits.[5]

The Arab community was barely touched by this surge in banking activity. Traditional money-lending to peasants by merchants and landowners, or exchange dealings, continued, the one exception being Barclays Bank (DCO), the government banker and currency agent, which sometimes stood behind the tobacco cultivators and provided agricultural loans, however short-term and expensive, to peasants in the absence of a national agricultural bank. Before and during the First World War, cash trading was common in the largest towns, and even in a small town, as Haifa was then, the income of some, mainly Christian, families was supplemented by earnings from the exchange market, but only at the most primary level.[6] In the coastal towns and Jerusalem, there is some evidence to suggest that the Arab community had begun to use banking facilities; short-term credits were granted against securities, but no advances on goods could be provided because of the lack of warehouses. Some of the traditional money services persisted long after the establishment of branch banking in many of the towns.

The major Arab banking success was the creation in 1930 of the Arab Bank, but even this was problematic. When 'Abdul-Hamid Shoman[7] first mooted his project of an Arab bank for Palestine, he found few supporters in his own community and far fewer among the foreigners he approached. He finally had to depend almost entirely on his own capital to fund the project with an investment of £P15,000. Fu'ad Saba, the accountant of the Palestine Arab Higher Committee, was appointed accountant, and Ahmad Hilmi Pasha,[8] a prominent Arab political figure, became manager, with Rashid al-Hajj Ibrahim as manager of the Haifa branch. The bank was promoted as a national institution in which Arabs were encouraged to invest,[9] but lack of funds and the Arabs' guarded attitude towards banking meant that the Arab Bank was not as influential in its first years as 'Abdul-Hamid Shoman had hoped. He also had to contend with the attempts by his executives to use the bank to further their own political careers, particularly by promising credit facilities of various kinds.[10]

The underdevelopment of Arab banking, and the political obstacles that prevented a more effective channelling of Arab resources in order to prevent further Jewish encroachment, were no more than contributory factors to the impoverishment of the Arab economic sector and the development of separatism. The Jewish sector had at its disposal large funds specially earmarked for investment in modern industries, and it also had access to funding institutions and banks, both local and foreign. In addition, many of the Jewish immigrants were experienced in the handling and management of banking transactions. The Arab sector was deprived of all these advantages. It had no tradition of banking activities and, in view of the economic policy practised by the Administration, it had no opportunity to accumulate or generate capital. In Haifa, the balance was strongly tipped in favour of Jewish industries backed by protective legislation and modern financial transactions. Haifa's character as a centre of Jewish heavy and market-oriented industry persisted until the end of the Mandate.

Foreign trade

Trade statistics for Palestine during the 1919–38 period, as given in Table 9.1, demonstrate the exceptional nature of the prevailing economic conditions, especially when compared with the trading accounts of neighbouring states.[11] The shift to a persistent deficit is explained by the large volume of capital and investment goods brought into the country by the Administration, quasi-official (mainly Jewish) institutions, and the growing numbers of immigrants. In contrast, exports stagnated

Table 9.1 Palestinian imports and exports 1919–38 (£P)

Year	Imports	Exports	Trade balance
1919	4,298,523	793,275	-3,505,248
1920	5,350,392	791,488	-4,558,904
1921	6,022,439	1,452,685	-4,569,754
1922	5,724,238	1,388,070	-4,336,168
1923	4,948,907	1,172,548	-3,776,359
1924	5,401,384	1,231,602	-4,169,782
1925	7,526,657	1,330,830	-6,195,827
1926	6,594,098	1,308,333	-5,285,765
1927	6,184,454	1,899,759	-4,284,695
1928	6,770,818	1,487,207	-5,283,611
1929	7,166,593	1,554,262	-5,612,331
1930	6,958,258	1,896,095	-5,062,163
1931	5,940,000	1,572,061	-4,367,939
1932	7,768,920	2,381,491	-5,387,429
1933	11,123,489	2,591,617	-8,531,872
1934	15,152,781	3,217,562	-11,935,219
1935	17,853,493	4,215,486	-13,638,007
1936	13,979,023	3,625,233	-10,353,790
1937	15,903,666	6,449,628	-9,454,038
1938	11,356,963	5,683,585	-5,673,378

Sources: compiled from S. B. Himadeh (ed.), *Economic Organization of Palestine* (Beirut, 1938), p. 390, Table I; also for 1937–8, from Government of Palestine, *Statistical Abstract of Palestine, 1939* (Jerusalem, 1939), p. 55, Table 66.

at first and began to rise only in the early 1930s, following expansion in citrus production and export promotion campaigns by heavily protected local Jewish industries, such as diamond cutting.

As the volume of trade, and particularly imports, increased, so did the importance of the ports. Haifa's role was now enhanced by its capacity to handle imports, just as before the war it had flourished as the agricultural export centre. The consolidation of an extensive road and rail network servicing the town, and the building of the deep sea harbour, led to its outstripping Jaffa as the main port, particularly after it began to establish a secondary role as an entrepôt for transit trading.

Permanent supremacy over Jaffa was achieved only in the mid-1930s (see Table 9.2). During most of the 1920s, Haifa lost ground, largely as a result of the new British policy of curbing grain exports at the same time as promoting citrus exports, for which Jaffa's easy access to the maritime plain made it the natural export outlet, accounting for between 72 and 80 per cent of the total value of Palestinian exports during the period.[12] Haifa, on the other hand, was the gateway to the granaries of

Table 9.2 Imports and exports for Haifa and Jaffa 1920–38 (£P)

Year	Imports		Exports	
	Jaffa	Haifa	Jaffa	Haifa
1920	2,055,100	1,854,345	276,079	270,666
1921	2,141,620	2,335,045	385,669	172,448
1922	–	2,430,635	–	–
1923				
1924				
1925				
1926	3,462,248	2,018,092	836,764	250,764
1927	3,127,413	1,963,970	1,131,995	496,581
1928	3,455,689	2,167,845	963,565	269,851
1929	3,591,942	2,461,833	877,285	412,812
1930	3,585,905	2,410,470	1,098,256	480,763
1931	3,055,626	2,085,055	953,117	425,437
1932	4,130,249	2,893,543	1,575,972	586,634
1933	5,832,868	4,260,045	1,540,213	893,541
1934	7,629,142	6,216,055	1,824,755	1,208,721
1935	7,719,886	8,455,765	2,285,073	1,707,421
1936	3,182,817	8,627,065	1,613,507	1,690,025
1937	2,144,211	9,300,274	1,678,094	3,167,225
1938	2,525,600	6,884,187	1,418,001	2,618,651

Source: statistics compiled from Government of Palestine, *Statistical Abstract of Palestine, 1939* (Jerusalem, 1939), p. 79, Tables 79 and 80.

the Marj and Hauran and the outlet for cereal exports. In the 1920s, however, new international boundaries and customs agreements with Syria, bad harvests and increased local demand caused a drastic cut in cereal exports; in fact, wheat and flour had to be imported, in increasing amounts, to meet local needs. This contraction had a far-reaching effect on Haifa and its Arab commercial community, as we shall see in the following pages. In the short term, it certainly influenced the propensity to import. In the long run, Haifa restructured its export trade to concentrate on citrus, especially after some of Jaffa's traffic was diverted in 1936-7 during the six-month Arab strike (see Chapters 14 and 15). Attempts were also made to develop industrial exports.

Transit and re-export trade, which had been linked traditionally to the grain trade, comprised only a small part of the city's overall commercial activities.[13] Towards the end of the period under study, however, it began to grow in significance, the main maritime re-export being Iraqi crude oil, which began to be moved through Palestine with the opening of the IPC pipeline in 1934. The importance of the transit trade in strictly commercial terms lay in the specialized services it engendered: the establishment of dry and cold storage units and bonded warehouses, the management of complex monetary transactions and the expansion of a service market for this trade.

While this may have added sophistication to commercial services in the city, it was the import trade itself that had the greatest impact on the transformation of the commercial sector as a whole. About a third of Palestine's imports passed through Haifa in the 1920s, rising to about a half in the 1930s. Britain was the main source, with some 40 per cent in the early period of the Civil Administration, and later – until 1937 – around 25 per cent.[14] The bias in favour of British goods was enthusiastically promoted by the Administration as part of its overall Palestine policy. Significantly, the expansion of this trade link necessitated the development of a commercial infrastructure in the importing cities able to deal directly with British manufacturers and exporters.

Of the neighbouring countries, Egypt and Syria were the two most important exporters to Palestine, both of re-exports, foreign manufactured and luxury goods, and basic food supplies as well as cloth and tools. However, the establishment of this trade pre-dated the new political frontiers and Haifa was particularly damaged by the new conditions covering trade with Syria. The British Administration acknowledged the difficulties provoked by the tariff and other barriers to free trade set up by the new political units.[15] The Syria-Palestine Customs Accord of August 1921 calmed some of the Arab community's apprehension, and Syrian exports recovered after 1922, although the Accord remained the subject of controversy throughout the decade. In the early 1920s, re-exports from Syria which avoided the prescribed customs tariffs damaged government revenue sources and also posed a threat to the nascent Jewish industries. By the 1930s, when the Accord was renewed, it had become an asset to these same industries, which saw Syria as a useful market.

That Palestine was an undeveloped country with a transplanted sophisticated population is clearly illustrated by the high percentage of imports of food (average 25 per cent) and manufactured items (55 per cent).[16] The cities consumed the largest part of these imports, but even village stores began gradually to stock the cheaper and more useful foreign goods. In Haifa, the economy became highly dependent on foreign goods, with an inevitable impact on the tastes, needs and demands of the Arab community. In order to cater for its own as well as the immigrant communities, the Arab trading sector had to deal with a far more complex process involving knowledge of the foreign market, its language, methods and supplies, and presupposing strong financial backing and the services of modern banking facilities. In the following pages we see how a growing sophistication and undoubted resilience were not sufficient of themselves to counter certain British policies and the emergence of racial exclusivity in certain areas of trade.

Development of Arab trade: the erosion of commercial control

Before 1920, trade in Haifa, especially in cereals, was controlled by various powerful families who derived their income from landholdings in the Marj and agricultural villages around the city. Often these families were directly involved in trade; in other cases, local agents (European and Arab) for European firms and shipping agents acted as collectors of exportable goods, either from Palestinian producers or from the Haurani peasants who brought their grains to the city. France and Germany were the main customers for these exports, simply because some of the francophone Christian families and some Germans worked in this line of trade, and family, religious, or cultural connections in the importing countries were vital for the clearing of business and the handling of remittances.[17] Certain Arab francophone families were appointed consuls for European governments interested in the cereal trade with the Palestinian hinterland: the Germaine family for France, the Skovinich and Khayyat families for Spain.[18] Individual links between Haifa merchants and the peasant villages were also important in building up the trust on which unsophisticated credit and loan operations were conducted for pre-harvest financing, and in enabling the merchants to judge import demand in the villages.

In the perception of Haifa's Arab trading community the first decade of the Civil Administration was the most crucial period in the process of change initiated by the new political conditions. The direction of this development became more a response to expanded demands resulting from new policies than an enhancement of already existing trades. In fact, those same policies which led to further consolidation of Haifa's trading position as a whole had a deleterious effect on the major traditional branch of Arab commerce, the cereal trade, as well as on many of the families and villages that depended on this trade in one way or another. Disruption of the cereals export trade and of the links between exporter, producer and importer had a much more far-reaching effect on the local Arab economy than the development of new industry.

By 1920, Palestine was separated from Hauran by international frontiers and customs regulations. The French authorities who now controlled the Syrian section of the Hijaz Railway imposed a 25-percent increase in freight rates on the Hama–Dera'a line,[19] while at the same time leaving unchanged, and later reducing, all rates on freight to Beirut, thus detracting from Haifa's importance as the principal import-export centre for Damascus and Hauran. But this action was nowhere

near as serious for Haifa's merchant community as the British Administration's decision in the autumn of 1920 to prohibit the export of
cereals and meat and to regulate the placing of local contracts by the
military authorities.[20] Introduced ostensibly to assure local supplies of
essential foodstuffs and in fact to provide for the expected flow of
Jewish immigrants, the order was looked upon by cereal traders as the
major cause of their dwindling revenues. Sir Herbert Samuel was
reported to have discussed the decision with the Haifa Chamber of
Commerce. The Arabs expressed their fears that the measure would
have an extremely detrimental effect on Arab commerce, but the HC
had based his decision on the statistics of the Director of Commerce,
himself Jewish. The reporter who was present at the meeting is understood to have told the HC that the director was ignorant of the nature
of the country and its peasantry, who could survive on very little.
Moreover, since the Palestinian harvest preceded that of Sudan and
Morocco, the country was able to import cheaply from these countries
later in the year, after exporting at the higher prices. He is also
understood to have suggested that if the government passed this law in
order to feed the expected immigrants, it ought to buy the crops at
present prices and store them and not make the Arab peasants and
merchants bear the expense.[21]

By December 1920, prices of cereals in the city had fallen to less
than half those at the beginning of the season because of the abundance
of local produce, which now had to be disposed of in the local market.[22]
The restrictions were waived a year later, but by then a great slump
had hit the cereal market; world prices had fallen and Palestinian
exporters found it impossible to get the prices they had expected for
their stocks. Australian flour undersold locally grown wheat, and consequently cereal merchants were forced to sell at a loss.[23]

Before the emergence of the slump, Arab criticism of the export
prohibition was able to put the blame explicitly on British policy. The
Executive Committee of the Haifa Congress (see Chapter 12), during a
meeting with Secretary of State Churchill on 28 March 1921, presented
him with their official stance on his government's policy:

> Palestine is an agricultural country and depends largely on her export of
> cereals for a living. Now Jewish immigration has raised the cost of living, and
> the government, in order to keep prices down in the interest of the Jewish
> consumer has prohibited the export of certain cereals, with the result that
> the granaries of the land are stocked with products and merchants cannot
> find an outlet for trade. Consequently a financial crisis set in and hundreds
> of merchants were bankrupt.[24]

The Congress also expressed the fear that the whole Arab mercantile
community would suffer from competition from wealthy Zionists.

Churchill's response glossed over these objections, although vague promises were made to the effect that the Arabs would share in the general prosperity that would be generated through Zionist funds, and it would therefore be in their best interest to 'take a wise and tolerant view of the Zionist movement'.[25] The Arab reaction was minimally reported, except in the Arab press. Even then, recognition of the extent of the loss dawned only when a general deterioration of the Arab economy set in. Local production of cereals was diminishing annually and larger amounts were being imported to meet the growing consumer demand and to keep prices in check. By 1931, a similar crisis in the soap industry and trade reactivated Arab fears of the threat to traditional Arab trades. The experience of the cereal merchants was seen as a model to be avoided. In Haifa, some of the best-established and traditionally sound merchants were facing financial problems and even public embarrassment. Barclays Bank auctioned off the olive oil of Fu'ad Sa'd, a prominent cereal merchant, in order to meet payment on a loan. Raja Rayyis had to sell land in order to meet his payments, while the Khalil brothers and Anis Houri, all of them prominent merchants, faced financial pressures.[26]

The situation of the Arab cereal merchants concentrated in the northern cities of Nazareth, Acre and Haifa deteriorated throughout the 1920s. Not only had they to contend with British policies which depressed prices, but they were also faced with the challenge posed by the Jewish land-purchasing policy in the Marj, which saw many of the cereal-producing villages pass into Zionist hands.[27] Crops from these new settlements, especially wheat, were sold directly to the Zionist Grands Moulins de Palestine or to Jewish warehouses in the city, bypassing the traditional wholesale merchants and commission agents. When the Grands Moulins first started in 1923, it depended on Arab commission agents to collect and buy the Marj grains, an occupation in which they were skilled; the flour was then sold to merchants and bakeries in the town, many of whom were also Arab. However, this situation proved short-lived and a significant part of Arab trading activities was undercut by an exclusive alliance between Zionist producers and distributors. Apart from the adverse effect of the Grands Moulins on smaller and more primitive mills, its main influence stemmed from the significant control it gradually acquired over flour and wheat price movements. Although in itself it was not a particularly efficient organization,[28] the size of the Grands Moulins venture and its tolerant treatment by the British Administration accorded it a near-monopoly in the market, which it used to keep flour prices low and to break the Arab producer-merchant chain. The situation was summed up by an Arab merchant from the Eastern Gate, the area where grain merchants had their stores:

The Arab trade in grains has died because of the transfer of the Marj villages into Zionist hands. All products are sent to the Jewish mill which thus places the peasants at its mercy. This mill has been importing flour in increasing amounts from Europe for prices cheaper than the merchants can afford to sell and thus causes stagnation of local produce.[29]

Even though a good number of Haifa cereal merchants still operated in the city, by the end of the decade they had to diversify their activities.

During the early 1920s, the tremendous increase in the city's population, both Jewish and Arab, served to conceal the onset of a structural recession. As noted in Part Two, Jewish immigration doubled the Jewish population between 1920 and 1926, a large proportion being European urban immigrants with the means for investment, either in new industries or in trade.[30] Haifa's apparent potential also attracted a large number of Arabs from the surrounding countryside and further afield, many relocating in desperation at the collapse of their livelihoods in their home towns. The agricultural towns of the north provided the bulk of the new Arab population, with an emigration of leading families: Acre (Mukhlis), Nazareth ('Azzam, Jarjura), 'Iblin (Sahyoun, Nashashbi), Shefa 'Amr ('Asfour, Habibi, Karkabi), Kufr Yasif (Boulos, Itayyim), Umm al-Fahm (Sa'd), Tirah ('Abdul Rahman, Akhal).[31] A considerable number of Nabulsis (Karaman, Abu Ghazala) also moved to Haifa following the earthquake of 1927 and after the local soap industry had been badly hit by competition from the Shemen works in Haifa itself (see Chapter 8). During the early 1920s, Damascene merchants found a ready outlet in Haifa for Syrian exports, and various export firms, such as Saraqibi and Sba'i, opened branches in the city.[32] As for those inhabitants who were of Lebanese origin and had been residing in Haifa for at least thirty years before the British occupation, their ranks were now being swollen by the arrival of relatives and members of the same villages.[33] There was undeniably a strong trading inclination in the population of Haifa during the 1920s. This characteristic was an even more striking feature of the 'non-Haifa' inhabitants, both Arab and Jewish, for whom it had more appeal than either Jerusalem or Jaffa–Tel-Aviv.

Customs returns for Haifa in 1921-2 (see Table 9.2) showed an increase over the previous years, but the increase in imports was handled almost exclusively by Jews,[34] with only a small group of Arab merchants dealing with minor volumes. Nearly all Haifa's traditional Arab traders registered a decline. It was not only the grain merchants who were affected, nor was the decline wholly attributable to lack of capital and credit, and the depressed world markets. Arab retail business was also experiencing the premonition of being 'frozen out' by Jewish imports and Jewish ambitions to take over the entire market.

Accurate and consistent statistical data on Haifa's trading sector are not available. However, special supplements of the *Commercial Bulletin* give lists of 'industries' in Haifa (1922), and of the main importers and exporters (1929 and 1933).[35] While not fully comprehensive, these provide some basis for tracing the evolution of commercial activities in each community. The 1922 listing shows the main lines of merchandise produced and sold on the market in Haifa to be: basic foodstuffs, clothing and shoes, furniture and kitchen utensils. As noted in Chapter 8, there was specialization by the religious communities in certain lines of production, with Arabs specializing in the more traditional and labour-intensive areas, while Jews, especially the 'Amal' co-operative, were involved in machine production. This was the trade distribution among the communities at a time when the main Arab trade, the export of cereals, had started to feel the effects of the damage done in 1920. The growing realization that trade was proving inadequate as a means of providing a livelihood created a depression among the merchant class that spread to other levels of Arab society, and which was recorded both officially and by individuals and organizations of the commercial community.[36]

Officials in Haifa and Jerusalem noted the abortive attempts of a few politically and economically oriented residents to establish an Arab economic society. The Arab Economic Development Association drew up a comprehensive programme covering the encouragement of agricultural production and tree-planting, the establishment of trade and labour unions, the founding of an Arab bank and the building of Arab bonded warehouses. The AEDA of Haifa was largely inspired by the editor of *al-Karmil*, Najib Nassar. The promoters of the Association were nationalists who saw economic development as a means of raising Arab status as producers and citizens in order to withstand the economic and cultural pressures of Zionist competition. The Association had very limited funds at its disposal and few means to enhance the peasant means of production, and its achievements were confined to airing Arab disapproval of government policy which encouraged Jewish development schemes.[37] During the early 1920s, fear of an uncertain future compounded by the lack of liquid funds and a tighter competitive market temporarily paralysed the local economy.

The ineffectual Arab response to Jewish commercial encroachment was not caused by any innate characteristics of resignation, but simply by a total lack of means when confronted with Jewish imports of capital and expertise. British policy and world markets had combined to bring down the Arab economy at a time when funds for the Jewish community were buoyant. From 1924, when the improvement in cereal prices coincided with less happy times for Zionist finances, the situation stabilized in Haifa and Arab firms began to examine the opportunities open to them in the extended market. Improved returns were also recorded in the traditional Arab retail market, the performance of which always closely mirrored the agricultural cycle, a fact that had sometimes been forgotten in the general social and economic depression of the early 1920s.[38]

Moreover, with the stimulus of a further large influx of immigrants in 1925, several earlier tentative attempts at trade diversification began to show results. Certain established importers such as Boutagy, Melikian, Hannoush, Zahlan and Za'balawi had taken the first opportunity to expand their businesses by catering to the tastes of the wealthier strata of the Jewish and British population. These firms were particularly aggressive in their new marketing ventures, aiming to become known as the local agents for certain European factories and brands of goods.[39] A few other general agencies emerged on the market, usually specializing in one brand of imports such as groceries, machinery or building materials.

Growth in the building industry was in fact providing a lifeline for many cereal exporters as early as 1922, as they turned their attention to importing building materials.[40] Factories servicing the building industry were also set up and these required raw material imports for the manufacture of bricks, ceramics, pipes, etc. But this trade was also cyclical in the sense that it was closely linked to the various waves of immigrants and the capital they brought with them. Imports directly related to the trading process – power generators, teak wood for display, adequate locks and rolling metal gates for stores – also began to feature in the statistics as the trading environment became more sophisticated and European-oriented, and more competitive.[41]

Changes in the traditional composition of imports were reflected in the local press, which was used as a means of publicizing new import ventures and of informing the public of the advantages of buying from firms importing directly from Europe.[42] Agents from Syria, Lebanon and Egypt also advertised their services, and trade literature was made available to the business community through a Government Catalogue and Sample room in Jerusalem, established in 1921. Government bias in favour of British goods inevitably influenced this publicity, but other exporting countries sent trade missions to the Haifa Chamber of Commerce in an attempt to facilitate trade, an incidental side-effect of which was a brief revival of the cereal export trade to new European customers.[43]

The trading centre, the old Suq, soon felt the impact of the expanded commercial community (see Chapter 6). The Municipality had already built an animal market and slaughterhouse to the extreme east of the town in 1921. By that date, plans to extend the commercial area were under way. A Jewish development company bought the site of a Catholic convent in the western part of the town in order to develop a new commercial centre.[44] Adjacent to this development, 'Aziz Khayyat, in 1923, built a four-storey office block – a new departure for Haifa. By 1926, various retail shops stocking modern items of groceries, luxury goods and building materials had sprung up. This whole commercial complex was intended to be strikingly different from the Arab traditional market situated to its east in the vicinity of the old town.

Arab emulation of the large Jewish trading initiatives was usually frustrated by lack of capital. Arab firms could not aspire to a fraction of the capital invested by non-Arab firms. The few attempts at similar trade projects were undertaken by wealthy entrepreneurs, but such projects as Fu'ad Sa'd's ice factory, 'Aziz Khayyat's property developments, Tahir Karaman's trading concerns, and 'Aziz Miqati's import business were lightly capitalized and boasted only modest turnovers.[45] Once the depression of 1920 and 1921 had abated, some attempts were made to tackle the problem of undercapitalization. Partnerships and companies were formed to pool resources, breaking the former strictly family character of Arab trade. In general, however, such solutions were implemented only by the more educated and better-off strata of the community. There were few partnerships between Arabs and Jews, and even among Arabs a clear preference was shown for association with members of the same religious community or town of origin. Up to 1928, it was mostly wealthy Christian Arab merchants who formed business partnerships among themselves, although they did strike up associations with a small number of wealthy Muslim merchants such as Karaman, Hunaini, Wardi, Reno and Abu Zaid.[46] By the early 1930s, partnerships among Muslims were becoming more common, especially in new lines of trade such as tourism, transport, insurance, car servicing and maintenance, and the import of textiles and building materials.[47]

The larger and more sophisticated Arab firms also adopted modern European marketing techniques as introduced by the European immigrants. They also adapted quickly to more rapid means of communication, such as the telephone, the telegram, and the motor car, and the system of payment by instalments was instituted by many of the larger firms to widen the market for their more expensive goods – a system made possible only by the gradual conversion of the larger Arab trading concerns to the use of credit and banking facilities.

For the many traditional Arab firms and trading families resistant to change, the period under study was one of increased vulnerability to economic cycles that were very much out of their control. Their main concern was often to maintain a trading location, for rents rose rapidly between 1920 and 1939. However, during much of the decade 1925–35, Arab merchants, both traditional and modern, managed to share in Haifa's general prosperity. The economic depression that set in in 1927 and 1928 following the failure of the Polish zloty in 1926 tended to affect the Jewish economy more than the Arab merchants.[48] A decline in building and industry did, of course, create Arab unemployment and reduce Arab purchasing power, but it was in the Jewish sector that actual cases of commercial failure were reported. The Arabs who had resisted the temptation to expand beyond their traditional activities were least affected by this particular recession, while those who had engaged in the import of building materials or European foodstuffs on a large scale found themselves over-extended. But for the tradition that difficulties should be solved privately among families, there might have been more obvious casualties of the economic downturn.

By the end of the first decade of the British Administration, the commercial life of Haifa had changed substantially. The 1929 *Commercial Bulletin* listing of importers and exporters indicates that, in addition to the introduction of modern trading methods, Arab merchants had diversified their lines of business and even initiated the import of novelties to the Arab market. Most of the trade was consolidated under three main categories: foodstuffs, household and personal goods, and building materials for the construction industry. Until the end of the Mandate, food remained the main area of Arab trading interest. Arabs still controlled the cereal trade, although by 1933 Jewish firms were involved through their contacts with European brokers.[49] There were equal numbers of Arab and Jewish importers of meat and spices, but there was fierce competition in grocery goods, where by the 1930s Arabs were losing their supremacy as a result of the influx of Western Jews, who invested in large importing firms and established grocery stores in the Jewish quarters.[50] It is worth noting that Sephardic Jews had been active in the food trade since before the Mandate; as Arabic speakers with access to the peasant producers, their activities tended to be more like those of the Arabs than those of the new wave of Jewish food merchants.

Considerable changes in the marketing of household necessities can be observed from the mid-1920s to the mid-1930s. While Arabs and Sephardic Jews were equally represented in the sale of basic and small household items, there was fierce competition between importers of personal and household goods, and of goods destined for the Administration.[51] Arab importers were usually established firms such as Karaman, Saraqibi, Boutagy, Farsun and Zahlan; by 1933 Jewish firms with stronger financial backing outnumbered the Arab firms.

One result of this failure of the Arab importers to capture a dominant share of the new market was that they, in turn, were forced to become more specific in their import business. By the late 1920s, such firms as Boutagy began to specialize in imports of medium-sized household goods, musical equipment and clothes, almost all imported direct from England; Zahlan concentrated on predominantly French toilet items and clothes; Saraqibi, Wardi and Kabab imported Syrian household goods and East European glassware. Another area of Jewish encroachment was in stationery goods and printing and building services. Trade in building materials experienced the greatest expansion in size and variety, especially during the construction boom of the 1930s, and Jewish firms in Haifa also gained a significant numerical advantage in their importation.[52] Jewish immigrants also established a clear superiority in almost all new trades and in fields requiring technical skills and substantial funds. Imports of photographic equipment, optical instruments, refined leather goods and specialized foodstuffs were entirely in Jewish hands, as were any moves towards local production or assembly of such items. In 1929, Haifa had only one Arab pharmacist to four Jewish, and six Arab commission agents to 13 Jewish. The only new market in which Arab merchants did establish parity with Jewish importing agencies was in motor cars.[53]

Thus, by the mid-1930s Haifa's trading market was very active, with both traditional and modern firms working side by side. Nevertheless, certain trends differentiating the activities of the two main communities were also recognizable. While the Jewish traders made their greatest inroads in the areas connected with imports in modern commercial activities, the Arabs still controlled the labour-intensive trades and those based on local produce. As the Jewish quarters became more exclusive, Jewish retailers of basic and perishable foodstuffs set themselves up, but in general they were dependent on the Arab wholesale market. In building materials, the situation was reversed, and it was Arab retailers who bought from Jewish importers.

Much of this activity, especially in the Arab sector, came to a halt during the six-month strike in 1936 and was adversely affected by the disturbances of the 1936-9 revolt. While the boycott of intercommunal exchange of commodities and labour was not total, it created conditions ultimately detrimental to the economic well-being of the Arab community and weakened its financial position. Wholesale trade was by and large less affected than retail business. The wealthy Arab wholesalers (in cereals, vegetables, fruits, groceries) experienced a sharp drop in turnover and had difficulty in servicing their debts,[54] but they possessed strong collateral in the form of immovable property and were ultimately assured of bank support. It was the middling to small retailing businesses which were hardest hit, and which could not sustain losses for an extended period. In spite of calls from the Strike Committee[55] not to pay rent, they faced closure by the banks and confiscation of their goods by wholesalers. These conditions provided Jewish traders with easy entry into various branches previously controlled by Arabs. The Jewish community's need for consumer goods, especially perishables, encouraged Jewish settlements to diversify their agricultural production to meet local demand rather than concentrating on produce for export, and Jewish merchants to enter the wholesale vegetable and fruit markets.

By 1939, it was becoming increasingly clear that the rearguard action of Haifa's Arab merchant class was faltering against the irrepressible forces of the Zionist movement backed up by a pro-settler Administration. It is academic to question whether the Arabs could have resisted more effectively if they had shown a greater willingness to change their traditional trading habits, although certain practices such as the preference for using commission agents rather than importing directly did ease the entry of Jews into the trading sector. In fact, the Arab trading sector had been losing ground ever since it lost its main item of exchange – cereal exports. Arab purchasing power became dependent on employment by Jews. More generally, the British Administration facilitated an import of capital that totally swamped anything the Arab merchant class could lay claim to or could hope to accumulate in the prevailing economic conditions of the period.

The development of separatism

In the pre-war period there was a comparatively healthy spirit of co-operation and competition between Arab and (mainly Sephardic) Jewish merchants.[56] Almost always informal, co-operation took the form of ordering on the same consignments, making common adjustments to commodity price rises, relying on each other's supplies in times of need and agreeing on quotas for the distribution of local cereal production. Competition for customers in a confined market with limited purchasing power led to gentle manipulation of prices and credit terms. This helps to explain the special relationships Sephardic merchants were able to maintain with the Arab community up to the end of the Mandate period; they felt themselves to be a part of – and understood the cultural setting of – the Arab trading class and consuming public. But these Sephardic merchants were soon outnumbered by new Jewish industrialists and small traders, and their voice was rarely heard during the communal struggles that followed the events of 1929 and 1935.

As early as 1921 the joint Chamber of Commerce in Haifa had split into two, one for Jews and one for Arabs, largely as a result of the demands by the growing Jewish trading population, and the growing influence of the more aggressive Ashkenazi merchants and representatives of organized Zionist economic interests within it, for changes in the status quo. The slow process of racial exclusivity in commercial affairs had begun. The policies of both chambers lacked consistency and clarity throughout the period, largely because the trading pragmatism of their members was often out of step with any political and separatist positions that circumstances forced them to take. The policy of the Jewish Chamber gradually fell into line with the more politicized Zionist elements and consolidated into an all-out struggle for the crystallization of a Jewish Haifa. To this end it both overtly and covertly backed the various campaigns to boycott Arab trade, labour and services or to promote Jewish attempts to conquer the market. But at the same time it was persuaded by leaders from organized labour, industry, banking, construction companies and marketing co-operatives of the necessity for maintaining a degree of co-operation with Arab traders operating in sectors where Jewish capacity was still low or negligible.

The membership of the Arab Chamber was particularly heterogeneous, which meant that, despite the presence within it of several aspiring Arab politicians, it was not in itself a particularly potent political force. Unlike its Jewish counterpart, its emphasis was not on the development of a purely Arab Haifa, but on promoting the town's commercial prosperity, which it saw as dependent on both Arab and Jewish contributions. All its Muslim members and most of the Christians were from Haifa and the northern district; the non-Palestinian Christian members were of Lebanese origin and had long been resident in the town. All were united by an undefined anti-Zionism and apprehensions of Jewish designs on the market. At the same time, there was intense and bitter rivalry among the main trading families; it appears that for at least some years in the early 1920s an important section of the Arab population was actually boycotting its own Chamber of Commerce.[57]

From about 1925 the membership began to change with the infiltration of merchants from other Palestinian cities and from Syria, and these new elements contributed to the shaping of a more aggressive policy, especially during periods of crisis. Even so, the Arab commercial class had no well-defined strategy, and influence was further weakened by a confusion about its real enemy: the Zionist immigrants or the British Administration.

Nevertheless even when the two Chambers of Commerce had developed segregated attitudes towards each other and towards trading interests in the town, contacts continued between some of the active members of both. There were isolated instances of co-ordinated requests and objections being presented to the Administration on matters of common interest; even as late as 1933 and 1934, at the height of the construction boom, joint proposals were made for rent restrictions on commercial premises. Contacts were few and superficial and did not indicate any genuine attempt by either side to overcome their differences. The Jewish Chamber still insisted on maintaining a façade of cordiality in order not to antagonize further Arab consumers and their trade market, on which Jewish consumers continued to depend. But such a refined strategy could not be expected from an Arab Chamber which was divided on basic principles.

In any event, official segregationist positions meant that relations between Jewish and Arab merchants could exist only on an individual basis, such as the partnership of Karaman with Solel Boneh in Even ve Sid (Stone and Lime),[58] and various other informal contacts, especially during the periods of prosperity in the early 1930s. Expansion in the building industry created more complex relations which are difficult to trace, but there are indications that at one level a system of client-patron relationships was being formed. Construction companies such as Solel Boneh would employ Arab contractors or even buy materials from Arab merchants in payment for other services, political and economic, rendered by associates of the contractor or merchant.[59]

In the new highly competitive environment, the political integrity and economic livelihood of the individual merchant were threatened; commercial ventures in the form of companies, co-operatives and partnerships became more common. Early in the 1920s, Sephardic cereal merchants organized themselves into a company, thus giving their business financial clout. Over the next two decades, some large partnerships were formed, such as the Levant Bonded Warehouses and Hiram Ltd; but the majority of Jewish trading projects were fairly small. By the mid-1930s, however, the Zionist Organization's producer and marketing co-operatives as well as most small partnerships and private firms had become part of a loose network identified with Zionist aims. In the Arab sector too, political events played an important role in the development of economic investment. Whereas, in the early 1920s, Arabs of all religious groups went in for very few partnerships, in the 1930s a number of partnerships were registered among members of the various religious communities, and there was an even more dramatic increase in Muslim/Christian partnerships, especially at times of high national feeling. Nevertheless, the Arab trading community never constituted a single comprehensive body either in its political or its economic interests.

One exception, however, was in the transport sector. With the commercial and industrial development of Haifa, it was clear that transport would become a remunerative line of trade, though it obviously required large resources of capital and trained staff. Some of the established commercial firms, such as Boutagy, tried to move into transport as early as 1921.[60] The bus and taxi services formed from the mid-1920s on were separately owned, either by Jewish or Arab companies or co-operatives, and each company serviced the quarters of its own community. Hadar HaCarmel, for instance, had its own bus company, and its co-operative frequently petitioned the Administration for concessions for its transport company. The Zionists were anxious to ensure that certain branches of road transport work should remain exclusively in Jewish hands, while certain Arab families, Silbaq, Armali,

Fustuq and Kildawi, controlled other bus routes.[61] Initially, Arab companies were made up of people of the same religion or town of origin, but by the 1930s merchants of all religious groups and the new wealthy professional stratum were investing in the transport business.[62]

The Arab trading community in Haifa tended to be more consistent than the Jewish Chamber in its criticism of the British Administration's economic measures, which it persistently showed to be prejudicial to the cause of local Arab commerce. Its struggle to maintain its commercial base through constant petitioning of the Administration can be likened to the Jewish sector's attempts to acquire concessions for industry. The vital difference, however, was that in the Arab case the numerous delegations, voluminous correspondence, and in-depth analyses of particular measures rarely if ever elicited a positive response from the government.

Arab criticism was not limited to the policies the Administration applied for revenue purposes or to support the Jewish economy but also focused on the Administration's apparent lack of concern with the Arab economy. The Arab commercial community had no official department it could turn to, and its activities were hindered by unnecessary bureaucracy in the Customs Department and by inefficient postal and road services. The government's dependence on the Crown Agents for its supplies was often used as proof of its lack of support for local traders. These criticisms, as repeated in editorials in the Arab press, were intermingled with fears of the government's collusion with Zionist plans to infiltrate the market.[63] Imports discouraged local production and impoverished both rural and urban populations; this, in turn, often led Arabs to sell their land and emigrate in search of work, which, it was argued, was the purpose of the measures. By 1933, these fears were reinforced when the Administration conceded to the Zionists a share in public works equivalent to their estimated contribution to public revenues (see Chapter 11). In Haifa, the political campaign to boycott Jewish and promote Arab imports was stepped up in order to show a higher Arab contribution to customs revenues, and so undermine any official justification of pro-Jewish bias on purely financial grounds.

Unfortunately, a measured Arab response to the series of rebuffs at the hands of the Administration and to the general conviction that Arab commerce was threatened by British actions and Jewish designs was not forthcoming. Instead, the espousal of segregationism was all too easy. In Haifa, the propaganda battle always eschewed all concepts of racial pluralism; the town had to remain Arab or become Jewish. An appeal was mounted to attract Arabs with funds to invest in Haifa as well as the funds of Palestinians living abroad, a further encouragement being the newly exploited Iraqi oil, which, it was argued, was bound to provide trading possibilities that would pass through Haifa.[64] However, while spokesmen for Arab commercial and political interests emphasized the importance of economic co-operation in order to establish sufficiently strong Arab trading companies, the popular appeal went out as 'Develop Haifa as the Jews have developed Tel-Aviv'.[65]

As a result of the 1929 disturbances, an all-out campaign was mounted to boycott Jewish products and trades, directed by the Arab Executive Committee and emphasizing the cessation of all land sales to the Jews. This first major public statement of inter-racial differences on the part of the Arabs became a rallying cry for many of the poorer stratum, despite the objections of Arab merchants who realized the dangers of what could be only a partial boycott. The boycotts of 1929 and 1935 led to a politicization of the situation in Haifa which paid scant attention to actual economic conditions, and led to much inter-Arab recrimination.

Various attempts at the national and local level were made to achieve a united Arab approach, but with no success. While certain commercial circles continued to reap economic benefits from land, building and trade investment in the city, the number of dispossessed and indebted Arab small merchants and agriculturalists increased.[66] More significantly, the events of 1936 established segregationism as a principle of economic life, precluding the possibility of a development in which all sectors of the population would be included.

Notes

1. S. Hoofien, 'The Question of a National Bank in Palestine', Memorandum to the Advisory Financial Committee, Zionist Organization, 3 November 1919 (CZA Z4/1163 I), p. 24.

2. When the Zionists tried to persuade the CO to legislate for a mortgage bank in 1922, the response was negative. Clauson minuted: 'Government should not be put to any expense, Government should interfere as little as possible in legitimate commercial enterprise and absolutely refrain from legislation' (PRO CO 733/18, Clauson's minute in despatch of HC to CO, 26 January 1922). This principle was further endorsed by Churchill in S of S to HC, 12 April 1922 (CO 733/18).

3. B. J. Smith, *The Roots of Separatism in Palestine* (Syracuse, NY, 1993), p. 31.

4. G. Hakim and M. Y. el-Hussayni, 'Monetary and Banking System', in S. B. Himadeh, *Economic Organization of Palestine* (Beirut, 1938), pp. 464–5.

5. Ibid., p. 474.

6. Oral information from family members.

7. 'Abdul-Hamid Shoman came originally from Beit-Hanina near Jerusalem. He made his fortune in America, where he emigrated in 1911 and remained until 1929. His first hope was to create a large institution with the experienced co-operation of Tal'at Harb of Bank Misr. This did not materialize because of the disturbances of 1929. However, Shoman, carrying 3,598 shares along with four members of his family, and Ahmad Hilmi Abdul-Baqi Pasha, carrying 125

shares, started the Arab Bank in July 1930. The Arab Bank, *Arab Bank Limited 1930–1980* (Beirut, 1981), pp. 6–8.

8. In 1933, Ahmad Hilmi Pasha established the Agricultural Arab Bank, which did not last long. The political commitments of this leader often dictated certain practices that were far from being economically sound and might explain his split from the Arab Bank and the failure of both the Agricultural Bank and a later project, al-Bank al-Watani (The National Bank).

9. *Al-Karmil*, 6 May and 28 November 1931; 22 March 1933.

10. *Al-Karmil*, 22 March 1933. Rashid al-Hajj Ibrahim promised to give credit to any co-operative organization equivalent to double its capital. He also assured these organizations that Hilmi Pasha endorsed this scheme because of Hilmi's political commitment and the fact that such loans would be guaranteed by means of chain vouchers.

11. By 1935, Palestine's trade deficit had risen to £P13.64m. Per-head imports stood at £P14.90 against exports of £P3.53, compared with £2.04 and £2.32 for Egypt and £2.53 and £1.02 for Syria respectively. *Palestine Royal Commission Report*, Cmd. 5479, July 1937 (The Peel Report, Jerusalem, 1938), Appendix 3.

12. H. Sawwaf, 'Foreign Trade', in S. B. Himadeh (ed.), *Economic Organization of Palestine* (Beirut, 1938), p. 416, Table XIII.

13. The average annual value of the Palestinian transit trade from 1920 to 1931 was only £200,000. In 1934 it increased to £239,000 and in 1935 to £428,000. (For statistics pertaining to 1920–27, see Department of Commerce and Industry, *Commercial Bulletin* (hereafter *Com. Bull.*), 1 November 1928, and for 1927–31, see Naval Intelligence Division (NID), *Palestine and Transjordan* (London, 1943), p. 290. However, during the Second World War, the value rose from £550,000 in 1939 to £6.9 million in 1944 (Government of Palestine, *Great Britain and Palestine 1915–1945*. Information Paper, No. 20, pp. 72–3). Much of this latter trade was made up of oil and military stores and passed through Haifa. Also see Sawwaf, 'Foreign Trade', pp. 422–3.

14. See Smith, *The Roots*, Table I, p. 22; and Sawwaf, 'Foreign Trade', Table VII, p. 406.

15. In a letter to Lord Curzon in 1920, Herbert Samuel wrote: 'Commerce and travel between Palestine, the Hauran and Syria have hitherto been untrammelled by frontiers, and there is resistance to the economic inconveniences that would be likely to follow from political separation'. Sir H. Samuel to Lord Curzon, 2 April 1920, Headquarters OETA (South), Jerusalem (Samuel Private Papers, St Antony's College, Oxford).

16. Sawwaf, 'Foreign Trade', p. 398.

17. Arthur Ruppin, *Syria: An Economic Survey* (New York, 1918), p. 58.

18. Oral information, E. Abou-Fadil Seikaly, May 1982.

19. Administrative Report, October 1921 (PRO CO 733/7); *al-Yarmuk*, 9 October 1924; *al-Karmil*, 18 February 1933. The French authorities instituted various measures to secure Beirut's superior position by facilitating imports and exports by means of lower taxes and freight rates.

20. *Report on the Economic Situation in Palestine at the Close of the Financial Year 1920–21*, 4 August 1921 (PRO CO 733/5).

21. Abdallah Mukhlis, 'The First Disaster', in *al-Karmil*, 22 November 1930.

22. *Al-Karmil*, 21 December 1920; 19 November 1927; 22 November 1930.

23. *Com. Bull.*, Vol. III, No. 28, 7 February 1923, p. 160.

24. Deedes for HC, Political Report, 8 April 1921 (PRO CO 733/2).

25. Reply by Mr Churchill in Despatch No. 32, 8 April 1921 (PRO CO 733/2).

26. *Al-Karmil*, 28 February and 25 April 1931.

27. Owing to these purchases, Haifa received a large number of immigrants from the Marj villages as well as from the towns (such as Nazareth) that were negatively affected. See: Yazbek, *Al-Hijra al-'Arabiyya ila Haifa* (Arab Migration into Haifa) (Nazareth, 1988), p. 77; *al-Karmil*, 23 April 1932.

28. S. Schama, *Two Rothschilds and the Land of Israel* (London, 1978), pp. 249–51.

29. *Al-Karmil*, 11 March 1925; 21 February 1926; 11 September 1929.

30. Y. Washitz, 'Jewish-Arab Relations in Haifa during the Mandate' (unpublished manuscript, n.d.), Chapter II, pp. 14–15.

31. Oral information, Gabriel Seikaly, Farid al-Sa'd, Hanna 'Asfour, Amman and Beirut, 1975–77.

32. Administrative Report, October 1921 (PRO CO 733/7).

33. Archives of the Maronite and Protestant Churches (Haifa, May 1975); oral information, Tannus Salama, Haifa, May 1975.

34. Governor of Phoenicia, Symes, to Civil Secretary, 5 February 1922 (PRO CO 733/38).

35. Special Supplements to *Com. Bull.* (Vol. II, No. 14 and No. 15, 14 and 21 July 1922) and *Com. Bull.* (Vol. VI, October 1929 and November 1933). The list of customs clearing agents in Haifa in 1930, *Com. Bull.* (Vol. VII, September 1930), endorses the conclusions of the 1929 and 1933 listings.

36. Political Report, CO to FO, May 1922 (PRO FO 371 E4829/582/65); *Com. Bull.* Vol. III, March 1923.

37. However, as recorded by the chief of the CID, this policy posed no threat since pro-British elements among the members would militate against any agitation that might result if it were financially strong. CID Report by G. P. Quigley, 28 January 1922, and Correspondence between Symes and Samuel between October and December, 1922 (ISA 2/159 Pol/2).

38. *Com. Bull.*, Vol. I (new series), November 1924, and K. W. Stead, Director of Customs, *Report on the Economic and Financial Situation of Palestine* (London, 1927), p. 9.

39. *Al-Karmil*, 19 and 30 November and 19 December 1920. Oral information from A. Zahlan, London, 1990–92; Yazbek, *Al-Hijra al-'Arabiyya*, pp. 25–6.

40. Administrative Report, 9 March 1922 (PRO CO 733/19), and *Com. Bull.*, Vol. I, February 1922.

41. *Com. Bull.*, Vol. I, May and June 1922; *al-Yarmuk*, 15 January 1925.

42. *Al-Karmil* and *al-Yarmuk* assigned at least one page to advertisements, which were printed free. The Jewish press and official publications, especially the *Commercial Bulletin*, were also means of trade information, aimed at a public other than the Arabic reading communities.

43. *Com. Bull.*, Vol. IV, 21 July 1923.

44. The Palestine Development Company had purchased 2,000 pics (one sq. pic = 56025 sq. cms.) of land (*Com. Bull.*, Vol. I, April 1922), financed by a loan of £E30,000 over ten years at an interest rate of 8 per cent (*Com. Bull.*, Vol. I (new series), January 1925). It also undertook various projects to build Jewish workers' quarters in various parts of the town.

45. The projects of these wealthy entrepreneurs are mentioned in many issues of *al-Karmil* and *al-Yarmuk* for the period under study. This was also confirmed

by oral information (Fawwaz al-Sa'd, Haifa, May 1975, and other respondents in Amman, 1975–77).

46. Reno and Abu Zaid were two families which were traditionally involved with the lighterage and tugging business. By the mid-1920s, development in transport requirements, especially for the import business, expanded their work. The Far'un brothers became their partners in 1927 in order to administer their large and complex business of lighterage and coastal transshipment (*Com. Bull.*, February 1927). In the same field, Christian Marshi joined forces with Muslim Umbarji (*Com. Bull.*, August 1929) to do stevedoring services at the Haifa port. Similarly, Karaman and Wardi and Kabab entered into partnerships with Christian merchants Haddad and Mansur (*Com. Bull.*, August 1925 for the first and December 1928 for the second) to administer firms for general trading.

47. *Com. Bull.*, January, June, July, August, September and December 1929, April, May, July and October 1930, and January and October 1931. After 1931, partnerships were no longer reported in the *Commercial Bulletin*.

48. A. M. Hyamson, *Palestine Under the Mandate 1920–1948* (London, 1950), p. 62; N. Weinstock, *Zionism: False Messiah* (London, 1979), pp. 134–5.

49. In 1929, there were 16 Arab and 6 Jewish merchants or firms involved in cereal imports; in 1933, the ratio was 17 Arabs to 7 Jews.

50. Oral information (Hanna 'Asfour, Beirut, June 1977, and Fu'ad 'Attallah, Amman, July 1975).

51. *Com. Bull.*, Vol. IX, January 1932, List of Manufacturers, and *Com. Bull.*, Vol. X, November 1933, pp. 72–3.

52. In the 1929 *Commercial Bulletin* listing, 13 Jewish firms are mentioned as against 9 Arab firms; in 1933 the numbers were 8 and 5 respectively.

53. *Al-Karmil*, 26 November 1927, and *Com. Bull.*, Vol. VII, October 1929.

54. *Ha'aretz*, 19 July 1936.

55. This was the local committee set up by the Higher Arab Committee (HAC) to supervise the activities and public observance of the strike. In Haifa, it had two centres, one next to the Istiqlal Mosque and the other in Allenby Street. The committee paid workers weekly wages while they were on strike and tried to alleviate the hardship of traders by encouraging them not to pay rents and urging landlords and money-lenders not to press charges.

56. In the pre-war period, there was co-operation mainly in the cereal and cloth trades. Sephardic merchants, such as Catran, Halfon, Negri and Tayyar, traded alongside the Arab wholesale merchants Sahyoun, Tuma, Sa'd, Abu Fadil and Hajj Ibrahim.

57. *Al-Karmil*, 5 July 1924, reported this dispute, which it said had erupted two years before. See Part Four for an analysis of Arab political development.

58. See D. HaCohen, *Time to Tell* (New York, London, 1984), pp. 41–9, on the takeover of this company by Solel Boneh in partnership with T. Karaman.

59. David HaCohen to Lifshitz, 26 August 1936 (CZA J16/68). In this letter, HaCohen asked Lifshitz to buy building stones from Jiryis Tannus, a partner of HaCohen's friend Shihadeh Shalah, then a member of the Haifa Municipality.

60. *Al-Karmil*, 22 October 1921.

61. CZA J16/6; Thischby to Sacher, 31 January 1928 (CZA 24/10, 264/1). Oral information, Habib Khayyat, Haifa, May 1975, and other contacts in Beirut.

62. J. 'Asfour, *Palestine: My Land, My Country, My Home* (Beirut, 1967), pp. 105–6.

63. Oral information, Khalid al-Hasan, London, March 1982, and various respondents who wished their names to be withheld.

64. *Al-Karmil*, 3 September 1930.

65. *Al-Karmil*, 27 April 1929.

66. *Al-Karmil*, 7 January 1931 and 24 February 1932. Various cases of peasants having to sell their daughters in the city because of the economic crisis were reported in *al-Karmil*. Appeals to the Administration from indebted landowners and agriculturalists, seeking aid against exorbitant interest rates, were also published in the Arabic press.

10

Land and Housing Policy

The establishment of a British Administration committed to facilitating the creation of a Jewish National Home in Palestine revolutionized trade in land, both urban and rural.[1] The purchase of land privately by Jewish immigrants or on a more systematic basis by Zionist organizations represented a much more concrete displacement of the Arab population than the gradual erosion of its share in foreign or domestic trade. Moreover, the building of homes for immigrants on the land purchased was one of the fundamentals of the Zionist settler movement. The correlation between Jewish immigration, building activity, and the general expansion of the economy is shown clearly in Figure 10.1. What is not in evidence is the effect of Jewish land purchases and construction activity on the Arab population in towns like Haifa. Some Arabs gained from this economic activity, as labourers, importers of construction materials or property developers on a limited scale, but they also had to contend with the fact that Arab landlords were often choosing to sell land to the Zionists, thus liquidating their stake in the future of Palestine. The fate of Arab land created the greatest tensions among the Arab community and crystallized their socio-political orientations.

Land prices had begun rising in Haifa at least two decades before the advent of the British Administration, as a result of the growth of the Arab community and early attempts by Jewish organizations to establish the nucleus of a Jewish presence in the city. By 1918, they were the same as in Jerusalem and slightly less than those prevailing in Damascus.[2] During the First World War and in its immediate aftermath, it was purchases by the Jewish real-estate companies, particularly the PLDC, which managed to keep land a marketable commodity.[3] As we saw in Chapter 6, these companies would parcel up their acquisitions and sell the plots to individuals, co-operatives and construction companies, the details being published exclusively to the Jewish buying public.[4] By 1925,

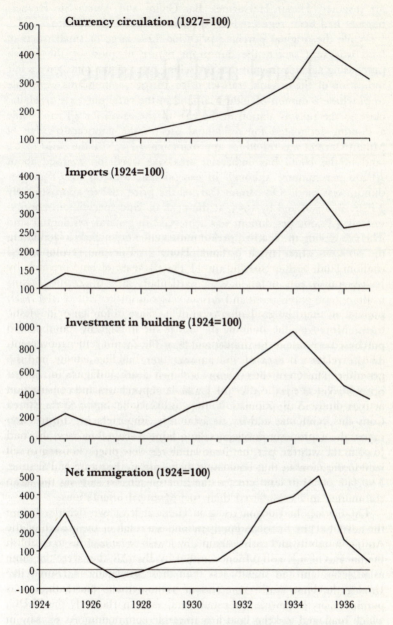

Figure 10.1 Correlation between building and other activity 1924–37 (compiled from graph by D. Horowitz and R. Hinden, *Economic Survey of Palestine* (Tel-Aviv, 1938), p. 107)

for instance, Hadar HaCarmel, Bat Galim and Ahuza Sir Herbert Samuel had been registered as co-operative building societies.[5]

While the original purchase price for these large or small tracts of land was kept secret, the non-profit nature of most of the Jewish purchasing agencies meant that the selling price of the plots gave a fair indication of the original transfer price. In 1920, immigrants were able to purchase a dunum of industrial land in the rural outskirts of Haifa, close to the railway station in the east of the town, for £P7.10, while a dunum designated for residential use on the panoramic ridge of Mount Carmel was resold for approximately £P55.[6] By the early 1930s, land in the Haifa Bay industrial area was worth on average about £P200 per dunum, although in exceptional cases up to £P300 per dunum was paid.[7] On Mount Carmel the price rose to approximately £P400 in 1930, and by 1935, at the peak of land speculation, approximately £P1,000 per dunum was achieved.[8] In general, residential land in Haifa during the 1920-39 period remained cheaper than in Jerusalem or Tel-Aviv, where trade in land played a more central role in the economy, but higher than in any of the all-Arab towns.

Apart from private landowners, particularly those absentees residing in Beirut, the government and various religious institutions proved ready sources of marketable land. As early as 1922, state land in Haifa, including residential areas in the old town, in Mawares and on the outskirts, was put on the market and leased by auction. In 1933-4, plots on the reclaimed area of the harbour were also leased for business premises. The Carmelite monks sold their land at Bat Galim on the open market in 1925, unlike the Catholic convent which had been sold in 1921 direct to the Zionists. In 1933, property belonging to the Greek Catholic church was sold in one lot to a Jewish purchaser.[9] In the early 1930s, the Latin church began selling large tracts of its land at Wadi Jmal in the western part of the town at very low prices to members of its congregation so that they could build private houses.[10] Much of it, however, found its way into the hands of speculators and was resold on the market to the highest bidder (see Maps III and IV).

On the whole, the market was open to all comers with sufficient financial backing, and competition and speculation were particularly strong in the town's commercial zone and in mixed areas such as Hadar HaCarmel and Mount Carmel. Arabs played the role of both middlemen and, in some cases, property developers. Investors like Ibrahim Sahyoun and 'Aziz Khayyat competed with Jewish buyers for various tracts of land in the commercial area, in Hadar HaCarmel, in Wadi Jmal and on the coastline around the promontory of Mount Carmel, on which they then built commercial premises, residential quarters or beach resorts. The depression of 1927, however, hit many of the speculators hard, and by 1929, many Arab landowners, both

Christian and Muslim, had been forced to relinquish part of their landholdings.

Only rarely were land transactions between Arabs and Jews made public; more often than not, they were concluded through middlemen, and only when they concerned outstanding community figures, such as the Salams, the Khalils, or the Shuqairs, or particularly large tracts of land, did they attract public attention.[11] In the 1930s, sales of land around Haifa and also on Mount Carmel between Arabs and Jews contributed to the tense political atmosphere.[12] The years 1924-6 and 1934-5 were peak years for land sales, with pronounced market troughs following both periods.

Almost all building activity in Palestine during the Mandate was commercial and depended on private or community investment. Most of it was concentrated in residential housing.[13] This investment had a vital effect on the economy in general, as shown in Figure 10.1, since it was through building activity that imported capital was distributed through the different strata of the population, thus increasing the general purchasing power and promoting an active trading market. With the government bound to an extremely conservative fiscal and budgetary policy, building activity became almost the only distributor of wealth and engine of economic activity after the collapse of the cereal export trade. To that extent, the correlation between building investment, immigration, imports and currency circulation, illustrated in Figure 10.1 and evident in almost any statistical series for the period, is not so startling. More interesting is the fact that, at the end of the second construction boom in 1936, the indices for imports and currency circulation did not fall off so sharply as those for building investment and immigration. This phenomenon can be taken as a sign of the consolidation and diversification of the Jewish economy, with the help of entrepreneurs, financiers and surplus imported capital, whereas the Arab capital stock was slowly being liquidated to cover high operating costs and falling profits, with few mechanisms for using small savers' funds.

During the 1920s, building activity in Haifa lagged considerably behind that in Jerusalem and Tel-Aviv, although in general, as shown in Table 10.1, it mirrored that experienced in Palestine as a whole (compare Table 10.1 with Table 10.2). House building restarted in early 1921 and was brisk up to the spring of 1923,[14] when a slump set in owing to a lack of liquid funds brought about by over-speculation. Such mismatches of supply and demand were inevitable. In 1928-9 Arab investors, who had built houses since 1925 in expectation of a new wave of Jewish immigrants, found themselves in severe financial straits as a result of the general economic depression. Nevertheless, in the first half of the 1930s, Haifa experienced a greater boom in building activity than the other main cities. Part of the reason for this was clearly the

Table 10.1 Building Activity in Palestine and Haifa 1924–38

Year	No. of permits issued		Value (£P)		Municipal expenses (£P)	
	Palestine	Haifa	Palestine	Haifa	Palestine	Haifa
1924	4,069	438	874,994	58,665	93,754	11,950
1925	5,742	514	2,002,237	113,950	111,100	9,041
1926	4,678	580	1,112,441	160,005	217,528	12,913
1927	5,841	368	770,064	79,825	76,928	11,234
1928	5,550	444	692,462	94,555	62,608	6,165
1929	4,193	310	1,741,687	166,160	61,535	9,323
1930	4,954	466	2,440,544	193,000	90,525	12,905
1931	4,912	307	2,715,015	213,500	96,436	10,915
1932	5,912	832	2,939,363	318,300	115,544	18,609
1933	7,330	1,210	5,532,637	1,152,000	109,928	12,801
1934	8,128	1,453	6,947,258	1,600,000	312,292	20,429
1935	8,685	1,611	8,428,606	2,528,000	274,224	26,367
1936	5,987	1,557	5,687,774	2,171,929	235,290	40,690
1937	6,655	1,568	4,120,241	1,757,340	256,974	30,571
1938	3,992	1,002	1,883,500	406,275	258,875	25,900

Sources: Figures for this table covering 1924–9 were compiled from different issues of the *Commercial Bulletin*: 1924–June 1925, Vol. II, No. 6; 1925–June 1926, Vol. III, No. 6; 1926–June 1927, Vol. IV, No. 6; 1927–July 1928, Vol. V, No. 7; 1928 and 1929–October 1930, Vol. VII, No. 10. For the period covering 1930–38 the statistics were compiled from Government of Palestine, *Statistical Abstract of Palestine, 1939* (Jerusalem, 1939), pp. 52–3, Table 63.

fact that building costs in the city were relatively low in view of the relatively low cost of land, the proximity to a major port, and the availability of cheap Arab labour.

From the peak of building activity in 1935, Arab building and its allied industries came to a total standstill in the Arab quarters during the disturbances of 1936–9, while Jewish and Arab building in the Jewish quarters continued at practically the same level. Building materials still came through the port, which had not fully suspended its activities; the large limestone quarries, whether in purely Arab or Arab-Jewish ownership, continued working; and cement and tiles continued to be produced in local Jewish factories. The suspension of building in Arab Haifa during the 1936 strike and the following years of unrest nevertheless had a devastating effect on the whole Arab economy. Arab rentals, already high, rose still higher. Not only was building limited to Jewish areas, but the distribution of building funds became restricted to Jewish labour and Jewish merchants. Quarries which before the strike had employed mostly Arab labour now hired a Jewish labour force, and

Table 10.2 Comparison between the building activities of the three major cities 1933–8

Year	Number of permits issued			Approximate value in £P			Floor area in sq. metres		
	Jerusalem	Tel-Aviv	Haifa	Jerusalem	Tel-Aviv	Haifa	Jerusalem	Tel-Aviv	Haifa
1933	1,368	2,290	1,210	2,118,843	1,776,600	1,152,000	145,037	353,322	197,350
1934	1,203	2,113	1,453	1,239,906	2,578,400	1,600,000	164,070	424,504	323,425
1935	1,293	2,078	1,611	1,433,327	3,154,900	2,528,000	182,115	448,459	390,071
1936	1,225	1,400	1,557	1,384,909	1,567,000	2,171,922	140,593	261,224	282,868
1937	1,270	1,209	1,568	844,000	1,034,000	1,757,340	147,451	180,745	213,387
1938	582	863	1,002	425,000	795,376	406,275	80,333	150,994	94,121

Sources: Adapted from Government of Palestine, *Statistical Abstract of Palestine, 1936* (Office of Statistics, Jerusalem, 1937), pp. 36–7, Tables 44 and 46; for 1936–8, adapted from Government of Palestine, *Statistical Abstract of Palestine, 1939* (Jerusalem, 1939), p. 54, Table 65.

many Arab unskilled seasonal workers went back to their villages. The Arab market drastically contracted, with the loss of economic contacts between the Jewish and Arab commercial communities and the diminished purchasing power of the Arabs themselves.

Cost of living

The only available statistical information on the cost of living is the Index of Retail Prices collected by the Administration from the early 1920s.[15] While this provides a reliable scale for fluctuations in the prices of basic commodities, it is an inefficient means of assessing the overall cost of living, because it does not include vital items such as rent and newly acquired urban needs such as transport. Clearly, however, all prices were subject to the conditions of agricultural production and its seasons, to world price trends and currency movements and, most of all, to local administrative policy and the activity of the market.

Even though food prices experienced a continuous downward trend when compared with the war years, prices were high when compared with those in neighbouring Arab countries and when viewed within the framework of a highly stimulated peacetime economy subjected to unusual and innovative demands. Furthermore, Haifa, where most of these conditions were intensified, experienced higher prices for most living expenses than Jerusalem and Jaffa in the 1920s and ran parallel to Tel-Aviv in the 1930s.[16] Any fall in prices was often caused by flooding the market with cheap imports of food, clothes and implements and was accompanied by a leap in the rents of business and residential accommodation – a situation experienced in the cities from early 1921. The outcry against high prices for food, fuel, rents and transport was constantly expressed in the press.[17]

The Administration's conservative economic policy and the protectionist measures it awarded Jewish industry account for much of the high cost of living suffered by all sectors of the population. Basic foodstuffs were directly and indirectly affected by customs policy. Concessions to Nesher raised prices in the building industry, which translated into higher rents. Moreover, the entry of large numbers of Jewish immigrants without proper arrangements for their accommodation and employment added to the congestion in the cities and thus to rental costs.

Rent profiteering was an endemic problem which was most intensely felt during 1925-6 and 1933-5, when large waves of Jewish immigration and land prospecting raised the demand for housing and caused overcrowding. By the mid-1930s, the average housing density in Haifa was 2.13 persons to a room in the better-off quarters and 2.65 persons to a room in the Arab old city; at the same time, the ratio of rental to income was as high as 40 per cent, with the poorer classes paying an even higher percentage.[18]

Haifa's business rents had increased drastically immediately following the occupation, causing the then military governor, Colonel Storrs, to prohibit any rise beyond 50 per cent above the pre-war charge.[19] Controls were first imposed generally in June 1919, but until the early 1930s, little use was made of the rent ordinances intended to protect tenants against excessive charges.[20] Under the pressure of the 1933 housing crisis the Law for the Protection of Tenants of April 1933 and the Landlords and Tenants (Ejection and Rent Restriction) Law of 1934 were issued,[21] but these rules were made valid only for short periods.

Small businessmen[22] and the poorer members of the Arab community were worst hit by the rent inflation. By the early 1930s, the impoverished immigrants from the countryside, living in shacks in and around the old quarters, and especially in the shanty town of Ard al-Raml, had attracted serious official concern, particularly when they became a threat to public health following the construction of the harbour and when the land on which their huts were situated was required for industrial purposes.[23] By 1937, a site in the vicinity of Balad al-Shaikh, which was a Muslim *waqf*, was chosen for their resettlement. For the Administration to come to the aid of displaced Arabs, whose unfortunate condition was principally brought about by its own policy, the situation had to be desperate indeed.

By the 1930s the economic boom brought a respite to the Arab community, whose incomes and economic expectations improved accordingly. However, the cost of living in the city had not abated, and while the majority of the impoverished Arab sector had acquired a higher standard of living, they had not acquired equivalently higher incomes. At the same time, there was no one within the Arab sector with sufficient authority or foresight to see that the high rents charged by landlords in boom periods merely restricted the purchasing power of tenants and weakened the Arab trading market. Even then the measures were never fully implemented and no housing for the poor was provided until the end of the Mandate.

The general insecurity of the times, coupled with the pressure on land and building prices exerted by the Jewish immigration, no doubt left little room for such 'enlightened' economics, but the Arab community was also hampered by the existence of a stratified political hierarchy and by the lack of any effective means to collect or harness financial resources. As noted in Chapter 9, whereas Jewish private developers could turn to more than one source for investment funds, Arabs were by and large deprived of facilities such as building societies and savings and mortgage banks, local or foreign.[24] Arabs wishing to build in Haifa and unable to raise funds would often sell one piece of real estate in order to build on another. Another means was to combine the resources of the whole family; borrowing from private individuals of long acquaintance and usually of similar religious background was a less common option, and raising money through the banks was the last resort. The inflated cost of living, of real estate and construction, was an additional factor in the difficulties faced by the Arab economic sector. As this and the preceding two chapters have illustrated, the Arab capital base was swamped by new imported capital, and the Arab economy was incapacitated by the separatist attitudes inherent in Zionist theory, the help Zionist authorities received from the British Administration, and the inability of the Arab political leadership to forge a common response to threats that it often recognized too late.

Notes

1. The need to provide Zionist and Jewish organizations with preferential immigration rights and land-purchasing and leasing terms was the concern of the British government soon after the occupation (Louis Mallet for Mr Balfour to the British Delegation, Paris, 2 April 1919; ISA 2/34). Later, in 1920 and 1921, the policy of granting these organizations leases for industrial and agricultural development was also established; however, it was suggested by S of S Churchill that this should be carried out discreetly (CO to CS, 1 March 1921; PRO FO 371 E2742/32/88). For a thorough study of British policy towards land acquisition by the Zionists, see: B.J. Smith, *The Roots of Separatism in Palestine* (Syracuse, NY, 1993), pp. 86–115. For an understanding of the Zionists' approach to land-purchasing philosophy, attitude and tactics, see: Kenneth W. Stein, *The Land Question in Palestine 1917–1939* (Chapel Hill, NC, 1984).

2. A. Ruppin, *Syria: An Economic Survey* (New York, 1918), p. 82.

3. For a detailed survey of PLDC land purchases on Mt Carmel and in the Bay area through the services of J. Chankin, see A. Ruppin, *Three Decades in Palestine* (Hartford, CT, 1936; reprint 1975), pp. 182–3. Also oral information from family members and various respondents.

4. A report on 'Industrial Statistics and New Ventures in 1920' for the ZO, 14 March 1922 (CZA A226/15).

5. Department of Commerce and Industry, *Commercial Bulletin*, Vol. II, December 1922; Vol. IV, December 1923; Vol. I (new series), February 1925.

6. One dunum was approximately equivalent to 919 square metres. Report on 'Industrial Statistics in 1920', 14 March 1922 (CZA A226/15) .

7. A. Granovsky, *Land Policy in Palestine* (New York, 1940; reprint 1976), p. 43.

8. R. Nathan, O. Gass and D. Creamer, *Palestine: Problem and Promise* (Washington, DC, 1946), p. 249.

9. This sale created tension among the Greek Catholic community and between them and the other Arab communities. It was finally decided that the whole property would be sold to one buyer, the JNF. *Al-Karmil*, 10 and 17 May and 19 July 1933.

10. This land was the property of the Carmelite order, and was parcelled into

one-dunum or half-dunum plots and sold at £P25 per dunum. Oral information, Father Cyril Borg, Administrator, Latin church, Haifa, May 1975.

11. An article in *al-Karmil*, 18 September 1924, mentions the possibility of land sales by As'ad Shuqair to the Zionist middleman Chankin. The sale of the Khalil lands created a controversy in the community and compelled the family to make a public statement explaining the conditions causing them to sell (*al-Karmil*, 2 November 1929 and 29 March 1930). The Salams, landowners residing in Beirut, sold a prominent building in the main commercial zone to the Zionists. The transaction was carried out quietly.

12. Farah Bros, from Beirut, sold the land of Koskos Tab'un to the JNF in 1930; the Jarrah family, from Acre, sold the land of Abu Sharshuh and the Dabbana family sold the Shallala land on Mt Carmel in the 1930s (oral information, Fu'ad Attallah, attorney involved in court cases concerning most of these transactions, Amman, July 1975). Also see *al-Karmil* and *al-Yarmuk* from 1928 to 1935, when articles on land sales were a constant feature.

13. See *The Anglo-Palestine Year Book*, 1946 (London, 1946), p. 163; Appendix, Table VIII, for these figures and for a comparison between private and municipal expenditure on building in Haifa.

14. Building activities were considered important signs of development and religiously recorded in the Reports of the Department of Customs, Excise and Trade (PRO CO 733/6, September 1921; PRO CO 733/25, August 1922; PRO CO 733/75, September 1924) and in *Com. Bull.* (Vol. II, September 1922; Vol. III, June 1923, and Vol. IV, July 1923). In 1923, Haifa issued building licences for 5,748 rooms and 310 shops. J. Shiffman, 'Building Activity in Palestine', *Palnews* (Tel-Aviv, 1935), p. 141.

15. The *Commercial Bulletin* was the Administration's means of regular reporting on price fluctuations in both the retail and wholesale markets. See *Com. Bull.*, Vol. III, 21 February 1923, pp. 166–7. Also, for a detailed study of the price indices, see R. Szereszewski, *Essays on the Structure of the Jewish Economy in Palestine and Israel* (Jerusalem, 1968), p. 68.

16. *Com. Bull.*, Vol. IV, July 1923.

17. *Al-Karmil*, 2 February 1921. In Haifa, in 1921, prices of vegetables were three times and meat and fish twice those of Jaffa. Landlords were demanding between £E50 and £E80 a year for two rooms which had cost them £E30 to build (*al-Karmil*, 14 May 1921). Rents had risen three to four times pre-war levels for both residential and commercial premises (*al-Karmil*, 19 September 1925). While mutton sold in the Haifa market for £P2.5 per oqqa (a weight equivalent to 1.283 kg) and rose to £P4 by early 1928 (*al-Karmil*, 8 January 1929), it went for £P1.5 in Syria and Lebanon (*al-Karmil*, 7 August 1927), and in the other Palestinian towns did not exceed £P1.5; in Beirut it was £P1.0 an oqqa (*al-Karmil*, 11 October 1930). The price of wheat was on the rise too, and in Haifa it suddenly rose from £P 2.0 a kilo in 1924 to £P 6.0 in 1925 (*al-Karmil*, 11 March 1925). Also, fuel and petrol were a cause of complaint by the general public and transport lobbies (*al-Karmil*, 7 November 1926; 13 February 1928; 23 February 1929; 6 March 1929; 10 June 1931; 17 June 1931).

18. Granovsky, *Land Policy*, pp. 20, 26; D. Horowitz and R. Hinden, *Economic Survey of Palestine* (Tel-Aviv, 1938), pp. 110–14.

19. *The Palestine News*, 31 October 1918.

20. Granovsky, *Land Policy*, pp. 62–4. Also see Sir H. Samuel to Earl Curzon, 1 January 1921 (PRO CO 733/9), and *Com. Bull.*, Vol. I (new series), November 1924.

21. HC to S of S, 18 April 1933. Landlords and Tenants Ordinance 1933 (PRO CO 733/242); Bye-Law to Landlords and Tenants (Ejection and Rent Restriction) Ordinance, 1934 (ISA 2 G/28/34); HC to S of S, 4 March 1935 (PRO CO 733/282).

22. M. Yazbek, *Al-Hijra al-'Arabiyya ila Haifa* (Arab Migration into Haifa) (Nazareth, 1988), pp. 31, 45–56, and 132–43.

23. Town Planning Adviser, *Annual Report*, 1936, p. 12; *Annual Report*, 1937, p. 18.

24. The Palestine Building Loan and Saving Association advanced £10,000 to a group of individuals building thirty houses at Bat Galim in 1922 (*Com. Bull.*, Vol. II, September 1922). Also in the same locality, the Italian firm of Gambin and Co. built ten houses in 1923 by advancing loans redeemable in five years (*Com. Bull.*, Vol. IV, July 1923). A South African company granted £15,000 in loans for building in different quarters of the town (Administrative Report, 30 September 1924, PRO CO 733/75).

11

Labour Policy

The British Administration's involvement in Palestinian labour affairs was a matter not of choice but of necessity. In Palestine, unlike the typical colonial setting, the British had to deal not only with the 'natives' but also with an enclave of Westerners whose views on labour matters were relatively sophisticated. As a result, previous colonial experience was harder to transfer to this complex and shifting situation.

The Administration's attitude

At first, the Administration tended to minimize its role. Only in the mid-1920s, after a period of relative economic prosperity, was it forced to view labour matters as a national issue: labour strife was bound to affect the economic well-being of the country. At the same time, it was not ready to grant any concessions that might affect the capitalist structure of the economy or involve the government in any expense. Two bills were drafted in 1925, one for the prevention of intimidation in labour disputes and the other for workers' compensation. Together with a 1927 ordinance passed for the protection of women and children and a law safeguarding machinery, these were the only labour laws passed by the Administration until the 1940s. A memorandum of 1922[1] had summed up the 'attitude of impartiality' the Administration was determined to preserve in the face of the increasing number of strikes and lock-outs, which, strengthened by a more explicit ideology for 'conquest of labour'[2] in the Jewish labour movement, often disrupted production. This situation ultimately forced the Administration to discard its spectator role in favour of a more direct approach.

More than any other Palestinian town, Haifa was the scene of intense labour activity during the period of this study. It was here that the first attempts at union activities on any sort of intercommunal basis were started. The Administration's adamant refusal to recognize the Railways, Telephone and Telegraph Workers' Union throughout the Mandate demonstrated its ambiguous position vis-à-vis the two communities.[3]

Even though it was never a champion of the General Federation of Jewish Labour, it was obliged, for political reasons, to accept that organization and recognize its worth in focusing on labour problems within the Jewish sector. While it could not completely ban Arab workers' organizations, it nonetheless tried to limit their activities. Arab efforts tended to be more successful where Jewish workers, with previous labour experience and the backing of the Histadrut, also worked. However, the fact that most such organizations in Haifa (the Bakers' Union, founded 1924; the General Workers' Club, founded 1924; the Sea Workers' Union, founded 1932) were sponsored by the GFJL, and the rest, such as the Railways, Telephone and Telegraph Workers' Union, were infiltrated by Zionist-oriented workers, caused Arab workers to look for alternative unions. According to a prominent figure in the Haifa Arab labour movement, the Palestine Arab Workers' Society (PAWS) was founded in 1925 in order to combat the Histadrut's negative influence on Arab labour.[4] Some politically ambitious Haifa lawyers, such as Najib al-Hakim and Mu'in al-Madi, joined the PAWS and offered their services free to the organization. Within the Palestinian Arab political arena, the PAWS had acquired a position challenging that of the Supreme Muslim Council (SMC) in Jerusalem by the late 1930s and the 1940s.[5]

By the mid-1930s, Histadrut policy towards Arab labour had become more explicitly racist. Nevertheless, it could not ignore the need to co-operate with organized Arab labour. If Jewish wages were to be increased in such trades as building and the railways, Arab competition had to be eliminated, and one method of achieving this was to co-operate with the PAWS to demand higher wages for Arabs. Attempts were also made by the Histadrut to recruit politically ambitious members of the PAWS, by promising support in local elections, such as the Haifa municipal elections of 1934,[6] and other advantages.

The Administration imposed very strict regulations on PAWS' activities in order to limit its political role, and at the same time depreciated its influence. Despite its having held a national labour conference in Haifa on 11 December 1930, sent protests to the Secretary of State and supplied the Administration with a monthly roster of its unemployed members, its existence was officially stated in 1932 to be merely nominal.[7] Its constant demands for parallel wages for Arab and Jewish workers, shorter working hours and better health insurance and compensation in case of injuries were neither supported by the Administration nor put into practice on government works. Furthermore, the official position as laid down by the 1928 Wages Commission set the Jewish minimum wage at least one-third higher than that of the Arabs because of the informally accepted dictum that Jewish workers were accustomed to a higher standard of living. The Administration's static perception of Arab standards and development continued until 1948, becoming progressively more out of step with the changing social realities of the 1930s and beyond.

The private sector

The official position towards both municipal and private-sector labour in Haifa was again an extension of the Administration's overall policy. Irrespective of the obvious hardships endured specifically by Arab labour, the Administration refused to move. Early in 1923, for example, the wages of 'local' labourers at the Grands Moulins de Palestine were reported as 300 mils for a 10–12-hour day (12–15 hours for porters). Child labour (aged 12–13) worked 8–9 hours a day for 100 mils a day, while skilled labourers were paid 300–355 mils/day at a time when the accepted wages were 500–600 mils/day. This situation did not move the Administration to act; it was the Haifa Labour Council (local branch of the GFJL) who came to the rescue by setting minimum wage rates. Arab labour within the Arab private sector did not fare much better. It was here that class differentiation was most clearly perceived. The Arab entrepreneurial class took full advantage of the defenceless condition of Arab labour, and cases of protests, strikes and lock-outs in Arab industrial and building firms were reported from the mid-1920s on.[8] An extreme case occurred in the building industry in 1932, with one of the wealthiest Arab contractors in the town exacting an 11-hour day from stonecutters paid at the minimum rate of 220 mils/day. When these labourers struck for better conditions, he dismissed them and brought in workers from Jerusalem.[9] Champions of Arab labour in the Arab community were few, however. Even the Arab press, which led the political campaign against Zionist encroachment, was reluctant to support the demands of Arab workers. The spectre of Zionism's political aims stifled attempts at social reform. However much the PAWS tried to protect Arab labour rights, its success was limited because of the composition of its own leadership and the constraints imposed by sociopolitical conditions.

The GFJL, on the other hand, was consolidating its position within the Jewish sector all through the 1920s. In addition to its efforts to secure the employment of Jewish labour on public works, it supported intimidation against Jewish employers. The District Commissioner, in a confidential report in October 1923, stated:

> ... there are too many Jewish workmen unemployed at present. With the anxiety of the JLCA to relieve distress on this account one can fully sympathize without endorsing their policy and methods. At the same time there is a feeling amongst Jews here that the JLCA are endeavouring to exploit the present situation in order to extend the authority and political scope of their

organization, and a rather fierce resentment at the 'dictatorial Russian' attitude adopted by members of the association.[10]

By the 1930s, Jewish labour in Haifa had attained a high degree of organization and a firm ideological base. Nevertheless, ideological zeal was constrained by the availability of work; in the inter-boom periods municipal and later relief projects were the main employers.

The public sector

The Administration, with its many departments and projects, was the major employer in Haifa. It had a high preponderance of Arab workers, owing, in part, to the economic situation of the Arab sector, which could not provide employment to absorb its working population, and also to the fact that this sector was the largest source of cheap unskilled labour, a situation thoroughly exploited by the Public Works Department. One feature of all government institutions employing Arab labour was their strict adherence to the principle of thrift. Casual labour was the principal means to this end; it was easier to manipulate and was not stable enough to organize and become a potential political threat.

The growing problem facing the Administration was that of the allocation of the available opportunities between the two communities, taking into account political considerations, the amount of unemployment among both groups (but mainly the Jewish one) and its possible repercussions, and the cheapest method of undertaking public works with the least complication. The Administration's attitudes and practices were affected only fractionally by events. As an employer, it did not maintain a uniform labour policy; heads of departments such as the railways, the PWD and the Haifa harbour could adopt their own recruitment measures and working conditions. Different priorities were adhered to at different times. The early period of the Civil Administration, 1920–23, was a time of generous expansion under Sir Herbert Samuel, with the railways enjoying a major share of public expenditure. The Zionist Executive staked its claim for a preferential share in public works as well as military projects.[11] It was clearly the concern of the Civil Administration to provide openings for Jewish labour, since immigration depended on employment opportunities, and as a concession to Zionist demands the Egyptian Labour Corps (ELC) was gradually phased out from the railways and partly replaced by Jewish labour. The experience proved expensive but served to establish a political precedent.[12] Jewish labour also attempted for a time to capture a share of employment in the Haifa harbour porterage works. Here too Jewish workers were unable to compete with the cost-effectiveness of Arab unskilled workers.

By the beginning of 1923, retrenchment was applied to all government expenditure. The first department in Haifa to be affected was the Railways Department, where a number of workers were discharged. With increasing unemployment, particularly in Haifa and Tel-Aviv, a general fall in wages led to a weakening of labour's bargaining power. In the following two years, a boom in the Jewish economy diverted much of the unemployed Jewish labour and some Arab labour to new private-sector enterprises. A number of industrial disputes were recorded in Haifa (at the construction site of the Nesher cement factory, at the Grands Moulins and at the Shemen oil factory), but these were of purely Jewish concern.[13] Arab labour was considered only as an alternative to be used for strike-breaking purposes.[14] The demand for government work had diminished visibly.

These fluctuating conditions corresponded to a deterioration in the output and stability of the countryside, a wave of inflation in the prices of basic commodities, and the growing appeal of urban economic opportunities. A continuous trickle of rural labour found unskilled employment on the roads and other government works at reduced wages.[15] In the same spirit of retrenchment, government tenders were now automatically given to the lowest bidder, and contracts were won by Jewish labour only when Zionist capital subsidized the difference in cost.

A long period of economic distress followed. Jewish unemployment was growing, a fact kept hidden by the Zionist Executive lest it affect immigration schedules. Initially, the GFJL introduced projects to employ Jewish labour; later it set up measures for work rotation and dole payments to relieve the situation. Nevertheless, by 1927, it was on the brink of bankruptcy. The Administration then acknowledged its responsibility and committed itself to a programme of relief works and an assurance of a Jewish share in government projects, especially in the Haifa harbour.

Unemployment problems

It is impossible to gauge Arab unemployment during the early Mandate period because of a dearth of records, which suggests a lack of interest on the part of the Administration. Even by the end of the 1920s, when District Commissioners supplied unemployment figures for their districts, statistics for the Arab sector covered only regular workers; the majority, casual seasonal workers from the countryside, were ignored. Jewish labour organizations limited competition for work distribution to a very small section of Arab labour; irrespective of employment conditions, Jewish labour demanded at least a 50-per-cent share of government projects, notwithstanding the fact that it was less cost-effective.

The unemployment returns for June 1927, as computed by the District

Commissioner, showed that, although Haifa was second only to Jaffa in the number of unemployed among all Palestinian cities, it had the highest rate of Arab unemployment. Furthermore, the unemployment statistics provided by the mukhtars of the various Arab communities in the city were three times those of the District Commissioner.[16] By the end of the year, Arab unemployment – mainly in the building industry – was reported to be on the increase. The attitude of the Administration was a further confirmation of its lack of interest. The OAG, writing to the CO on 2 June 1927, stated:

> There are no new works coming up and financial provision merely for relief works is politically bad, looks like supporting Jews. Until Arab unemployment becomes a considerable factor the Government will give, whenever possible, preference to Jewish contractors and to employ Jewish labour at ordinary market rates.[17]

It took a long time for the Administration to regard Arab unemployment as considerable, and various contracts in Haifa were handed over to Solel Boneh as relief projects, while some public works programmes, such as the Haifa–Acre road, were brought forward to employ 400 Jewish labourers in December 1927. (On account of the higher rates paid to Jewish labour, it was possible to construct only six kilometres instead of the eight scheduled for PWD projects.[18]) Another project handed over as relief work was the Mount Carmel Road, executed in 1928, for which the Municipality provided a betterment tax to reimburse the government.[19] These projects set the pattern for a percentage to be given to Jewish labour in future municipal works, for instance, the Law Courts (1931) and the Government Hospital (1936).

As a result of these tight conditions, the wage rates of both communities dropped; nevertheless, Jewish rates for urban unskilled labour continued to exceed Arab rates by one-third to one-half. Only the Railways Administration refused to concede different wages and paid the market minimum to both sectors. The concentration of such large blocks of unemployment in urban centres posed serious worries for the Administration. The Zionist Executive had insinuated threats of violence if certain basic needs of Jewish labour were not met. During 1927-8, approximately 1,000 Jewish labourers were sent from Haifa on relief works to neighbouring settlements, and a small number of Arab workers, approximately 70, were despatched to Nablus to carry out repair work on government premises following the earthquake.

The harbour project

It was in the Haifa harbour works that the Zionist Executive hoped to find an ample outlet for the relief of Jewish unemployment. Zionist activities in London on this matter proved fruitful. The Palestine and East Africa Loans Act (1926) financing the project included a stipulation for fair labour conditions, which was interpreted as meaning a fair proportion of Jewish labour paid at what was considered as a Jewish living wage. As expressed by Whitehall:

> There has been a considerable amount of unemployment among Jews who have settled in Palestine in consequence of the scheme for a National Home for the Jews, and the opportunity which the proposed harbour works will afford of providing work for Jewish labour is one which cannot be neglected. Owing to the different standards of life that prevail among Arab and Jew respectively, special provisions as to wages etc will have to be made if the project is to be secured, and it would be difficult if not impossible to include such provisions in any contract which could be made with a firm contracting for the whole work.[20]

The persistent manoeuvres of the Executive and the GFJL in Palestine kept the Administration well aware of Jewish demands and the potential turmoil resulting from labour problems. Here again the Administration was confronted with a dilemma; the harbour had to be built as cheaply as possible while employing a fair share of expensive Jewish labour and at the same time making full use of cheap Arab labour. Through a major campaign in the press, delegations to the High Commissioner in Jerusalem and similar activities in London, Jewish demands, at least at the minimum, set the framework for the harbour works employment policy by late 1928. The three main principles finally formulated by the Administration were: prohibition of imported labour; exclusive use of Palestinian stone and cement as far as possible; and setting the minimum wage for unskilled labour at 150 mils/day with the promise of a fair, though unspecified, share for Jewish labour.[21]

Given the Jewish community's contribution to revenue, and the Zionist argument that, as opposed to the casual labour of Arab fallahin, Jewish labour constituted the majority of the permanent labour force in the city, the Zionists demanded 50 per cent of the work as a minimum. They also endeavoured to show that the increase in cost due to Jewish employment would not be as high as was assumed by the government.[22] The High Commissioner, in his despatch to the Colonial Office on 15 May 1929, recommended the same minimum wage of 150 mils/day for a 54-hour week for both Arab and Jewish unskilled labour, with a further suggestion that Jewish labour be accorded the contracts for other public buildings to be constructed by piecework. This was seen as solving the issue of the Jewish proportion of labour on public works by ensuring that the total Jewish labour employment on the harbour and other government works would be 30 per cent of all government employment in Haifa.[23] Up to June 1930, Jewish employment on the harbour works amounted to 14 per cent of the total, a proportion the Administration considered fair in view of the 1929 demographic statistics, which showed that the Jews constituted 19 per cent of the whole Palestinian population.[24]

In the bickering over the wage rates and labour distribution between the Administration and the Zionists, the inherent motives of each side were starkly expressed. The Arab exclusion from these discussions once more demonstrated the paternalistic colonial attitude towards the Arab community, and led to a further divergence between the economic development of the two communities. The roots of the dilemma lay in the attitudes of both the Administration and the Zionists towards Arab labour. To the Administration, Arab labour, with its low standard of living and high level of dependence, was the ideal source for the major part of the unskilled work; to the Zionists, Arab labour was a major threat to the Jewish conquest of work in a city which they hoped to make into a Jewish centre. Moreover, Arab labour on government works tended to hold back the rise in wages of organized Jewish labour. A delicate and precarious formula had to be worked out to accommodate both these attitudes.

Between 1928 and 1929, the Administration struggled to find a formula that was both economically feasible and at the same time acceptable to the Zionist Organization. The principle of Jewish rights to a higher wage rate was well established. Nevertheless, the Administration shied away from applying this principle overtly, because of its moral implications and in view of the expected Arab reaction. While the CO was reconciled to the fact that the 'National Home' policy was going to be costly, and that the price would have to be paid by Palestine, it was not ready to carry out a blatantly discriminatory policy, for instance, bonus payments to supplement Jewish wages, where the cost could be shown in round figures.[25] With the Zionist Organization also refusing to concentrate Jewish labour in the skilled sections of the works, as was the case in the Nesher cement factory and the Rutenberg project (see Chapter 14), the Administration found itself in a quandary.[26]

Shares in employment

Up to 1930, unskilled labour in the Athlit quarries was almost entirely confined to Arabs, at wages below the Administration's minimum stipulation of 150 mils/day and even below the Wages Commission's living wage of 120 mils/day. Of 470 Arab labourers in the quarries in late 1929, 50 were paid 100 mils/day, 80 110 mils/day, 300 120 mils/day and 40 an unspecified wage above 120 mils/day.[27] The fact that this was the scale after substantial pay increases had been effected leads one to speculate on conditions during the previous eighteen months. Wage increases had been instituted to give the labour force an incentive for higher productivity and stability, but the minimalist approach left much to be desired. The maximum increase over the thirty months of construction was to the minimum approved wage of 150 mils/day, and it was only following the High Commissioner's instructions in January 1930 that this was to be achieved.[28] Nevertheless any savings accumulated by employing Arab labour were later expended on experimenting with Jewish piecework in the quarries. This was first conceded in November 1929 to meet some of the Jewish demands for a share in the unskilled work of the harbour and to ward off attacks by the Trades Union General Congress in London. Following assurances from the Prime Minister to Dr Weizmann in February 1931, the Administration pressed the resident engineer to augment Jewish participation in the harbour works. Whereas in June 1931 only 34 Jewish labourers were day earners out of 338 workers, the number grew to 81 in July, along with 200 Jewish labourers on piecework – a method which enabled Jewish labour to gain wages substantially higher than Arab daily labour, but which did not necessarily mean higher production at a lower cost to the Administration.[29] A similar arrangement for Arab piecework, proposed by the High Commissioner and the resident engineer, was never carried out.

By 1931 the CO and the Administration seemed exasperated at the Zionists' persistent demands.[30] This mood was reinforced by the High Commissioner's concern about the condition of the Arab rural class and the power of the Zionist lobby in shaping the course of government in Palestine,[31] and his opposition to the piecework system at the quarries, which he considered economically unjustified.

It was in relation to the construction of the harbour that Jewish claims to a share in employment equivalent to the community's contribution to revenue began to be voiced most clearly. The GFJL suggested an arbitrary figure of between 20 and 40 per cent as the percentage of Jews to be employed on public works, a figure based on the 1932 population ratio and the ratio of Jewish to Arab wage-earners. On this score, the Administration had to give way to political considerations. The High Commissioner found it hard to translate the Prime Minister's undertaking to Weizmann into practical policy:

It is very difficult – more so than the 'colour bar' question with which I am familiar in South Africa. It is possible to lay down some principles as a basis of action but it is, for political reasons, almost impossible to state them frankly without exposing ourselves to charges of unfair discrimination.[32]

The actual formula worked out in 1933 between the Jewish Agency and the Treasurer and finally the High Commissioner stipulated that the Jews should have 30 to 33 per cent of employment on government projects. This percentage was arrived at by taking into consideration a multitude of variables, the most significant being the level of unemployment among Arabs and Jews. Economic measures, however meaningful, had to take second place now that racial tensions were directly connected to economic satisfaction.[33]

Although the application of this agreement was not immediate or complete, its significance for the Arab working class was crucial. For one thing, it added to the Arabs' feelings of insecurity and legalized what they considered the cause of their oppression. The emphasis in labour affairs had shifted from a concern with wage rates between Arab and Jew to the allocation of work between Arab and Jew. To the disadvantage of the Arab worker, his struggle now was to ensure employment before demanding wage parity. Between 1931 and 1936, the gap between the Arab and Jewish working classes widened and the struggle for employment intensified. The 1936 strike was the expression, in more violent terms, of this feeling of dispossession on the part of Arab workers.

In the racially mixed areas, such as Haifa, this gap was most sharply felt as a result of government recruitment practices and work conditions. Added to this were the contrasting economic situations of the two communities. Arab unemployment, while highly volatile, was on the increase, maintaining a level of 16,000 to 17,000 against the Jewish figure of 600 to 1,500 between 1932 and 1935.[34] Economic boom in Jewish areas and cities was contrasted with adverse conditions in the countryside and the Arab towns. There was a considerable movement of population, mostly Arab – especially from the towns of Gaza, Nablus, Nazareth, Hebron and Jenin – to the orange-growing districts and the port cities, where building activities were flourishing. In Haifa, Jewish – and to a lesser extent Arab – building attracted a large number of these migrant workers. Even though unemployment figures for Haifa were low, and in comparison with those for Jerusalem and Jaffa did not merit serious concern, the unemployment in the northern countryside and the large influx of migrant Arabs to work on government projects and in the private sector flooded the ranks of unskilled labour and altered the character of the city.

By March 1936, unemployment was seriously affecting both Arab and Jew. About 30 per cent of Arab labour was estimated to be unemployed, and able to be hired for 70–110 mils/day instead of the market rate of 150–200 mils/day. Jewish wages, too, had fallen by around 50 per cent, and many were working only two or three days a week. To alleviate the situation, Jewish labour kitchens were reported to offer meals at one-third of the usual price.[35] It was in this atmosphere of discontent that the strike and the political disturbances were bred.

In spite of the Administration's commitment to the allocation of work in the proportions laid down by the High Commissioner, and persistent Zionist demands to that effect, the allocation continued to be affected by the general economic conditions in the country and by the policy of cutting down expenditure. In departments where employment was mixed, Jews tended to be grouped in the skilled, better-paying positions and the Arabs in the unskilled positions. Certain concessions to Jewish labour were made, however, such as employing exclusively Jewish labour in Jewish areas. No charges of discrimination could be levelled against the Administration in these instances, since Arabs and Jews did not work on the same site and consequently differences in wages did not come readily to light. On the whole, however, the principle of the lowest tender was still employed; according to the High Commissioner, its abandonment for the sole purpose of paying un-economic wages to Jewish workmen was indefensible on any ground and would in fact amount to discrimination in favour of Jew as against Arab.[36] It was intentionally overlooked only in 1936, when Jewish unemployment had grown to 6,000 because of a serious slump in the building industry.[37] The Administration found it expedient to devise a specific method of ensuring a fair share of public works, for 1936-7, to Jewish workmen; a number of road construction projects in the Jewish areas of the town were directly assigned to Jewish labour. None were assigned in the purely Arab areas, and those in the mixed areas were subject to tenders on the open market.[38]

When the harbour construction was completed in late 1933, only a small number of the workers were re-employed inside the harbour area. Of 380 labourers on the Haifa Harbour Development Works in May 1936, only 10 were Jews.[39] The modern port provided new labour opportunities especially for stevedores and porters, a branch primarily manned by Arab labour. Until 1933, all porterage activities were allotted by open tender, under the management of the Department of Customs. An Ordinance of September 1933 authorized the Director of Customs to appoint an overseer to carry out the work. The appointee, an Arab, employed 80 Arabs on a regular basis and several hundred daily casual labourers, almost all Arab, at a wage averaging between 130 and 200 mils/day in 1936, a rate considered abnormally high by the government.

The 1936 strike came to Haifa on 29 April, when some one hundred porters at the harbour stopped work. During the six months of the strike, most of the Administration's Arab employees joined it at some time or other. The immediate result was the infiltration of Jewish labour into areas of work which had previously been purely Arab and en-couraged by the Administration to stay that way. Such was the case with certain jobs, mostly unskilled, in the railways, the port, the Public Works Department and the Municipality,[40] which a number of Jewish workers took over conditional on assured tenure thereafter. The Administration was reluctant to commit itself to more than a small percentage of Jewish workers, who had to be paid higher wages; to ensure a foothold in all departments, the Histadrut subsidized the wages paid by the Administration.

The case of Arab labour at Haifa Harbour is a good example of the Administration's attitude during and after the strike. The initial approach to the porters' strike was once more paternalistic and condescending. At no time were the authorities ready to assess the deeper underlying cause of the strike and the Arabs' real fears and grievances. Again, the Administration's direct concern was the smooth working of the system and the maintenance of as normal a façade as possible. Arab labour was still preferred and considered profitable and manageable. The remaining 250 porters who had not struck were boarded and lodged at the port,[41] thus severing their contacts with the strikers and ensuring the service of a vital government project.

Still with economy as the main guiding principle, the Administration did not hesitate to employ 200 Haurani labourers alongside the Palestinian Arab workers. The Hauranis were a cheap labour force whose high productivity on unskilled work was well known. It was only as a result of the ZO's complaints in the British press that the Administration dismissed this non-Palestinian labour force and employed Arabs from the depressed Nablus district[42] instead. Jewish workers had to be introduced to supplement the workforce, and also now as a matter of right. Nevertheless, the Administration maintained its policy of segregating Arab from Jew while paying them different wages. The Jewish labourers were paid by the piece after an agreement with the Jewish Agency which provided them with labour-saving devices, thus enabling them to receive higher wages for fewer hours of work. In addition, Jewish labour was now in a position to impose work conditions in order to ensure higher profits and a steady income to a permanent labour force. The effect of these arrangements was to increase the casualization of Arab porters; they were expected to turn out in sufficient numbers, but only on the days when they were required. In effect, Arab porters were used for work which was in excess of the capacity of regularly employed Jewish porters.[43]

Following the strike, labour conditions in Palestine did not improve significantly. As one authority put it:

> By 1937 it was becoming clear that the volume of immigration, despite the privations which the Jewish population was prepared to suffer in order to support it, was beyond the capacity of the country. Considerable unemployment began to show itself among both Jews and Arabs. As early as 1935 wages began to fall. By 1938 unemployment and underemployment among both Jews and Arabs had become a matter of concern even though among the Jews the situation was, to some extent, mitigated by the large number of

temporary police that were recruited, the government and military works that were instituted and the replacement of Arabs by Jews in the Jewish owned orange groves.[44]

This situation provoked the Arab workers further, and found expression in their violent reaction during the revolt.

British labour policy was an expression of the generally anomalous policy practised in Palestine. By adopting a dual approach towards the communities, the Administration put the Arab working class in a position to be exploited by both the colonial rulers and the immigrant community. On the one hand, the Administration's exploitative attitude towards labour organizations, legislation and conditions of work eroded the capacity of the Arab working class to accumulate a surplus and stunted its chances of development. On the other hand, its non-interventionist policy in the face of the development of the Jewish labour movement promoted another means for Arab exploitation.

Notes

1. Memorandum by the Controller of Labour, 19 May 1922 (ISA LEG/3 1188/N).

2. *Kibush Avoda*, Hebrew for 'conquest of labour', was the labour slogan of Zionist ideology, and second only to the 'conquest of land' in the philosophy of building the Jewish National Home. The application of this principle differed from one area and one period to another. Conquest of the labour market signified the creation of an exclusive domain.

3. This union, organized by Jewish workers early in 1919 to include both communities, was banned initially by resurrecting Ottoman laws forbidding persons engaged in public service to found trade associations (Memo on Conditions of Railway Workers, December 1928; PRO CO 733/162), and was then accused of being organized by local Bolshevik sympathizers (Postmaster General to Clauson, 9 September 1926; PRO CO 733/125). Finally, at the insistence of the GFJL and the International Transport Workers Federation, the government consented to the formation of unions from one department only in order not to undermine the authority of department heads (OAG to HC, 22 July 1929; PRO CO 733/174). In this way, it had better control over situations where Arab workers could learn modern union tactics. For further review of this organization, see R. Taqqu, 'Arab Labor in Mandatory Palestine, 1920–1948', Ph.D. thesis, Columbia University, 1977, pp. 82–5.

4. J. 'Asfour, *Palestine: My Land, My Country, My Home* (Beirut, 1967), p. 31; M. al-Sharif, 'Mu'tamar al-'Ummal al-'Arab al-Awwal' (The First Conference of Arab Workers), *Shu'un Falastiniyya*, No. 50/51, October/November 1975, p. 297. Also see Listing of Palestinian Societies (ISA 61/52).

5. See pp. 152–3 on the establishment of the SMC by the Administration. Also see: U. M. Kupferschmidt, *The Supreme Muslim Council* (Leiden, 1978). The political role and significance of the Council will be further expounded in Part Four. For the role of Arab lawyers in the PAWS see *Haifa* (Workers' Magazine), 15 December 1924.

6. 'Asfour, *Palestine: My Land*, p. 102.

7. Official Parliamentary Report, 14 April 1932, enclosure to HC's letter to S of S, 29 July 1932 (PRO CO 733/221).

8. See *al-Karmil*, 10 October 1925; 11 November 1928; 4 October 1930; 8 October 1932; 20 August 1932.

9. ISA 95 DISP/4/1/2 and DISP/5/A.

10. The Jewish Co-operative Labour Association (JCLA) was the precursor of Solel Boneh (established 1925), the building branch of organized Jewish labour. It was founded in 1920 as an association of Jewish building workers in order to carry out contracts, primarily for the Administration. District Governor, N.D. (PRO FO 371 E11360/206/65).

11. Conference on Labour, Government House, Jerusalem, December 1921 (PRO CO 733/8).

12. Correspondence between District Governor, ND and CS, May–July 1922 (ISA LEG/3 1185/N), and Report on Military Labour, 19 December 1920 (ISA 11 DIT/111/3 1155/U). Also, for a detailed discussion of the Egyptian Labour Corps, see: B. J. Smith, *The Roots of Separatism in Palestine* (Syracuse, NY, 1993), pp. 146–7.

13. Symes' minute on Secretariat Paper, 27 May 1925 (ISA 95 Disp/1/1).

14. HC to CO, 20 April 1925 (PRO CO 733/92).

15. Report of the Wages Commission enclosed in HC to CO, 17 July 1928 (PRO CO 733/152). District Commissioner, ND Report No. 8, 30 September 1925 (ISA 11 WAG/5).

16. Unemployment Statistical Analysis (ISA UNE 1/1 Immigration and Labour). The returns for unemployment for June 1927 were:

	Jews	Non-Jews
Haifa	2,072	700
Jaffa–Tel-Aviv	4,741	450
Jerusalem	1,092	–

Returns for Haifa's non-Jewish community as reported in *al-Yarmuk* No. 197, 12 April 1927, were: Muslims 1,500; Christians 1,060. According to the above source, Jewish unemployed skilled labour exceeded its Arab counterpart.

17. OAG to CO, December 1927 (PRO CO 733/142), and HC to CO, June 1931 (PRO CO 733/203).

18. Ibid.

19. Meeting between GFJL and the HC at CO Conference, 22 October 1928 (PRO CO 733/161).

20. FO to American Ambassador Houghton, 29 January 1929 (PRO FO 733 164/67026). As early as February 1927, the Colonial Office had been advised by the consulting engineers to carry out the project departmentally; this was seen as the most workable arrangement because it would give the government the freedom to use Arab unskilled and Jewish skilled labour with discretion (Harding's minute of 28 February 1927, PRO CO 733/132).

21. OAG to ZO, 20 September 1928, and CO Conference, 22 October 1928 (PRO CO 733/161).

22. Merkes Avoda, Haifa, to Secretary, ZE, 7 September 1928 (CZA Z4/3469). Kaplansky to Lord Passfield, 11 July 1929 (PRO CO 733/174).

23. HC to CO, 15 May 1929 (PRO CO 733/165).

24. CO notes, June 1930 (PRO CO 733/189).

25. The scheme of bonus payments to increase Jewish wages was opposed by Grindle because it would show just how much the Zionists cost HMG. Minutes by JES, and G. Grindle, 30 October 1928 (PRO CO 733/161).

26. Meeting of ZO with HC and GFJL, 7 May 1929, and CO to HC, 16 May 1929 and HC to CO, 15 May 1929; see also Williams' and Shuckburgh's Minutes, May 1929 (PRO CO 733/165).

27. Resident Engineer to CS, 23 October 1929 (PRO CO 733/165).

28. Resident Engineer to CS, 27 January 1930 (PRO CO 733/189).

29. The estimated labour cost of Jewish piecework for March to May 1930 was 101, 90 and 88 mils/cubic metre respectively, while the corresponding Arab cost was 96, 90 and 70 mils/cubic metre. Jewish man-production was estimated at double that of the Arabs, in view of the incentive and facilities provided by piecework. Resident Engineer to CS, 26 May 1930, and CO minutes, June 1930 (PRO CO 733/189). By 1931, wages for Jewish pieceworkers averaged 245 mils/day and for Arab day workers 160 mils/day, including bonus, both for a 9-hour day. Confidential memo of meeting between Acting Treasurer, Chief Accountant and Consulting Engineers, 1 August 1931 (PRO CO 733/198).

30. Demands for observance of the Sabbath upset the work schedule of the resident engineer, who wished to maintain supervision of Jewish piecework. HC to CO, December 1930 (PRO FO 371 E6684/5671/65); HC to S of S, 8 January 1931, and Thompson to CS, 16 February 1931 (PRO CO 733/198).

31. HC meeting at CO, 7 May 1931 (PRO CO 733/197).

32. HC to Shuckburgh, 10 July 1931 (PRO CO 733/203).

33. HC to S of S, 10 August 1933 (PRO CO 733/238), and HC to S of S, 25 April 1936 (PRO CO 733/307).

34. In early 1933, Arab unemployment was roughly estimated at 16,000 and Jewish unemployment at 600. HC to S of S, 18 February 1933 (PRO CO 733/238). By the end of the year, the number of Arab unemployed rose to 16,800 and of Jewish unemployed to 2,050. Memo on Employment Conditions, December 1933 (PRO CO 733/249). The statistics furnished by the Commissioner for Migration and Statistics give a very different picture, with Arab unemployment in June 1934 at 14,000, while by July it had jumped to 17,000. Jewish unemployment in both months was 100. Statistical Summaries of Unemployment by E. Mills (PRO CO 733/249). In Haifa, statistics for Arab unemployment show an erratic situation from one month to the next: 1934, 1,700, June 1935, 1,830. Figures for Jerusalem and Jaffa in 1934 were 1,825 and 1,386 respectively, by December 1935, 1,850 and 3,416. Comparative Estimates of Arab Unemployment in 7 Towns, 1935 (PRO CO 733/269). These figures should be viewed with circumspection and can give only a picture of the broad lines of employment conditions. Prior to the 1936 strike, unemployment was very high in Jaffa, and administrative measures for alleviating only Jewish unemployment further exacerbated the situation. The outbreak of 1936 seemed a predictable result. G. Mansur, *The Arab Worker under the Palestine Mandate* (Jerusalem, 1937), pp. 38–9.

35. Political Summary, 6 March 1936 (PRO FO 371 E1293/19/31).

36. Meeting of GFJL with HC, 26 June 1931 (PRO CO 733/203).

37. By September 1935, and because of the Italo-Abyssinian conflict, a short-

age of liquid funds led to a slump which particularly affected Jewish businesses because, more than the Arabs, they depended on a system of extended credits. Report on Unemployment, September 1935 (PRO CO 733/269).

38. HC to S of S, 25 April 1936 (PRO CO 733/307).

39. HC to S of S, 27 June 1936 (PRO CO 733/307).

40. Abba Khoushi, 'Capture of Labour in Haifa', and Ben Dov, 'Penetration to Conquer Labour', *Davar*, 2 November 1936.

41. HC to S of S, 29 April 1936 (PRO FO 371 E755/755/31).

42. Mansur, *The Arab Worker*, p. 11. In describing the incident of the Haurani labour, Mansur gives an account of the very high level of unemployment in the Nablus district. When the 200 Hauranis were being replaced, 1,200 labourers came from the Nablus area hoping to find employment at the port.

43. Report on Jewish Labour in porterage work. F. O. Rogers, 18 June 1937 (PRO CO 733/328).

44. A. M. Hyamson, *Palestine Under the Mandate 1920–1948* (London, 1950), p. 76.

PART FOUR

The Political Transformation of Haifa's Arab Community

Prologue

While, as Parts Two and Three have shown, socio-economic changes strongly affected the development of Palestinian society, these changes occurred within a highly charged political atmosphere. It may, therefore, be useful to give a brief outline here of the leading political events highlighting the evolution of Palestinian history during the period under study.[1]

Under a League of Nations Mandate, Britain assumed in 1917–18 a role which was in some respects unique in its imperial experience: with its occupation of Palestine it took on the thankless task of being responsible for two communities of divergent development and aspirations. In the triangle of Arab-British-Jewish/Zionist relations, British policy was rooted in its commitment to the establishment of a Jewish National Home (JNH) in Palestine, as promised in the Balfour Declaration of 1917. The Arab party in this triangle fought what it conceived as a battle for survival against both British and Zionist implementation of the JNH policy. Between 1918 and 1920, the option of Arab solidarity seemed a possibility as the Palestinian Arabs sought to ally themselves with the mainstream Arab nationalist movement in Syria, their hopes pinned on the government of King Faisal, son of Sherif Husain of Mecca, set up in Damascus in October 1918.[2] However, these pan-Arab fantasies were dashed with Faisal's defeat by the French at Maisaloun on 20 July 1920 and the collapse of his government.[3]

Palestinian goals now focused on Palestine itself and solutions within it. The course of events gave the Arabs continuous cause for protest which became progressively tinged with despair. Such was their reaction to the anniversaries of the Balfour Declaration, Jewish land purchases, the eviction of Arab peasants, legal and illegal Jewish immigration, Arab-Jewish labour disputes or arms smuggling for the Zionists. The accumulation of Arab resentment and frustration, as well as the slow erosion of their economic base, built up to the violent collisions of 1918, the early 1920s, 1929, 1933 and the long revolt of 1936–9.

The earliest nationalist organization, the Muslim-Christian Association (MCA), represented the main anti-Zionist current led by the more moderate conservative trend of the notable class. It was during national congresses that the guidelines of the struggle were to be formulated and during the third congress, held in Haifa in December 1920, that an Arab Executive (AE) was elected. Between 1921 and 1923 three delegations from this Arab leadership went to London in the hope of reversing Britain's support of the JNH policy, only to return empty-handed.

The politics of the Jerusalem notable class had been dominated by competition between the Husaini and the Nashashibi families even before the British occupation. With the new situation after 1918, this same family antagonism aligned itself into two opposing camps according to their interpretation of national issues and their attitudes towards the Administration and its policies. From the outset the Husainis proclaimed a firmly nationalist, anti-Zionist orientation – an ideology which appealed to mainstream Palestinian thinking, from the more educated, young committed nationalists to the poor dispossessed peasants and urban labourers. The Nashashibis, on the other hand, headed a wide platform which ranged from a conciliatory attitude towards the Administration and its JNH policy to collaboration with it and with the Zionists. The supporters of this second current, which came to be known as the Opposition, i.e. opposition to the main line, represented a plethora of shifting political orientations. Under this umbrella congregated those elements that had personal, family or interest feuds with the Husainis; those nationalist elements who hoped for some compromise solution to the Palestinian impasse, or who could not abandon their faith in British goodwill; as well as those who had been offended by the tone of the nationalist trend, whether pan-Arab or pan-Islamic. While both currents claimed to be working for the national good, there were leaders in both camps who were moved by personal and family interest or by straightforward ambition for power.

The Administration exploited the rivalry between the Jerusalem families in its dealings with the Arabs. When Hajj Amin al-Husaini was appointed mufti of Jerusalem by the first High Commissioner (HC), Sir Herbert Samuel, on 8 May 1921,[4] this move was largely to keep the balance between the two factions, since Ragheb Nashashibi had been appointed mayor the previous year, replacing, and humiliating, an older member of the Husaini family, Kadhem Pasha.[5] In addition to the position of mufti, the Administration reinforced Husaini influence by setting up the Supreme Muslim Council (SMC)[6] under his leadership, with control over religious affairs and, in particular, endowments (waqfs) and the appointment and dismissal of judicial officials (Qadis). In other words, the SMC was permitted the financial power that could give it political control. In fact, the Administration succeeded in creating an Arab political body able and willing to maintain peace in the country for at least a decade. Throughout the 1920s the SMC used its powers of patronage to build up its strength against the opposition. It entered all the arenas of the national struggle: it allied itself with the AE's political line to the point of complete identification with it; it gradually came to oppose the MCAs and mounted the campaign against the Advisory and Legislative Councils which the opposition supported in 1922–3; and it challenged the opposition in municipal elections in 1927 and 1934.

The opposition also built its initial power on support from the Administration. Ragheb Nashashibi's appointment as mayor of Jerusalem in 1920 secured the loyalty of the Nashashibi clan for the British presence, when they had been, until then, known supporters of the French. However, following the sudden prominence of Husaini influence, the opposition began to attract new elements, who were not involved in the feud of the two families but who, nevertheless, had lost out with this new development. The strongest support for the opposition, or rather the strongest opposition to the SMC and Husaini hegemony, came from the north. Traditionally the northern districts had economic, social and political contacts and common interests with Syria and Lebanon, rather than with the south in Jerusalem. Their traditional leaders, as well as the emerging Christian notables, had ambitions for a stronger role in Palestinian political life, ambitions which were curbed by the SMC/AE nepotistic and exclusivist practices. While these elements were united in their antagonism to the Husaini faction, they differed drastically in their political orientations. There were those who maintained a pro-Ottoman Islamist position, irreconciled to the nationalist movement and some of them with close contacts with the Zionists. There were also some who were persistent supporters of the British Administration, among them committed nationalists, some with religious overtones and some with pan-Arab orientation, but whose ambitions had been deflated. Many members of the emerging Christian merchant class, though on the whole anti-Zionist, were wary of any pan-Arab or pan-Islamic calling, which might challenge their newly acquired wealth and status.

In general, the opposition faction had the moral and financial support of the Zionists, a fact made clear in the platform of its organizations and a cause of its lack of appeal. The 'Muslim National Association' was the first such organization, with branches in the north and centre of the country. Following the AE's success in the boycott of the Legislative Council elections, the opposition adopted a new political approach, led by elements which preferred a middle path between the nationalist stand of the AE and the overtly compromising position of the Muslim Associations. A new 'National Party' became their platform in late 1923, sharply anti-Zionist, but opposed to pan-Arab orientations and supporting the Administration as well as pragmatic approaches to the country's political and economic problems. Its line was satisfactory neither to the Zionists nor to the committed nationalists, however. Starting in 1924, therefore, the Zionists set up other short-lived political platforms among the Arabs, such as the 'agricultural parties', to support their policy.[7] By 1925 the opposition was gaining in status when it challenged the elections to the SMC and won a moral victory when they were invalidated. Furthermore, it had become a clearly recognized actor in the Arab political arena when the Administration appointed a temporary SMC with two representatives from each camp. What set the future scene for each party was the municipal elections of 1927, in which the opposition won an overwhelming victory, thus giving its whole ideological spectrum a recognized channel comparable to that of the SMC and the AE.

Up to 1923, and particularly during the administration of Sir Herbert Samuel, the government attempted to find ways of achieving peace and stability by encouraging those elements that were willing to co-operate and participate in the government. One significant attempt was the Advisory, and later Legislative, Council, proposed by the British government to the first delegation to London in August 1921 as a means of providing the Arabs with representative institutions through which they could participate in the government of their country. In its final form the Legislative Council was regarded by the Arab nationalists as falling short of their expectations, since it gave only limited legislative and no executive powers to the Arabs. At the same time, an uncompromising current within the nationalist movement, clearly evident in the Fifth Congress in August 1922,[8] was leading the debate against participation in the election of such a council or any co-operation with government policy based on the principle of accepting the Balfour Declaration. The AE used all means at its disposal in its successful campaign to boycott the elections. Again, when the HC suggested in October 1923 the establishment of an Arab Agency, on the model of the Jewish Agency, to advise the government on policy, this was also refused on the ground that it lacked any formal status in the Mandate system.[9]

The paralysis that settled over the Arab nationalist movement after 1923 was rudely shaken in the confrontations of the Wailing Wall incident in 1929. Writers seem to have reached a consensus on the reasons for this inertia. A main cause appeared to be the changed fortunes in the JNH policy as an economic crisis in Zionist circles affected the rate of immigration and Jewish employment. Jewish emigration exceeded immigration in 1927 and demonstrated itself in more visible signs of Jewish moderation and less anxiety on the Arab side.[10]

In the political arena energies were diverted to factionalism and political fratricide between the two nationalist currents, leading to inactivity on both sides, particularly after the ratification of the Mandate, with its Zionist policy, by the League of Nations. It should also be noted that after August 1925, when Lord Plumer took over as HC from Samuel, no new conciliatory overtures were made to the Arabs, and Plumer's military background and approach inhibited overt Arab political objections.

However, these outward signs of inactivity hid a gradual accumulation of factors that were heading for more radical grassroots Arab outbursts. The economic constraints which the Arab community had experienced since the early 1920s, with land sales, trading restrictions and an increasingly proletarianized labour force with diminishing opportunities, were beginning to affect an ever wider circle of the Arab community.[11] Furthermore, a younger, dispossessed and embittered generation of better-educated Arabs was coming of age and, being less inhibited by the social restrictions of the older generation, was questioning the political path of the nationalist movement.

By 1929 conditions had drastically deteriorated, as was confirmed by the commission, headed by Sir Walter Shaw, which investigated the causes of the violence of that year. The subsequent report of Sir John Hope Simpson on the land and agricultural situation, as well as the British White Paper of October 1930, indicated that the worsening economic and political conditions were the underlying cause of Arab discontent and violence.[12] The 'Passfield' White Paper of 1930 was intended to appease Arab opinion, promising measures that would limit the JNH and alleviate the depressed conditions of the peasantry and the urban working class. However, all was repudiated by Prime Minister MacDonald's 'Black Letter' of February 1931 to Dr Weizmann, which came in the wake of a wave of heated Zionist objections to the 1930 White Paper.[13]

During the chain of events following this setback, practically all sectors of the Arab community closed ranks in opposing the British policy. The unprecedented growth of both legal and illegal Jewish immigration (see Chapter 4) caused extreme anxiety among the Arabs.[14] Furthermore, an intensification of Zionist measures to colonize land, labour and the market accompanied the demographic changes, together with signs of Zionist stockpiling of arms. By 1935, when international events brought economic crisis to Palestine,[15] the widespread depression among the urban and peasant city workers had radicalized the Arab political stance.

This overt radicalization hid a deeper and more serious change in the Arab socio-economic structure. Widening class differentiation had exacerbated antagonisms in Arab society, highlighting and enlarging the schisms between traditional competing elites, between rural and urban societies, between the increasingly destitute and proletarianized peasantry at the periphery of urban society and the newly emerging urban bourgeoisie, both Christian and Muslim, and between Christians and Muslims. In short, as a result of overwhelming challenges and its own dynamism, Arab society was experiencing a transformation of class and consciousness.[16] The radicalization also changed Arab socio-political structures. On one level, a larger stratum of the population had become politicized and involved in protest against what they conceived to be the cause of their worsening conditions, namely the Zionists and the Administration. On another level, the traditional leadership and their socio-political structures were overwhelmed by this new mood and forced either to accommodate themselves to it or leave the political arena. Both the AE and the opposition organizations slowly disintegrated and by 1935 new political groupings emerged, reflecting the new mood and a new stage in the struggle.

During the 1930s the escalating violence and its repercussions were a testimony to the popular state of radical combustion. By 1936 it found an outlet in the national strike, called by the radicalized urban politicians as a last attempt to reassemble all Arab political ranks in an unprecedented act of civil disobedience. Involving most strata of society, whether willingly or otherwise, this action revealed to the Arabs the political state of affairs which two decades of British control, Zionist development and their leaders' smoke-screens had achieved. More significantly, it exposed the threadbareness of the nationalist movement, the lack of a united ideological commitment and the impotence of the Arab Higher Committee (AHC) to achieve solutions.

When partition of Palestine was recommended by the Royal Commission in July 1937, a wave of violent protest ensued, especially in the north (the area that was allotted to the Jewish state), sweeping away the traditional politicians in its path.[17] As a result the British authorities exiled members of the AHC for supposedly fomenting rebellion. By so doing the Administration only redeemed their status by investing them with heroic martyrdom, thereby giving the traditional leadership a new lease of life to continue their role in the national struggle from exile, up to the end of the Mandate.

By late 1937 and throughout the months of the Arab revolt of 1938–9, the leadership was hijacked by rural-based activists and sometimes makeshift leaders who found themselves in the forefront because of the absence of the traditional politicians. The country was swept by violent action, initially against the British Administration and the Jewish presence, and later degenerating into political cleansing, fratricide and acts of revenge.

Militant reaction had remained the only method not attempted by the Arab nationalists and was generally recognized as such; however, it clashed with the interests of a widening circle of the settled population, both urban and rural. For the Arab politicized communities, the revolt was a vindication, but at the same time it challenged what they had achieved in the previous two decades. Nevertheless, in the light of the coherent reaction of the entire Arab society to the long strike, to the government's repressive measures and to the hardships these entailed, there was clearly a general endorsement of radicalization which reflected deep changes in political orientations. By the early 1930s not only peasants and workers were negatively affected by the JNH policy; the urban lower strata of the commercial bourgeoisie were also identifying with the same grievances.[18] While the traditional leadership had become ossified in its futile tactics and procrastination, it was being overwhelmed by this new current in which the orientations of intellectuals, professionals, the lower middle classes as well as peasants and workers had coalesced.

While the rebellion was a genuine expression of the socio-political alienation of the whole Arab society, the form it took and the circumstances surrounding its activities reflected the direction of the most militant and the worst-affected sectors. The rebels challenged the social norms and economic concerns of the urban society; they also threatened the peace and quiet in which the Christian communities and the newly established bourgeoisie lived, and, most importantly, they overthrew the traditional political channels and flung the social order into upheaval. During the final stages of the revolt in 1939 the activities of some of the fighters degenerated into family, personal and regional animosities, or they simply became agents of the exiled political leadership.[19] The more pressure was applied to them, the more deviant and unsynchronized their activities became. Vandalism and criminal actions were committed against the Arab communities in the name of the rebellion.

The Arab civilian population suffered on all fronts, being increasingly terrorized from within their own society and by government policies. By late 1939 they had lost all chance of economic recovery and any semblance of social cohesion; their political movement had become fractured and dependent on outside Arab political manoeuvring. On the Zionist side, the rebellion was used to strengthen the independent stance of the Jewish community, to develop its fighting arm (the Haganah) from a defensive into an offensive machine, and to control a wider range of the country's economic activities. This hastened the implementation of Zionist plans. For the Arabs, the political gains were nominal and temporary. They were embodied in the White Paper of 1939, which seemed to come closer to Arab demands than any previous policy statement under the Mandate; however, by then the international power structure had changed and other forces were now conspiring against the Arab cause. By the end of the Second World War Britain's imperial power had declined, to be replaced by the United States – a staunch supporter of a Zionist state in Palestine, especially following the Nazi atrocities in Germany. Furthermore, the Mandatory authority now faced a militant, well-armed and well-trained anti-British Jewish community set on achieving independence from British control.

Notes

1. The political history of the Palestinian impasse has been researched, analysed and published from practically all angles of the debate. However, for selected works that have thoroughly reviewed this period, see: A. M. Lesch, *Arab Politics in Palestine, 1917–1939* (London, 1979); Y. Porath, *The Emergence of the Palestinian Arab National Movement, 1918–1929* (London, 1974) and *The Palestinian Arab National Movement, 1929–1939* (London, 1977); E. Tuma, *Sittun 'Aman 'ala al-Haraka al-Qawmiyya al-'Arabiyya al-Filastiniyya* (The Last Sixty Years of the Palestinian Arab Movement) (Beirut, 1978); C. D. Smith, *Palestine and the Arab–Israeli Conflict* (2nd ed. New York, 1992); A. W. Kayyali, *Palestine: A Modern History* (London, 1978); W. F. 'Abboushi, *Filastin qabla al-Dayaa'* (The Unmaking of Palestine) (London, 1985); P. A. Smith, *Palestine and the Palestinians 1876–1983* (New York, 1984); N. 'Allush, *Al-Muqawama al-'Arabiyya fi Filastin 1917–1948* (The Arab National Struggle in Palestine 1917–1948) (Beirut, 1970).

2. Smith, *Palestine and the Arab–Israeli Conflict*, pp. 70–71; Porath, *The Emergence*, pp. 70–103.

3. Ibid., p. 100. Also see S. Al-Husri, *Yawm Maisalun* (The Day of Maisaloun) (Beirut, n.d.).

4. Porath, *The Emergence*, pp. 184–207; Lesch, *Arab Politics*, pp. 91–2.

5. Porath, *The Emergence*, pp. 100–103; Smith, *Palestine and the Arab–Israeli Conflict*, pp. 70–71.

6. U. M. Kupferschmidt, *The Supreme Muslim Council* (Leiden, 1978).

7. Porath, *The Emergence*, p. 227; Lesch, *Arab Politics*, p. 51.

8. Porath, *The Emergence*, pp. 148–9.

9. B.N. Al-Hoot, *Al-Qiyadat wal-Mu'asasat al-Siyassiyya fi Filastin 1917–1948* (Leadership and Political Institutions in Palestine 1917–1948) (Beirut, 1981), pp. 165–8; Lesch, *Arab Politics*, p. 166.

10. Porath, *The Emergence*, pp. 243–4; Kayyali, *Palestine*, p. 136; Lesch, *Arab Politics*, p. 96.

11. Kayyali, *Palestine*, p. 108; Smith, *Palestine and the Arab–Israeli Conflict*, pp. 94–5; Smith, *Palestine and the Palestinians*, pp. 51–62; 'Abboushi, *Filastin*, pp. 89–114.

12. Lesch, *Arab Politics*, pp. 169–70; Porath, *The Palestinian Arab*, pp. 27–39; Hoot, *Al-Qiyadat*, pp. 221–9.

13. See N. Weinstock, *Zionism: False Messiah* (London, 1979), pp. 119–20; Kayyali, *Palestine*, pp. 155–63; Porath, *The Palestinian Arab*, pp. 27–39.

14. J. L. Abu-Lughod, 'The Demographic Transformation of Palestine', in I. Abu Lughod (ed.), *The Transformation of Palestine* (Evanston, IL, 1971), pp. 150–51; Porath, *The Palestinian Arab*, pp. 39–40; Lesch, *Arab Politics*, p. 56.

15. The Italo-Abyssinian war, which broke out in the autumn of 1935, heralded growing tensions in Europe and exposed Britain's weakness.

16. For an analysis of changes within the Palestinian Arab society at this period, see: Smith, *Palestine and the Palestinians*, pp. 51–63; E. Zureik, 'Reflections on Twentieth-Century Palestinian Class Structure', in K. Nakhleh and E. Zureik (eds), *The Sociology of the Palestinians* (London, 1980), pp. 52–8; T. Nashif, 'Palestinian Arab and Jewish Leadership in the Mandate Period', *Journal of Palestine Studies*, Vol. 6 (iv) (1977).

17. Lesch, *Arab Politics*, pp. 120–24; Tuma, *Sittun 'Aman*, pp. 132–45.

18. For a class analysis of the revolution of 1936–9 see: G. Kanafani, *Palestine: The 1936–1939 Revolt* (London, Tricontinental Society, n.d.).

19. Lesch, *Arab Politics*, pp. 224–5; Porath, *The Palestinian Arab*, pp. 249–60.

12

Transition into
the British Orbit

Early political orientations

The social structure of Haifa made the task of setting up a new administration in 1918 an easy and smooth one. There was no strong, historically established Muslim religious structure supported by public recognition and respect, as there was in Jerusalem.[1] The Military Administration was careful, however, not to give cause for Muslim discontent on a religious basis.[2] In Haifa, the Muslim religious dignitaries were not the only leaders of socio-political movements in the town, or even in the Muslim community itself. The traditional Muslim notable families, Khalil, Shukri, Hajj Ibrahim, Mukhlis and Taha, shared leadership with the recognized religious families of Murad, Khatib and Imam in guiding the political direction of the Muslim community. In early 1919, the Muslim Association (al-Jam'iyya al-Islamiyya) was established to deal with Muslim community and national affairs.[3] Its members included representatives of all political currents among the economically and socially privileged strata of Muslim society. From the start, it was influenced by the political orientation of its president, the mufti of Haifa, Muhammad Murad, and other powerful Arab nationalists among its members. Though practically all the prominent members of the Muslim elite publicly expressed their support and admiration for the British occupying forces and the Administration,[4] their subsequent activities and alliances were to reveal divergent and bitterly conflicting political orientations and commitments vis-à-vis the principal issues of the British, Zionism and Arab identity.

On one side stood the notable families of Turkish extraction from the Ottoman bureaucracy, who, even when they recognized the necessity of restructuring the Muslim leadership to safeguard their own and the community's interests at this juncture, stayed aloof from the Arab leadership of the town. An example of this tendency was Hasan Shukri, who, in his official capacity as mayor of Haifa, handed the town over to General King, the military officer leading the occupying forces. Symbolically, the General immediately reconfirmed him in his post and effectively transferred his allegiance to the new Administration by handing back to him the sword of surrender. Except for one short lapse, Shukri, until his death, loyally performed his duties in the manner he considered to be in the best interests of the new Administration, acting either on his own personal initiative, as with the congratulatory telegram he sent to the High Commissioner,[5] or at the instigation of the Zionists, as illustrated by his role in the pro-Zionist 'Islamic Patriotic Society' (al-Jam'iyya al-Islamiyya al-Wataniyya) (see Chapter 13).[6] At different periods of his career, he was able to attract around him people, mostly Muslims, who saw his influence as a means for personal advancement or as an instrument in the rivalry for leadership among the Muslims. Members of another family of Turkish origin, the Khalils, also joined the board of the Muslim Association, but they were not politically active.

Among the remaining body of Muslim leaders, two trends in political thinking were emerging, both conservative, anti-Zionist and Arabist. One group, which congregated around 'Abdallah Mukhlis, found support from 1922 onwards outside Haifa, in the opposition movement to the political control of the Jerusalem Arabs, and specifically of the Husainis and the Supreme Muslim Council (SMC). In Haifa it won support among the more educated pro-British Muslim and Christian elements. Mukhlis, a well-known historian and writer on national and Muslim affairs,[7] had served in a number of official posts under the Ottoman regime.[8] His political position was halfway between the strongly pro-Ottoman, even anti-Arab, nationalist position of As 'ad Shuqairi of Acre and the extreme anti-Zionist, nationalist stand of Shaikh Sulaiman al-Taji al-Faruqi, a member of the famous 'alim family from Ramleh. Like these two prominent wealthy figures, Mukhlis' political orientation was determined by his own personal background and ambitions as well as by the specific socio-political features of northern Palestine. Unlike them, Mukhlis did not possess family, financial or religious power to attract traditional supporters in Haifa, but he was able to take an intermediate position by appealing to the conservative literate stratum of the upper middle-class Muslims and members of the Christian lower middle class. He found a special ally in Najib Nassar, who shared his generally conservative, nationalist leanings as well as a growing antagonism to the Jerusalem leadership.

The second group exhibited an Arab nationalist tendency which was more in line with the mainstream nationalism of the educated Muslim circles of Jaffa, Nablus and Jerusalem. This nucleus expressed a growing anti-British trend, ranging from the mild to the extreme, depending on individual orientations. Its focal members were Mu'in al-Madi, Rashid al-Hajj Ibrahim, Ahmad al-Imam and Muhammad Murad. While all four were Palestinian nationalists with strong Muslim feelings, the first two were linked to the Syrian pan-Arab movement of which they had been members. The group as a whole was closer to the Jerusalem leadership than any other political group in Haifa.

Mu'in al-Madi and Rashid al-Hajj Ibrahim, both prominent in Arab nationalist circles since before the occupation, had to accommodate their political thinking to the changed circumstances. Initially, Madi's activities had centred on the Hashimites. He began his career in the entourage of King Faisal, under whose short-lived government in Damascus he was appointed governor of the Karak district; afterwards he returned to his family seat of political and economic influence in Ijzim. This background, coupled with his education, allowed him to take controversial stands without damaging his position as a nationalist; he was one of the few members of the Arab nationalist movement who compromised on the question of the Legislative Council but maintained their credibility.[9] Hajj Ibrahim was from the start a Muslim Arab nationalist, with emphasis on both aspects. He was closely related both to the Arab nationalists in Syria and Palestine, the forerunners of the Istiqlal party, and to the Muslim circles of Haifa.[10] Initially, like most of the politicized Muslims in the town, he assumed a pro-British stand, as illustrated by his political position during the Palestine Congress of 1919.[11] Only later, in the late 1920s, did he become more anti-British.

Ahmad al-Imam, a professional journalist, and Shaikh Muhammad Murad, a traditional semi-educated mufti, were the two most active members of the Muslim Association, the former as its acting secretary and nationalist ideologue, the latter as its president. As mufti of Haifa, Murad met the HC, Herbert Samuel, in 1920 when, with an eye to gaining Muslim approval, the local administration of the *awqaf* (Muslim endowments) was being reviewed and some moribund *awqaf* were being revived in Haifa.[12] In view of his Islamic orientation and position, his livelihood depended on these sources and on the Supreme Muslim Council in Jerusalem, which explains his allegiance to the Husaini leadership. Imam was also a part of this Muslim current, but his commitment to Jerusalem was less whole-hearted. Like Hajj Ibrahim, he was a Muslim Arab nationalist and in 1922 he joined him in the 'Comité de Caiffa', a short-lived committee representing the Istiqlal nationalist party of Syria for the purpose of making propaganda against the French.[13] He also moved towards an anti-British position in the late 1920s.

From early 1919, the Muslim nationalists in Haifa, whether expressing pro- or anti-British sentiments, were blacklisted and watched by the police.[14] Al-Hajj Ibrahim, Imam and Murad were singled out as a 'bad lot'; furthermore, Murad was considered a dangerous leader to be closely supervised. Mu'in al-Madi was listed as a milder troublemaker, but was also watched after his return from Transjordan in May 1921.

In addition to these, a growing number of silent political elements made up the membership of the Muslim Association and its youth and literary subcommittees. In December 1920, the CID reported the membership as 700, possibly the largest community organization in Palestine.[15] While the board of the Association, comprising wealthy landowners and merchants, was moderate and conservative, its rank and file was guided by the Islamic fundamentalist teachings of the mufti and the chauvinist Arabism of Imam. The chances that more radical, even militant, nationalist groups would emerge from this Association were thus great. There are indications that the underground militant organization 'al-Kaff al-Aswad' (The Black Hand), active in Jaffa in early 1919, had a branch in Haifa, but very little is known of its operations. In 1922, a 'Muslim Self-Sacrificing Society' was reported to have also been active in Haifa.[16] Not only Muslims were members of the Black Hand, and later, in 1934, some members – both Christian and Muslim – set up 'Nadi al-Shabab al-'Arab' (The Arab Youth Club).[17]

The first political groupings among the Christian communities followed the norms traditional to their society. As in the Muslim community, overall political orientation was determined by religious and family allegiance and alliances, but the lead was primarily taken by the appointed religious leaders, who, in accordance with their communities' traditions, assumed a political status along with their spiritual and social roles. Political awareness was more pervasive among the Christians than among the Muslims, because of their favourable educational and economic background. Christian political structures during this early period therefore reflected a generally cohesive orientation and practice; this was particularly true of the Greek Catholics.

Haifa's Christian communities had no reservations, however, when it came to one topic, Zionism, which most of them passionately opposed for ideological, economic, patriotic or religious reasons. Opinions on this matter were expressed by recognized secular and politically articulate spokesmen such as Najib Nassar, Wadi' Bustani, Fu'ad Sa'd and Teofil Boutagy, the first three of whom were blacklisted by the police for opposing government policy.[18] The number of Christians signing public statements against the Balfour Declaration and joining the various protests against Zionist activities in Haifa often exceeded that of the Muslims, and included religious leaders and a large number of the wealthiest merchants and even some of the landowners.[19] The fact that Haifa had such a large Christian population, many of whom were educated with an Arab cultural orientation and francophile leanings, explains the strongly anti-Zionist tone of political life, which persisted with varying degrees of intensity throughout the Mandate period. To the francophile elements, this anti-Zionist line was also intended to embarrass the British and their support for the policy of the Jewish National Home. In contrast, Najib Nassar, whose passionate hatred of Zionism was well known and whose hopes in the British were initially boundless, refrained from keeping up the pressure in his anti-Zionist campaign, took no part in the statements submitted to the Administration, and kept a low profile on political matters during the early period. By this behaviour he intended to lend support to the British Military Administration.

On political issues concerning British rule and the Arab orientation of the nationalist movement, the Christian educated and politicized sectors held a wide spectrum of opinions. The differences cannot be wholly explained in terms of religious communities or socio-economic class, and neither were they unaffected by them. While the dominant group in the Catholic communities had strong French sympathies, many of their members came out publicly on the side of the British. Wadi' Bustani, a Maronite lawyer employed by Haifa's military governor in the early period, Colonel Stanton, as his private adviser, was highly appreciated by the British.[20] As an open anti-Zionist with a strong awareness of his Arab background, his position was resented by the Jewish community of Haifa and a demand for his dismissal was submitted to the governor. He was accused of being an Arab nationalist who influenced the military governor by intriguing against the Jews and meddling with affairs that did not concern him.[21] Most probably, it was also to Bustani that Herbert Samuel referred when he spoke of the harmful effects upon Zionist interests of 'levantine' officials who worked in the offices of the military governors.[22] Other Greek Catholic entrepreneurs and landowners, such as 'Aziz Khayyat, seem to have had pro-British sympathies. But, while Khayyat took part in the common protests against the Zionists, his business contacts with the West, especially Britain and the United States, led him to keep a low profile in the politics of the Greek Catholic community.

The anti-British feeling was significant only during the first five years of the occupation, when the francophiles believed there was a chance of reversing the situation in favour of France. Even then, this option was not considered very seriously and the expression of these feelings was confined to general pro-French sympathies and disapproval of British practices. Bishop Hajjar, an ambitious politician in his own right, led this current of thought, and the Christian Association headed by Fu'ad Sa'd expressed his views.[23] Hajjar's position as spiritual head of the largest Christian minority, the Greek Catholics, plus his personal charisma and compelling powers of persuasion,[24] gave him prominence over the other Christian religious leaders.

The issue of identifying with the Arab aspect of the national movement was ambiguously treated in these circles. It should be remembered that the Christian communities had only recently become free to participate with the Muslims in public and political affairs on an equal footing. The caution, suspicion and lack of self-confidence which characterized Christian attitudes towards Muslim political movements were often translated into a general timidity in public expression and action on political issues. Though Christians identified with Arab culture, they were wary of any attempt to define this identity in an exclusivist Muslim way. Co-operation between Muslims and Christians in Haifa was at its best in the early days of the occupation, when both communities felt the same intense national and economic threat.

A British Administration, however, gained the approval of a sector of the notable and merchant class, both Muslim and Christian. Linked to the overriding concern with the economy among Haifa's leading families was their commitment to a moderate and stable political structure. On the one hand, British rule promised stability and economic prosperity for Haifa in particular; on the other, British political influence had gained adherents early on among these strata in the town, most probably before and during the war. In November 1918, the 'Anglophile Party' was formed in Haifa by the Greek Orthodox-turned-Protestant Najib and Rashid Nassar and the Muslim Amin 'Abdul-Hadi and 'Abdallah Mukhlis. They believed the Arab nation's success was dependent on binding it to Britain and seeking British protection, and emphasized the need to unite Arab demands and develop the economic life of the Arab countries, while at the same time respecting British interests in the region.[25]

The moving spirit behind this organization was Najib Nassar, who had planned its establishment before the end of the war.[26] Clearly, even if it was not set up at the instigation of the British military authorities, the party was in close contact with the local military governors and heeded their advice to keep out of politics, especially matters concerned with the Zionists.[27] It is also clear from its records, however, that the main orientation of the membership was strongly Arabist and anti-Zionist. It sought to appeal to the educated Christian and Muslim strata by capitalizing on the Muslim-Arab character of the nation and the role of Britain in liberating that nation from the Turks. The two outstanding dates in the party's calendar were to be that celebrating the alliance between Sherif Husain and Britain and the birthday of the Prophet, seen as the founder of Arab unity.

Even though it was in Haifa that the party was founded, the Nazareth branch was the most active and had the largest membership. This branch was also successful in spreading the party's principles among most of the Christian and Muslim villages of the Nazareth sub-district[28] and in setting up a nationalist school and agricultural and civic committees. Jubran Kazma, a young Arab nationalist and trained agronomist, was the president of this branch, and during the last weeks of 1918 and in early 1919 he collaborated with Nassar in attempting to spread the influence of the party to the other main Palestinian towns. Their success lay mainly in maintaining a network of friendly contacts with other organizations, clubs and political currents in the major towns, and it was through this means that Arab nationalist circles in Haifa and the north became acquainted with organized public and secret nationalist societies in Jerusalem and Nablus so early on in the occupation. Nassar established a link with Jam'iyyat al-Ikha' wal-'Afaf (Association of Brotherhood and Purity) and with al-Muntada al-Adabi and al-Nadi al-'Arabi of Jerusalem, and concluded an arrangement with the latter club for its premises to be used for the meetings of the 'Arab Anglophile Party'[29] – a clear indication of the unity of purpose and political direction of the two organizations. The Jerusalem organizations were violently anti-Zionist, with somewhat varying degrees of animosity towards British rule. Nassar's choice fell on al-Nadi al-'Arabi, which had a large number of Husainis among its members and which demonstrated pro-British tendencies. Even so, Nassar regarded the Jerusalemites' attitudes as more negative vis-à-vis the British than he would have liked.[30]

In Haifa, where the membership continued to be limited to a small circle around Nassar and Mukhlis, the political orientation of the group was conservative; it adhered strictly to the military governor's request not to indulge in political, especially anti-Zionist, activities, and its emphasis was on economic and social development. The more youthful and zealous nationalist elements in Haifa and Nazareth, however, could not be confined to such a programme, and attempts were made to change the character and activities of the party in both localities. In February 1919, the Haifa branch of the party proposed to change its name to 'The Muslim-Christian Society', the better to express the political mood in the town, which was affected by the general trend towards unity with Arab Syria. This marked a move towards a more radical Arab position, but not an abandonment of the pro-British stance. The line of the party in Haifa was intended to reconcile the demands of both the Muslim youth and the francophone elements, who were wary of the call for political unity with Syria, which would ultimately mean Muslim rule under Faisal.

But the more explicitly pan-Arab Nazareth branch of the party favoured the name 'Southern Syrian Society' as a more appropriate title following the first Palestine Congress of the Muslim-Christian Associations, held in Jerusalem in January–February 1919, where the idea of unity with Syria as 'Southern Syria' had gained strong support.[31] In the event, neither name was adopted, but the party in Nazareth continued to act in accordance with the new political spirit. Damascus was referred to in their correspondence as 'our capital', and their contacts with al-Nadi al-'Arabi in Damascus, especially through Mu'in al-Madi, were close and friendly.

The pro-British elements in Haifa were not confined to this current of thought, and various Protestant merchants and entrepreneurs supported the British Administration wholeheartedly and publicly. Such was the case of the successful businessmen Teofil Boutagy and Sulaiman Nasif, whose background and economic interests drew them into the British orbit. While Boutagy exhibited genuine sympathy with the Arab movement and was active in it,[32] Nasif aspired to a political role at the national level and behaved in a condescending fashion towards the local organizations. A Protestant of Lebanese origin who had come to Palestine only with the British occupation, Nasif had previously been employed with the British in Egypt and the Sudan, and this experience, plus his entrepreneurial pragmatism, coloured his attitude towards the Administration. He was among the very few Arabs in Haifa who co-operated with British and Jewish investors in large-scale projects.[33]

The followers of the pro-British line in Haifa, whether members of the Anglophile Party or not, found it hard to reconcile their feelings with the pro-Zionist declarations of British policy.[34] After September 1919, the strength of the party dwindled and its active members began to look for different channels for their activities. The 'Economic Society' was established in June 1921, with much the same people as had been active around Najib Nassar. It had an elaborate programme of social, economic and labour reforms, but, again, it failed to recruit much support. Once more in July 1922, this same group were discussing the establishment of an Arab bank which did not materialize. Finally a 'Literary Circle' was founded as a branch of the Economic Society; its members were educated Christians and Muslims who were active in the political circles of their communities and were known for their (qualified) pro-British stand.[35]

Another organization in which these elements came together was the Carmel Masonic Lodge, part of the Grand Masonic Lodge of Scotland but not associated with a previous attempt in April 1922 to establish a branch of the Grand Lodge of Freemasons of Egypt in Palestine.[36] The Masonic lodges in Palestine, which were affiliated to British lodges and whose membership lists were entirely Arab, protested against this attempt. In Haifa, the Carmel Lodge remained active until the end of the Mandate and was under the influence of the Boutagy family (both father and son, Teofil and Emile, held the office of Master). The membership was predominantly Protestant, plus a few Greek Orthodox and Muslims. Rashid al-Hajj Ibrahim and the governor of Haifa, Symes, were members at one point.[37]

The best spokesman for the pro-British policy was the newspaper *al-Karmil*, especially through Najib Nassar's editorials during the first few years of the Administration, before he became disillusioned with Britain's lack of even-handedness. In spite of his attempts to accommodate and justify measures which were seen as unfavourable to the nationalist cause, he felt compelled to voice his group's apprehensions in regard to the Administration's pro-Zionist policy. His criticisms became progressively more strident and give a vivid picture of the frustrations experienced by moderate Palestinian Arab nationalists.[38]

The phase of national cohesion

Immediately after the British entry into Haifa the Arab notable and educated strata were galvanized into political action, following in the footsteps of Arab activists in the other major towns. The seriousness of the political change drew the different communities together. This happened in other cities too, but whereas in Jerusalem, Jaffa and Nablus the Arab political community – both Christian and Muslim – was represented in united Muslim-Christian Associations, in Haifa, with its Christian predominance, two separate societies emerged. One was the Muslim Association, led by the mufti and including secular elements which in fact had more weight in the community than the religious leadership. Among the Christians, each denomination set up a representative committee, headed by a clerical leader, all of which combined in an umbrella Christian Association chaired by Fu'ad Sa'd, the head of the Greek Catholic committee. During periods of intense national activity, however, proclamations from Haifa were issued under the combined name of 'The Muslim-Christian Association of Haifa', as in other towns.

Such public expressions of solidarity occurred in the period 1920–22, when the nationalist front in the town was very cohesive, and communications with the Executive Committee of the Palestine Congress came from one body represented by the chairmen of the Muslim and Christian associations.[39] The occupation by Britain, a Western and Christian power, led to a certain sense of relaxation, however tentative and cautious, among the Christians. The relative strength and independent outlook of the Christian community structures in Haifa at this stage allowed an equitable representation between religious and secular, Muslim and Christian, elements in the political arena. This was a confirmation of Haifa's heterogeneity and the need to maintain a *modus vivendi* among the various communities and socio-political currents, irrespective of long-standing reservations and communal differences. It was also an indication of the deep-seated apprehension among all sectors of the population towards a new ruling power which supported, however ambiguously, the dreaded Zionist policy.

Between January 1919 and June 1923, five Palestine Congresses took place, and Haifa's contribution to the national movement reflected the specific development of political orientations in the town. The First Congress in January–February 1919 came soon after the occupation, when many of the town's political leaders had not yet returned to their homes or had not yet recovered sufficiently from the impact of the war to absorb the significance of the British occupation. The two delegates from Haifa to that congress – the Muslim Hajj Ibrahim and the Greek Orthodox Iskandar Manassa – represented their own political positions and those of their immediate religious and socio-economic circle. Both had a strong commercial background and were staunchly pro-Arab, anti-Zionist and pro-British.[40] This was not exactly the general political mood among the Greek Catholic community led by their francophile bishop, Hajjar, however, nor did it express all the divergent political feelings among the Muslim community.

By December 1920, when delegates of the Muslim-Christian Associations met again in Haifa for the Third Congress, developments in the town had dramatically united the population behind the notable and upper-middle-class leadership in the uproar against Zionism. Events in Palestine as a whole, and activities and reactions in Haifa, accelerated the crystallization of this united front. Following the anti-Zionist demonstrations in Jerusalem in February 1920 and the outbreak of violence at the Nebi Musa pilgrimage in April, passions were roused in Haifa and the anti-Zionist movement took on a more active form. In February, over fifty Muslim and Christian leaders in the town sent a strongly worded letter to General Bols denouncing his statements on Zionism to the Jerusalem newspaper, *Mir'at al-Sharq*.[41] Two weeks later, the Chief Political Officer, Colonel Meinertzhagen, took it upon himself to drive home to the Haifa Arabs HMG's policy on Zionism.[42]

Even though, to the inexperienced eye of the military governor, the Arabs appeared to have acquiesced and accepted the policy with a good spirit, despite a number of veiled threats, a series of protests resulted from this affair which swept Arab Haifa into a stage of wider popular activity in its opposition to the Zionist policy. A peaceful demonstration scheduled for 8 March 1920 aroused great controversy in the town and exposed the depth of Arab feeling and the strength of the local Jewish community. By the time the demonstration finally took place, restrictions had been imposed on its itinerary and the slogans it carried, reflecting the influence exerted on the Acting Military Governor, Major Kinsman, by the local leaders of the Jewish Committee. These same leaders felt it their duty to help the Governor in 'his responsible work of maintaining order' by reporting on all aspects of the demonstration, even supplying him with samples of leaflets distributed and names of activists among the participants.[43] These actions did not go unnoticed by the Arabs and in turn they accused the Administration of being intimidated by the Jews. Such incidents increased the polarization of the Arab and Jewish communities and drew the Christians and Muslims closer together in public expressions of social and political solidarity.[44]

In an attempt to defuse the situation, the new High Commissioner, Sir Herbert Samuel, met representative notables of Haifa on 8 July 1920, and tried to calm their fears. This was part and parcel of Samuel's policy of gradually gaining the confidence of the communal leaders, providing them with social and economic benefits, and unobtrusively binding them to the system. Nevertheless, the anti-Zionist campaign in the press and at the public level continued unabated, and was reflected in the Third Palestine Congress, held in Haifa and at which it was strongly represented. The congress underlined the conservative outlook of the established leadership and their myopic approach to the Administration.[45] While Muslim-Christian unity and anti-Zionism were emphasized, self-government under British hegemony was called for. These resolutions received the approval of the pro-British current in the town, which had been strengthened by the fall of the Arab government in Damascus to the French earlier in the year. On the one hand, this event diminished Christian fears of Muslim domination, and on the other, it highlighted the vulnerability and isolation of the Palestinian Arabs. This isolation was felt particularly strongly by the large Greek Catholic community, who, while supporting France, found themselves under British rule in Palestine and now had to face increased anti-French feeling on the part of the local Muslims and Arab nationalists. Those same groups which, until a few months earlier, had been calling for union with Syria now turned their sights on internal solutions. For the next few years, the national movement in Haifa revealed two simultaneous tendencies: an enlarged and intensified opposition to Zionism which was beginning to identify Britain's role in bolder terms, and a growing need to assert a regional and independent line.

The anti-Zionist current was accelerated by the strengthened position of the Zionists and what was gradually perceived by the Arabs as British duplicity. Co-operation between organizations and members of the political community was at its height at this time. When the representative character of the communal associations was challenged by the opposition movement, they were given overwhelming popular support.[46] But what most cemented the Christian and Muslim communities was their shared experiences in the violent clashes when a Christian youth and a Muslim man were shot dead by the British police during an illegal demonstration against Secretary of State Churchill's visit to Palestine on 25 March 1921.[47] The brutality of the police action[48] embarrassed pro-British political circles and prepared the mood for a more radical orientation. At this stage, the Christian and Muslim Associations of Haifa were leading the movement of confrontation in opposition to the Balfour Declaration and went so far as to hold the demonstration even though it had been banned by the government. In an open letter to Churchill on the day of the ill-fated demonstration, *al-Karmil* wrote:

> Those of us who are thoughtful recognize Britain's purpose in maintaining its influence over the Arab lands. It is to transform Palestine into the port of Iraq, the Arabian Peninsula and India. It is to hold control over this bank of the Suez Canal. It is to exploit Iraqi oil and to establish British factories in Iraq and to create in the whole Arab region and Palestine a market for British goods. Thoughtful Arabs do not begrudge you this, but putting the port of the Arab countries in foreign [Zionist] hands so that they exploit our economic resources ...

Such outspokenness seemed to be more characteristic of Haifa political circles at this time than of those in other Palestinian cities. Both Christians and Muslims openly discussed political ideas, expectations and apprehensions.[49] It was not coincidental that, from that date on, more rigorous censorship was applied to the Arab press in Haifa.

The mounting anti-Zionist feeling intensified. Arab reaction to changes brought about by the Zionists, following the fresh wave of Jewish immigration, took the form of protests in the press and elsewhere against the infiltration of Bolshevism, gun-running, and the threat posed to the economic life of the community by the scale of immigration and land sales. The preferential treatment awarded the Zionists in respect of immigration and acquisition of land, monopolies and concessions was stated as the premise for British policy in Articles 4, 9, and 11 of the Mandate. It was in furtherance of these aims that the Civil Administration lifted the ban on land purchase in 1920 and initiated steps towards exploiting the country's natural resources through concessions. Arab reaction to the first attempts to implement this policy was immediate and sharp. In Haifa, the Rutenberg electrification concession (1921), the Athlit, Caesaria and Kabbara land concession (1924),[50] and the sand dunes in Haifa bought by the Shemen Company in 1920 directly touched the life and political awareness of the Arab inhabitants.[51] Politicized Arab circles were aware that, in addition to the economic consequences of these concessions, they established the principle of a Jewish right to formulate the direction of the country's development and to transfer state land into the inalienable ownership of the Jewish people. Such official support only supplemented other Zionist efforts in the private sector, for example the acquisition of the Marj Ibn 'Amir land from the Beirut merchant family Sursuk, and individual transactions in regard to residential quarters in the cities.

Arab recognition of these realities spurred political campaigns at the local and national level to oppose the electrification of Haifa through the Rutenberg concession, to highlight the plight of the Arab cultivators and bedouins living in the area of the Kabbara and Ard al-Raml concessions[52] and to mount an outcry against local personalities involved in land sales to Zionist organizations.

Most political circles in Haifa immediately concentrated on opposing concessions of government land situated to the south and east of the town, as well as private sales by absentee notables. The sand dunes near the Bat Galim settlement became a cause of local debate when the new settlers turned back Arab workers who had traditionally used the public sand on the beach for transporting to building sites; the conflict was exacerbated when the police enforced the new prohibition and prevented Arabs from using the beach sand.[53] Other concessions that preoccupied Haifa's press and political circles were the Caesaria concession to the south of Haifa and the marshy land to the east (Dastariyya), both granted to Zionist organizations for development.[54] Many of Haifa's politically vocal citizens were involved in negotiating with the central and local government in an attempt to nullify these concessions or at least to preserve the rights of their evicted inhabitants, which Wadi' Bustani, employed by the Arab Executive Committee, was to defend.[55]

Teofil Boutagy, Rashid al-Hajj Ibrahim and Najib Nassar were on the lookout, supplying the AE with information on local developments and reporting them in the press. The fact that important social and political personalities were also identified as selling land to Zionist organizations, such as the Maronite Khuri brothers, who sold their land in Yajur to the Shemen Company, aroused condemnation in the press. What worried the nationalist circles in Haifa was that the number of Arabs selling land to the Jews was growing and that the status of these influential individuals remained intact in spite of what was seen as their perfidy.[56] Such events were undermining the structure of the nationalist front, in whose policy the preservation of land in Arab hands was a major pillar.

Britain's immigration policy was justified by the government on the grounds of building up the economic base of the country, by importing both skilled individuals and capital.

> It was always realized that for a developing country such as Palestine, with very few local resources and a small population, an influx of both capital and labour was necessary and there was for long an endeavour to secure some sort of balance between them.[57]

However, the general Arab feeling in Haifa was that the Administration was successful neither in securing this balance nor in warding off the negative effects of the immigration. By 1921, Jewish immigration had become a politically sensitive issue which engaged public opinion and could produce popular discontent and possible disorder.[58] As already discussed in Chapter 8, the economic life of Haifa's Arabs was immediately affected by this influx. More than other towns, Haifa felt the immediate impact of the new immigrants, since many who disembarked there stayed on during this early period. Apart from the protest against Jewish immigration in principle, Arab objections to the resultant increase in the cost of living, the threat to Arab commercial activities, the usurpation of labour from Arab workers and the unfair distribution of public works rose with the growing number of immigrants.[59]

A further effect worried the Haifa Arabs: the infiltration of Communist elements among the new arrivals, with proselytizing ambitions. Early in 1920, with the arrival of 650 Jews from Russia, a good number of whom were committed Bolsheviks, unsuccessful attempts were made to attract Arab adherents to secret cells and to infiltrate the working classes by underground propaganda activities.[60] Their most prominent activity in Haifa was the May Day demonstration of 1921 and the circulation of a manifesto calling on Arab workmen to rise against the effendi class.[61] A large number of Communists were deported following this event, but Communist proclamations continued to be distributed, inciting the Arabs against British imperialism and exploitation by the rich notable class. This served only to intensify Arab bitterness, especially among the economically privileged classes, against Zionism, Jewish immigrants and even the Administration that provided them with a haven.[62]

Some members of the Administration linked these Communist activities to the Jewish labour movement, which encouraged dissension between peasants and landowners, while at the same time endorsing the establishment of illegal military structures.[63] In addition to the secret Jewish defence force, the Haganah, organized by Jabotinsky as early as 1919, certain unions of the labour movement were notorious for their arms smuggling. Such was the reputation of the Haifa carpenters' union, which was connected with the incident of arms caches smuggled in December 1921 to a Mr Rosenberg – a prominent member of the Jewish labour office in Haifa, who, when arrested, was attending a meeting which looked to the police very much like a Communist gathering.[64] In 1924 the War Office reported on other Jewish firms involved in arms running between Danzig and Palestine for the benefit of Communist organizations in the country.[65]

The issue of arming the Jewish colonies in the north had been the subject of public vexation among the Arabs since early in 1920 and was brought up at every protest against government policy. In Haifa these protests arose from incidents when Arab employees at the port accidentally discovered arms smuggled in with agricultural and building equipment; more significantly, while indicating a serious programme of arms stockpiling by the Zionists, the incidents inflamed Arab suspicions that similar previous activities had been successful. Nevertheless certain government circles were prepared to turn a blind, if not approving, eye on such activities. During a meeting at Government House, Jerusalem, on 8 December 1922, Dr Weizmann reported that he had expressed his concern to the Colonial Office.

> The CO had, however, assured him that there is no necessity for him to distress himself on this matter because the Jews had to defend themselves. The CO authorities gave him the impression that in their view this was a matter that needed no special action and was not to be altogether discouraged. Lord Balfour, Mr Churchill, Lloyd George, with all of whom he had spoken on the subject, treated the matter lightly, even jocosely.[66]

The public uproar became more urgent as Jews accused of smuggling or illegally possessing arms were often acquitted for lack of evidence, while Arabs convicted of much lesser crimes had harsh sentences passed on them.[67]

Such incidents further exacerbated the communal antagonisms between Arab and Jew, and while they drove the traditional leadership to feel more frustrated and impotent in regard to government policy, they certainly promoted ideas of militancy and revolt. Official political reports from Haifa in 1922, when the Administration felt it had established its grip on the country and the governor, Symes, seemed in control of the political currents in the city, indicated this exasperated mood among an increasing section of the public and the leadership:

> ... the Governor suspects that the party which is prepared to run risks is greater than it was last year and is also prepared to run greater risks than it cared to face a year ago and that there is an organization perhaps only known to a few of the leaders to control and wage definite conflict.[68]

Even if Arab antagonism was not immediately translated into violence, the ground was being prepared for the revolutionary potential that emerged at a later date. The common threat that such activities among the Jews engendered drew the Muslims and Christians closer in their campaigns against the joint enemy, and this convergence seriously disturbed the Zionists. As a result, the pro-Zionist 'Muslim National Society' of Haifa felt compelled to denounce the attitude of the Muslim and Christian Associations which had 'aggravated and agitated the population over an insignificant incident' which, they claimed, was used to spread anti-British propaganda.[69] Attempts to undermine the united front against Zionism, and the British policy of support for it, took various forms in addition to the formation of dissenting Arab parties. It was only after 1923, however, that these attacks and splits in the nationalist movement depleted its inner strength and arrested its development.

It was during the Fourth Palestine Congress, held on 29 May 1921, that the nationalist front experienced its first public split, which exposed its shaky foundations. The success of the Muslim-Christian united front encouraged the Haifa delegates, especially the Christians among them, to try for a more prominent and central role on the national political scene. On one level, the Christians attempted to press for a more important contribution, as implied in Najib Nassar's suggestion that the vice-chairmanship of the executive committee of the congress should be assigned to a Christian member, and in Fu'ad Sa'd's persistent attempts to have Bishop Hajjar appointed president of the delegation which was being sent to London to negotiate with the British government. On another level, the Haifa delegation, including its various Muslim members, felt secure enough to challenge Jerusalem's hegemony and to claim a more prominent role.[70] These attempts proved unsuccessful and only Fu'ad Sa'd was nominated from the Haifa Christians to join the delegation. The failure to secure for Haifa's Christian leadership, which was dominated by the Greek Catholics, the means of exercising political power beyond the traditional limits, diminished the involvement of that sector of the Haifa political community and added another element to the growing opposition front. The immediate reaction was that Fu'ad Sa'd, in protest, refused to join the delegation, of which he had been elected a member. These frustrated Christian groups gradually over the period 1922–3 distanced themselves from active political participation, especially after the circulation of pan-Islamic ideas by Muslims encouraged by the Kemalist victories in Turkey, which were viewed as a Muslim challenge to Christian-Western encroachment.[71] Nevertheless, the Christian community of Haifa as a whole remained adamantly and actively anti-Zionist.

After the congress, the northern opposition to Jerusalem, personified in 'Abdallah Mukhlis, Sulaiman al-Taji al-Faruqi (Ramleh), As'ad Shuqairi (Acre) and Hasan Shukri, found support among some of Haifa's Christian elements, who now shared with them a common antagonism towards Jerusalem. This situation encouraged a more public exposure of political differences at a time when a similar opposition movement had appeared in other parts of Palestine. As a result, the solidarity of the national political front was weakened by the insistence on control by the Jerusalem leadership, on the one hand, and by the attempts of the political circles in Haifa, specifically the Christians among them, to become independent of that leadership, on the other. Nevertheless, these cracks were still minute and, at least formally, Haifa's political leadership maintained some unity during the Fifth and Sixth

Congresses, held in August 1922 and June 1923. The nationalist front in Haifa was still able to win popular support for the boycott movement in 1923 against the two administrative attempts to provide the Arabs with self-governing institutions, the Legislative and Advisory Councils. By the end of the year, however, the challenges facing Muslim-Christian solidarity were further emphasized by the growing strength of the Zionist movement and the consolidation of the Mandate.

Notes

1. R. Storrs, *Orientations* (London, 1943), p. 320. During the last week of September 1918, a few days after the occupation of Haifa, Col. Ronald Storrs (later appointed military governor of Jerusalem) was despatched there by Allenby to establish the military administration.

2. *The Palestine News*, 7 November 1918. When the Hijaz Railway was extended to Haifa in November 1918, it was diverted from the approved route, which would have necessitated the demolition of one side of a mosque.

3. *The Palestine News*, 20 March 1919: in this issue, the 'organization of the Muslim Society Association, [which was] an educational and cultural institution [that] will take care of waqfs' was announced. Also, Ahmad al-Imam, secretary of the Muslim Association, to the Governor, ND, No. 289/1, 10 August 1928 (ISA 61/547). Al-Imam specified that Governor Stanton had approved the Association's licence on 31 March 1919, and that public gatherings had been held on the Association's premises since October 1919 (*al-Nafir*, 1 October 1919).

4. Military governors were met and seen off at gatherings where the mayor, the religious leader, Muhammad Murad, and the political spokesmen of the Muslim community, such as Ahmad al-Imam and 'Abdallah Mukhlis, expressed the feelings and aspirations of their community towards the British. *Al-Nafir*, 1 October 1919, and *The Palestine News*, 14 November and 19 December 1918.

5. Hasan Shukri to Herbert Samuel, 23 March 1920, and Herbert Samuel to Hasan Shukri, 26 March 1920 (ISA, 2/30 CS 5). Six other 'leading townsmen' joined Shukri in sending the congratulatory telegram: Najib 'Ammun (advocate), Mahmud Yasin, Salim Jahil, Husain Ahmad, Faris al-Yasin and Jamal Sadiq.

6. 'The Islamic Patriotic Society' was the English name this society gave itself, although it also called itself 'The Muslim National Society'. The Haifa branch was registered in November 1921 and its political line was pro-Zionist and pro-Administration.

7. Z. Vilnay, *Khaifa Be'avar Ve Bahoveh* (Haifa in the Past and the Future) (Tel-Aviv, 1936), p. 5.

8. As superintendent of stores for the Hijaz Railway central office in Haifa (Q Khuri, *Al-Dhikrayyat* (Memories) (Jerusalem, 1945), p. 235) and then employed by the local *waqf* Administration until he was dismissed by the SMC (*al-Yarmuk*, 13 November 1924).

9. Y. Porath, *The Emergence of the Palestinian Arab National Movement, 1918–1929* (London, 1974), pp. 145, 221. Intelligence reports during this period give contradictory information on his political alliances and orientations. In 1919 he had been active in the nationalist movement in Damascus, and in 1921 he was

reported to be supporting a Muslim-Jewish entente and to be in close contact with Kalvarisky. Report on the Fourth Arab Congress, 21 June 1921 (CO 733/13).

10. In 1921 he was appointed co-director of the Sahli *waqf* in Haifa (*al-Karmil*, 11 May 1921). He was also a member of the Muslim Association from its inception and later was active in the Young Men's Muslim Association. List of Societies (ISA 61/141).

11. Col. Waters-Taylor to Chief Administrator (OETA, South), 3 February 1919 (ISA 2/155 Pol 2185).

12. Report to Foreign Office, 8 November 1920 (PRO FO 371 628/1579/88).

13. Herbert Samuel to CO, Despatch 714 – Administrative Report for August 1922 (PRO CO 733/25).

14. E. P. Quigley (ADPS) to District Commandants of Police, 6 November 1919 (ISA 2/157).

15. Quigley ADPS (CID – Palestine Police) to ACS (P), Report on 'Moslem-Christian Associations in Palestine', 23 December 1920 (ISA 2/155 Pol 2185).

16 District Commandant of Police-Samaria to Director of Public Security, CID, 29 July 1922 (ISA 2/166 Pol 12). The Arabic name of this militant organization was not recorded. But one of its branches, opened in Nablus, carried the name 'al-Jam'iyya al-Rahiba' (The Fearful Society). Started by Hilmi Fityani, the aims of the society were reported as being 'to kill Britishers and Christians who were pro-British'.

17. See List of Palestinian Societies (ISA 61/152). The connection between members of this organization and earlier underground militant groups, such as the Black Hand, in Haifa in 1929 (*al-Karmil*, 10 December 1929) was reported by oral information (names withheld by request).

18. E. P. Quigley (ADPS) to District Commandants of Police, 6 November 1919 (ISA 2/157).

19. Protest submitted to the Military Government to be forwarded to General Bols, CA (OETA-South) by the representatives of the Muslim and Christian communities of Haifa, 27 February 1920 (ISA 2/30 CS 5) and 8 March 1920 (ISA 2/30 CS 5). Also see Correspondence on the protests and demonstrations in Haifa in reaction to Col. Meinertzhagen's address to representatives of Muslims and Christians in Haifa concerning HMG's policy with regard to Zionism. 3 March 1920 (ISA 2/155 Pol 2185), 6 March and 8 March 1920 (ISA 2/30 CS 5).

20. The military governor praised Bustani's services very highly in 1919 (*al-Nafir*, 1 October 1919). However, by 1920 his role in the nationalist movement was unfavourably viewed by the Administration and he was considered an agitator. Report of Fourth Arab Congress, 21 June 1922 (PRO CO 733/13).

21. Quoted in B. Wasserstein, *The British in Palestine: the Mandatory Government and the Arab–Jewish Conflict 1917–1929* (London, 1978), p. 174.

22. Report by Herbert Samuel to the Zionist Commission in London on 'Our Relations with the Authorities' (Cairo, 7 November 1919).

23. For the role played by Fu'ad Sa'd and Najib Nassar in promoting the nomination of Bishop Hajjar to the Palestinian delegation sent to Europe, see Report on the Christian-Muslim Delegation from Palestine to the UK, 22 July 1921 (PRO FO 371 E8441/8364/88).

24. Oral information, Hanna 'Asfour, Beirut, May 1974. See Report on the Muslim-Christian Delegation from Palestine to the UK, 22 July 1921 (PRO FO 371 E8441/8364/88).

25. *The Palestine News*, 28 November 1918.

26. I have in my possession the original documents and correspondence records of the Nazareth branch of 'al-Hizb al-'Arabi al-Muwali li-Britania', translated as 'The Arab Anglophile Party'. In a letter from Najib Nassar of 18 November 1918, dealing with a technical matter of membership, he intimates that this party had been in the making by him and a group of sympathizers before the British occupation.

27. Records of the meetings of 27 November 1918, 20 December 1918. J. Kazma to Military Governor, 10 December 1918.

28. The branches of the party in the villages were very active in explaining the dangers and significance of the Zionist activities in the rural areas of northern Palestine. Reports of party activities of the Haifa, Tiberias and Safad branches on 21, 22 and 23 December 1918.

29. For details on the make-up and ideology of these clubs, see Porath, *The Emergence*, pp. 74–9.

30. Report by Nassar to the Nazareth branch of the party at the meeting of 20 December 1918.

31. A.W. Kayyali, *Palestine: A Modern History* (London, 1978), pp. 60–63.

32. Teofil Boutagy to Khalil Sakakini (Sec. of Arab Executive Committee), 24 October 1923 (ISA 65/1 3589). From this correspondence it is clear that there was no love lost between Boutagy and Nassar, most probably because of a clash in ambitions.

33. Nasif's recent arrival in the country was often brought up by nationalist circles as proof of his lack of allegiance to the Palestine cause. This was especially emphasized when he agreed to serve on the Advisory Council in 1923 (*al-Karmil*, 9 June 1923), even though his name was not mentioned. He was in close contact with the Zionist Executive and relayed information about the Arab nationalist circles in an attempt to achieve recognition as a moderate politician (F. K. Kisch, *Palestine Diary* (London, 1938), p. 67). However, correspondence between Nasif and the Palestine Arab Executive on this role shows the bitterness between them. Nasif to Arab Executive, 7 March 1925 (ISA 65/1 3589). In business he was a partner in the Bonded Warehouses (1921) and the Haifa Chamber of Shipping (1932) and in the late 1920s he was awarded the Hamma concession (*al-Karmil*, 8 June 1929).

34. *Al-Karmil*, 2 July and 1 October 1921.

35. Political Report for April 1922 (PRO CO 733/21); *al-Karmil*, 5 July 1922; J. Bahri, *Tarikh Haifa* (History of Haifa) (Haifa, 1922), p. 30. The active members of the 'Literary Circle' were Ahmad al-Imam, 'Abdul-Rahman Ramadan, Yusif al-Khatib, Tawfiq Zaibaq, Rafiq Tamimi, Qaisar Khuri, Adib Jada' and Jamil Bahri.

36. Members of the Egyptian Lodge approached the HC in April 1922 to establish a branch in Jerusalem, but upon investigation by the CID and Col. Storrs, this request was refused. It transpired that the Egyptian Order was 'nothing more or less than part of the Arabic "Syrian Union Party" in Cairo and which is known to be a Zionist Organization, for the spread of its propa-

ganda throughout Arabia and the Near East.' P. B. Bramley (Director, Public Security) to ACS (Pol), 20 April 1922 (ISA 2/162). Also see Political Report for April 1922 (PRO CO 733/22).

37. *Al-Karmil*, 12 January 1924.

38. *Al-Karmil* issues of 1920–36. An article illustrating this condition was the editorial addressed to Secretary of State Churchill in the issue of 25 March 1921 (see note 47 below). The close contact between Nassar and the local administration is shown in the special interviews accorded to him by Symes (governor of Haifa 1920–25) concerning various local issues. Nassar abided by the governor's request to withhold or publish certain items of news. Symes to CS, 30 November 1922 (ISA 2/180).

39. *Al-Karmil*, 7 September 1921, and Correspondence of Executive Committee, 1 March 1921, 13–14 July 1922 (ISA 65/1 01058). Also see Public Proclamation to the Arab Nation from the Muslim-Christian Association of Haifa, on 11 July 1922 (ISA 65/1 01026).

40. The Haifa delegates joined some representatives from Jerusalem and those of Gaza in dissenting from some of the resolutions proclaimed by the congress. They did not approve the change of name from Palestine to Southern Syria, and wanted only a form of cultural union with Arab Syria while leaving the Palestine government independent and autonomous, with Britain as protector and Zionist immigration prohibited. See (ISA 2/155 Pol 2155) Reports on the Palestine Conference, 31 January and 25 February 1919.

41. Protest submitted to General Bols, CA (OETA(S)), 27 February 1920 (ISA 2/30 CS 5).

42. Col. Stanton to HQ (OETA (S)), 3 March 1920 (ISA 2/155 Pol 2185).

43. For reference on the demonstration of 8 March 1920, see ISA 2/30 CS 5 and ISA 2/155 Pol 2185.

44. Religious events such as the birth of the Prophet were celebrated by all communities as a national feast (*al-Karmil*, 30 November 1920). Also, when the prisoners accused of complicity in the Nebi Musa events were transported through Haifa to Acre prison, they were met by huge crowds cheering them as heroes (oral information, Wadi' Jabbur, Haifa, April 1975, and in J. 'Asfour, *Palestine: My Land, My Country, My Home* (Beirut, 1967), p. 59).

45. For references on the Third Palestine Congress, see pertinent files in ISA 65/1 01058; Porath, *The Emergence*, pp. 108–10; *al-Karmil*, 16 December 1920.

46. See Correspondence of the Christian and Muslim Associations of Haifa to the Executive Committee of the Palestine Arab Congress, 19 and 20 March 1921 (ISA 65/1 01058). Also see *al-Karmil*, 22 March 1921.

47. *Al-Karmil* expressed shock at the deaths on the streets of Haifa on 25 March 1921 and could not but criticize, however covertly, government practices. The solution proposed confirmed the conservative attitude of the paper and the political notables it represented. It advised the Arabs to strengthen their communal unity and to abide by the law (*al-Karmil*, 5 April 1921). Also see Bahri, *Haifa*, pp. 17–18.

48. The Commandant of Police was accused by many of the Haifa nationalists of having deliberately shot the two people at the demonstration. Iskandar Majdalani of Haifa reported having heard Bishop Hajjar level this accusation at the Commandant himself (oral information, Iskandar Majdalani, Haifa, May 1975).

Also, Mrs Moody reported in her diaries that 'Mr. Sinclair stopped the Haifa riots by a few well placed shots'. Moody Diaries, MSS Brit Emps 382, Box 1 File 2, entry for 28 July 1922 (Bodleian Library, Oxford).

49. CO to FO, February 1921 (PRO FO 371 E3882/35/88) and Report of June–July 1921 (PRO FO 371 E7618/35/88).

50. S of S to HC, 1 March 1921 (PRO FO 371 E2472/32/88). Also see B. J. Smith, *The Roots of Separatism in Palestine* (Syracuse, NY, 1993), Chapter 6, and A. H. Jader, 'Siyasat Tawzi' Imtiyazat al-Mashari' al-kabira fi-Filastin Ayyam al-Intidab' (Policy of Distributing Large Concessions during the Mandate), *Shu'un Falastiniyya*, March 1976, Vol. 55, p. 184.

51. This Arab awareness and the mounting protest in Haifa against these concessions and land sales were the subject of many Reports to the CO by the District Governor, Symes. Political Reports, December 1922 (PRO CO 733/41), June 1922 (PRO CO 733/23), G. S. Symes to CS, 30 November 1922 (ISA 2/180), CO to FO, Political Report, April 1923 (PRO FO 371 E5650/206/65).

52. For Rutenberg see Chapter 13; for Kabbara and Ard al-Raml see Chapter 14.

53. Teofil Boutagy to Khalil Sakakini, Secretary of Executive Committee, 24 October 1923 (ISA 65/1 3589); also *Jirab al-Kurdi*, 8 October 1923.

54. Confidential letter from Symes to CS, 30 November 1922, on his discussion with Najib Nassar on the Kabbara concession and the disturbed Arab public opinion on the subject (ISA 2/180). Teofil Boutagy to Khalil Sakakini, 4 October 1923 (ISA 65/1 3589).

55. For Bustani's role in defending the Arab claimants, see the correspondence on the subject, 1 March and 11 June 1923; 27 February, and 4 March, 13 June 1924; (ISA 2/231) .

56. *Al-Karmil*, 4 January 1922; 8 June 1929.

57. A. M. Hyamson, *Palestine Under the Mandate 1920–1948* (London, 1950), p. 73.

58. Report on the political situation to the FO for August 1921 (PRO FO 371 E9807/35/88).

59. *Al-Karmil*, 14 and 21 May 1921.

60. The early (1919–23) activities of Communist cells were carried out secretly in the town, and meetings were held at night under the trees on Mount Carmel (oral information, Pnina Weinhauss, Haifa, May 1975).

61. Report by Admiralty, March 1920 (PRO FO 371 E1223/164/44); CO to FO, 1 May 1921 (PRO FO 371 E888/35/88); Report from Dept. of Public Security, May 1923 (PRO CO 733/44).

62. For the Arab view on Communist activity in Palestine and its link to the Zionists and the British Administration, see *al-Karmil*, 5 and 25 May 1921, and *Jirab al-Kurdi*, 8 October 1923.

63. Report by E. Richmond on 'The present tendencies and dangers of the Jewish Labour Movement in Palestine', 30 June 1922 (PRO CO 733/39).

64. Report by District Governor, Haifa, 15 December 1921 (PRO CO 733/33).

65. War Office to FO, March 1924 (PRO FO 371 E2536/2536/65).

66. Memorandum on meeting at Government House, 8 December 1922 (PRO CO 733/41). This same official attitude concerning arms smuggled into Haifa

and Jaffa continued in 1925. American Consul at Haifa, Oscar Heizer, American Consular Reports, 30 April 1925.

67. For Arab protests, see Muslim-Christian Association to HC, 24 December 1921 (ISA 2/158).

68. Political Report for June 1922 (PRO CO 733/23).

69. Muslim National Society to Sir W. Deedes, 27 February 1922 (ISA 61/547).

70. For details of the Fourth Congress, see Report to CO, 21 June 1921 (PRO CO 733/13) and Report to FO, 22 July 1921 (PRO FO 371 E8441/8364/88).

71. See Political Reports for the Northern District for December 1921 (PRO CO 733/8), April 1922 (PRO CO 733/21), September 1923 (PRO FO 371 E9049/65).

13

The Phase of Political Fragmentation

Cleavages and splinter movements in the national front

The previous chapter has demonstrated how, during the early years of the British occupation, Arab opposition to the Zionist movement took precedence over other political sentiments and expressed itself in the creation of united national structures which rose above old inter-communal antagonisms. Anti-Zionist feeling created a political alliance among Haifa's heterogeneous population in spite of their diverse political orientations and attitudes. But the post-war developments which encouraged the formation of this front resulted, at the same time, in the emergence of a wide range of new political-social currents in the various strata of Haifa society. During the period of transition, up to 1923, the nascent Arab nationalist movement in the town faced problems resulting from its own social composition, from that of the society at large and from the political realities of the occupation. By 1923, when the Mandate was officially instituted,[1] when the Arab experiment in Syria had been defeated, when the ideologues of the broad national movement had been weakened and when the attempt at a united anti-Zionist front had momentarily expended itself, the stage was set for concentration upon local issues and the resultant splintering of the new-found unity. During the period 1923-9, political life in Haifa concentrated on the problems created by British policy and Zionist practices and their solution within the political society of the town itself as well as of Palestine. This situation limited the options and the room for manoeuvre and accelerated the process of internal diversification.

The cornerstone of dissension

The first signs of cleavage appeared in late 1921 with the establishment of the 'Islamic Patriotic Society' (IPS). This society gained the approval of the Administration in October 1921 for its stated object, namely, to work with the government and to promote good relations between the different sections of the country. The High Commissioner repeatedly expressed his opinion that these

> societies [the Muslim National Societies] owed their origins largely to the influence of Mr Kalvarisky of the Jewish Colonization Association, a Jewish member of the Advisory Council. He is convinced that their activities will prove of value in bringing together the Arab and Jewish communities.[2]

Hayyim M. Kalvarisky, the head of the Arab Department in the Zionist Executive, saw these societies as a means of promoting pro-Zionist propaganda in opposition to the Muslim-Christian organizations, and he provided the funds to run them until the latter part of 1923. Thereafter, as the Zionist Executive faced straitened circumstances and curtailed its financial support, the societies ceased to function.[3] Throughout their short life-span the Administration continued to be doubtful about their effectiveness because of their obvious financial dependence on the Zionists.

Branches of the society were opened in all the major towns of Palestine in the course of 1921, and those towns with the strongest opposition to Jerusalem produced the most active branches. Nevertheless, this opposition was not the only characteristic common to members of the society, nor were all Palestinian elements opposed to the Jerusalem leadership likely candidates for membership. The society was distinguished from all other political movements in Palestine by its vehement support of the Zionist movement and the principles it embodied, by its exclusively Muslim membership and its obvious anti-Christian bias, and by being made up of former political figures who had been excluded from the nationalist mainstream.

The make-up and role of the Haifa branch of the IPS reflected these characteristics better than any other branch, thanks to the contribution of Hasan Shukri, the mainstay of the society in Haifa. Shukri depended for his livelihood on his post as mayor, which he had held previously during the Ottoman regime. This source of income and prestige was suspended in April 1920 when he was dismissed by Colonel Stanton after sending a welcoming telegram to the new High Commissioner, Herbert Samuel, who was himself a Jew. The military governor took this step following pressure from the local 'Muslim-Christian Association'.[4] The dismissal rankled with Shukri, and alienated him further from the nationalist current in the town, which was, after all, Arab with strong Christian backing. He had sympathized with the Zionist movement prior to the occupation, and his sympathy could be allowed free expression now that the new Administration publicly sanctioned the movement. He was valued by the Zionists as an ally; regular subventions were paid to him until 1925,[5] and his case for a government post was pleaded by the Zionist Executive.[6] Shukri's family background, as the son-in-law of the wealthy landowner Mustafa Pasha al-Khalil, who, along with him, had close relations with the Zionist land-purchasing agencies, assured him of Zionist support.[7] For his part, Shukri loyally tried to further Zionist aims and to recruit supporters for the Zionists among the respected Muslim circles of Haifa.

Initially he was able to attract a number of Muslim dignitaries to join the Islamic Patriotic Society, all of whom stood to gain from associating with this type of dissident body. Hajj Khalil Taha, a respected Muslim merchant, even hosted the founding meeting on 15 November 1921. Another important figure who joined at this date and was elected chairman was Shaikh Yunis al-Khatib, former qadi of Mecca and in 1921 the representative of the *ulama* in Haifa.[8] Both these men had lost their previous influence over the Muslim community to new leaders associated with the nationalist movement, such as Hajj Ibrahim and Shaikh Murad. The society also appealed to members of the Abu Zaid family, which engaged in fishing and stevedoring business in partnership with the Renno family, also Muslim Arabs. The Zionist Executive had used the services of these families in the off-loading of goods and immigrants at the Haifa port, and in 1924 a formal agreement was concluded between them[9] – a partnership which in 1930 was instrumental in permitting the Salonica Jewish stevedores to acquire a footing in Haifa harbour.[10] In addition to the Arabs involved in this society, a Jewish associate of Kalvarisky, Saphir, who lived in Haifa, helped in the local organization.

Following the IPS's first public statement of 27 February 1922, condemning the agitation against the Zionist movement and the smuggling of arms,[11] the ranks split, and al-Khatib, who had not signed the statement, resigned.[12] Shukri thereafter assumed the leadership and continued with the society's stated policy until it petered out of existence in 1923. The membership remained small and had limited influence, the only well-known personalities being Taha and Shukri. The fact that such a society could be set up, however, clearly indicated the availability of elements among the local Muslim community who – primarily for personal and financial reasons – felt alienated by the Muslim nationalist current in the town and the Christian prominence in both the economic and the political arenas[13] – an anti-Christian bias which was now encouraged by officials and the Zionist authorities.[14] These elements became identified with the pro-Zionist, pro-Administration current in the town. Even though they were mostly Muslims to begin with, a few prominent Christians took the same line, men like Sulaiman Nasif, who solicited Zionist financial aid for the opposition newspaper *Mir'at al-Sharq* in 1923.[15] Supporters of this political position could always be found among both sectors of the Arab community; after 1923, however, it was a role performed more by individuals than by organized parties.

By the end of 1923, therefore, the political communities of Haifa were already in an advanced state of ideological disunity as a result of external influences as well as their own make-up. Zionist and British attempts to attract the interest of what they considered 'moderate' Arab elements were partially successful. The 'Islamic Patriotic Society' scored the first success for Zionist plans and forged the nucleus of a pro-Zionist group, which was later enlarged and strengthened by gradually coming to control the municipality. The Administration did not actively encourage the society, but it suited its purposes to have elements identified which it considered 'moderate' and 'reasonable', and which naturally supported the Mandate policy. In Haifa, the Administration contributed to the splintering of the national front by a deliberate policy of neutralizing the undecided and conservative elements within it. For this purpose, various means were used, not least economic and social incentives for employment,[16] educational opportunities, and repressive regulations. These latter, which gradually restricted the options for political expression in the town, ranged from press censorship to the Ordinance of Collective Responsibility[17] and the prohibition of any government employee from joining or contributing to the nationalist organizations.

Opposition party: a feature of national cleavage

The Jerusalem leadership also contributed to this splintering of the national forces in Haifa, by creating its own allies and spies within the political community, and so accelerating a polarization into the pro-Jerusalem current and its opposition.[18] Antagonism against the hegemony of the Jerusalem leadership was strong in Haifa and the northern districts and had been a latent force for some time before 1923. The northern political community had traditionally had its own leadership, which, until recently, had looked towards Beirut or even Damascus for guidance. The attitude which continued after separation from Syria sprang from the make-up of Haifa's literate and politically conscious strata. Family and economic relations were common between the northern towns and the Syrian cities, and this led to an exchange of ideas and political orientations. As we saw in Chapter 6, Haifa's Arab commercial community was enlarged during the 1920s by the advent of a substantial number of Damascene Muslim families and smaller numbers of Lebanese Christians, many of whom sought employment in the public sector. These new elements, whether Muslim or Christian, were even less inclined to follow the Jerusalem leadership.

Another feature was the strong personal animosity many of the northern political elites felt towards the southern leadership. It would be erroneous, however, to correlate the opposition movement with the pro-Zionist current among the Arab political community, or with the anti-nationalist or non-nationalist orientation of some of the traditional and even pro-Ottoman circles of the Arab leadership, as Porath seems to conclude.[19] Opposition was a characteristic and an expression of the northern political movement and included members of all political persuasions. Among Haifa's political leadership, the opposition camp was the largest, and was represented by people in the Arab nationalist movement like Mu'in al-Madi as well as individuals like Hasan Shukri who subscribed to a pro-Zionist policy. Opposition in Haifa, however, did not automatically mean alliance with the opposition in Jerusalem or complete concurrence with all political leaders of the opposition in the north. As has been reported by various members of Haifa's Muslim and Christian political circles, opposition was often against both factions of the Jerusalem conflict, the Husainis and the Nashashibis.[20]

The diverse political orientations and the personalization of ideo-logical struggles after 1923 led to the dismemberment of the fragile coalitions hastily concluded in the wake of the British occupation and the challenge posed by the transfer of sovereignty to a government supporting Zionist goals. Differences between political groups often degenerated into personal animosities which were made public and polarized supporters of individual leaders rather than the supporters of a political current or orientation. These differences created their own momentum and were exacerbated by long-standing communal, family, social and economic divisions, which were often particular to the situation in Haifa and to the changed conditions resulting from eco-nomic developments. In addition to the trend represented by Hasan Shukri and some of his associates (his supporters were not limited to those who came out publicly in favour of the Zionist policy), other political currents expressed themselves in the form of parties, associ-ations or groups influenced and led either by articulate or notable spokesmen or by political currents and orientations.

The opposition front, at the national level, organized itself into the Palestinian Arab National Party (PANP), which was convened in November 1923.[21] Haifa played a significant role in this, with 'Abdallah Mukhlis elected its secretary and *al-Karmil* becoming its mouthpiece in the north. The party's platform was very similar to that of the national-ists in the Arab Executive and the Muslim-Christian Association. In fact, it competed with the latter by taking a more extreme anti-Zionist stand against the Balfour Declaration. However, it opposed the policy of non-co-operation with the Administration and expressed its dis-satisfaction with the manner in which the political leadership had represented the Arab case. Its line was 'to receive from the government all that it is possible to receive and to make the strongest possible stand for those things which it has not yet been possible to secure.'[22] Although it demanded the establishment of a national government and an elected parliament, this was sought under British protection, a proviso held to demonstrate the party's moderate pragmatism. Sulaiman al-Taji al-Faruqi was elected president and As'ad Shuqairi, who joined it early in 1924, became its pillar in the north.

Notwithstanding the large number of Palestinian sympathizers with the opposition front, the PANP did not attract many members, especially in Haifa. Its platform was seen as deficient by such people as Sulaiman Nasif, who sought an organ which was even more favourable to the Administration and the Zionists.[23] Mu'in al-Madi also withheld his support, probably because the party's platform fell short of his proposal for achieving an appropriate representative legislative council via negotiations with the government. By 1924 however, it was clear that al-Madi was anxious to create his own nucleus of influence in his family seat of Ijzim, an agricultural town close to Haifa, together with a base in the city. For a long time the al-Madi family had persisted in expressing nationalist, anti-Zionist feelings, at a time when the Zionist-sponsored 'Associations for Village Co-operation' (Jam'iyyat ta' awun al-qura) were very active in the Nazareth region.[24]

The fact that some members of the PANP, especially in Jerusalem, had been previously associated with a sympathetic stand on Zionism, put off some would-be followers and affected the general attitude towards the party. More significant still was the lack of support shown by the Christian leadership of the town. Admittedly, the Christian community, in all its demonstrations, was still represented by the Christian Association, headed by Fu'ad Sa'd at the Palestine Congresses in 1922 and 1923, but its participation was becoming nominal only and a Christian withdrawal from the political arena was conspicuous. Officially, the Christian leadership remained noncommittal towards the new party, though there was general sympathy for its anti-Jerusalem position.[25] But various features caused the Christians to hold back, especially after what was seen as a setback during the Fourth Congress. The association of the PANP leader al-Faruqi with the newspaper al-Jami' a al-Islamiyya, which followed a strong Islamic line and often printed virulent articles on the subject, as well as the former religious status and persistent personal ambitions of the party's patron al-Shuqairi, caused the Christians considerable uneasiness. Even al-Karmil did not lend its whole-hearted support during the first year, and it was only in mid-1924 that Nassar embarked on his frontal attack on the Arab Executive and the Supreme Muslim Council. What aggravated the Christians' hypersensitive feelings even more was the fact that, while they regarded with apprehension the growing power of the SMC at the

expense of the AE and the possible Islamization of the national movement, the Kemalist achievements in Turkey, which were regarded in
Palestine as a victory for an Islamic nation, strengthened the status of
the pro-Ottoman conservative elites, many of whom were prominent in
the opposition movement.[26] Moreover, they felt that they would do
better if they were not identified with a party whose stand on Zionism
was, to say the least, suspect.

The two main supporters of the party in Haifa were Mukhlis and
Nassar, whose influence belied its lack of numerical strength. Most of
the party's views, which gradually became more radical, were issued
through its secretary, Mukhlis, and published in al-Karmil and in Mir'at
al-Sharq of Jerusalem. While active supporters were few, sympathizers
were many, and Haifa's political circles were tolerant of the strong
campaign mounted in al-Karmil by Faruqi, Shuqairi, Mukhlis and Nassar
against the SMC and its supporters in Haifa. Nassar remained consistent
in his basic political stand against Zionism and used the party to
strengthen his position, especially when he felt justified in attributing a
pro-Zionist approach to his opponents. This was the weapon he used
when attacking the AE's pro-Hashimite stand and its support for the
Anglo-Hijazi treaty in 1924.[27] In short, Nassar presented the party's
political platform from the perspective of his own deep personal commitment. His objections to the structure and activities of the SMC
stemmed from his perception that the Husaini leadership was attempting
to monopolize the national movement and its financial resources by
methods which led to popular confusion. The Jerusalem leaders, in his
view, lacked the attributes of leadership, which should be concerned
with the economic, social and educational well-being of their followers.[28]
This campaign grew more personal and bitter at times of intense
competition between the two fronts, as in 1926-7 during the activities
preceding the municipal elections, and in 1928-9 during the events
surrounding moves for reconciliation between the two parties and the
Seventh Palestine Congress, and prior to the bloody events of September
1929.

At the local level the party established an 'Association of Muslim
Youth',[29] but there are no records of its activities. Through al-Karmil
Nassar and Mukhlis exposed the position and allegiances of their
opponents, especially those active in the Muslim Association. The attack
on this society was no less vehement than that on the SMC and would
often cite its members' acts of perfidy, such as sales of land.[30] An
interesting development in Nassar's political orientation during this
period was his growing opposition to the British Administration. Initially,
his criticisms were limited to the Governor, Symes, whom he considered
unsympathetic to the Arabs, while recognizing him as a diligent officer
serving British policy. During the trying years of the economic de-

pression, 1926-8 (see Chapter 8), he became more direct in his attacks on the British occupation or 'colonization' and its methods of impoverishing the economy and aggravating the situation further by employing British personnel.[31]

For their part, the political circles in Haifa which supported the Jerusalem leadership reacted in a similar fashion, and this confirmed the earlier splintering of the united front. Embodied in the Muslim Association guided by Shaikh Muhammad Murad, this group saw itself as the steadfast upholder of the pristine nationalist demands of the Arab population. Acknowledging the signs of break-up in the nationalist front in Haifa, Ahmad al-Imam had made great efforts since 1920 to bring out a newspaper that would become the voice of the association. On 3 August 1924 al-Yarmuk was first published in Haifa.[32] Its introductory issue presented its purpose as being: 'to serve Palestine, the Arab East and Syria, by whose dismemberment the Arab and the Muslim countries have been negatively affected'. Among its main supporters were Rashid al-Hajj Ibrahim, 'Abd a-Rahman al-Hajj (mayor of Haifa following Shukri's dismissal), and Sulaiman al-Salah (president of the Muslim Association since 1924), as well as the mufti and Ahmad al-Imam. In addition to vilifying the members of the opposition, in particular Shuqairi, Mukhlis and Nassar, both personally and for their political views,[33] al-Yarmuk attempted to demonstrate that political life in Haifa was still dependent on the nationalists led by the Muslim Association, and that disruption was caused by the aberrant behaviour of just a few members of the opposition. To this end, the association attacked the campaign mounted by the opposition against the SMC, and organized a number of petitions against the PANP, which were sent to the Administration.[34] For its part, the Administration looked favourably on this process by which the nationalist front was being neutralized. In Haifa, Symes was anxious to emphasize to each and every party that they did not represent all sectors of the Arab community. His contempt for, and apprehension of, what he called 'the Effendi class' explain his harsh attitude towards the political leaders. When the Muslim Association called for a public meeting on 30 November 1923 in the Great Mosque to hear Musa Kazim al-Husaini, Symes prohibited the use of religious premises for political purposes.[35] This was a new limitation on the Muslim community, for whom the mosque had traditionally been a gathering place for all communal activities; no such prohibitions had been issued in 1920.

In a more constructive way, the Muslim Association, by projecting itself as the mainstream political current in Haifa, tried to impart confidence in itself and in the Jerusalem leadership. It continued to court all elements of the Arab community, officially to express solidarity with the Christian communities, and to take up the case of Arab workers and employees laid off by the Administration.[36] At the same time, it promoted the political positions assumed by the Arab Executive, praised the Hashimites, and accused Ibn Sa'ud of false patriotism.[37] The SMC elections in 1926 were also a subject of concern until the Jerusalem leadership succeeded in getting Murad reaffirmed as mufti. Clearly, in addition to local nationalist concerns such as land sales, the distribution of work opportunities and economic development, matters of Palestinian national interest also played an important part in the politics of this group.

The leaders associated with this political line were under no illusions about the strong opposition they faced in Haifa, whether expressed overtly or simply by withdrawal from the political scene, and they tried from early 1924 to work out a formula for reconciliation. They repeatedly called for changes in the procedures for electing representatives so that all sectors of the community should have a share in public decisions, and also for the unity of all nationalist elements.

In June and December 1924, two conferences, the first of the Arab press, held in Haifa, and the second of political leaders, held in Nablus, failed to achieve a settlement. Other meetings in Haifa between leaders of the opposition and local and national politicians supporting the AE met the same fate.[38] Many of al-Yarmuk's editorials bemoaned this situation, and would either bitterly attack the opposition or try to placate them and call for reconciliation. It was clear from the mood in Haifa, however, that these calls were merely gestures of political expedience, while none of the political elements were ready to meet in a single front. A wide spectrum of political orientations existed in Haifa at the time: those, like Shukri, in support of the Administration and its JNH policy; those in the PANP of Mukhlis and Nassar, who attempted to reconcile their support of the Administration with a rejection of its policy; those in the Muslim Association with its adamant rejection of the JNH policy and its administrative support; as well as the Christian leadership which supported the nationalist cause loosely, with an ambiguous attitude towards the Administration, and subordinated its political stance to what was viewed as sectarian interest. It took all these elements four years of estrangement and the shock of 1929 to reunite their forces.

Sectarian differences

The antagonism between these various political elements was leading towards a more introverted and insular ideological approach in Haifa. What was of most concern to the group involved in the Muslim Association was the issue of the local Muslim community, and its economic, social and political well-being. This was an inevitable result of the nature of the association, which at this stage was the only organization exclusively for the Muslim community and representing a nationalist-Islamic orientation. As already stated in Chapter 12, the association, through the influence of the mufti – who had been strengthened by his Jerusalem allies both as a religious and as a national figure[39] – and Ahmad al-Imam, had assumed a prominent role in the consolidated nationalist front which was active in the period 1918-23. It was natural that, when the other political forces in the town turned to alternative influential groupings, this association should turn back to its own community and supporters, and emphasize its main characteristic – its Islamic affiliation. This was further aggravated by a near-boycott by the Christian community of political life in the town and the leadership of the association. Furthermore, the association tried to project the image of being the only genuine nationalist organization free of financial links with foreigners, especially since its most outstanding member, Shaikh Murad, and the SMC administered the Muslim endowments (awqaf), the only administrative department fully controlled by Arabs.[40]

Ironically, it was precisely over this department that the Muslim community in Haifa splintered, a situation that assumed serious proportions in the 1930s. While the mufti and the president of the Muslim Association, along with a number of its board members, were supporters of the Jerusalem leadership and the SMC, other board members did not follow the same preferences, and most of them usually assumed a neutral, non-partisan approach. This was the case with the members of the Khalil family, who were always well-represented on the board. Their family connections with Hasan Shukri, however, prejudiced them in his favour, even though they had never come out publicly in support of his party. Furthermore, on various occasions they remained allied to members of the Muslim Association trend, as was the situation during the 1927 municipal elections, when Tawfiq al-Khalil ran on the ticket supported by the association, who opposed the nomination of Hasan Shukri.[41] By trying to remain independent of local partisanship, however, members of this family found themselves in confrontation with Jerusalem. In 1924 Ibrahim al-Khalil, the administrator of the local waqf, which was endowed by his family, undertook a large and economically remunerative project of building a mosque and stores in the heart of the eastern business quarter on the site of the Muslim cemetery.[42] There were indications that the project, which created one of the most valuable pieces of real estate owned by the Muslim community of Haifa, was not included under the central control of the SMC.[43] For this reason, the mosque waqf was called 'Istiqlal' (Independence), to indicate its freedom from SMC control, a fact not particularly appreciated by the Jerusalem leadership. Other members of the Muslim community shared al-Khalil's

attitude towards Jerusalem, most of them newly arrived from Damascus
and Beirut, and relatively wealthy merchants.

The isolation of the nationalist elements of the association gradually
engendered a somewhat intolerant approach towards the Christian
community. Initially this expressed itself in a zealous campaign to
promote everything that was Muslim for the good of the Muslim
community; the organization of Muslim commercial companies, Muslim
co-operatives, Muslim schools and hospitals, and the like.[44] But by 1925
it was turning into bitter attacks against the employment and promotion
of Christians by the Administration, and the right of Christians (i.e.
Nassar) to criticize the SMC or take part in the political life of the
country.[45] This was not a sustained policy, however, for at the same time
articles were published in the Muslim press condemning confessionalism
and advocating the dissolution of the Muslim and Christian Associations.[46] Some prominent Christian personalities in Haifa, such as
Bustani, retained close contacts with Muslim national circles. The
negative aspect of Muslim attitudes towards the other communities did
not spring from any premeditated principles; it was the result of socio-
economic changes during the period (see Part Three), as well as the effect
of guidance by leaders with narrow and limited perceptions. But attitudes
towards the Christians were a matter of policy for the 'Islamic Patriotic
Society', and it was they, encouraged by their Zionist allies, who started
the public outcry against the large number of Christians employed by the
government. The spirit of tolerance that had pervaded Christian-Muslim
relations prior to 1923 was clearly wearing thin, especially now that
economic pressures and the growth of a generation of better-educated
Muslim youth drew both communities into competition.

The Christian community itself was moving in a similar direction.
Following the brief experience of the consolidated political front during
1918–22, some Christian leaders, in particular Hajjar and Sa'd, were
left with a sense of having been betrayed and excluded from political
participation. Furthermore, they felt entitled, by virtue of a growing
commitment to the Arab cause among the Christians, to a prominent
role on the national scene. The Christian community of Haifa, in
particular, was adamant in asserting its role as the better-educated,
wealthier and numerically larger sector of the town's population, more
so than the Christian communities in other Palestinian cities. As noted
in Chapter 12, such ambitions were thwarted in the Fourth Palestine
Congress in May 1921, when the candidacy of Hajjar as a national
political leader was rejected. As a result, the Christians deliberately
kept themselves aloof from the political life of the town and concentrated
their energies on community development in the social and economic
fields, exploiting the Mandate's need for their skills, if only their knowledge of English and French.

A certain attitude became characteristic of the Christian leadership, especially the Catholics among them; they felt secure in the protection of the Mandate to the point of discarding compromises and becoming selective in their alliances with local movements and parties. The increasingly Muslim character of the Muslim political community isolated the Christian community and encouraged their political introversion. While the Christian Association maintained its official relations with the Arab Executive and responded to its calls for strikes against Balfour's visit to Palestine in April 1925, their contacts were reduced to the minimum and the sympathies of most of the leaders lay elsewhere. The Christian sympathy in general was with the opposition front, but without being committed to any one specific organization of that front. Nevertheless, Christian political circles persevered in their struggle against Zionism, considering it a threat to the Christian and the Arab character of Palestine. During the visits of prominent Haifa Christians to Europe in the 1920s and 1930s they were known to have presented the Arab case and reported on Zionist propaganda.[47]

This political fragmentation, however, was an expression of the bankruptcy of leadership among the elite. The cleavages reflected personal, family and regional ambitions and overshadowed issues of national concern. But the most significant aspect of the situation was the effect that two external and independent elements, the Zionist movement and the British Administration, had on the local political scene by influencing coalitions, alliances and rivalries. It was in the pre-election campaign for the Municipal Council, and the composition and behaviour of its members concerning vital local concerns, that the splintering of the national front was most clearly demonstrated.

Role of the Municipality

As noted in Chapter 5, the municipal councils which existed at the time of the British occupation were reinstated, unaltered in their composition and duties. Throughout the Mandate period, the official attitude towards local institutions stemmed from Britain's colonial experience,[48] with some concessions in deference to Zionist demands, such as allowing women's suffrage in the Jewish town of Tel-Aviv. Local institutions were subordinated to the British Administration and made dependent on the decisions of the Colonial Office. Whenever the issue of self-governing institutions was raised by the local populations and the Palestine Administration, the response from the Colonial Office fell within the general paternalistic colonial framework.[49] Moreover, various officers of the Administration looked with suspicion at any Arab attempt to achieve self-government, for fear of its being used by the political strata to strengthen their opposition to the Administration.[50]

However, a major aim of Sir Herbert Samuel's administration was to achieve the co-operation of the Arab population in the government of the country, which would entail their tacit approval of the Mandate policy. To this end, he tried to coax Arab leaders and potential leaders to participate in the Legislative and then the Advisory Councils, but to no avail. He was therefore left with municipal councils as the only other administrative means to provide the Arab communities with some form of self-governing institutions, however limited, and a platform for Arab-Jewish co-operation.

In the early period of his administration, Samuel proposed to the CO that no change in the municipalities be made until the Order-in-Council on nationality was promulgated, which would confer citizenship on legal immigrants and make them eligible to vote and stand for election. At the same time, the proportions of voters of different communities in the towns would have had time to shift in favour of the minority. The Ottoman electoral law, which was based on the *millet* system, provided for proportional representation according to communal size. This the HC considered to be unfair to minorities in the towns: for example, in Haifa, 'where Jews are in a small minority, it is possible that no Jews would be elected to the Municipality, although they constitute one of the most important elements in the town and vice versa at Tiberias'.[51] Changes in the electoral law to divide the municipal area into wards, with elections to be carried out on a geographical basis, were strongly opposed by the Arabs and by the Advisory Council when it was approached on the subject.[52] Municipal Councils, therefore, continued to be made up in proportion to the number of Muslims, Christians and Jews in the electorate, with representatives of minorities, as deemed necessary, appointed by the Administration. In Haifa, two Jewish council members, Shabatai Levy and Raffoul Hakim, were appointed by the Military Administration at the same time as a larger number of Jews and Christians than before were being employed in technical capacities by the Municipality.[53]

In December 1924, Sir Herbert Samuel wrote to the Secretary of State on the need to draw up a Municipal Amendment Ordinance for the purpose of regularizing the electoral procedure and holding elections. This request he presented again and again to the CO until, in his final report of 5 March 1925, he strongly criticized the British government for perpetuating the system of nominated municipalities, as started by the Military Administration, which resulted in the people having a far smaller share in the government than had been the case in Turkish times,[54] and, moreover, contravened the third article of the Mandate, which required that local autonomy should be encouraged.[55] The Colonial Office response argued that Arab co-operation in the government of the country depended on the Arabs themselves and not on concessions granted to them, while the peculiar circumstances in the mixed towns precluded municipal elections, since the government was not convinced that there was 'a genuine demand for the institution of Municipal elections except among that small class which would use such elections solely for the purpose of promoting anti-government feeling'. At the same time, the government was anxious, at this stage when the country was quiescent, to let matters rest and not to hold municipal elections which were bound to expose complex problems, such as the issue of granting citizenship to Jewish immigrants and the resultant change in the municipal electoral composition of the towns.[56] The CO clearly did not share the HC's approach on this matter. Sir Herbert Samuel was anxious to leave Palestine with some organs of democratic representation and to confirm his belief in Arab-Jewish co-operation, while the officials of the CO were convinced that the only form of municipal government to be tolerated by the Administration was the one in existence, and that changes would be considered only in order to benefit the Administration and aid it in its task.

In March 1926, the new High Commissioner, Lord Plumer, deemed the time and conditions opportune to resume municipal elections by the end of the year, with a higher tax qualification for voting eligibility in order to improve the quality of the electorate. As he put it in a confidential despatch to the Secretary of State:

> I have come to the conclusion that the rates previously suggested would have led too early to the enfranchisement of a number of persons who possess little sense of civic responsibility and only a small interest in the well fare [sic] of their respective towns.[57]

This suggestion was included in the Municipal Franchise Ordinance of 1926, which was still derived from the Ottoman Municipal Law of 1877, but differed in that the new voters and candidates were to be Palestinian citizens paying higher rates of taxation.[58] Arab reaction to the ordinance was critical of two main items: the rule governing eligibility for voting and nomination, which it was feared was intended to enfranchise the largest number of Jewish immigrants regardless of any previous criminal record,[59] and that regarding the appointment of the mayor by the governor. In Haifa there was the fear of having a non-Arab appointed mayor; at the same time, the two major political groups among the Muslims each had their own candidates for mayor. Elections took place in 22 towns between January and June 1927.

Even before this formal change in the composition of the municipalities, they had already been substantially changed by administrative interference, whether by dismissing members and/or whole councils or by imposing additional members on existing councils.[60] The Municipal Councils Validation Ordinance, enacted in February 1925, in addition to validating the acts of municipal councils appointed (or reaffirmed) since the British occupation, read:

> Pending the holding of municipal elections, the District Commissioner, with the approval of the High Commissioner, may nominate or suspend a municipal council or a president or any member thereof, and may replace a president or member who has been suspended.[61]

These prerogatives were put to use by the local British administration. Haifa provides a cogent example of this process.

Working of the Haifa Municipality

By 1927, a number of major confrontations had occurred between the Haifa Municipal Council and the local administration. From the early 1920s, although Arab nationalists and moderates held prominent positions in the Municipality, it was gradually being manipulated by the Administration and the Zionists with the hope of serving Zionist plans for the town. It was also to become the arena for inter-Arab political competition and an instrument of national fragmentation.

The first interference in the affairs of the Municipality was the dismissal of its mayor, Hasan Shukri, by the military governor in 1920 (see p. 183 above). This action also confirmed the political role that the local council exercised in the life of the city and was a triumph for the nationalist elements. Even though he sympathized with the Arab nationalist current, 'Abdul Rahman al-Hajj was appointed to succeed Shukri; however, his power and independence were curbed and changes were made in spite of his objections. The Administration was adamant that the plans for the town's development along the lines it saw fit should be carried out. This did not happen without resistance from the mayor and the other members of the Council who were, on the whole, supporters of the anti-Zionist camp.

Although there must have been at least four Muslim, four Christian and two Jewish members in the first Municipality, the only names that can be traced among the Muslims are the mayor al-Hajj, 'Aziz Miqati and Amin 'Abdul-Hadi, all of whom were members of the Muslim Association. Iskandar Barghash, Yusif Ishaq and Ilyas Mansur were Christian members representing the three main denominations and were generally sympathetic to the national, anti-Zionist current. Of the two Jewish members, Shabatai Levy, an important employee of PICA and a land agent, was of Turkish origin, and Raffoul Hakim was a Sephardic merchant; both of them knew Arabic and maintained social relations with Arabs along with their strong ties with Zionist institutions.

The most serious challenge the council members faced was the electrification of Haifa through the Rutenberg concession and its endorsement by the Administration. It gradually dawned on the active political groups in Haifa that the Administration was intent on having Rutenberg as the sole provider of electricity to Haifa. As early as 1919, Fu'ad Sa'd had approached the military governor with a proposal for a 40-year concession to light Haifa electrically, but his request was not considered seriously by the government.[62] Another attempt was made by Teofil Boutagy in December 1922 and transferred by the District Governor, Symes, to the Chief Secretary for consideration; it met the same fate.[63] This makes it clear that neither the Arab population nor the local British administrators were fully aware of the significance of the monopoly granted to Rutenberg and the government's total commitment to the 1921 concession, which gave him monopolistic rights over the supply of electric power over the whole of Palestine (apart from Jerusalem). The intention to grant Rutenberg the concession had been communicated to the Haifa Municipality during the HC's first visit to the town. The immediate reaction was negative, but no further steps were taken to implement the project and Arab protests therefore died out. The obvious reluctance to consider other projects or initiate one by the Administration kept public opinion on the alert, particularly after the political uproar in Jaffa caused by a similar problem.

Meanwhile, Haifa's growing community and its improved economic situation created a more urgent demand for electricity. The longer it took to be installed in Haifa, the weaker became the objections to Rutenberg, as no other company was allowed to put forward a project. The two above-mentioned proposals were not the only ones from the private sector in Haifa, but as the governor, Symes, commented in December 1922, 'I have had to turn a deaf ear, or to discourage, tentative proposals made to me and to the Municipality by private individuals'.[64] Since it was stipulated in the 1921 concession that the lighting project did not need to come into operation until 1923, during which time Rutenberg should have formed his company, local attempts at similar development were put off until then. The decision to hold off local proposals came direct from London and was fully endorsed by the HC, whose commitment to the success of the Jewish concession went even deeper than that of the CO.[65]

In order to expedite municipal participation in the project and to ensure the success of the concession, the HC put forward a draft ordinance authorizing the raising of loans for municipal purposes on the security of municipal property and revenue, especially in view of the proposed participation of the major towns in the electric lighting schemes.[66] However, the Administration was not ready to go further in its political support of the Zionist project and refused to endorse the ordinance, though the CO pointed out to the Anglo-Egyptian Bank, which was providing the loans, that Rutenberg's project would be adequate security without further government guarantee.[67] Apart from the financial aspects, the CO and the Administration in Jerusalem worked closely with Rutenberg to ensure the success of his project and its acceptance by the Arab municipalities; draft agreements between these municipalities and Rutenberg were drawn up by the Jewish concessionaire and the Administration and approved by the CO.

In spite of Symes' persistent attempts, starting in November 1921, to contact Rutenberg in order to hasten the execution of the project, it was only in mid-March 1923 that Rutenberg visited Haifa and invited its Municipality to participate in his plans. By that time anti-Zionist feeling in the town had somewhat quietened down and Arab economic prospects had become more promising. Nevertheless, the District Governor was unable to persuade the majority of the Municipal Council (i.e. the Arab members) to enter into discussion with him. They admitted that their motives were political, based on their belief that a subsidiary agreement between the Municipality and Rutenberg would imply Arab recognition of the validity of his larger concessions to harness the Jordan-Yarmuk waters. Nevertheless, it was clear to the governor that certain elements, 'the more progressive among the local – including of course the Jewish population', were amenable to further discussion, and that, if matters were allowed to rest for a while, public opinion too would have changed.[68]

Between March 1923 and November 1925 the controversy over the Rutenberg scheme consumed the political life of the town and made public the differences and dilemmas of the supporters of the various ideologies. While opposition to the same scheme in Jaffa became a campaign carried out in the mosques and streets by the intense nationalist elements in the town against their opponents in the Municipality,[69] in Haifa the committed nationalists were represented by the mayor and certain members of the Municipal Council. Initially, the Muslim Association endorsed the position of the Municipality by organizing public protests and the signing of petitions. Most sectors of the community, Muslims and Christians, landowners, merchants, professional people and craftsmen, were represented in protests to the Municipality, demanding a legal end to the concession.[70] Arab public opinion, at this stage, as recorded in the local press, diverged from the official attitude towards the powers and role of the Municipality. Naively, the Arabs regarded the Municipality as an independent democratic institution which was protected from government interference.[71] However, it was precisely in regard to this independence that the Arabs of Haifa were made to face up to the inadequacy of their own leadership and the meaning of administrative controls.

Unlike Jaffa, where the Arab Municipal Council took the decision to participate in the Rutenberg scheme, in Haifa the decision was taken by the local administration and made to look as though it was an independent decision of the council. Nevertheless, this did not mean that all members of the Municipal Council supported the nationalist call for a boycott. Clearly the mayor, at least, maintained an adamant rejection of the project, and officially all the other Arab councillors followed suit.[72] But differences among them were emerging, especially in 1924-5 when the opposition to the Jerusalem leadership was also evolving. In addition, the attitude of many of the councillors, both Muslim and Christian, towards this dispute was individualistic and lacked any sense of socio-national consciousness and organization. In most instances, being a councillor carried with it social prestige and a means of economic betterment, and if an individual's attitude transcended his personal ambitions, it would still stop at loyalty to his religious sect or socio-economic class.[73] Such behaviour, at these early stages in the search for a national identity, was doubly detrimental to the already weakened nationalist front.

By 1925, the Muslim Association had its own doubts about the role played by the Arab councillors in the matter of the Rutenberg concession.[74] The Christian councillors were obviously in a dilemma. They opposed a project which was nationally labelled as a Zionist enterprise, but their economic interests (and they were all merchants) dictated a pragmatic approach. It should also be remembered that, as noted above, the Christians as a community had at this time withdrawn somewhat from the political scene, while their attitude had become more accommodating towards the Administration and less tolerant of the nationalist Muslim current. Even though the debates on the subject in the Municipality were held in secret, Arab political circles were informed of the positions taken by the Arab councillors. It became clear that the Christian members took a feeble, non-committal position, while the Muslim members, apart from the mayor, did not present any significant opposition either. The attitude of the Muslims was a cause of recrimination in the community, since they were aligned to the nationalist group in the town represented by the Muslim Association.[75] The controversy gave rise to a political conflict between the opposing camps, and a race by each side to prove its followers' adherence to nationalist principles while attacking members in the opponents' group. Al-Yarmuk, while it constantly supported the Muslim members of the council, still criticized – though without providing names – the other Arab members who stood in fear of the Administration. When it became clear that the project was going through, it laid the blame on public opinion as represented by the Municipality.[76] Najib Nassar, on the other hand, mounted his attack on the Muslim Association for its support of the Muslim councillors, and because its officials, especially the mufti, were trying at this critical period to placate the Administration by holding

farewell parties for the departing governor, Symes.[77] When the laying
of the transmission cables finally started he besought the Municipality
and its mayor to desist from using the temporary disagreements in the
nationalist movement to satisfy the rapacity of a few rich land agents
(*samasira*) and for the sake of luxuries.[78]

Despite all this political activity, the execution of the Rutenberg
project in Haifa was not altogether in the hands of the Municipality.
Even though its public approval was sought and its denial delayed the
project's completion, the preparatory work for erecting the poles in the
streets had been started on the orders of the governor alone while the
discussions were still continuing. After Symes and his assistant (Eric
Mills), and after June 1925 the new governor, Albert Abramson, and his
assistant (Edward Keith-Roach), had held numerous discussions and
meetings with the Council, agreement was reached, on a tentative
basis, to light the town, while a committee was formed to study the
project further.[79] According to Keith-Roach, the method used to force
the Municipal Council to abide by the concession was that proposed by
him to Abramson, namely, to refuse to sanction the purchase of oil for
street lamps from a certain date, and to instruct Rutenberg to turn on
the current from that date without formal agreement.[80] This was done
and the agreement held.

This precedent of administrative interference became a constant
feature after 1925. When the Greek Catholic councillor Yusif Ishaq
died in early 1926, Abramson appointed Ibrahim Sahyoun in his stead
without consulting the community, who for their part had nominated
Khalil Sanbar for the position.[81] When they objected to this arbitrary
practice, the governor informed them that appointment by him was all
that was legally required. By this time, political circles in Haifa had
become more critical of administrative measures to incapacitate the
Municipality. In June 1926, a project, again by Rutenberg, to supply
Haifa with an electric transport system between the town and the top
of Mount Carmel was discussed in the Municipality. The manner in
which the project was brought to the attention of the council was by
the governor informally introducing the subject as a *fait accompli*, with
the only decision to be made by the Municipality being whether it
should be built in the eastern or western part of the town.[82] Although
the project did not materialize, events like this drew the attention of the
Arabs to the rights the Administration was assuming over the Municipality in various fields and the methods it used for that purpose.

Municipal elections and political manipulation

The municipal elections of 1927 were another step in the process of
eroding the authority of the Municipal Council. It was at this stage that

the Zionist elements in the town took a more public role in manipulating local politics in the interests of the Jewish community and Zionist plans for the town. Furthermore, these elections and the campaign that preceded them came at the height of the conflict between the Muslim political groups, especially between the supporters and opponents of the SMC, and gave them the chance to use their differences as weapons in the campaign, further increasing the fragmentation of the community's national front.

After December 1926, when the governor appointed an electoral committee to draw up the voting list for the Haifa municipal area,[83] the campaign sprang into action. In all, 4,590 people were registered to vote, 3,771 of them Arabs and 819 Jews.[84] Among the Arabs, the Muslims had the highest number of voters, larger than all the Christian voters combined; the Greek Catholics came next, followed by an equal number of Greek Orthodox and Maronites.[85] Among the nationalists, the Muslim Association nominated Tawfiq al-Khalil, 'Abdul Rahman al-Hajj (the incumbent mayor), Sulaiman al-Salah and Rashid al-Hajj Ibrahim, and the opposition group nominated Amin 'Abdul-Hadi, Hasan Shukri (the ex-mayor), 'Uthman al-Khamra and 'Abdallah Mukhlis for four Muslim places.[86] Among the Christians, eleven candidates were nominated, also for four places,[87] while the Jewish candidates, Shabatai Levy and David HaCohen, ran uncontested.[88]

The chances of the Muslim nationalist candidates were slim from the outset, because of the convergence of opposing elements from all sectors of the community against them. On the one hand, it suited the Administration to have the nationalist current weakened, especially if it was denied control of an institution like the Municipality that could recruit opposition on a popular level. On the other hand, the local opponents of the nationalists, whether moderate Muslims, Christians or Zionists, in spite of their inherent and tactical differences, joined in the same campaign to defeat the candidates of the Muslim Association. For their part the Muslim nationalist candidates were not totally united, nor did they run on a single ballot. For example, as noted already, though Tawfiq al-Khalil ran as a candidate of the Muslim Association, his allegiance to the Jerusalem SMC and his opposition to the candidacy of Hasan Shukri were suspect. It was tacitly understood in the town that the Khalil family supported Shukri; socio-political alliances were still made very much along family lines.[89] Furthermore, the platform that the nationalists supported was the same as that of the SMC and the Arab Executive in Jerusalem, which refused to take into consideration the changed composition, in size and social characteristics, of the population and the altered economic conditions, which demanded innovative approaches and policies. In Haifa specifically, the developments of the preceding ten years had drastically altered both the human make-up and the economy of the town, particularly as regards the minorities. Unlike Jerusalem, where the nationalist leadership hoped to avert the possible defeat of their candidates by attempting to confine the elections within each religious community,[90] this move would not have helped in Haifa. The Christians stood as one bloc against the Muslim Association, a position which was duplicated by the Jews.

The Christians, for their part, while voting together for the non-Christian candidates, differed among themselves in their votes for members of their own community. However much the Christian leadership might try to present a communal united front, the new stratum of wealthy entrepreneurs and ambitious merchants had a mind of its own on the running of the elections.[91] The various Christian communities were showing signs of the clerical leadership's control weakening in relation to the emerging merchant class, whose alliances were growing beyond the confines of their *millets*. Two of the outstanding new Christian figures who were destined to affect the direction of the Municipality were the Greek Orthodox Mikha'il Tuma and the Greek Catholic Ibrahim Sahyoun. Both ambitious merchants had grown very wealthy during the early 1920s through the sale of land[92] and investment in the building industry. At the same time, they retained both their traditional grain trade and their social prestige within their communities (see Chapter 3).

All the Christian candidates in the 1927 elections were from the emerging merchant class, and reflected its social characteristics. In addition to being hyper-conscious of their religious-social affiliation, the Christian merchants were very anxious for the continuation of the economic conditions which the British Administration had brought, and they actively defended their particular interests by the most reactionary reasoning.[93] Though the Muslim candidates shared these characteristics, they all came from older established families and had not acquired the rapid wealth accumulated by some of the Christians. Members of the newly wealthy Muslim entrepreneurial class achieved prominence in the second elected Municipality under the Mandate, which took office in 1934 (see Chapter 14).

The large number of Christian candidates gave rise to an intense election campaign within the Christian community – and one which deteriorated into a family and personal leadership (*za'ama*) struggle.[94] This promoted the cult of personality, of individual economic and social prowess, a trait developed to unprecedented proportions among the Christian leadership. Even though in essence the campaign among the Muslims was also carried out on the basis of support for the individual, his family and his network of patronage, it was projected as a nationalist struggle. The Christian struggle, on the other hand, was dictated by social, economic and also latent political motives, an impression confirmed by the fact that very few of the Christian candidates had previously been associated with nationalist activities in the town, and also by the recent lack of political commitment on the part of their community as a whole.

The election also revealed the changes which had taken place in the Jewish community in Haifa. Since 1923, it had grown in size and, more significantly, in economic and political strength. The spread of Jewish quarters, surrounding the Arab areas, and the extension of the Jewish economic presence in the market had become a tangible reality (see Chapters 4 and 14). Furthermore, the Administration's promotion of Jewish economic and political assets, such as its policy towards Jewish industrial projects, Jewish labour and Jewish participation in the Municipal Council, all contributed to the changing fortunes of the community.

These characteristics were reflected in the attitude towards the 1927 elections. Even though various voices in the Hadar HaCarmel local council had suggested in 1926 the creation of a separate Jewish municipality on the model of Tel-Aviv, which had split from Jaffa, the arguments against separation and for the introduction of organized Jewish influence into the municipality prevailed. The way in which the Jewish candidates were elected uncontested was a measure of the community's cohesiveness and discipline. Shabatai Levy, a Sephardic Jew of moderate Zionist leanings, and David HaCohen, an Ashkenazi Jew, a labour Zionist and an administrator in Solel Boneh, were chosen after a process of deliberation in the community organizations and with the help of a special 'Va'ad Leumi' (Jewish National Council) committee sent from Jerusalem for the purpose.[95] In addition to the aim of presenting a strong united front, the Jewish community intended, by this method, to weaken the chances of opposition from the Arab sector; it precluded the possibility of the Arabs dissipating Jewish votes by striking separate agreements with opposing candidates. The two candidates were also chosen because of their ability to reach compromises with the Arab councillors while representing the two extremes of Zionist demands, the minimum as represented by Levy, and the maximum by the stance of HaCohen.

The next step in this direction was for the Jewish political elements to support Arabs who would be likely to come to terms with their general requests. The Zionists' search for allies in Arab political circles in Haifa was not unsuccessful, as illustrated by their experience with the Islamic Patriotic Society and other organizations. The Zionist Executive tried to persuade the Administration to recognize these allies and recompense them for their support. Early in 1923 the head of the Zionist Executive tried to impress upon the Chief Secretary the necessity of giving public appointments to two supporters of Zionist policy in Haifa: Muhammad Sha'ban, ex-mukhtar of the eastern quarter, and

Hasan Shukri, both of whom had lost their posts because of their unpopular political views.[96] When the opportunity presented itself in 1927, Shukri – at the head of a list of supporters, members affiliated to the Arab political opposition – was supported by Jewish political elements, and thus they were assured of a unanimous Jewish vote. It was important, from the Jewish point of view, not only to secure the mayoralty for Shukri, but to ensure the exclusion of the anti-Zionist mayor, 'Abdul-Rahman al-Hajj, and councillors Rashid al-Hajj Ibrahim and Sulaiman al-Salah, who supported his political line.[97]

Even though the other candidates who ran with Shukri on the opposition platform – al-Khamra, 'Abdul-Hadi and Mukhlis – did not share his pro-Zionist feelings, they were considered acceptable by the Zionists because of their opposition to the Muslim Association. Since 1923, the opposition groups, while still maintaining a belligerent attitude towards the Zionist movement, had turned the venom of their attacks against the extreme nationalists, and consequently by implication became partners with the Zionists in the same struggle. Even Shukri, whose pro-Zionist history went back a long way, could not run and win on a pro-Zionist platform, however. He was promoted by *al-Karmil* as a moderate opposition leader, endowed with the skills of compromise and capable of reconciling the good of the Municipality and the people with the wishes of the Administration.[98] The programme that he and his supporting candidates promised dealt mostly with civic improvements for the town, with only cursory reference to political matters. Even in its campaign against the SMC and the Muslim Association, the opposition confined its attacks on its opponents to their administrative and economic inefficiencies and their sectarian policy.[99]

The results of the elections were predictable.[100] All the prominent nationalist Muslims were defeated, and Tawfiq al-Khalil was the only one of the Muslim Association candidates to win. 'Abdallah Mukhlis, however, was the only opposition candidate to lose, demonstrating that, in the last resort, family and economic influences were the determinants of success. Among the Christians, the elected councillors – Khuri, Sahyoun, Abyad and Tuma – belonged to the enriched merchant class. Hasan Shukri was appointed mayor and Ibrahim Sahyoun deputy mayor.

The significance of the outcome on Arab political life was manifold. On one level, it meant the eclipse of the vocal nationalist current as an elite political class. Its leaders were deprived of the only administrative organ they controlled, and their uncompromising attitude hardened. At the same time, this situation gave popular leaders a chance to encourage the development of community organizations such as the Young Men's Muslim Association (YMMA).[101] On another level, it meant the emergence in the town of new socio-political forces which saw the

Municipality as a means to further their individual and group objectives. The attitude of the merchants who already belonged to the council was reinforced by the mentality of the high-powered and economically motivated new members, both Muslim and Christian, who were pragmatic businessmen rather than politicians and resented the Jerusalem leadership's political influence. This attitude, of course, found a positive echo among the Jewish and pro-Zionist members of the council. It also fell in with the Administration's initiative to curb Arab nationalist feelings. The electoral process highlighted the fragmentation of the national front, and the council which emerged from it was the type of organ that the Administration was able to manipulate.

The attitude of the Arab councillors was moulded by the spirit of their class and its prejudices. Until the municipal elections of 1934, most of these same councillors remained in their posts without further elections – another example of administrative manipulation. Since the 1927 elected councils had fallen in smoothly with the Administration's policy, in 1930, when new elections should have taken place, it was considered undesirable in view of 'present circumstances to hold municipal elections throughout the country'.[102] This sense of permanence bolstered their self-confidence, and gave them the opportunity to view municipal affairs from their individual and class self-interest. Their conservatism was compounded by inexperience and ignorance. Improvements entailing financial expense were resisted strongly, especially when such projects would have changed the socio-economic balance. It is interesting to note that the Oriental Jewish councillor Levy, whose family had been settled in Haifa for a long time, sided with the more commercially oriented Christian councillors on matters relating to wage increases and improvement in labour conditions, while the Muslim members, whose sympathy was with the Arab – mostly Muslim – municipal labour, sought reform, however moderate. It was, however, the labour councillor, HaCohen, who demanded large wage increases for Arab workers in an attempt to create conditions which would satisfy the claims of labour Zionists that Jewish workers would be able to conquer the labour market only if pay and work conditions were improved.[103]

The greatest change resulting from the elections was the unprecedentedly powerful position acquired by the Zionist vote in the town, through both the Muslim mayor and the Jewish councillors. Political realities imposed on the other opposition members a tacit acceptance of, and accommodation to, the new Jewish strength. The Jewish councillors were thus able to effect great improvements in the status of their community. For one thing, the Hebrew language was introduced as a third medium (in addition to English and Arabic) for council meetings, and all Municipality proclamations were translated and printed in both

Arabic and Hebrew. Even though this came in gradually, since both Jewish councillors spoke Arabic, it was the first step towards giving a dual character to the Municipality and it familiarized the population with these changes. In any case, it was a necessary change, since a much larger number of Jews, some of whom did not speak Arabic, were employed at the Municipality through the efforts of the new mayor.[104]

While Shukri was the Zionists' man in the Municipality and supported their proposals, the other Arab councillors, especially the Christians, were far from co-operative when it came to projects benefiting purely Jewish areas. During the 1928 financial crisis in the Zionist Organization, the Administration offered to lend the Municipality £P12,500 to build the Mount Carmel road in order to help Jewish labour.[105] The Council disagreed on the principle of accepting the loan (which was to be repaid by the Municipality). Shukri sided with the Jewish councillors in their demand for the project, while the other Arab members wanted to delay the decision and study the loan's conditions, which were obviously intended to benefit Jewish quarters and Jewish labour. Nevertheless, up to the end of the 1920s, there were few causes for serious splits in the council and all members were anxious to achieve working agreements. The moderation of the Arab councillors and the deliberate determination of the Jewish members to maintain good relations were clearly the reasons for this smooth running of the town's affairs.[106] Not until the 1930s would greater friction arise within the council, and it was then that the people's dissatisfaction with its performance would mount.

The elected council of 1927 was the answer to the Administration's policy. It was made up of less-politicized Arab members whose economic interests were linked to the continued stability of the system, even if they were not in complete agreement with the Mandate policy. The Jewish councillors, representing the minority in a mixed town, knew that their success depended on a gradual process of setting precedents with the Arab members but, above all, on the support of the Administration. For this reason, they put up no serious opposition to the Administration's measures to control the Municipality, when in fact they were in a better position than the Arabs to do so. By 1929, when the Administration started discussing a new municipal bill to limit the powers of local councils,[107] the local administration had already encroached in some instances on municipal rights and the prerogatives of the council. One such case was that of the sanitary inspector, Oakey, the problem of whose employment was finally resolved by the Administration, which switched him to the Health Department while the Municipality continued to pay his salary (see Chapter 5).[108] After 1929, the council's lack of ability to deal with increased responsibility, and the weakness of its members in maintaining a stand against such interference, gave the local administration even wider scope to interfere in municipal affairs.

Coalescence of the national forces

Immediately following the 1927 elections, the nationalist elements within the victorious opposition groups called for regrouping. This, however, was sooner said than done, for the animosity of the previous five years went very deep among the various political groups in the town. It had become clear that the Muslim nationalists had been drastically weakened and the influence of their leaders seriously reduced; at the same time, the situation allowed the opposition to expect a regrouping of the national forces, with more concessions in their favour. For this reason, the opposition press called for and debated the conditions of reconciliation on the one hand while maintaining its campaign of defamation against the Jerusalem leadership and their allies in the Muslim Association on the other.[109] The platform of this campaign remained the same, calling for moderation while refuting any proposal for a legislative council which would implicitly accept the political structure of the country. The Muslim nationalists, for their part, moderated their attacks on the opposition and refrained from competing with it by means of exaggerated expressions of nationalism. It had become important to create an atmosphere in which all sectors of the Palestinian Arab political movement could take part in the Seventh Congress in June 1928, which had been agreed upon by the two fronts in Jerusalem.

This proposed Congress had become a cause for heated debate among the Arab political forces in Haifa. The supporters of the SMC were only too ready to see an end to the damaging attacks by the opposition and to achieve a unanimous voice in local politics. It was, the opposition, however, that put obstacles in the way of convening the Congress. Strong repugnance at the Jerusalemites' high-handed manner of assuming the leadership and their method of setting up the proportional representation of the various districts was expressed in public.[110] The opposition were adamant in rejecting what they considered to be a repetition of the SMC's nepotistic and authoritarian style of carrying on national political affairs. This position was endorsed by the organization of a Christian front represented in Haifa by a Christian committee under Fu'ad Sa'd, which demanded proportional representation for the Christians. This decision on the part of the Christians, who for the first time had come out publicly in rejection of the policies of Jerusalem, strengthened the anti-Christian feeling of the vocal nationalists in the town and caused them to mount a strong campaign against the Haifa Christians.[111]

It was finally agreed to hold the Congress in Jerusalem on 20 June

1928, and the demands of the opposition and the Christian front were fully accepted. All sides of the political arena were anxious to achieve national cohesion and were hopeful of better results from the Congress. Najib Nassar, who was among the opposition spokesmen in Haifa, now saw his role as ended, since all partisan groups had met amicably and Shaikh Shuqairi had been given the opportunity to serve in the Congress.[112] Unfortunately, the deliberations and resolutions of the Congress did not meet with the approval of many members of the opposition, and criticism was immediate and rigorous. It was frustrating that the same members of the Jerusalem elite were reinstated, albeit in an enlarged AE. Another objection was to the emergence of radical youth spokesmen whose demands went beyond those of both currents in the national movement. The youth group was outspoken in demanding full independence within the framework of Arab unity, a demand that struck fear into the heart of all conservatives, even someone as adamantly nationalist as Nassar.[113] These same people had opposed the organization of the Young Men's Muslim Association in Haifa because of its radical stance and its extremist leadership in the person of Rashid al-Hajj Ibrahim.[114]

The conflict between the two political leaderships did not come to an end. It quietened down noticeably, however, during 1928-9, until the outbreak of racial violence on 23 August 1929. The intensity and the matters of contention also changed. Religious antagonisms seemed to take over from the purely political causes of discord; they revealed themselves mostly in the form of Muslim objections to the large number of Christians employed by the Administration. Meanwhile, a definite anti-British feeling was being more persistently expressed and analysed by followers of both currents. More than ever before, criticism of Britain's role in the region and its exploitative, imperial policy in Palestine was voiced in strongly hostile terms,[115] reflecting the atmosphere of frustration and despair that in part explains the outbreaks of 1929. Even though the cause of the disturbances in Haifa was the repercussions of the religious uproar concerning the Wailing Wall (Buraq) incident of September 1928, the roots of the hostility that wrecked the delicate intercommunal relationships went deeper and dated from further back. The religious sentiment acted as a catalyst to reactivate popular frustration at political, economic and social privations.

The violence shocked all the Arab political circles in Haifa and pushed them into immediate coalition. Public opinion became sharply anti-Zionist and anti-Jewish, a condition sustained by a media campaign to that effect.[116] The role of the British Administration and the police, though deplored, was not the Arabs' main grievance. All the latent fears of Jewish economic and political ambitions came to the fore and prompted boycott and segregation. Zionist projects in the town became the targets of attack, the more so because it was from these locations that Arabs were assaulted.[117] The Rutenberg power station was reported to have housed Jewish guerrillas who used the company's cars to enter Arab quarters and shoot passers-by. The Grands Moulins was also rumoured to have been the scene of sniper activities in which six Arabs were killed. Rumours exacerbated conditions and inflamed both communities. Clashes between Arabs and Jews took place in the old quarters of the town and in Hadar HaCarmel on 25 August, and a company of the Green Howards was despatched to quell the violence.[118] The result was twenty-one Arab and seven Jewish deaths.

The Arab press

As this chapter has shown, the political atmosphere among Haifa's Arab community had become highly charged, with clearer differentiations, by 1929. It was the Arab press that kept public opinion abreast of developments; it was through *al-Karmil* that the northern opposition to Jerusalem was spread, through *al-Yarmuk* that the SMC communicated its views and propaganda, and through *Mir'at al-Sharq* that support for the Administration was proclaimed. But the most significant role of *al-Karmil* and *al-Yarmuk,* in particular, lay in reflecting the grievous political, social and economic conditions of the Arab community, especially of the worst-hit sectors.

The Arab sense of injustice at the Administration's unequal treatment of Arab and Jew was sharply portrayed.[119] But the main service provided by the press was to keep alive the issue of national unity in the face of what was seen as Zionist aggression backed by Britain's pro-Zionist policy throughout the whole Arab region. In spite of the highly inflammatory nature of these messages, the institutionalized leadership was sluggish in its reaction. Haifa's Muslim and Christian leaderships met in November 1929, in response to a call from Ibrahim al-Khalil and Fu'ad Sa'd to consider a constructive approach to the problem.[120] Once again these meetings resulted in promises of united action, but little effective action followed.

While the traditional leadership was obviously unwilling to commit itself to the national struggle, it still clung to its status. Some militant strands of the more radical national movement had appeared in Haifa by the end of 1929, in response to the overwhelming passivity of urban political society.[121] But even these were easily suppressed by the Administration. The press was similarly intimidated by administrative suspension, fines and legal action.[122] The Administration recognized that, since it was determined to impose a policy which was contrary to majority public opinion, it would be folly to allow a free press not liable to censorship.[123] The fact that Edwin Samuel, son of Sir Herbert Samuel, was the Administration's press censorship officer only added to the nationalists' bitterness. Even this ultimate outlet for popular discontent was kept within limits, a measure which increased the impotence and frustration of urban political society.

Notes

1. At the San Remo Conference, April 1920, Britain was nominated as Mandatory for Palestine, and on 29 September 1923, the Mandate was confirmed and came into operation.

2. HC Herbert Samuel in a secret despatch to the CO, 18 November 1921 (PRO CO 733/7).

3. Confidential secret despatch from Central CID, Jerusalem, to E. Richmond, Assistant Sec. (Pol.), 17 August 1923 (ISA 2/158).

4. Kisch to Deedes, 21 March 1923, with material gathered for a draft reply by Ernest Richmond (ISA 2/151). Another version of Shukri's dismissal lays the blame at the door of General Bols, who was accused by the Zionists of being an anti-Semite and under the influence of his Arab girlfriend (oral information, David HaCohen, Haifa, April 1975). Since there were two associations in Haifa, the Muslim Society and the Christian Society, what was referred to here was a representative body of both societies.

5. Kalvarisky to Shukri, n.d. (CZA S25/10298); Kisch to Schueli, 8 June 1925 (CZA S25/517), quoted in B. Wasserstein, *The British in Palestine: the Mandatory Government and the Arab-Jewish Conflict 1917-1929* (London, 1978), p. 175.

6. Kisch to Deedes, Confidential letter of 21 March 1923 (ISA 2/151); see also D. HaCohen, *Time to Tell* (New York, London, 1984), pp. 24-5.

7. Ibid., p. 25.

8. Yunis al-Khatib, chairman of the Islamic Patriotic Society to Phoenicia District Governor, 15 November 1921 (ISA 61/542). The founding members who met at the house of Hajj Khalil Taha on 15 November 1921 were: Yunis al-Khatib, Hasan Shukri, Mahmud al-Safadi, Mahmud al-Yasin, As'ad al-Salah, Mahmud al-Khatib and As'ad Abu Zaid. See Y. Porath, *The Emergence of the Palestinian Arab National Movement, 1918-1929* (London, 1974), p. 217, and communication, from the Islamic Society to the HC, 21 November 1923 (ISA 2/158).

9. Schueli to Customs Superintendent, Haifa, 17 July 1924 (ISA 202/24).

10. Y. Washitz, 'Jewish-Arab Relations in Haifa during the Mandate' (unpublished manuscript, n.d.), Chapter V, pp. 37-8, and oral information, Iskandar Majdalani, Haifa, May 1975.

11. Shukri, vice president of the 'Muslim National Society' in Haifa, to Deedes, 28 February 1922 (ISA 61/547).

12. Yusif and Yunis al-Khatib to Governor of Haifa, 27 March and 15 April 1922 respectively (ISA 61/547). In these letters of resignation from the IPS the two Khatibs expressed their opposition to the aims of the society which had become clear from its public statement, and confirmed their support of the Arab Palestinian delegation.

13. Porath, *The Emergence*, pp. 214-16.

14. As early as 1919 Herbert Samuel had felt that Syrian and Egyptian officials, many of whom were Christian, posed a threat to the economic and political ambitions of the Jews (Herbert Samuel to ZO, 'Our Relations with the

Authorities', Cairo, 7 November 1919, Samuel Private Papers, St Antony's College, Oxford). This feeling was reiterated by Kisch in his complaints against the Christian Arabs to Deedes in a letter of 30 January 1923 (ISA 2/151).

15. Porath, *The Emergence*, p. 224.

16. To gain legitimacy, the government was 'anxious to incorporate the leadership of *all* sections of Arab society within the established polity', with the effect that 'both toadyism and treachery became apparent qualifications for government office in Palestine'. 'The mere presence of Arab officials within the Administration was politically more important to the British than their level of bureaucratic efficiency'. Wasserstein, *The British*, p. 171 (emphasis added).

17. The Ordinance of Collective Responsibility was proposed by the HC and authorized by the Cabinet in order to enable District Governors to enforce the principle of collective responsibility upon tribal sections in villages and in tribal areas and where necessary to impose collective punishments (whether by fine or otherwise) for the misdemeanour of individuals. 5 March 1924 (PRO CO 733/83).

18. It is clear from the correspondence of the Arab Executive with members of the Haifa Muslim Association that these members were keeping Jerusalem informed of the activities of the opposition and its newspaper. See correspondence in ISA 65/1.

19. Porath, *The Emergence*, pp. 208–13.

20. Oral information, Khalid al-Hasan, London, March 1982, and other informants who requested that their names should be withheld.

21. For detailed research and analysis of the origin of the Palestinian Arab National Party, see Porath, *The Emergence*, pp. 208–303.

22. Political report on the Arabian situation for November 1923 (PRO FO 371 E11227/10395/65).

23. *Mir'at al-Sharq*, 28 July 1927.

24. Porath, *The Emergence*, pp. 28–9.

25. As early as December 1923, the Northern District Governor, Symes, reported on the Christians' withdrawal from 'active participation in the extremists' (Muslim nationalist) agitation'. Report of Northern District Governor to CS, December 1923 (PRO FO 371/737/65).

26. N. A. Badran, *Al-Ta'lim wal-Tahdith fil-Mujtama' al-'Arabi al-Filastini* (Education and Modernization in Arab Palestinian Society) (Beirut, 1969), p. 269.

27. *Al-Karmil*, 29 March 1924; 15 July 1925.

28. See the issues of *al-Karmil* for the period 1924–8. His most bitter criticism was registered in editorials of 15 September 1925; 5 and 19 September 1926; 3 April, 18 September and 5 November 1927; 6 and 19 February and 11 March 1928.

29. *Al-Karmil*, 5 April 1924.

30. *Al-Karmil*, 8 April and 19 August 1925; 24 April and 5 November 1927, to cite only a few instances.

31. *Al-Karmil*, 3 June 1925; 8 April 1925; and 5 December 1926; 20 February and 3 December 1927. In the last editorial cited here, he concluded that the British government's Zionist policy in Palestine aimed at creating barriers between the Arab regions and preventing their unity.

32. Ahmad al-Imam to the AE. 15 October 1922 and 21 August 1924 (ISA 65/1).

33. See the issues of *al-Yarmuk* for the period 1924–8, especially the issues of 1 and 18 September, 19 and 23 October, 13 November, and 1 December 1924; and 5 February 1925.

34. Sulaiman al-Salah to HC, 26 November 1923, and a number of petitions against the National Party (ISA 2/172).

35. Symes to CS, 4 December 1923 (ISA 2/172); see also Political Report by Symes to CO, June 1927 (PRO CO 733/142).

36. *Al-Yarmuk*, 1 September and 26 November 1924; Wadi' Sanbar to the AE, 21 September 1924 (ISA 65/1).

37. *Al-Yarmuk*, 19 November 1924.

38. *Al-Yarmuk*, 16 and 19 November and 1 December 1924; *al-Karmil*, 4 July 1926; 22 January 1928. See also Jamal al-Husaini to Mary Adelaide Broadhurst, president of the National League (Britain), 30 May 1926 (ISA 65/1).

39. Muhammad Murad, in addition to being mufti of Haifa and member of the SMC, was elected to the AE at the Fourth Congress (1921), the Sixth Congress (1923), and the Seventh Congress (1928).

40. *Al-Yarmuk*, 22 November 1924.

41. *Al-Zuhur*, 12 January 1927.

42. *Al-Yarmuk*, 3 August and 18 December 1924; also oral information, Suhail Shukri, Haifa, May 1975.

43. See Abramson to Bowman on government education in Haifa, November 1926 (PRO CO 733/117). Abramson mentioned that the Muslim Association was a local body totally independent of the SMC. According to Suhail Shukri, his uncle, Ibrahim al-Khalil was the moving spirit behind the financing and building of the Istiqlal *waqf*. In 1936, Hajj Amin al-Husaini attempted to incorporate this *waqf* into the rest of the country through the agency of the SMC but was opposed by al-Khalil. The assassination of al-Khalil soon after led to a period of terror among the Muslim community of Haifa. (Oral information, Suhail Shukri, Haifa, May 1975.)

44. *Al-Yarmuk*, 18 and 25 December 1924 and 1 January 1925.

45. *Al-Yarmuk*, 1 January 1925; 23 October and 1 December 1924.

46. *Al-Yarmuk*, 25 September 1924.

47. During Bishop Hajjar's visit to Rome for the 16th centenary of the Council of Nicea in 1925, he presented the Palestine case, showing Zionist plans to buy land as a manoeuvre to weaken the Christian character of the Holy Land. Mr Dormer (official of the British Embassy in Rome) to FO, July 1925 (PRO FO 371 E4410/125/65). Fu'ad Sa'd and Teofil Boutagy, during visits to Europe in the 1920s, reported on Zionist propaganda and suggested methods of combating it (*al-Karmil*, 3 December 1923).

48. See E. A. Brett, *Colonialism and Underdevelopment in East Africa* (Bungay, Suffolk, 1973), p. 29.

49. See comments by Mr Blood of the CO (expert on local government) on the Report of the Commission of Local Government, 24 February 1925 (PRO CO 733/90). Blood said that 'the Eastern countries have no sense of local government because the idea of doing things for themselves is foreign to the eastern mind'. See also remarks by J. M. Farrell, Assistant to the Head of the Education Department, to Owen Tweedy on popular suffrage in the East, 2 December 1927 (Owen Tweedy Diaries, 'Second Odyssey', Book II, Private Papers Collection, St Antony's College, Oxford).

50. Clauson's minute on HC's report to CO of 5 March 1925 (PRO CO 733/110).

51. HC to CO, 14 February 1921 (PRO FO 371 2354/2345/88).

52. Telegram from HC, Sir Herbert Samuel, to CO, July 1921 (PRO FO E712354/2345/88). Also see Jamal al-Husaini to HC, 23 March 1923 (ISA 2/158).

53. Immediately after the occupation of Haifa, the authorities asked the Municipal Council, headed by Hasan Shukri, to elect two Jewish members to the Council 'in order to restore to that community its right for national participation' (*The Palestine News*, 7 November 1918). J. Chainkin and Shabatai Levy were then chosen, and their appointment approved by the military governor, who also reaffirmed the appointment of the whole council. Abraham Halfon, a native of Haifa who came from a Sephardic Jewish family, had been employed as secretary of the Municipal Council before the war. See Z. Vilnay, *Khaifa Be'avar Ve Bahoveh* (Haifa in the Past and the Future) (Tel-Aviv, 1936), p. 100. Also, the municipal engineer was a European Jew (*Jirab al-Kurdi*, 8 October 1923).

54. For HC's correspondence to CO on the issue of municipalities, see HC to CO, 6 June 1924 (PRO CO 733/69); HC to CO, December 1924 (PRO CO 733/52); and HC report to CO, 5 March 1925 (PRO CO 733/110).

55. HC report to CO, 5 March 1925 (PRO CO 733/110).

56. Despatch by S of S Amery to HC Samuel on the subject of municipal legislation, 7 March 1925 (PRO CO 733/87). Also see Clauson's minute on HC's letter of 28 May 1925 (PRO CO 733/93), and Keith-Roach's minute of 6 June 1925 (PRO CO 733/87).

57. Plumer to Amery, confidential despatch of 24 March 1926 (PRO CO 733/113).

58. *Palestine Blue Book*, Municipalities 1927 (Jerusalem), p. 63.

59. *Al-Karmil*, 3 October 1926.

60. The Arabic press protested against government interference in the local councils, a condition that generated popular resentment (*al-Nafir*, 8 September 1923). There were many instances of popular objection, especially after the Nablus council was summarily dismissed and a more amenable one appointed (*Haifa*, 13 March 1925).

61. Quoted in O. S. al-Barghouti, 'Local Self-Government Past and Present', in Viteles and Totah (eds), 'Palestine, A Decade of Development', *The Annals of the American Academy of Political and Social Science*, Vol. 164 (November 1932), p. 37.

62. CO to HC in response to arguments of the Arab Executive, 1925 (PRO CO 733/93).

63. T. S. Boutagy to President (*sic*), Haifa municipality, 8 December 1922 (ISA 2/793), and Symes to CS, 26 December 1922 (ISA 2/793).

64. Symes to CS, 26 December 1922 (ISA 2/793).

65. S of S Churchill, to CO, 22 June 1922 (PRO CO 733/39). In this letter the S of S wrote, 'I, therefore, consider that, pending the formation of Mr. Rutenberg's Co., no applications for town lighting etc. ... should be accepted, and I shall be glad if you will inform these bodies accordingly'. Also see correspondence between HC and CO in April 1923 (PRO CO 733/44).

66. HC, Herbert Samuel, to S of S, Winston Churchill, 16 December 1921 (PRO CO 733/8).

67. CO to Mr Fao of the Anglo-Egyptian Bank, April 1923 (PRO CO 733/44).

68. Symes to Director of Commerce and Industry, 24 April 1923 (ISA 2/793). For wider political and economic aspects of the Rutenberg concession see B. J. Smith, *The Roots of Separatism in Palestine* (Syracuse, NY, 1993), pp. 117–26.

69. Political Report for May 1923 (PRO CO 733/46).

70. *Al-Yarmuk*, 18 September and 9 November 1924. See also Political Report for January 1925 (PRO CO 733/89).

71. *Al-Karmil*, 11 June 1924; 8 August 1925; *al-Yarmuk*, 1, 8 and 19 February 1925.

72. *Al-Karmil*, 5 December 1923; 11 June 1924; *al-Yarmuk*, 19 February 19, 1925. David HaCohen, in his book *Time to Tell*, p. 24, accuses the mayor, whom he considered to be a strong supporter of the mufti of Jerusalem, of refusing even to open Rutenberg's letter of proposal for lighting Haifa.

73. Councillors in the Haifa Municipality were often accused of being opportunistic and lacking a sense of civic duty by the press and the less advantaged classes of society (*Jirab al-Kurdi*, 8 October 1923; *al-Yarmuk*, 19 February 1925; *al-Karmil*, 21 February and 5 August 1925). This became even clearer in the 1930s when economic conditions had perceptibly improved, thus giving many of the Arab councillors better chances to reveal their inadequacies as public servants. See HaCohen, *Time*, pp. 27–32; also confirmed through oral information (London, June 1982, names withheld by request).

74. *Al-Yarmuk*, 1 and 8 February 1925.

75. *Al-Karmil*, 21 February 1925.

76. *Al-Yarmuk*, 1 and 25 February 1925.

77. *Al-Karmil*, 27 June 1925.

78. *Al-Karmil*, 8 August 1925.

79. *Al-Karmil*, 28 November 1925.

80. Keith-Roach, 'Pasha of Jerusalem', Part I (Private Papers, St Antony's College, Oxford), p. 130.

81. *Al-Karmil*, 9 May 1926.

82. *Al-Karmil*, 6, 13 and 20 June 1926.

83. Religious denominations and political orientations were represented in the membership of the electoral committee. The members were Amin 'Abdul-Hadi (opposition camp), Hajj Khalil Taha (opposition camp, supporter of the Islamic Patriotic Society, Rashid al-Hajj Ibrahim (Muslim nationalist front), Khalil Sanbar (Greek Catholic), Yusif Ghammasha (Latin), Mikha'il Tuma (Greek Orthodox), Rev. Flaihan (Protestant), Samuel Pevsner (Ashkenazi Jew, early Zionist settler), and M. Hassoun (Sephardic Jew, merchant). *Al-Karmil*, 12 December 1926.

84. *Palestine Blue Book* 1926–1927, p. 66; CS to S of S on 24 December 1934 (ISA 2/G/114/34).

85. A tentative list of the numbers of voters and their communal breakdown was published in *al-Karmil*, 6 February 1927. Although the numbers did not correspond to the official final numbers of Arabs and Jews that voted, they provided an approximation of the communal breakdown.

86. *Al-Zuhur*, 12 January 1927. This newspaper, owned by the Greek Catholic Jamil Bahri, prided itself on being non-partisan concerning the political conflict

raging among the Muslim groups in the town. It represented a Christian viewpoint, however. In listing the names of the Muslim candidates, it reported erroneously the name of 'Aziz Miqati among the opposition candidates instead of 'Uthman al-Khamra.

87. *Al-Karmil*, 8 May 1927. There were five Greek Catholic candidates, three Greek Orthodox, one Maronite, one Catholic and one Protestant.

88. HaCohen, *Time*, p. 26.

89. Ibid., p. 25; oral information, Beirut, 1977.

90. The AE to CS, 6 November and 2 December 1926; CS to AE, 26 November 1926 (ISA 65/03076). The AE hoped that if voting were confined to members of one community only, their Muslim candidates in Jerusalem might win the election on the Muslim vote, since their opponents were supported by the Jewish and some Christian votes. However, the situation was different in Haifa, where the Muslim candidates could not get the full support of the Muslim voters.

91. *Al-Zuhur*, which was very close to the Christian clerical leadership (i.e. Bishop Hajjar), gave the impression that the Christians would only nominate a number of candidates equivalent to their seats and would hold no elections (*al-Zuhur*, 12 January 1927). Nevertheless, eleven Christians ran, of whom five were Greek Catholic (*al-Karmil*, 8 May 1927).

92. Vilnay, *Khaifa*, p. 100.

93. In his book, *Time to Tell* (pp. 27–33), HaCohen provides very pertinent examples of Sahyoun's and Tuma's behaviour in the Municipality. More than the other Arabs, they vehemently opposed all attempts at social and economic improvement in Arab working conditions in the Municipality. In fact, most of the Arab councillors were cautious about initiating any improvements that incurred expense or would in the long run cause the wealthier strata to share in their costs. See also Y. Washitz, 'Jewish-Arab Relations in Haifa during the Mandate' (unpublished manuscript, n.d.), Chapter IV, pp. 3–5.

94. The issue of personal leadership (*za'ama*) could be sensed in the press campaign of the period. See in particular *al-Karmil*, 20 February and 17 April 1927.

95. Oral information, David HaCohen, Haifa, May 1975.

96. F. H. Kisch to CS, Deedes, 21 March 1923 (ISA 2/151) and CS to ZE, 2 September 1923 (ISA 2/151), in which the cases of these two 'moderate' Arabs are detailed. The case of Hasan Shukri has already been mentioned; as for Sha'ban, the CS specified that he had been dismissed for irregular behaviour and had later lost the election when he ran again for mukhtar.

97. HaCohen, *Time*, p. 24.

98. *Al-Karmil*, 5 December 1926.

99. *Al-Karmil*, 3 and 17 April and 8 and 15 May 1927.

100. The numbers of votes scored by each successful candidate were: Nasrallah Khuri, 1,980; Ibrahim Sahyoun, 1,900; Hasan Shukri, 1,893; Jamil Abyad, 1,820; Amin 'Abdul-Hadi, 1,810; Tawfiq al-Khalil, 1,758; 'Uthman al-Khamra, 1,591; Mikha'il Tuma, 1,266 (*al-Karmil*, 22 May 1927).

101. Rashid al-Hajj Ibrahim to DC, 18 May 1928 (ISA 61/141). As the elected president of Jam'iyyat al-Shubban al-Muslimin (Young Men's Muslim Association), Hajj Ibrahim applied to the DC and received the approval and registration of the Association on 5 July 1928.

102. HC to CS, 14 February 1930 (PRO CO 733/189).

103. Minutes of Municipal Council meeting, 26 November 1929 and 16 December 1930, quoted in Washitz, 'Jewish-Arab Relations', Chapter IV, pp. 4–5. This situation arose when many municipal workers left to work in the harbour works and it was obviously necessary to improve working conditions in the Municipality in order to attract workers.

104. Ibid., Chapter IV, p. 3.

105. Al-Karmil, 11 November 1928.

106. Minutes of the Municipal Council until the early 1930s as quoted by Washitz, 'Jewish-Arab Relations', Chapter IV, pp. 11–14.

107. Al-Karmil, 10 April 1929.

108. Al-Karmil, April–August 1929.

109. See al-Karmil issues from June 1927 to May 1928.

110. Al-Karmil, 11 March, 8 and 29 April, 20, 27, and 30 May 1928.

111. Al Karmil, 10 and 17 June 1928.

112. Al-Karmil, 24 June 1928.

113. Porath, The Emergence, p. 254; E. Tuma, Sittun 'Aman 'ala al-Haraka al-Qawmiyya al-'Arabiyya al-Filastiniyya (The Last Sixty Years of the Palestinian Arab National Movement) (Beirut, 1978), pp. 65–6; al-Karmil, 24 June and 1 July 1928.

114. Al-Karmil, 27 May 1928.

115. Editorials in al-Karmil and al-Yarmuk from July 1928 to the end of August 1929.

116. Al-Karmil, issues of August through to the end of December 1929.

117. Al-Karmil, 14 and 21 September 1929.

118. Telegram from Mr Hoare (Cairo) to FO, 26 August 1929 (PRO FO 371 E4232/4198/65). Haganah units, which had existed in Haifa since 1919, repelled Arab attacks on the Jewish quarters, and sent carloads of armed men to attack concentrations of rioters inside Arab quarters. Washitz cites these incidents as documented in the Haganah archives (Washitz, 'Jewish-Arab Relations', Chapter III, pp. 5–6).

119. The disparity in the treatment of Arab and Jewish prisoners and those found carrying firearms was a main complaint of the Arabs (al-Karmil, 7, 14 and 21 September, 13 November and 3 December 1929).

120. Al-Karmil, 20 November 1929.

121. The militant organization al-Kaff al-Aswad (The Black Hand) put up posters on walls and in mosques in the town, threatening those who sold to or co-operated with the Jews (al-Karmil, 10 December 1929).

122. Al-Yarmuk was suspended from 5 December until the end of the month, when it had to pay a fine, for writing what the censorship authorities considered inciting articles. Al-Nafir was also fined for the same reason in mid-December, and al-Karmil was threatened with closure (al-Karmil, 7, 24 and 28 December 1929).

123. Keith-Roach, 'Pasha of Jerusalem', Vol. I, p. 290.

14

Radicalization of
the National Forces

Introduction

The 1929 disturbances set the pattern for the Arab opposition to British
policies which culminated in the 1936–9 rural revolt. The inevitability
of violence was gradually evolving as the ultimate solution to the
Palestinian grievances. While sporadic violent reaction had been recorded since the beginning of Jewish settlement, it was only after the
experience of British colonial administration and the implementation of
the Zionist settler colonization that this option was deliberately adopted
by elements of the dispossessed society.[1] Very early on in the occupation,
potentially violent Arab reaction to the policies of the Mandate was
taken into consideration by the British authorities. The Intelligence
Division of the Military Administration closely monitored all prominent
personalities involved in political activities; this practice was continued
by the police, the CID and district officers under the Civil Administration.[2] Opposition to the Mandate was a feature of certain Arab strata,
in particular the politicized sectors of Muslim society whose opposition
stemmed either from a Muslim or a pan-Arab orientation. However, it
was the Jewish National Home policy, which the Mandate imposed,
that was the main target of Arab opposition, both Muslim and Christian. For a number of reasons, this opposition did not pose a serious
threat to the regime during the first decade of British rule. The social,
religious and economic heterogeneity of the Arab population hindered
the development of a united national consciousness, a single political
platform and organized means of resistance during periods of relative
political tranquillity and economic prosperity. While Jewish immigration, land acquisition and economic control still had limited effect,
Arab reaction to the JNH remained sporadic and unco-ordinated. This
was encouraged by the Administration's carrot-and-stick policy to ensure
a balance between Arab acquiescence and militancy; opposition was
diluted by providing work in the Administration, by binding the interests

of the recognized political leadership to those of the government, and by ensuring that both parties of the polarized leadership retained equal political influence.

Nevertheless, instances of militant Arab reaction to the changes brought about by the new occupation did occur, mostly in the northern districts, where Zionist land purchases and agricultural settlements were directly linked to the economic hardship affecting the rural and urban communities. In Haifa, as was shown in Chapter 12, armed gangs appeared in 1919 and 1922 at periods of heightened deprivation, and British officials came to recognize that, in spite of the Arabs' apparent placidity, there was a current of militancy that became clearer at times of economic distress.[3]

In reaction to the 1929 events, the High Commissioner, Sir John Chancellor, proposed fundamental changes in the Mandate policy, which he perceived as unworkable in view of the violent Arab opposition.[4] This violence had come as a surprise, not only to the Administration, but to many of the Arab leaders themselves. Since 1922, nothing on the surface had indicated the deep-rooted frustration. Neither the Administration nor the Arab political strata were able to gauge the effects on the basic fabric of Arab society of a decade of British-Zionist policy. A number of factors contributed to the Arabs' sense of desperation by 1929: increased immigration, land purchases, smuggling of arms and immigrants, and signs of a Zionist military build-up. In addition, what appeared to the Arabs as an increasingly repressive regime endorsed a policy resulting in the impoverishment of the countryside and of the middle and lower strata of the urban communities, which was compounded by the self-interested attitude of the fragmented Arab leadership (see the Prologue to Part Four above). While the nationalist elements among the Palestinian leadership had been weakened, these conditions radicalized the lower strata of society and encouraged the emergence of religious leaders who led the struggle under the banner of religious solidarity ('asabiyya). The disturbances of 1929 had religious overtones which appealed to those who felt frustrated at a time when the incompetence of the urban leaders had left an obvious political vacuum. Irrespective of the immediate causes of the August 1929 riots, these events were seen as a nationalist uprising by the Arab population.

Conditions deteriorated drastically following Ramsay MacDonald's letter to Dr Weizmann in February 1931, dubbed by the Arabs 'the Black Letter'. By 1936 even British officials in the Northern District acknowledged, in retrospect, the deleterious effect of this British repudiation of its earlier promises.[5] Press campaigns mounted against Zionist arms smuggling and immigration and the government's policies resulted in suspensions of individuals and press controls. Boycotts, strikes and sabotage became everyday events in the towns. The expulsion of peasant and bedouin Arabs from lands purchased by Zionist organizations only stiffened Arab resistance. Most of the coastal land in the Bay between Haifa and Acre (Ard Jidru) was sold by the Sursuk family to various Jewish companies in 1928. The land was occupied by 'Arab al-Raml, who claimed ownership of certain areas, and the Ghawarneh Arabs, who claimed a prescriptive title to other parts. The former group were evicted in November 1931 and the latter, who put up a stiff resistance to their dispossession, were forcibly evicted by 1936.[6] Such events often led to violent clashes and deaths, exciting public opinion and culminating in the street demonstrations of October 1933, which the police suppressed harshly, with many deaths.

In response to this more militant opposition, the Administration decided on a course of repression.[7] Violence had become an integral part of Palestine's special political situation, with militant activity in one sector promoting its counterpart in another. Whereas in the 1920s Zionist measures to take over land, labour and the market remained largely inconspicuous, in the 1930s they became more obvious as Jewish organizations amassed arms and engaged in military drill and organized acts of reprisal.[8] Violence was the prerogative of no one sector or party on the Palestine scene.

This chapter will trace Arab action and reaction to this process of radicalization. Paradoxically, it was in Haifa that a strong radical movement existed in the early 1920s, although it was overshadowed by a conservative trend among the mercantile stratum of the political community. While the particular socio-economic atmosphere of Haifa nurtured political orientations that were accommodating to the new order, it also created antithetical militant trends that shook the basis of society. For a proper understanding of the process of change that the Arab community had undergone since 1919, it is important, at this point, to trace the more subtle developments in the ethos of both ethnic groups of Haifa society.

Socio-political transformation of the two ethnic communities

While Arab circles generally had been preoccupied with internecine struggles since 1923, the political and economic realities in the country had drastically altered. In Haifa these changes had a special significance, because of the composition of its population and the development of its industry and commerce. Local political events highlighted the changed conditions among the communities, especially after the election campaign of 1927.

The Jewish community had experienced drastic and obvious changes during this period. By 1927 it can be safely surmised that the Jews in

Haifa made up a little less than one-third of the population. The Arab quarters of the town, excluding the sea front, were being encircled on all sides by Jewish quarters (see Map III). The claustrophobia the Arabs were experiencing was acknowledged by British officials, who reported that Haifa 'was ringed round by Jewish enterprise and Jewish-owned land'.[9] In Hadar HaCarmel, the oldest of the Jewish quarters outside the old town, a community structure was set up to service the needs of the Jewish community; the corporation of Hadar HaCarmel, essentially a company to provide water to the Jewish quarters, developed into a municipal-type body in which the various Jewish political orientations were represented. Even though the other Jewish quarters such as Bat Galim and Neve Sha'nan established local councils to collect dues for communal services and improvements, the larger concentration of politicized and better-off Jews in the Hadar became the focal centre of Jewish Haifa. The Va'ad Leumi (Jewish National Council) had had a democratically elected local Community Committee there since 1922.[10] In 1931, it reorganized its structure, according to the regulations confirmed by the government that year, so that its composition was explicitly based on party distribution representing the whole spectrum of Jewish political affiliations.[11]

By the mid-1920s the social make-up of the Jewish community in Haifa was homogeneous, unlike the situation in Jerusalem and Tel-Aviv. Ashkenazi Jews now outnumbered the original small Oriental community and had brought with them their social institutions, into which Sephardic Jews such as the Halfouns, Tayyars, Hakims, Raffouls and Abu-Tubouls were incorporated. In a mixed town, where the Jews were still in the minority, the advice and know-how in traditional affairs of these Orientals were often sought by the more politically sophisticated and pragmatic Ashkenazi immigrants. Social cohesion was exemplified by co-operation between workers and progressive businessmen.[12] After 1923, the Bolshevik elements had been weakened by developments within the Zionist socialist movement. The elections for the local labour councils in mid-1923 were won by the 'Ahduth Ha'avodah' party, with a markedly high membership in Haifa, despite the fact that only 75 per cent of the workers in the party participated.[13] Known to be moderate, with a strong nationalist orientation, the party's victory indicated the tendency of a major part of the Jewish labour force in Haifa towards a less radical stance.

Among the Arab community the changes had been more subtle. By 1929 a middle-class Christian and Muslim stratum had emerged to engage in entrepreneurial activities, thus linking itself to the permanence of the Mandate system and indirectly to its corollary, the JNH. The leadership of all political currents came from this class of merchants and landowners, among whom individual and family interests took precedence over societal and even communal concerns. Features peculiar to these interests were developing, as could be seen in the refusal of many municipal councillors and suddenly enriched businessmen to involve themselves in politics as well as in their attempts to justify their accumulation of wealth. This class alliance had not, however, become firm by 1929, and at the first signs of violence the new bourgeoisie reverted to their communal and religious allegiances. Nevertheless, these links too had been weakened by a decade of political infighting.

Haifa Arab society as a whole, however, had a somewhat different experience. In the 1920s, the town was a haven for labour from the countryside, especially the dispossessed peasantry of the northern district, and from the economically depressed southern towns of Palestine. However, the large influx of workers made exploitation possible, as was the case with the government and municipal labour force,[14] as well as the large body of workers in the building industry. Conditions worsened during the economic crisis of 1927-9 and the Zionist campaign to 'conquer labour', when work sites were picketed by Jewish workers and job opportunities and wages decreased. The Arab workers, who bore the immediate brunt of the Zionist policy, were the most susceptible to the influence of the conservative leadership.[15] The incomers from the villages were made unpleasantly aware of the precariousness of their existence in comparison with those already settled and the more privileged strata of the town. The anonymity of urban life pushed them to seek reassurance in religious leadership, which was the strongest link with their village life. Lacking the initiative and the means as yet to organize themselves, the urban workers were easily exploited by the leadership and harshly suppressed by the government. Even though the first Arab labour union was established in Haifa in 1925, its influence remained limited until the mid-1930s.

It was among what might be called the lower middle class, who neither benefited significantly from the system nor were in a state of destitution, that signs of change could be detected and that Arab frustration became apparent. This large sector of the population was less homogeneous than either the bourgeoisie or the poorer working classes. It also lacked a conscious identity. On the whole the better-off section was an extension, though an economically deprived one, of the bourgeois class with which it shared a common social and cultural background. As a result, it tended to be envious or obsequious in its dealings with this class, and at the same time to exhibit a sense of superiority towards the manual labour class. The mercantile mentality was quite strong among this heterogeneous sector, especially in a trading town like Haifa.

It had become clear to the politicized elements of this stratum that the Mandate policy, with its Zionist aspects, was detrimental to their interests in the short run and to the whole of society in the long run. The more radical, so-called 'left nationalist' stratum, especially those in youth movements such as the YMMA and the Scouts, emphasized their anti-British feeling rather than an anti-Zionist attitude;[16] they saw British colonization as the root of all Arab grievances. During the five years preceding the violent outbreaks of 1929, these grievances had grown increasingly bitter. A major request by the Arab and particularly the Muslim community of Haifa, repeatedly presented to the Administration, was for improvement of the education system. The significance of this request was deeper than might appear on the surface. The nationalists argued that Haifa's sectarian school system precluded the development of a generation conscious of its heritage. It also produced only one stratum of citizens, young people who shunned manual labour but were not trained for white-collar jobs, a situation that resulted in a truncated society.[17] Even more than other cities, Haifa was short of government schools, a deficiency bitterly criticized by its Muslim community;[18] while missionary schools were many and varied, their standards and teaching materials were regarded as inefficient and inappropriate.

Such complaints became even more bitter when compared with developments in the Jewish sector of the town. Wadi Salib, the Muslim quarter, felt the effect of these injustices most; the community was too poor to carry out the necessary road and sanitary construction, and very few of the municipal improvements introduced into the other quarters, such as electricity, police stations and a sewerage system, were extended to it.[19] Among these poorer Arab classes the policy of the local administration was seen as intended not only to deprive the old quarters of improvements but also to divest them of already established services, for example, by moving the post office headquarters to the Hadar HaCarmel area.

Resentment was mounting at the contemptuous way in which the local British authorities had come to treat matters of Arab welfare. Officials were never available to hear Arab complaints, while Arab society was feeling the economic pinch resulting from the Administration's policy of allotting emergency funds for Jewish aid and for bailing out the Tel-Aviv municipality.[20] The peak of this ferment came in 1929, in the period preceding the events of August. At this stage, Arab opinion, irrespective of political alliances, was acutely critical of the deteriorating conditions in the town, which were reflected in social regression. The crime rate had risen drastically and cases of indecent assault, especially on women, had increased.[21] It had become common for officials and even the Arab police to treat Arabs with disrespect, especially the less wealthy among them, while the more powerful Jews were treated differently. These feelings were the result of a slow process, whereby the economic prosperity of a small stratum of Arab society and the segregationist policies of the Jewish sector emphasized the privations of the poorer strata of the Arab community. Their political fragmentation added to their sense of crisis and desperation.[22]

The disturbances provided an outlet for this state of mind. Even though it was mainly the more destitute who took an active part in events, the whole Arab population became involved in the political debates surrounding them. But in contrast to the events of 1921, when a nationally cohesive anti-Zionist front was formed from all religious communities and social classes, the events of 1929 did not result in unity. The political cohesion of the society had been deeply fractured in the interim, and even more significant was the social differentiation that had taken place. Not only had a new entrepreneurial class made up of both Christians and Muslims emerged, but a stratum of the elite class, mostly Muslims, had also aligned themselves with the system by their tacit endorsement of the Zionist movement. In spite of their political frustrations, they were anxious not to endanger their new economic status. The upper strata of the middle class, in particular those who belonged to the new, better-educated and aspiring generation, were faced with a dilemma. On the intellectual level, they opposed the Administration's policy and sympathized with the Arab expressions of anger, but they also recognized that their welfare was dependent on a stable political structure. When a number of Arabs were to be brought to trial on charges of looting during the disturbances, the Arab lawyers of Haifa refused to defend them;[23] the legal profession had become yet another channel for the politically ambitious new generation.

Forging a political identity

On the surface, political conditions in Haifa did not change as a result of the 1929 disturbances. Nor did the attitude of the 'moderate' strata of Arab society, whether Muslim, Christian or secular nationalist tendencies, change in any concrete sense. Nevertheless, change had been progressively affecting all other strata of Haifa society and gradually introducing a spectrum of political movements which shared a common articulate national consciousness. It was in the less wealthy, though educated, stratum of the middle class and among the poorer urban working class, as well as the lowest strata of peasant workers in the town, that this development took place. The process was sharpened by the acute socio-economic differentiation resulting from the pro-Zionist policy; it was also enhanced by the events surrounding the 1929 uprising, but most of all it was nourished by the cultural, religious and social composition of society. The Arab character as well as the Muslim identification of these strata acted as a cementing bond. Until 1935, when the first organized militant movement was exposed, these strata experienced a cyclical process of radicalization, which, though tempered at every violent juncture, evolved into a single-minded opposition.

The peasant stratum, whether temporarily or permanently resident in Haifa, constituted the lowest layer of the town's social scale. There is little information on the detailed make-up and origins or on the evolving infrastructures of this fringe 'society'. Nevertheless, the gradual assembling of poor peasants attracted by Haifa's work opportunities at periods when they were deprived of some or all of their traditional sources of livelihood is recorded in official and private documents from the mid-1920s. Their main characteristics were their extreme destitution, their rootlessness and their lack of any legal protection or municipal help. In 1924, peasant labourers were harassed by the police because they slept in the streets and presented a nuisance to the modern town.[24] By 1936, the District Commissioner reported that seven or eight thousand Arabs were compelled to sleep in the streets or live in the shanty-quarters of the old town in hovels made from wood and petrol tins, with no drainage, water or basic facilities.[25] In his opinion, this was 'a disgraceful blot, not progress, when a pastoral people are turned into town dwellers with no resources'.[26]

As we saw in Part One, Haifa had had a drifting labour community of peasant stock since the early 1900s, drawn by the construction boom and the laying of the Hijaz Railway, but with the British occupation they became a more permanent addition to the population. This community did not reach noticeable size until the mid-1920s, however; by the mid-1930s it had become a potential source of social disequilibrium. During this decade Haifa became a melting pot and fermenting cauldron for the frustrated and embittered peasant city dwellers.

In the city, people from the same village gathered in the same area[27] and filled the most menial jobs, in particular for the port and the railway. These people led a precarious existence; they depended on their daily wages during boom periods and were reduced to begging when the job market shrank. In these conditions, 'peasants, uprooted from the villages, found themselves homeless, penniless and in many cases friendless in the large towns'.[28] During the economic depressions of 1927–8 and 1935, they endured great economic distress in addition to sporadic campaigns by the local Administration to clear the town by destroying their huts without providing them with alternative dwellings.[29] These experiences fed their resentment and brought home to them the social and economic disparities which were glaringly apparent in the town. The social and political forces behind the changes in their lives were not beyond their comprehension, but they lacked a leadership and a structure that would transmit their grievances. By leaving their villages, these peasants had shaken off the control of their traditional leaders and of the feudal landowners. By entering a heterogeneous stratum with no real ties to Haifa's established elite, they acquired an independent and radical orientation with little control from the notable landowning families, whose monopoly over the resources crucial to the life of the Arab worker and peasant had come to an end with the migration. In this situation new leadership structures sprang up, such as officials in the municipality, owners or contributors to the few large Arab industrial projects and leaders in the labour organization, the Palestine Arab Workers Society (PAWS), which weakened the control of the Arab notable families in Palestine as a whole, and particularly so in the case of Haifa.[30]

The lower layer of the Arab urban working class was aligned with the peasant proletariat. Arab skilled manual labour, however, had achieved a slightly higher status by its longer period of more or less steady work in the city. This labour force had been attracted to work opportunities in the government projects, public facilities and the Municipality, and had increased with the growth of the town's service infrastructure. The building industry, both in materials production and construction itself, was another major field which absorbed Arab labour. In Haifa, this stratum acquired characteristics different from those of labour in other towns. For one thing, because of the large work sites – in the railways, the port, the IPC, industry and in private building – Arab labour came up against intense competition from organized Jewish labour. The growing disparity in wages and working conditions between Arab and Jewish workers sharpened Arab political consciousness, in spite of efforts by the Histadrut to lessen the animosity by helping to organize Arab workers.

The PAWS played a part in sharpening the social and political awareness of this stratum. Problems facing the Arab workers were given public coverage and workers were instructed in the methods of united action and in developing an assertive attitude towards employers.[31] Solidarity among Arabs was emphasized. This underlined, on the one hand, the sense of socio-economic separation which the workers felt vis-à-vis the Jewish working class and the rest of Arab society; it also gave them self-confidence, as a group, which they often translated into action. Arab workers employed in the railways, the quarries, the IPC and the Municipality formed the bulk of the participants in the 1929 and 1933 disturbances, and with the peasants in the attacks mounted by followers of the Qassam movement in 1936 and after (see Chapter 15).

Even though its effectiveness was limited, the PAWS was a vehicle for circulating radical and innovative ideas, not only for its members but also for the handful of communists active in Haifa and the younger generation of educated activists. From the beginning, the PAWS had been under the influence of a few Palestinian communists and some young men who had experience in Western labour affairs.[32] During its first congress, in January 1930, communist members publicly accused the rich bourgeois strata of collaborating with the British colonial power. This extremist position, however, did not reflect the general attitude within the PAWS, which was hostile to communist involvement in labour affairs.[33] Their rank and file were conservative and moved more by the power of religion than by the little-understood precepts of communism. By the time the PAWS had become more powerful, and had more bourgeois, politically ambitious leaders, it had assumed a moderate line.[34] However much these leaders tried to keep out of the endemic Jerusalem power struggle between Husainis and Nashashibis and to remain independent of both, the PAWS was often pulled into the national conflicts. In addition to the Histadrut's attempts to organize Arab workers in the GFJL, supporters and opponents of the SMC also tried to create their own labour unions in Haifa for partisan purposes. During the IPC strike, Fakhri Nashashibi (nephew of Raghib) tried to win the PAWS over to the opposition by negotiating on behalf of the Arab workers, but was denounced by the society.[35] Such activities were a major cause of the weakness of the whole Arab labour movement and its failure to maintain a consistent socializing programme free from political infighting.

In the 1930s, a generation of educated nationalists, critical of the traditional leadership and their elitist politics, grew up in the cities of Palestine. It was no coincidence that the radical youth movement arose after 1929, when the impotence of the Jerusalem leadership was exposed, and that most of the young activists came from the north and the Nablus region. The first organized youth protest against the British pro-Zionist policy and the dwindling effectiveness of the Arab Executive took place in Nablus in August 1931. It was organized by young radicals of the town, some of whom had been associated with the pan-Arab nationalist movement that had swept the region at the end of the Ottoman period. Its anti-government orientation impelled the AE to try and contain the youth movement. This resulted in the first National Congress of Arab Youth at Jaffa in January 1932. Branches of the Congress were established in the main towns where Arab Boy Scout organizations were also set up.[36]

The movement's public denunciation of the tactics of the national politicians evoked a response in Haifa's already politically conscious circles of educated, mainly Muslim, youth. At this level, the radical process was manifested in two currents which overlapped and whose messages were interlaced. At one end of the spectrum stood the religious nationalist current represented by the YMMA and its inner circle of

Qassam followers (see below); at the other, the more secular, though Muslim, current of the Istiqlalists. Both expressed, in a general sense, the Arab/Palestinian nationalist, anti-Zionist orientation, but now with a sharper and more articulate anti-British flavour – an attitude mainly represented up to now by the AE, the SMC and the Husaini faction, with whom the radical groups maintained links of varying intimacy. It is important to consider in more detail the structure and role of these two currents in the radicalization process.

The Young Men's Muslim Association was established in reaction to the YMCA and in response to the need for a structure that would express the views and demands of urban Muslim youth. In the YMCA, Christian young men were provided with social, cultural and educational facilities which worked towards reinforcing Christian separation, facilitating employment and consequently weakening the nationalist front.[37] These associations, with their proselytizing activities, were regarded with suspicion and hostility by the Muslims, especially in the early 1930s, when educated young Muslims were finding it hard to secure jobs because of competition from non-Muslims, especially Christians.

It was in Haifa, with its large increasingly prosperous Christian community, that the YMMA was most aggressive in its opposition to the YMCA and to the excessive employment of Christians by the Administration and the concessionary projects.[38] Moreover, in Haifa, unlike the Christian communities of Jerusalem and Jaffa, Bishop Hajjar and a number of prosperous Christian merchants restrained their communities from political participation. The clannish and often fanatical attitude of the Muslim Association, and after 1928 of the YMMA, was reciprocated among the Christians.

Both communities were emboldened by their numerical strength in the town and by attitudes which they had brought with them to Haifa. Whereas many of the Christians had come to Haifa from Lebanon and from the northern Palestinian villages, where they had always been a strong minority, many of the Muslims had come from Damascus, Nablus and the Muslim villages of Palestine, and were unfamiliar with the special intercommunal relations prevalent in the town. These relations were exacerbated in 1930 when the president of the YMCA, Jamil al-Bahri, a Greek Catholic journalist, was murdered by Muslims connected with the Muslim Association, in a dispute over a piece of land contested between the two communities. The controversy that ensued opened up a chasm between them, with far-reaching consequences. Christian introversion was intensified to the point where some elements even came out publicly against the national movement.[39]

The constitution of the YMMA defined its activities as Muslim, social and cultural, with no involvement in political affairs.[40] Nevertheless, it was clear from the list of founders and from the specific grievances of the Muslim youth that the YMMA would not be able to divorce its social from its political role. In addition to established and respected merchants (Huri, Abu Muslih), among its founders were also nationalist (Hajj Ibrahim) and religious activists (Shaikh 'Izzedin al-Qassam).[41] Between 1928 and 1936 the YMMA was led by these two men,[42] both of whom were responsible for the intensely religious and uncompromising character of the Haifa branch. This also explains the deep suspicion in which the local Administration held the YMMA; to limit its influence, government employees, including teachers, were prevented from joining the association, a fact that affected the calibre of its membership and the type of its activities.[43]

Though the YMMA used the premises of the Muslim Association, it was relatively independent of that organization and of the SMC. In its public meetings, it tried to steer clear of politics, but in private and in the meetings of the Executive Committee of the Palestine YMMA, political issues were the primary concern, and the link with other nationalist groupings such as the Youth Congress and the Istiqlal Party was freely discussed.[44]

The Haifa branch of the Youth Congress, opened in 1931, collaborated closely with the YMMA, but there are indications that it was less independent of the SMC.[45] The Scout organization also played an important part during the turbulent events of the 1930s, whether in joining in demonstrations, enforcing strikes or guarding the sea coast against illegal immigrants. The scouts, the youth group and the YMMA were all closely watched by the police, and some of their members were even arrested under suspicion, following attacks on Jewish quarters and settlements. Though some members of the YMMA must have joined al-Qassam's underground organization,[46] no criminal offence was ever proved against any of its members in Haifa. Nevertheless, the growing militancy of the majority of young Muslims, their support and guidance by seasoned radical politicians and puritanical religious leaders, and the moral and financial support given them by respected Muslim professional men and merchants, caused great unease to the local Administration and the police.

In fact, the local Administration had been watching the escalating militancy of the Muslim community with apprehension. Religious leaders seemed to show no hesitation in inciting opinion against the pro-Zionist policy and its threat to Islam. Speeches delivered in the Istiqlal mosque were considered by the DC to be violent and seditious.[47] The press was also moved by the general radical mood, and editorials reflected the community's deep mistrust of the government. In retaliation, Arabic newspapers were intermittently closed down for the slightest reason. The feelings of the Arab community were best illustrated by the frequent street demonstrations after 1929, which were becoming more deliberate in their anti-government focus. In the October 1933 demonstrations the attack was against government property and the police, who responded by firing at those considered to be the ring leaders.[48]

These mass activities were the result both of a spontaneous popular reaction to the worsening conditions in the country and of organization by radical leaders, especially the Istiqlalists Mu'in al-Madi, Subhi al-Khadra and Rashid al-Hajj Ibrahim. The last two were particularly active in the YMMA, the Scout squads and branches of the Istiqlal Party in the north; they were also watched by the police because of their close relations with Shaikh al-Qassam. Al-Hajj Ibrahim, in particular, is singled out by writers on the Qassam revolt as having preached violence against the Jews to activists in the north since the early 1930s.[49] His possible collaboration with Shaikh al-Qassam is also insinuated by these same writers. Nevertheless, his only documented role is that of a somewhat conservative Arab nationalist with strong Muslim leanings. In Haifa he was able to influence a large number of progressive educated young men, especially those attached to the YMMA. Until the early 1930s, he was pro-Husaini and active in the Muslim Association, but he seems to have fallen out with Jerusalem at the time of the formation of the Istiqlal Party, when he demanded a more militant approach from the Arab Executive; nevertheless, he did not completely break away from the mainstream nationalists.[50]

Like many of the pan-Arabists in Palestine, the Istiqlalists were financially subsidized by more fortunate nationalists in the neighbouring Arab countries.[51] For many reasons, however, the Istiqlal Party – as an organization – proved short-lived in the partisan atmosphere of Palestine. It lacked the financial backing and personnel to attract popular support, and its leadership refused to open its ranks to new ideologues. Moreover, its members soon split into those who supported and those who opposed Amin al-Husaini and the SMC.[52] It was not able to secure the support of Haifa's older-established and more conservative politicians; it was popular only among the associates of Hajj Ibrahim and the young radicals, especially the members of the YMMA,[53] where it was successful in spreading its political ideology. In Haifa, the two currents coalesced to form an Arab nationalist, anti-British ideology which attracted even Christian young men.[54] Both the Youth Congress branch and the YMMA followed the same ideological line, whether guided by Istiqlalists or not.[55]

The role of power elites

As soon as the uproar surrounding the 1929 events subsided, traditional political life in Haifa resumed its old ways. The moderate and conservative nationalists returned to bickering for and against the Jerusalem leadership; the Christians remained detached and outside the main political arena; while the pro-Zionist elements had, by this time, acquired a complacency and a secure socio-economic status that allowed them a larger measure of political patronage. The impact of the change caused by 1929 was gradual, and by 1936, after al-Qassam's death, its radical aspect took all political circles by storm.

The radical voices in the town were raised immediately after 1929 by nationalist leaders and their young followers grouped in the Muslim Association. Following the death of the mufti, Muhammad Murad, in April 1929, elements less aligned with Jerusalem and more concerned with local politics appeared. Merchants of both Palestinian and Damascene origin, who had gained prominence with their newly acquired wealth and patronage, competed for political positions in the Muslim community.[56] Most members of this elite were conservative, and worried by Istiqlali attacks on British policy. At the same time, the credibility of any leader depended on his support, if only verbal, for the Arab, anti-Zionist and now increasingly anti-British stand.

The Muslim Association still retained its leading role as the main organization responsible for defending national and Muslim rights in Haifa. By 1934, when the feeling of despair among all political circles had become more acute, it took the initiative in convoking a meeting with the Christian Committee and the members of the Arab Executive to consult on national affairs; it was also able to maintain the tradition of a Muslim-Christian solidarity procession during the feast at the end of Ramadan.[57] It was the Istiqlal members in the Association who started assuming a more explicitly belligerent attitude towards the Administration. In 1932, members of the Association boycotted the parties held in honour of the High Commissioner at the Municipality.

The Muslim Association was perceived by some Muslim leaders as a source of community power, 'za'ama', similar to that which the Municipality, the Chamber of Commerce, the PAWS and other community organizations offered the new bourgeois leaders, both Muslim and Christian. Some of the old Muslim leaders, for example Ibrahim al-Khalil and Khalil Taha, were not necessarily identified with nationalist ideals, and among the new leaders most had achieved their status primarily by virtue of their economic prowess. It was also clear that some of these newly enriched entrepreneurs were involved in secret business deals which contradicted the nationalist image they projected.[58] The more such cases came to be known, the more they built up radical opposition to the traditional leadership on the part of the less privileged strata of society. When the youth organizers held their secret preparatory meetings in the major cities before the Jaffa conference in March 1933, Hajj Tahir Karaman, Ibrahim al-Khalil and Hajj Khalil Taha were excluded because of their Jewish contacts.[59]

Leaders of both the pro-Husaini faction and the opposition belonged to the conservative current; this drew them closer and blunted their differences. While Nassar and Mukhlis continued to expose and vilify the Jerusalem leadership and the practices of the SMC, and to bemoan the clearly deteriorating condition of Arab political life, the tone of these attacks was becoming more conciliatory.[60] The opposition in the north, in particular Shuqairi, attempted to revive the antagonism against Jerusalem by creating a new party, Hizb al-Ahrar (the Liberal Party). It attracted only a few ambitious young men such as Hanna 'Asfour, however, while it was denounced by the old supporters of the opposition, like Nassar,[61] who were obviously weary of the perpetual bickering and desperately looking for solutions. They tended to direct their attention towards local problems, especially those affecting the Arabs' economic status, employment, and education.

The press of Haifa reflected, at this juncture, the generally con-servative attitude of most political leaders and their followers in the emerging bourgeois class. Their explanation for the ills of society was the infiltration of communism among the Arabs and its deleterious effect on Arab labour. They strongly opposed strikes as a political weapon because they damaged the economy, especially the interests of the merchant class. Christians and Muslims were united in this stand.[62] Between 1930 and 1936, Haifa saw many strikes, some co-ordinated with action in other Palestinian cities but others carried out in Haifa alone. The press was the main vehicle expressing the growing anti-British feeling[63] and Arab discontent, sometimes the discontent of the working classes and not necessarily only of the bourgeois class. By June 1931, new steps to control the press were taken by the Administration,[64] but such measures only radicalized it further and fostered increasingly critical attitudes in the newspaper owners.

After 1929 Christian political circles remained unobtrusive, especially after the accusations directed against the community for its apathy during the disturbances. Muslim resentment at what they saw as Chris-tian privileges reached its height with the death of Jamil al-Bahri (see above). Thereafter Christians and Muslims reverted to introverted communal reactions, discarding the national solidarity built up between them for at least two decades. Al-Zuhur, Bahri's newspaper, published inflammatory articles demanding foreign protection for the Christian minorities and dissociating the Christians from the national movement. Muslim behaviour was similarly inflammatory. When a delegation from Jerusalem came to attend the funeral on behalf of the Arab Executive, a Muslim party encouraged by Rashid al-Hajj Ibrahim blocked its path and tried to prevent its attendance. It finally took the mediation of Hajj Amin and a nationwide campaign to cool the atmosphere.[65]

It was mainly the Greek Catholics who maintained their boycott of the town's political life. This in turn promoted a fracture in the Christian front, since the Greek Orthodox and Protestant communities were anxious to overlook Christian-Muslim differences.[66] By 1932, the Christian Committee was re-established, however, with proper representation of all communities. Even Fu'ad Sa'd, a staunch supporter of Bishop Hajjar, was encouraging participation in political life by 1933.[67] By then the general political atmosphere in the town had improved in preparation for the municipal elections.

The role of the elites in the Municipality

As shown in Chapter 13, the 1927 municipal elections brought in a sweeping majority of opposition sympathizers and gave the Zionists a determining voice in municipal affairs through the appointment of Hasan Shukri as mayor. As all the Arab councillors came from the emerging bourgeois class, for whom municipal office was mainly a means of achieving social status, the day-to-day operations of the council did not concern them overmuch, and this allowed the mayor and the Jewish members to create many precedents in the interests of the Jewish sector. These developments were gradual but had reached explosive levels by the end of 1931.

Disagreements occurred mainly over labour and the distribution of municipal projects, as well as employment policy in regard to minor positions in the service of the Council. Demands for a larger allotment of municipal projects and the employment of Jewish labour were pushed by the Jewish councillors, supported by the mayor (and sometimes by the local Administration) but often opposed by the Arab members. Finally, it was decided that a certain percentage (equivalent to one-third) of all municipal work was to be given to Jewish labour, a policy confirmed by the Administration in 1933.[68] The Arab public in Haifa became aware of the situation within the Council only towards the end of 1930, when irregularities in the finances of the Municipality were published in the press. Fu'ad Saba, an auditor and a nationalist supporter of the Jerusalem leadership, was employed to audit the municipal finances. His report accused council members and employees of corruption and bringing the Municipality to bankruptcy, the main indictment being against the Jewish engineer, who was attacked for fraudulent practices.[69]

These disclosures fuelled the Arabs' attacks on the general policy and performance of the Arab councillors. Whereas in 1927 Hasan Shukri had been put up for election as mayor with the qualification of being an experienced civil servant, capable of compromises while safeguarding Arab rights, in 1931 he was projected in the press as an ignorant, illiterate man and a stooge exploited by the Jewish councillors.[70] The fact that, because of Shukri, the Municipality's lawyer, engineer and veterinarian were Jews active in the Zionist organizations in the town, added to the condemnation. The Jewish engineer was replaced by an Englishman, and soon afterwards, Saba's services were also dispensed with.[71] These actions only confirmed Arab opinion that the Municipality was becoming a Jewish stronghold. Keith-Roach, who took office as DC in September 1931, dealt with the situation in a drastic fashion. He informed the mayor of the accusations against him, and threatened him with dismissal unless he regarded his first allegiance as being to the Administration and kept the DC fully informed.[72]

By 1933, the nationalist leaders in Haifa were preparing themselves for the 1934 municipal elections. As early as April 1929, the plans for a new municipal bill, limiting the powers of local councils, had been discussed in the Municipality and denounced by the local Arab press.[73] This measure was perceived as a weapon to be used by the Administration to intimidate representatives. By 1932, a Municipalities Ordinance was drafted which gave the High Commissioner large powers of appointment and dismissal and subjected municipal councils to strict administrative and economic control by the District Commissioners.[74] Despite objections from the mayors of Arab towns and the Tel-Aviv Municipality, the Municipal Corporation Ordinance was promulgated in January 1934, and the elections of that year were held under its terms. The Jewish councillors, who objected on principle to such a limitation of their democratic rights, accepted the right of government to interfere in municipal affairs, regarding the measure as safeguarding Jewish interests in towns where Jews were still in a minority; government interference would be sought to ensure a share for the Jewish sector in local projects and employment. After 1936, however, when the Jewish community had achieved numerical parity with the Arabs in Haifa, they objected to the power this Ordinance bestowed on the DC.[75]

The 1934 elections followed the procedure used in 1927, although the council was enlarged to include two additional Jewish councillors; 5,186 Arabs and 3,010 Jews voted for the new council of twelve,[76] and eight Arabs were elected and four Jews nominated by the Jewish community. The composition of the Arab part of the council was indicative of the changed political atmosphere in the town, especially the stepping up of nationalist activities. Several meetings were held by political and communal organizations before the elections in order to agree on candidates.[77] 'Abdul-Rahman al-Hajj (the ex-mayor), Rashid al-Hajj Ibrahim and Badri al-'Idi, a nationalist lawyer and a strong supporter of the al-Qassam movement, were the nationalist candidates; Hasan Shukri (the incumbent mayor) and Shihada Shalah, a Greek Catholic involved in labour affairs,[78] were the Zionist-supported Arab candidates; Ibrahim Sahyoun and Mikha'il Tuma represented the

Christians, and Hanna 'Asfour ran on the ticket of the Arab labour movement.[79]

Despite the changed composition of the council, the nationalist representatives were given no opportunity to promote their political interests until 1936. Decisions concerning urban improvements, labour distribution and employment were made amicably, even though criticism of the Municipality by the radical elements was increasing. By June 1936, however, all activities of the Municipality came to a standstill when the Arab councillors resigned en masse in support of the Arab strike. Even the pro-Zionist Arab members felt compelled, at this stage, to resign with the others. The four Jewish councillors and their two Arab supporters were reappointed to a municipal commission with four British members, which ran the Municipality until 1940, when Arabs representing the nationalist current were re-elected. Meanwhile, Hasan Shukri had died and Shabatai Levy had been appointed mayor in his place. Since that date the mayoralty had moved to the Jewish sector at a time of intense political radicalization of the Arab community. This was symbolic of the changed status of Haifa: Jewish ascendancy in the town, numerical, economic and political, had become a fact.

Notes

1. A. M. Lesch, *Arab Politics in Palestine, 1917–1939* (London, 1979), p. 198. See also the Prologue to Part Four above.

2. The Criminal Investigation Department (CID) operated in Palestine until 1922 and was re-established in 1930 as a result of the August 1929 disturbances. HC to CO, 28 June 1930 (PRO CO 733/180).

3. Political Report by Governor of Phoenicia, Symes, for June 1922 (PRO CO 733/23).

4. HC to CO, 17 January 1930 (PRO CO 733/182).

5. Reporting on the 1936 disturbances, Keith-Roach reveals the deep unease of some British officials about the application of the policy. 'We must admit that by the restrictions imposed in Mr. Ramsay MacDonald's letter to Dr. Weizmann we have failed in Palestine, otherwise there would be no need for a Royal Commission to examine into our doings'. Memo on the disturbances of 28 July 1936 by E. Keith-Roach, enclosed with letter to Sir Osmo Parkinson, 30 September 1936 (PRO CO 733/316).

6. DC to CS re Jidru land, 5 November 1935 (ISA L/262/ 34); E. Keith-Roach, 'Pasha of Jerusalem', Vol. I (Private Papers, St Antony's College, Oxford), p. 396. Raya Adler (Cohen), 'The Tenants of Wadi Hawarith: Another View of the Land Question in Palestine', *IJMES* 20/22 (May 1988), pp. 197–220.

7. H.C. Wauchope to S of S Cunliffe-Lister, 8 December 1934 (PRO CO 733/257). See also F. M. Moody's 'Diaries' (Private Papers Collection, Bodleian Library, Oxford), 20 April 1936, on the British army's brutal treatment of Arab villagers. In the opinion of Sydney Moody, the army carried out an irrational

campaign of terror in the towns, too – especially Jaffa. He tried to restrain the army from shooting into the houses in Jaffa at night to stop sniping, but the army had persuaded the HC to pursue this course of action.

8. Volunteers from Haganah were used by the British army for offensive action against Arabs in 1936–9 (J. C. Hurewitz, *The Struggle for Palestine* (New York, 1968), p. 93). This policy sanctioned Jewish violence against the Arabs.

9. Political Report by E. Mills, September 1924 (PRO CO 733/74).

10. Z. Vilnay, *Khaifa Be'avar Ve Bahoveh* (Haifa in the Past and the Future) (Tel-Aviv, 1936), p. 110.

11. Jewish Community Council, *Kehilat Khaifa Beasar Hashanim, 1932–1941* (The Jewish Community of Haifa in the Ten Years 1932–1941) (Haifa, 1942), p. 1.

12. Y. Washitz, 'Jewish-Arab Relations in Haifa during the Mandate' (unpublished manuscript, n.d.), Chapter II, p. 14; D. HaCohen, *Time to Tell* (New York/London, 1984), pp. 25–6; A. Khalifa (trans.), *Al Thawra al-'Arabiyya al-Kubra fi Filastin, 1936–1939: Al-Riwaya al-Israeliyya al-Rasmiyya* (The Great Arab Revolt in Palestine 1936–1939: An Official Israeli Account), From Books of the Haganah, Vol. 2, Books 5, 6 (Beirut, 1989), p. 233.

13. Political confidential report, June 1923 (PRO FO 371 E7682/206/65).

14. HaCohen, *Time*, pp. 24–33, 69, 91.

15. N. A. Badran, *Al-Ta'lim wal-Tahdith fil-Mujtama' al-'Arabi al-Filastini* (Education and Modernization in Arab Palestinian Society) (Beirut, 1969), pp. 220–22; G. Kanafani, *Palestine: The 1936–1939 Revolt* (London, n.d.), p. 7.

16. CS despatch on communist pamphlet on the disturbances to FO, November 1929 (PRO FO 371 E6558/4198/65); A. W. Kayyali, *Palestine: A Modern History* (London, 1978), p. 145.

17. See *al-Karmil*, 28 March and 4 July 1926; 11 and 29 May 1929; K. Sakakini, *Kadha Ana Ya Dunya* (Such I am, O World) (Jerusalem, 1955), pp. 246–7; oral information, London, September 1981 (names withheld by request).

18. District Commissioner to Head of Education Department, referred to CO, November 1926 (PRO CO 733/117); *al-Karmil*, 3 July 1929, and oral information, Khalid al-Hasan, London, March 1982.

19. *Al-Karmil*, 30 September 1928; 9 January and 5 June 1929.

20. *Al-Karmil*, 14 and 21 October 1928; 18 and 21 September 1929.

21. *Al-Karmil*, 26 January, 20 February, 1 May and 5 June 1929.

22. A reading of the local press in Haifa for the first six months of 1929 clearly reveals a sense of fear and wrath. See *al-Karmil* and *al-Yarmuk* for the period.

23. *Al-Karmil*, 25 September 1929. This referred to the 'Green Hand Band' of Ahmad Tafish that operated in the Safad-Acre region in mid-1929 (Kayyali, *Palestine*, p. 156; see also *al-Karmil*, 2 August 1930).

24. *Haifa*, 20 November 1924.

25. M. Yazbek, by studying the Shari'a Court records and extrapolating on the origin of the Haifa, mainly Muslim, population, gave a vivid picture of the background and miserable living conditions of the Haifa slum residents. M. Yazbek, *Al-Hijra al-'Arabiyya ila Haifa* (Arab Migration into Haifa) (Nazareth, 1988), pp. 132–43. See also Chapter 4.

26. Keith-Roach, *Pasha of Jerusalem*, Vol. I, p. 399, and 'Recommendations on Future Policy', Secret Report on 9 September 1936 (PRO CO 733/316). George Mansur reported that in the mid-1930s Haifa had over 11,000 Arab workers

living in these shanty towns. G. Mansur, *The Arab Worker under the Palestine Mandate* (Jerusalem, 1937), p. 14.

27. For example, the people coming from Saffouriyya lived in the huts to the west of Haifa, in Zawara, and the militant cells that sprang up in the 1930s among this stratum chose that area for their meetings (A. Mukhlis, 'Diaries', 1936–1940; Palestine Research Centre, Beirut); see Yazbek, *Al-Hujra al-'Arabiyya*, pp. 118–23, on the relationships and interdependence between these immigrant residents of the slums.

28. J. Marlowe, *Rebellion in Palestine* (London, 1946), p. 69.

29. *Al-Karmil*, 25 March 1933. Appeal by YMMA (Haifa) to DC to stop the demolition of huts in which the poor of Haifa live, on 9 April 1935. The response was negative on 1 May 1935 (ISA 61/141).

30. J. S. Migdal, *Palestinian Society and Politics* (Princeton, NJ, 1980), pp. 25–7.

31. Arab labour under the direction of the PAWS carried out various strikes, starting in the late 1920s. Examples of these activities were the strike of the Nesher workers in 1932 and those of the IPC in 1935. E. Tuma, *Sittun 'Aman 'ala al-Haraka al-Qawmiyya al-'Arabiyya al-Filastiniyya* (The Last Sixty Years of the Palestinian Arab National Movement) (Beirut, 1978), p. 98. See also Chapter 8.

32. Badran, *Al-Ta'lim*, p. 248.

33. M. Budeiri, *The Palestine Communist Party 1919–1948* (London, 1979), p. 54. Communist elements in Haifa continually tried to influence and infiltrate the labour ranks; however, they had difficulty in attracting adherents and arabizing their message and were persistently hunted by the police. Kanafani, *Palestine*, pp. 6–8; *al-Karmil*, 15 July 1930 and 25 February 1933. See also Police Summaries for July 1935 (PRO FO 371 E4436/154/31).

34. Badran, *Al-Ta'lim*, p. 248. J. 'Asfour, *Palestine: My Land, My Country, My Home* (Beirut, 1967), pp. 31–43. 'Asfour, a well–off advocate, was one of the leaders of the PAWS. Tuma, *Sittun 'Aman*, p. 84.

35. CID Report on IPC strike, 9 March 1935, and statement by Arab workers on the activities of Fakhri Nashashibi, n.d. (ISA 65/1 3578); J. C. Hurewitz, *The Struggle for Palestine*, p. 61; Report by DC to CS on methods to limit participation of municipal employees (i.e. Fakhri Nashashibi) in political affairs, November 1934 (ISA 2 G/184/34).

36. Tuma, *Sittun 'Aman*, pp. 101–16; Y. Porath, *The Palestinian Arab National Movement, 1929–1939* (London, 1977), pp. 119–23.

37. Badran, *Al-Ta'lim*, pp. 294–5; Porath, *The Emergence*, pp. 300–302; Lesch, *Arab Politics*, pp. 106–7.

38. Oral information, Beirut and Amman, May/June 1975 (names withheld upon request). *Al-Karmil*, 1 October 1932.

39. Porath, *The Emergence*, p. 303; Porath, *The Palestinian Arab*, p. 109; *al-Karmil*, 20 and 24 September 1930 and 21 January 1931; Yazbek, *Al-Hijra al-'Arabiyya*, pp. 116, 128.

40. A. W. Kayyali (ed.), *Watha'iq al-Muqawama al-Filastiniyya al-'Arabiyya didd al-ihtilal al-Biritani wal Sahyuniyya* (Documents of the Arab-Palestinian Resistance to the British Mandate and Zionism) (Beirut, 1968), p. 101.

41. YMMA to DC, 18 May 1928 (ISA 61/141).

42. Rashid al-Hajj Ibrahim was president of the YMMA until 1932; 'Izzedin al-Qassam became president in August 1932 and remained active in the associ-

ation until his death in 1935. See file on the YMMA in ISA 61/141; see also *al-Karmil*, 17 August 1932 and 19 July 1933; Police Summary, 17 February 1936 (PRO FO 371 E887/19/31). Another Istiqlalist, Subhi al-Khadra (an attorney and director of the *awqaf* in the north), helped in the organization of YMMAs in the northern district.

43. Lesch, *Arab Politics*, p. 107; Badran, *Al-Ta'lim*, pp. 295–6.

44. Police Summaries, March 1933 (PRO FO 371 E1455/111/31).

45. *Al-Karmil*, 14 November 1931; al-Hajj Ibrahim, who by 1936 was quite critical of the Jerusalem leadership and much closer to the militant circles of al-Qassam and the YMMA, and was a founding member of the Istiqlal Party, was reported to be in the process of reviving the YMMA, while at the same time he opposed the Muslim Association and the Haifa branch of the Youth Congress. Police Summary, 17 February 1936 (PRO FO 371 E887/19/31).

46. A. H. Ghunayyim, 'Thawrat al-Shaikh 'Izz al-Din al-Qassam' (The Revolt of Shaikh Izz al-Din al-Qassam), *Shu'un Falastiniyya*, No. 6, January 1972, p. 182.

47. See articles in *al-Karmil* and *al-Yarmuk* for 1930–33 on arming and training of Jews by the government and similar topics. See also Keith-Roach, 'Pasha of Jerusalem', Chapter XI, p. 398.

48. Report by DC, ND on the disturbances, 7 November 1933 (PRO CO 733/239). For the opinion of a British official on the 1933 disturbances, see Humphrey Bowman's 'Diaries' of 29 October 1933 (Private Papers Collection, St Antony's College, Oxford).

49. S. Lachman, 'Arab Rebellion and Terrorism in Palestine 1929–39: The Case of Sheikh Izz al-Din al-Qassam and his Movement', in Kedourie and Haim (eds), *Zionism and Arabism in Palestine and Israel* (London, 1982), p. 53; Porath, *The Palestinian Arab*, p. 132.

50. In July 1937, he was delegated by Hajj Amin al-Husaini and the SMC to meet with Kalvarisky in search of a solution to the dilemma of the Arab/Jewish situation. This was part of a tactical campaign by the Arabs to procrastinate until the meeting of the Permanent Mandates Commission. M. Cohen, 'Secret Diplomacy and Rebellion in Palestine, 1936–1939', *International Journal of Middle East Studies* 8, 1977, pp. 379–404.

51. Mu'in al-Madi, Subhi al-Khadra and Rashid al-Hajj Ibrahim were helped by financial subsidies from the Iraqi Prime Minister, Yasin al-Hashimi, who had a special secret fund for these purposes. S. A. al-Qaysi, 'Yasin al-Hashimi: A Study of His Role in Iraqi Politics between 1922 and 1936' (unpublished M.A. thesis, University of Basra, 1976), p. 202.

52. Porath, *The Palestinian Arab*, p. 126; Tuma, *Sittun 'Aman*, pp. 110–16; Badran, *Al-Ta'lim*, pp. 299–300.

53. Police Summaries for May 1933 (PRO FO 371 E2477/111/31).

54. Christian radical youths were beginning to identify with this ideology (*al-Karmil*, 11 May 1932, and *al-Nafir*, 9 October 1933). In addition to the few Christian members of the communist party and the labour movement, some joined the Arab Youth Club in 1934 where these beliefs circulated (see Chapter 12).

55. See the Youth Congress Manifesto (*al-Karmil*, 14 November 1931, and al-Kayyali, *Watha'iq al-Muqawama*, pp. 368–71) and the connection between the Istiqlal Party and the YMMA in Haifa (Police Summaries, March 1933, PRO FO 371 E1485/111/31). By the mid-1930s, Muslim youth were strongly influenced

by political conditions in neighbouring states, and Egyptian periodicals and newspapers like *al-Thaqafa* and *al-Ahram* were widely read (oral information, Khalid al-Hasan, London, March 1982).

56. One such leader was Hajj Tahir Karaman, a successful merchant and entrepreneur who was assured of the support of his employees and business associates when he ran for elections in the Municipality (he replaced Huri in 1931) and the Chamber of Commerce (*al-Karmil*, 12 June 1929). He built a mosque between the villages of Kasa'ir and Hosha to the north of Haifa in an attempt to gain the support of the rural population in that region (oral information, London, June 1982, names withheld by request). See also Arabs' *Who's Who*, prepared for the Jerusalem Secretariat, in PRO CO 733/248.

57. Police Summaries, January 1934 (PRO FO 371 E649/271/31). *Al-Karmil* (29 April 1933) reported an item of news that illustrated the state of panic the Arabs in the north were experiencing. It reported the intention of the Arabs of Acre to request, through the League of Nations, annexation to Lebanon, to which Acre had been linked in former times. This request was considered as a means of escaping the Zionist threat.

58. Sakakini, *Kadha Ana*, entry for 22 March 1933, p. 246. HaCohen, *Time*, pp. 79–91.

59. Police Summaries, April 1933 (PRO FO 371 E1993/111/31); Tegart Papers, Box 1, File 3(b).

60. The complaints against the SMC came from the traditional opposition in the north and from their supporters, mainly Muslim, in Haifa (Petitions against practices of the SMC, November 1931, ISA 2 K/186/3 and 2 K/44/31). For attacks on the Husaini political activities, see *al-Karmil*, 11 January and 23 July 1930; 31 October 1931; 18 June 1932.

61. Porath and Nassar mention the composition of this party in the north and the ambitions of 'Asfour (Porath, *The Palestinian Arab*, p. 50, and *al-Karmil*, 22 February and 18 July 1930; 18 July 1931). No mention of this party, however, was made by Hanna 'Asfour, the Haifa member, in his book giving an account of his professional and political careers, *Palestine: My Land*.

62. *Al-Karmil*, 16, 20 and 27 August 1930. The long six-month strike of 1936 was publicly opposed by some merchants in Haifa (Washitz, 'Jewish-Arab Relations', Chapter III, p. 12).

63. *Al-Karmil*, 7 June and 26 July 1930; 12 April, 18 May and 3 December 1932.

64. R. A. Furness, Report on the Control of the Press in Palestine, 20 June 1931 (PRO CO 733/204). See also *al-Karmil*, 3 June and 8 August 1931.

65. For details on the Bahri incident and its repercussions among the communities, see *al-Karmil*, starting in August 1930 and to the end of January 1931, especially the issues of 27 September and 11 and 18 October 1930.

66. *Al-Karmil*, 12 October 1932.

67. In a revealing interview with *al-Karmil* (22 July 1933), Fu'ad Sa'd explained the changing attitude of many Christian Arabs. While attending the Exhibition of Arab Industries in Jerusalem, he had become aware of the strength of Arab solidarity, increased by political conditions in the country. He emphasized that his contacts with foreigners had convinced him that being a Christian did not

afford him better consideration; on the contrary, it only aroused distrust among the Muslims.

68. Minutes of the Municipal Council for 1931–3, especially those of June 1932, quoted in Washitz, 'Jewish-Arab Relations', Chapter IV, pp. 4–5. HaCohen, *Time*, pp. 27–9 and 89.

69. Anonymous letter to the Haifa Municipality, 9 November 1931 (CZA J15/4205); see also *al-Karmil*, 6, 24 and 27 June 1931.

70. *Al-Karmil*, 20 May, 3 June, 14 November and 19 December 1931; 6 May 1933.

71. *Al-Karmil*, 4 May 1932.

72. Keith-Roach, 'Pasha of Jerusalem', Vol. 2, Chapter IX.

73. *Al-Karmil*, 10 April 1929.

74. Hasan Shukri to CS, 21 December 1932, and Mayors' petition to HC (enclosure) (ISA CS 2 G/99/33); Municipal Corporation Ordinance 1934 in HC's despatch, 26 April 1936 (PRO CO 733/302); *al-Karmil*, 13 May 1931; 23 November 1932.

75. Washitz, 'Jewish-Arab Relations', Chapter IV, pp. 6–9.

76. S of S to Col. Wedgwood, 6 July 1934 (ISA 2 G/114/34).

77. Police Summaries, April 1934 (PRO FO 371 E2173/271/31).

78. Tegart Papers, Box 1, File 3(c), p.5 (Private Papers, St Antony's College, Oxford).

79. 'Asfour, *Palestine: My Land*, p. 102. 'Asfour relates that he had been approached by leaders of the Histadrut, offering him support if he ran on their list of candidates, an offer he refused.

Conclusion: the Path to Revolution

Background

While the accelerating militancy of the Arab reaction since 1929 had shocked British officials, the Administration had been monitoring its mounting intensity closely.[1] British officials on mission were trained to dissociate themselves from involvement in the particular aspirations of the communities they governed, as demonstrated in the attitude of many District Commissioners and other senior officers.[2] Most of them saw acquiescence on the part of the Arab population as the natural behaviour among governed people; all the more shocking therefore was the intensity of Arab reaction during periods of crisis. They failed to grasp the significance of the impact of the Mandatory policy on the fabric of Arab society. As indicated in Chapters 13 and 14, the accumulation of economic, social and political grievances brought great socio-economic differentiations, radicalized large sectors of society and was to climax in the eruption of civil disobedience, spontaneous militant confrontations and organized rebellion. Such activities were considered by the Administration, and the Zionists, as the terrorist acts of brigands and lawless peasants.

To the Arab society of 1935, on the other hand, these conditions were the product of a sequence of events that was inevitable. While traditional leaders attempted by all means in their power to halt the course of radicalization, they found themselves carried away by the current. If the leadership was surprised by the concentric cycle of violence of 1929, 1933, 1935 and 1936, it was in fact caused by their myopic perspective on political reality, and especially on developments in the cities where they lived. Until the mid-1930s acts of violence were more often sporadic, unco-ordinated and mostly attributable to the poorer strata in the cities, those who bore the heaviest brunt of the Mandate policy. By late 1935, however, the onus of the radical mood had shifted, to peasant urban dwellers, to urban workers, to the lower middle-class, petty entrepreneurs and to the intellectuals, along with a widespread rural involvement. In the cities what had altered was the popular frame of mind, which now saw in militancy the only outlet left, enlarging the circle of participation and preventing those who wished to deviate from doing so.

Foremost among the cities during the 1930s, Haifa had witnessed the emergence of a Palestinian capitalist class, especially in the fields of commerce, import/export trade and construction, as well as in small industries servicing the Arab market, such as cigarettes. Wealth also accumulated among real-estate owners, who profited from the rise in land prices and the demand for rented premises, and from cheap labour for building. This emerging stratum was, by virtue of its economic interests, more aligned to the aims of the conservative traditional leadership; however, at this stage its potential growth had become restrained and contained by Zionist competition.[3]

While economic prosperity benefited this sector of the urban community, it did not extend to the lower stratum of the middle class: government employees, small merchants and craftsmen, who had been negatively affected by the economic pressures and the changing character of the city. The worst-hit were the displaced peasantry and the working classes. Within a decade, while these changes were glossed over by those benefiting from the status quo, other political realities such as the Jewish numerical presence, their economic and political strength as well as their control of vital resources of urban life had become actuality. The reality of the Jewish National Home policy, with its negative effects on the Arab community, could be overlooked no longer. In Haifa this state of affairs was concretely felt by 1935, when the physical, economic and political aspects of the Arab town were being squeezed, altered and slowly phased out. In this atmosphere differences in socio-political orientations had blurred somewhat and their focus converged.[4] The popular reaction to, and tacit endorsement of, Shaikh 'Izzedin al-Qassam's challenge to British authority were testimony to these altered conditions and indications of the widespread militancy in the city as well as in the countryside.

Shaikh 'Izzedin al-Qassam: symbol of radical response

It was against this background that the martyrdom of al-Qassam at Ya'bid on 20 November 1935 revealed the advanced stage of organization reached by the militant groups in the struggle against the British occupation and its corollary, the JNH policy.[5] The northern districts of Palestine had seen political violence against Jewish settlement from the outset. But organized militant activities with a coherent ideological commitment had gradually coalesced to combine the radical nationalist currents of the cities with the countryside, the proletarianized peasants and the urban workers. Though there had been reports of organizing for militant activities in various regions of Palestine since the violent events of 1929, it was in the north that such activities were most intense and produced long-lasting results.[6] In Haifa and its countryside, the history of Zionist implementation of Jewish settlement and conquest of the land, the market and labour had produced an inflammatory situation. As a centre for the port, the railway, the IPC refinery and large building activities, Haifa attracted an increasing amount of drifting, mostly unskilled, Palestinian labour in the 1920s and 1930s. Combined with the radicalization and introversion of the Arab nationalist strata, this produced a highly combustible situation. The struggle had emerged from its narrow opposition to Jewish settlement into an outright revolt against the Mandatory government, the upholder of the JNH policy. Urban political leaders were often the guiding spirits and the financial backers of these campaigns, but the peasant immigrants and the rural population formed the backbone of the revolt. Accordingly they paid the highest price for this involvement.

The special character of Shaikh 'Izzedin al-Qassam – a dignified, charismatic and morally motivated puritanical Muslim cleric[7] who had the uncanny ability to translate what he believed into steadfast commitment on the part of his followers – defined the spirit behind the whole revolutionary expression of the three years of the rebellion. He had moved to Haifa in 1921 from Jabala near Latakia in Syria, where his vocation as a Muslim activist against the French (1920-21) singled him out. Haifa provided ripe soil for his mission, especially among the most destitute strata of the urban community – men of little or no education, illiterate menial workers in the railways, the port, the Municipality, the construction sites and quarries, small shopkeepers and the large numbers of the unemployed. It was in the crowded shanty towns and the poor sectors of the old town that this motley collection of poor labourers and proletarianized peasants congregated, united in their resentment against British and Zionist policy which had deprived them of their traditional sources of livelihood and threatened their very existence, as well as a growing bitterness against the rich urban residents. Economic destitution bound together members of this group, and, as was to be proved later during the 1936 strike and the ensuing violence, religion was the framework in which they found licence to express their intense frustration and sense of injustice. Al-Qassam recruited followers from among them, and the organization he created endured after his death to mount a long-drawn-out campaign against the JNH policy and the more privileged strata of society.[8] However, his influence extended beyond this stratum to the growing number of

Muslim young men in the city, especially those associated with the YMMA, of which he was director.

Al-Qassam's teachings exhibited great humility, a sensitive appreciation of human strength and weakness and an overriding religious conviction. He felt strongly about foreign (non-Muslim) occupation of the Arab-Muslim homeland, thus investing his message with an Arab nationalist flavour in addition to the basic religious one. An effective orator and teacher, he started from the religious premise of Islam as the model for a puritanical way of life, helping deviants from the slums of Haifa to reform, giving the young a purpose and a defined cause, and calling for Jihad in order to redress the condition of Islam and the Muslims. This Jihad he defined in its military, ethical and spiritual dimensions, to be followed by those committed to the cause in the utmost secrecy.

Al-Qassam was a successful Muslim revivalist, a social reformer and a nationalist who interpreted the message of Islam to the uprooted dispossessed peasants of the shanty quarters of the old town, and to the politicized and frustrated Muslim youth of the poorer and lower middle classes in concrete pragmatic terms that made sense in the face of their dilemmas.[9] It was a message that he proclaimed loud and clear in his Friday sermons, in his private meetings, in his training of his secret cells of fighters, and while he toured the villages around Haifa as a marriage registrar (*Ma'thun Shari'i*), creating a network of followers and supporters there. The core group of his closest disciples, not exceeding twelve members, came to constitute the society of al-Qassam, through which the separate secret cells were interlinked.[10]

As a teacher at the Muslim (Burj) school until 1925, he had the opportunity to influence many students, but he was most effective in the Istiqlal mosque, where the Muslim *waqf* administration, run by the Muslim Association, employed him to lead prayers, preach sermons and look after the needs of the Muslim community. There, as well as in the other smaller mosques of Haifa, al-Qassam was totally dedicated to his mission, running evening classes for illiterates and giving religious teaching as well as maintaining close social contacts with his congregation and so building up his clandestine fighting circles. His idealism was combined with pragmatism, a philosophy he practised in his own life. Faith is the basic prerequisite to end transgression, and martyrdom in Jihad inspires other Muslims to continue the struggle even after a leader's death, thus creating the revolutionary focus which he initiated with his Jihad. For this purpose he chose his followers extremely carefully and trained them in faith, the use of arms and secrecy, enlisting the help of experts to undertake this training and of wealthy Muslims to subsidize it.

By his followers al-Qassam was obviously revered; however, in the eyes of the Administration, which had been watching his activities closely since 1929, he was 'a fanatical religious sheikh of the most dangerous type'.[11] His activities were also unsavoury to many wealthy Muslims of the town and to those who had aligned themselves publicly with Administration policy. His contempt for the impotent Arab leadership and their tactics was implied, even though he never confronted them, except in what is reported as his appeal to Hajj Amin al-Husaini to take up arms in the south while he carried on the revolt in the north, an offer that was turned down while the leadership awaited the outcome of diplomacy with the British.[12] It was in his adamant opposition to the British, their allies and collaborators that al-Qassam differed from the traditional nationalist leadership, and made common ground with the radical nationalists, the Istiqlalists and the growing younger generation, both Muslim and some Christian middle-class groupings. His call was to purge the national front of collaborators, land agents for the Jews (*samasira*) and those who were betraying the Muslim consensus.

From the start al-Qassam gave a religious legitimacy to his movement by acquiring a *fatwa* (religious sanction) from religious authorities in Damascus endorsing his call to Jihad and every planned assassination of Arabs considered to be collaborators and land agents. This was a formula to be followed by his disciples later on against informers and police officers. His approach to Christian Arabs was ambiguous; while it was obvious that they should not be considered as enemies, they were certainly not partners in the battle he was waging. His more virulent attacks were against the non-conformists who were Muslim, and seemed to ignore the Christians among them. His public career was brief and therefore failed to formulate definite policies concerning the Arab Christian communities, except to imply acceptance of them as long as they conformed to the Muslim consensus. He seems to have had careful but amicable relationships with Christian Arabs, who were symbols of the nationalist vanguard of their community, such as Najib Nassar, who published his writings, and Hanna 'Asfour, who defended his followers in the Nahalal case.[13] Nevertheless, his message was basically one of a Muslim solution, and he bestowed on his followers a particularly introverted Muslim outlook. The YMMA in Haifa and its branches in the northern district villages, which he had initiated, reflected an exclusivist Muslim perspective that bordered on anti-Christian feeling.[14]

Al-Qassam's real success was among the lowest economic strata. While he exerted influence on the radical nationalists in the YMMA and the Youth Congress, he was not able to recruit fighters from among them; they were his urban support group, the fund-raisers and propagators of his mission. It was with the respected Istiqlal leadership that he had the closest relationships, particularly Rashid al-Hajj Ibrahim, Subhi al-Khadra and Mu'in al Madi.[15] These Istiqlal leaders, while more radical than the traditional nationalists, still conformed to conservative behaviour and were respected members of the business and Muslim community structures in Haifa. Nevertheless, at this stage Haifa spearheaded the most radical response to the JNH policy, exposing the various political orientations and forcing all classes of society to face up to reality and take a stand.

Al-Qassam felt pursued by the authorities, and this led to the incident at Ya'bid which caused his death and the premature exposure of his movement. The significance of the event lies in the reaction it created in Haifa and the north, and among Arab nationalist circles. To the shocked confusion of the traditional leaders, the popular explosion indicated a large-scale demand for radical solutions and the existence of a network of militants between the city and its immediate villages. This reaction embarrassed the Jerusalem leadership, who seemed to look with disfavour on any radical challenge to their control of political events. Whereas they expressed their disapproval by not attending al-Qassam's funeral, conditions soon deteriorated, with al-Qassam proclaimed a popular hero, thus forcing these prominent leaders to come to Haifa to celebrate the fortieth day after the funeral, when huge demonstrations were held. A significant indication of Haifa's fragmented Muslim front was exhibited at these fortieth-day ceremonies, when the traditional nationalist trend, represented by the Muslim Association, a coalition of the political parties and the Haifa Youth Congress, held a first service, with speeches by the leaders, to be followed by another more inflammatory service, with double the attendance, organized by the Istiqlalists and the YMMA, at which vehemently anti-British, anti-Zionist speeches were delivered.[16] This was a clear signal from the extremist politicians and the young radicals and Islamists that the traditional leadership needed to get its act together or face serious dissension. It was also a signal to the other Arab communities and political currents in the city of the way the wind was blowing. It shocked the Christian political fronts into a less lethargic and more concerned mood at a time when certain elements in the community had already begun to reassess the situation.[17] A significant number of the Christian younger generation, the better-educated and the professionals, now viewed things in a more nationalist light.

Despite attempts by local leaders to keep matters under control, the masses under the influence of al-Qassam's followers began taking over immediately after his death and attacking police and government targets. In the following months, other militant groups on the same model as the Qassamites (or Ikhwan al-Qassam, as they called themselves) sprang up in other regions of Palestine, particularly in the Carmel area. The attitude of the Administration was summed up in the police report for January 1936:

It should be noted in this connection that Haifa consists of a large motley crowd of casual workers or temporary residents from various towns and villages in Palestine and Trans-Jordan who are prone to trouble and responsive to agitation, and unlikely at times to submit to the influence or direction of political leaders or parties.[18]

It was true that the local leaders were not influential among the turbulent masses, but others had sprung up from these grassroots elements. The Istiqlal leaders, along with Badri al-'Idi, leader of the Youth Congress in Haifa, 'Atif Nurallah, the local Scout commander, and Hikmat al-Namli, the secretary of the Muslim Association, were in contact with these emerging radical leaders, and helped in collecting money for their activities.[19] Under their direction the YMMA, the Youth movement and the Scouts reinforced the public demonstrations. The cause of al-Qassam was taken up by a wide variety of supporters: Muslim fundamentalists, poets and intellectuals, youth organizers and women.[20] What was not expressed was the tacit approval of these militant tactics by an ever-growing cross-section of the Haifa middle classes, both Muslim and Christian.

The strike: last resort of the urban leaders

The response of the urban leadership to the escalating violence took the form of the strike and the policy of civil disobedience, non-payment of taxes and boycott of the Administration and the Jewish community. This was not the choice of the bourgeois merchant leaders but of the leaders of the youth movement and the lower stratum, the under-privileged Muslim elements who were gradually coming to control the political life of the town. At a stroke political initiative, action and determination became the overriding priority in Haifa, drowning out every other concern. It was clearly a spontaneous reaction to the critical condition of the country, and was co-ordinated with organized agitation by Qassamite fighters and loosely aligned to the traditional nationalist movement, which was reasserting its role. Though a large number of volunteer Arab fighters flocked in from Transjordan, Iraq and Syria, including the veteran Syrian fighter Fawzi al-Qawqji, the Qassamites still operated independently, especially in the north, with links to the Higher Arab Committee.[21] The immediate response of the authorities was to arrest the middle-cadre urban leaders and organizers, and to hit hard at the poorer elements of the town.

The local Haifa Strike Committee, set up in co-ordination with Jerusalem, called a meeting of representatives of all nationally organized bodies on 22 April 1936 to decide the policy to be followed.[22] Its purpose, in addition to encouraging all sectors of society to join the strike, was to raise funds for the support of the needy and the unemployed. Various other sub-committees, manned by volunteer students, women and activists in the youth organizations, were set up to run the strike and to achieve total observance, their functions ranging from fund-raising to vigilante teams to implement the severance of all economic and social relations with the Jews.[23] Proclamations were issued calling on workers in all sectors to join the strike, and whenever they did, announcements to that effect were made in an effort to build up cohesive, nationalist public support.

In view of the need to maintain a united front, prominent merchants and traditional politicians such as Karaman, al-Khalil, Taha and Hajj Ibrahim were appointed to the committee. Though many of them were lukewarm towards the principles of the strike, this role imposed on them a nationalist respectability even if it was against their economic interests. Furthermore, they were compelled by the militancy of the younger generation and the lower strata to go along with the hardline policy. Wealthy Christian merchants were not asked to shoulder any of the responsibility of the committees, but, like their Muslim counterparts, they were obliged to donate to the cause, even if reluctantly. The strike went a long way towards cementing the fractures in the town's social structure; however, it also gave occasion for promoting sharper socio-economic awareness between the social classes and the religious communities as well as between the city and the countryside.

From May until the end of 1936, Haifa was under the control of the radicals, and most normal activities came to a standstill. Violence erupted in a sustained fashion and took different forms. In the town the sabotage of communications, the cutting of cables and electrical connections, the burning of Jewish and British property, attacks and sniping on Jewish quarters, especially in the more isolated areas, and the ambushing of military and police personnel became daily occurrences. The town was gripped by an intense atmosphere of panic and upheaval, in which instances of violence, murder and destruction were escalating and unpredictable. What was happening in the city was, in fact, an extension of the campaign mounted in its immediate rural vicinity, mainly by Ikhwan al-Qassam, who often carried the armed confrontations into the city in whose shanty towns their supporters and fighters lived and from where their supplies and funds came.

The Al-Qassam society in Haifa, which had been the heart of al-Qassam's movement, was now led by a number of religious figures, including Shaikh Kamal al-Qassab, an old collaborator of al-Qassam, Hajj 'Abdullah Abu Younis and Shaikh Husain Hamadi. The latter attempted to continue al-Qassam's socio-political activities by building up new militant youth associations such as the 'Fityan al-Jazirah League' and 'The Youths of the Prophet Muhammad Society', but he was denied official approval. Another religious figure associated with al-

Qassam and the subsequent militant current in Haifa was Shaikh Mohammad al-Khatib, who throughout the revolt kept up a campaign preaching militant Islam, and is credited with the propagation of a strong Islamic flavour to the revolt.[24] Many of these Shaikhs were pursued by the authorities and were obliged to abscond to Syria, from whence, along with Dr Sa'id Odeh,[25] they carried on clandestine activities, supported by funds collected in Haifa. During the strike the society provided ammunition, provisions and military clothing for the participants in the struggle, both in the city and among the guerrilla gangs in the villages.

During 1936 and the subsequent years of the revolt (1937-9), Haifa remained a source of active fighters and saboteurs for blowing up bridges and the IPC pipelines, as well as for fund-raising, smuggling of ammunition and similar activities. The overriding majority were peasants from the villages but there were also workers who knew Haifa well, who lived in its slums and were sometimes employed in its menial jobs. CID investigations during the revolt revealed an intricate network of co-operation between the northern villages and towns, with a high level of secrecy. Individuals belonging to prominent families in Nazareth, Jenin and Haifa seemed to be part of this network, collecting funds and performing the more sophisticated aspects of operations. Inside Haifa the organized Istiqlalists were instrumental in providing the Arab inhabitants and the fighters with an operational network to smooth the running of everyday affairs during the strike and later on, during the early months of the revolt. Businessmen providing vital services to the Arab community were supplied with special permits to carry on their affairs and to move about without fear of harassment by the strike committees or the rebels.[26] Rashid al-Hajj Ibrahim took a prominent role in organizing this network and maintaining order in the town.

In the northern district, the revolt was undertaken by Qassamite fighters immediately after the death of their leader, their targets being the British army and police and Jewish settlements.[27] They were responsible for shifting the strike from a protest movement of non-co-operation into an open revolt. From June to September 1936, an increasing number of Qassamite attacks on the police and on Jewish quarters gave the impression that the government had lost control.[28] In fact, the traditional as well as the more radical urban leadership clearly wavered in their support of this militancy. Early on in the strike some members of the Haifa Strike Committee suggested ways of limiting the participation of all economic sectors, for fear of its detrimental effect on the Arab economy. Others known for their nationalist leanings went so far as to support strike-breaking actions.

The result was a campaign of recriminations, terror and murder against those considered to be dissenters from the militant consensus.

Some were attacked for supposedly selling land to the Jews, for having business and social dealings with them, or for being wealthy and lukewarm towards the rebels; others, such as the Arab police, were accused of collaborating in uncovering Qassamite cells and informing on rebel activities.[29] Such happenings, which occurred in broad daylight, intensified fear in the town, especially in the eastern quarters that housed the Arab old town. In reaction, many members of the Arab police either joined the strike or refused to take part in action against their communities. Many middle-class Muslims moved out of their traditional quarters into the mixed or mainly Christian quarters of Wadi Nisnas, and the 'Abbas area. Another side-effect was the flight of wealthy merchants, landowners and prominent government employees, Muslim and Christian, to Lebanon and Syria. The course of revolution was obviously leaving behind some sections of the city's Arab community which could not stomach the radical process and were becoming marginalized by it.

Nevertheless, the overall picture of Arab, Muslim and many Christian attitudes to the strike was one of support for the radical approach and a feeling of patriotism in which all Arabs were united. An objective observer of the situation at the time, the principal of the English High School in Haifa, was highly sympathetic towards the Arabs' patriotic readiness to endure deprivations; their determination to persist with the strike, despite the communal fines and harsh sentences, was seen as an indication of their desperation and loss of faith in the goodwill of the Administration.[30]

The strike in Haifa was not total, a fact of which the town was continuously accused and an indication of its complex economic and political situation. In the port, the Arab workers refused to stop work, except for a short period, for fear of losing their jobs to Jewish workers. The Histadrut, in anticipation of a larger Jewish share in the port employment, and as part of its labour conquest philosophy, had already started encouraging Salonica port workers to emigrate and set themselves up in Haifa, and it was from among them that any replacements came.[31] Some government employees did not strike; nor did Arab employees of the IPC who held tenured jobs. Even though municipal workers did not join the strike at all times, services for the Jewish quarters were taken over by Jewish workers. Those most adversely affected by the strike were the poorer strata and the small businessmen.[32] The larger enterprises were able to sustain reduced business and still meet their loans and financial commitments, something that small merchants and the many petty craftsmen could not manage. During the early period of the strike, the local committee, helped by funds from Jerusalem and from local merchants, was able to meet payments to the unemployed, but as time went on this became more difficult.

Intimidation to join the strike also became more common. Employees, teachers and businessmen gradually joined the ranks of the radicals, even though it was obviously not a path they would have chosen willingly.[33]

The Administration tried by various means to discourage workers from striking and provided them with protection; it also imprisoned leaders of the labour movement who supported the strike.[34] What aggravated its attitude was the violence that accompanied the strike, and this led to closer co-operation with the Jewish community and the Zionist organizations in the town. It was at this particular time, and in the light of the strike's repercussions on the political orientation of both communities, that the altered character of Haifa was revealed. To the Zionists, Haifa was a model of Arab-Jewish co-operation and the success of the Zionist experiment. This explains the many attempts by the Histadrut leadership and other Zionist bodies to find compromises and solutions to immediate problems arising from the strike. Nevertheless, violence created barriers difficult to surmount in the heat of the moment, and left legacies which were hard to forget in the long run.

Violence was also instrumental in speeding up the final changes to the city. From 1936 the old Jewish quarters within the Arab town, Harat al-Yahud and Ard al-Yahud, were the first targets of attack, as well as the new Jewish quarters and settlements on the eastern periphery.[35] By the end of 1936 the residents of both old Jewish quarters had fled in panic to the Hadar HaCarmel mixed or purely Jewish areas.[36] This move was discouraged by official Zionist policy, which was promoting a campaign of self-control and not conceding victory to the Arab rebels.[37] By physically segregating the two communities, other aspects of communal relations were negatively affected. Social relations were strained, reinforcing the economic boycotts and separations that the strike and the rebellion imposed. Furthermore, the situation reawakened fears of enclosure and defeat within the Jewish community. Its allies within the Arab community were being targeted as well, and could not depend on government protection.[38]

Jewish organizations at that stage were concerned with intensifying their armed protection, in which the British authorities were helpful. Locally, the Haganah organized its committees under emergency regulations to guard Jewish quarters. The Firemen's Society, set up by the Haganah, was the legal umbrella under which secret military recruitment, training and protection services were hidden; by late summer 1936, a huge number of volunteers, mostly students of the Technion, had joined and were being trained to face the emergency. The British authorities often depended on this body to supplement their own activities, a situation used by the Haganah to arm itself officially.[39] The job of protecting the Jewish community had become more difficult, because of the distribution of Jews in practically all areas of the town. Not only did Jews live among Arab quarters, but the main work sites were in the harbour, the IPC and the old commercial centre within range of Arab Haifa. Furthermore, labour settlements in the Bay area were still newly developed and therefore targets that needed protection. The activities of the Firemen's Society and other para-military bodies therefore extended over a large area, with different forms of military activity. Within the town, the all-Jewish quarters of the Hadar were not attacked because of this effective protection. This was another physical form of segregation reinforcing the socio-political separation of the two communities. By late 1937, with the resumption of violence during the second stage of the rebellion, Jewish militancy in Haifa expressed itself in retaliatory excesses which revealed careful preparation and sophisticated equipment.

It was not only the Jews who felt the need for this protection. By late 1937 Arab 'moderates' from among the wealthier notable and merchant strata also sought armed protection. When a few of them returned to Haifa at the end of the strike, in late 1936 and early 1937, they made this need known to the authorities. It has been reported that they also asked for, and were authorized to set up, their own armed police force; however, this has not been endorsed by any respondent.[40] Only in 1939 were the 'Peace Bands' organized to defend the Nashashibi front in co-operation with the British army. Though the Arab community through-out the period of the revolt suffered from the activities of informers and collaborators with the authorities, there are no indications that these were part of an organized body. Nevertheless, the 'moderate' stratum, both Christian and Muslim, felt cornered and threatened; they were walking a tightrope of attempting to be loyal Arab nationalists on the one hand and pragmatic merchants on the other. Many respondents from the Muslim and Christian middle class have stated that there was an urgent need among the Arabs to arm themselves against growing Jewish attacks at a time when emergency laws were introduced pro-hibiting and harshly punishing Arab acquisition of such defence items.

When the strike was called to a halt on 11 October 1936, the violence ceased and Haifa took stock of the aftermath. The communities had been cut off from each other and there were no signs of immediate reconciliation. The Muslim radical and youth elements had been galvanized and for once had experienced organized action as a solution to nationalist demands. However, within this front the urban leadership seemed inclined at this stage to accept a political solution. Positive hopes were pinned on the diplomatic deliberations with London. The city's Christian community had also been incorporated within the patriotic front during these trying months and had, to a limited degree, paid the price by being subjected to intimidation and harsh treatment at the hands of the authorities.[41] This reaffirmed their national affiliation and their support of the radical strategy that had been pursued. However, confessional apprehensions, fear of the unknown elements that had carried out the revolt, and often panic and paralysis concerning the future were features of the reaction within this community.[42] It was the elite strata of both communities, who had fled the city along with their families, who did not endorse the revolt, even though they were cautious not to express this publicly.

As for the Jewish community, segregation had intensified the application of the Zionist philosophy. The community was alerted and organized for self-defence and retaliation. As recorded by official Zionist writers,[43] there was a general feeling among the politicized elements of the Yishuv, that Haifa was already a Jewish town and that at this crucial time it was a national priority to prove this to the weakened Arabs.

On the whole, the strike and the early period of the revolt failed to achieve their purpose, because they were not able to paralyse the entire economy of Haifa and thereby force the government to meet Arab nationalist demands. Once again it was proven that the urban leadership was incapable of successfully following through a comprehensive, radical policy that did not serve its immediate interests. As a result, the rural elements in the radical movement took over the reins of the struggle. The strike committees were transformed into boycott committees, signalling the continuation of the struggle by political means. The radical elements of the youth movement were adamant about ensuring the application of this policy by creating blockades between the Arab and Jewish sectors of the town; for a few months in 1937 it was necessary to obtain a permit from the committees in order to cross from one area to another. Tension did not lessen during 1937, even though the physical violence had abated. The Arabs of Palestine, particularly those in the cities, were clearly in a state of high agitation as they awaited the decision of the Royal Commission.

The die had been cast, and the traditional urban politicians could no longer retrace their steps to the period prior to the strike and the events of 1936. In Jerusalem, the political leadership was more fragmented than ever, and all would have preferred an acceptable political solution to save their face. Within the Husaini camp, which had had the strongest influence during the early part of the revolt, the dilemma was intense. Decisions were being appropriated by the more radical, middle-cadre younger generation who had been involved in the activities of the previous year, and they pushed for intransigence and a radical solution. This was, of course, endorsed by a hardline British official stand vis-à-vis the Husaini leadership and by a more belligerent Zionist approach. As a result of the Peel Commission's recommendation of the partition of Palestine and the establishment of a Jewish state, the choice was removed from them with the overwhelming popular rejection of partition. Earlier on, the Nashashibi party had resigned from the Higher Arab Committee in a clear indication of its accommodating position, giving cause for future recriminations by the militants.

The rebellion 1937–8

The whole situation was aggravated in late September 1937, when L. Andrews, the Acting District Commissioner for Galilee, was assassinated in Nazareth, probably by Qassamite rebels, because of his alleged attitude towards the Arab cause and the partition plan. The urban political leadership, under threat of arrest, took the only option available: resumption of the revolt and flight from Palestine, while maintaining nominal leadership and some control from Lebanon and Syria. Damascus became the headquarters for the leadership of the revolution, the Central Committee for the National Jihad,[44] which attempted to direct the course of the armed revolt by providing and manipulating the finances and supplies of the rebels. The fact that Hajj Amin al-Husaini, the traditional nationalist and religious leader, still headed this co-ordinating committee goes a long way to explain the peasant acceptance of his direction. Palestinian peasants remained strongly motivated by conservative affiliations to religion, the family, the village and the clan.

From late 1937 until early 1939 the revolt in Palestine was the closest the Arabs ever came to victory. Armed activities were particularly intense in the north, the areas intended by the Peel Report for transfer into the Jewish state. Conditions had crystallized political orientations, and the situation had become a matter of survival for some, especially the peasants and urban workers. In Galilee in particular, the urge to persist in the fighting was strong, and the urban populations of the northern cities threw in their lot with the rebels by tacit and sometimes active support. In Haifa most of the prominent figures in the radical camp were exiled, leaving the field vacant for lower-stratum cadres and the peasants. This situation diminished the circle of experienced organizers, thus devolving responsibility to politically as well as socially less sophisticated peasant leaders. In fact, the peasants were in almost complete control of the revolt, while the urban middle and lower bourgeoisie became gradually alienated. Even the most radical among the urban nationalists confined their support to organizational and verbal activism, and rarely participated in actual fighting. Nonetheless, the Arabs of Haifa, especially in the Muslim areas, as well as in the mixed Christian-Muslim quarters such as Wadi Nisnas, 'Abbas and Wadi Salib, suffered harassment and arrests by the authorities, sniping and attacks by Jewish bands and sometimes violence from the rebels themselves.[45] By the end of the revolt many people from these strata were not only alienated but had even retreated from the arena.

The year 1938 proved definitive in the course of the rebellion and in the final destiny of Haifa. It was during this year that the fiercest confrontations occurred, in the streets of the town, in its railways, alleys and old marketplace, in its prisons and the woods of its mountain, the Carmel, and first and foremost in its countryside.

The whole country was immersed in a full-blown rebellion which reached its peak in the summer of 1938, when the rebels controlled most of the roads and many of the towns and practically the whole of the countryside. Railway communications were almost completely destroyed, police stations were raided, and arms, ammunition and, when available, cash were stolen. The IPC pipeline was repeatedly blown up, as well as bridges and other installations. In the mountains, the stronghold of the rebels, they set up their camps, courts and training grounds. Rebel activities were intense in Galilee, motivated by the partition scheme and the previous experience and success of the Qassamite fighters there. This was made easier by the proximity of the northern borders with French-mandated Syria and Lebanon, which became a channel for traffic in supplies, arms and personnel. To thwart these activities the British sought the expert services of Charles Tegart, who implemented the erection of military police forts all around the country and a barbed-wire fence across the border with Syria and Lebanon. It was clear that the government was unable to control the situation; it called in reinforcements and depended more heavily on Zionist 'special squads' to terrorize the countryside.[46] Punitive government measures were also extreme in the villages and the Arab quarters in the towns.

In the Galilee villages, the surviving Qassamite fighters (Ikhwan al-Qassam) became more daring; they were able to control large areas of the northern villages. Of the four Qassamite centres in the north, those which affected Haifa most were the ones led by Tawfiq al-Ibrahim (Abu Ibrahim al-Saghir), who was active in the Nazareth and Haifa areas, and Yusif Sa'id Abu Dorra, who was active in the Carmel region and at some point in 1938 had a band active within the town of Haifa. Furthermore, the city was still the source of most of the Qassamite fighters in the Haifa area; out of 51 fighters there, 31 came originally from Haifa.[47] The proximity of the fighters to the city and their constant link with the Arab part of the old town kept tension and violence at a high level. In the long run, as happened by the end of 1938 and during 1939, with the diversification of the leadership and the lack of control and misuse of authority, this violence became directed against the Arabs in Haifa.

CID and Haganah records of events show a constant state of militancy within the city, especially in the old Arab part of the town.[48] They also show the concentration of rebel activities against British and Jewish positions. Another aspect that became more evident as the year went on was the violent activities of the special Zionist bands of the 'Irgun Tzvi Leumi', an extremist dissident group within the Haganah which perpetrated attacks in the old city and among civilian populations,[49] such as the placing of bombs in the congested Arab market, twice during 1938 and once during 1939.

Activities against Arabs who were considered unsupportive also increased noticeably during this period, reflecting the lack of control and the deteriorating conditions within rebel circles. As the situation of the rebels grew more difficult, owing to government and Zionist attacks and lack of funds and arms, their violence was increasingly directed against the most vulnerable elements, the Arab civilian population and those considered to be the cause of their plight. Their attacks and extortions often took the form of a class struggle, reflecting the bitterness of the peasant and working-class elements in a state of lawlessness. At this stage the revolt in Haifa began to acquire the tones of a social revolution, as the rebels demanded that Arabs should wear the distinctive peasant *kufiyya* and should abstain from paying rents to landlords and the like.[50] The town's Arab civilians were forcibly drawn into the cycle of violence and found themselves at the mercy of conditions over which they had no control. All observers of the period concur on the extreme state of panic and terror to which the civilian Arabs were reduced by the end of the revolt, because of the violence of all parties involved.

Aftermath: an altered Haifa

1939 was the year of retreat, retrenchment and containment of the radical currents that had held Haifa and the whole country in their grip for three years. The revolt petered out, though not without a period of violence which caused the embattled and now cynical Arab civilian population to view the ending of hostilities with private relief and sadness. In Haifa the end of the revolt, irrespective of its latter negative aspects, was a triumph for the Administration and its JNH policy. It was also a minor triumph for the mercantile and upper-class Arabs, who could now resume their business and their residence with no concern for what the future might hold. It was a moral, psychological and political defeat for the rest of Arab society, especially the radicalized younger generation, whose enthusiasm, hopes and beliefs were extinguished by powers that had become too strong to fight.

Haifa was altered after the events accompanying the revolt. It changed in its human components and the distribution of its population, and in its economic and political base. The balance had now tipped in favour of the Jewish character of the city, and it was set on a course which was dramatically achieved with the tragic expulsion of the Arab population in 1948.

The strike and the revolt were a challenge to both communities of Haifa, the Jewish and the Arab. Official Zionist literature on the strike features it as an unfortunate occurrence in a town where the Jewish people (the Yishuv) had achieved a formula of co-operation unprecedented in any other town of Palestine. From the Zionist perspective, Haifa had indeed provided the Zionist experiment of settlement and conquest of land, labour and the socio-political arena with many successes. Jewish residents of the city were spread out in all directions, having reached the numerical strength of at least half the population, and new quarters encircled the old town, where a completely Western Jewish life was led. In the economy, certain modern, capitalized industrial enterprises were totally Jewish, though the Arabs still maintained smaller industries that would service the larger economy. The one area of significant Arab advantage, the retail market and intensive labour projects such as building and the quarries, was also being slowly infiltrated by Jewish labour, with Jewish-Arab partnerships weakening the Arab stand as a community similar to the situation within the Jewish sector.[51]

In the 1920s and 1930s Haifa had bred a mercantile, pragmatic apolitical Arab stratum whose interests were more financial than ideological and who in 1936 were forcibly pushed into a radical situation to which they were opposed. While the radical current had been picking up momentum, this stratum had, ostrich-like, hidden away from the reality of the Palestine situation, until it exploded on the death of Shaikh 'Izzedin al-Qassam. Politically the Haifa Arabs had persistently revealed their ethnic and social fragmentation, especially in this newly formed mercantile class. By binding their interests and existence to the permanence of the Mandate system and its institutions, this stratum, both Christian and Muslim, had been neutralized since the early 1920s. Christian introversion helped the emergence of more intransigent Muslim attitudes, thus offsetting both. And the one forum for local political manoeuvring, the Municipality, had been nullified as a channel of community strength, thanks to the wise management of the local Zionist organizations and the Jewish community.

The strike unbalanced this situation and introduced into Haifa an intransigent Arab element – the proletarianized peasant workers and their supporters in the villages. The radical trend that supplied from among its followers the manpower that was determined to carry on the struggle was bred in Haifa. Unlike the political experience of the south, where traditional power structures set the pattern for a coherent, conservative political orientation, in the north a young, new and hetero-geneous community was less bound by tradition and more directly affected by the pro-Zionist policy of the Mandate. The region experienced greater human mobility than the south; the movement from the village to the city created conditions which contributed to the emergence of more radical and less controllable political elements. Despite the growth of a mercantile stratum whose conservatism gave the semblance of stability, the educated younger generation of all strata sympathized, if only ideologically, with the radical militants, and this gave further strength and direction to the revolt. They were also ready to challenge traditional political norms and forge new approaches to solve their national problems – a path which was to be followed by later generations of Palestinian activists, both within Palestine and in the diaspora.

Haifa, which was transformed during the period from a predominantly Arab town into a western-oriented, Jewish-controlled industrial city, underwent a process repeated in most Arab towns and communities that have fallen to occupation since then – the cities of Galilee since 1948 and those of the West Bank since 1967, particularly Jerusalem. The pattern is the same and the purpose unabashedly blatant: economic, social and physical encirclement; land expropriation with impunity; Arab community fragmentation, political coercion and the marginalization of Palestinian intellectuals and writers. Since the revolt of 1936–9 Palestinian society has reproduced an innate activism in many forms to redress its history in a struggle for national freedom and expression. At that early juncture in its history the hopes and dynamism of the radical spirit were compelled to wait for other generations to rekindle them, as happened in the Intifadah of 1988. Time has shown the endless resources of the society to deal with adversity and to improvise methods for its rejuvenation and perseverance. The revolt pointed the path for future generations and inspired what was to come in the highly charged history of the Palestinian struggle for freedom.

Notes

1. See CID reports (PRO CO 733/180). This is also confirmed in Charles Tegart's mission to Palestine at the time of the Arab Revolt. See Tegart Papers (Private Papers, St Antony's College, Oxford).

2. From the private papers of E. Keith-Roach, District Commissioner for the Northern District, F. Moody, officer in the Jerusalem Secretariat, and H. Bowman, Director of Education, this attitude is clear. (Private Papers, St Antony's College, Oxford).

3. M. H. Yacoub, *Nathra Jadida ila Tarikh al-Qadiyya al-Filastiniyya 1918–1948* (New Approaches to the History of the Palestinian Problem 1918–1948) (Beirut, 1973), pp. 103–4. Many of the emerging middle-class and entrepreneur families lacked sufficient capital, backing and skills to compete with Zionist enterprises,

and were obliged to move from their base in Haifa to find a better income and less competition in other purely Arab towns. This has been endorsed by many respondents. See Chapter 9.

4. See Chapter 14, sections on 'Forging a political identity' and on 'The role of power elites'.

5. See S. Yasin, *Al-Thawra al-'Arabiyya al-Kubra fi-Filastin, 1936–1939* (The Great Arab Revolt in Palestine 1936–1939) (Cairo, 1959); S. Hamouda, *Al-Wa'yi wal-Thawra* (Awareness and Revolution) (Jerusalem, 1985); S. Lachman, 'Arab Rebellion and Terrorism in Palestine 1929–1939: The Case of Sheikh Izz al-Din al-Qassam and his Movement', in Kedourie and Haim (eds), *Zionism and Arabism in Palestine and Israel* (London, 1982), pp. 52–99; S. F. El-Nimr, 'The Arab Revolt in Palestine: A Study Based on Oral Sources', Ph.D. thesis, University of Exeter, 1990; T. R. Swedenberg, 'Memories of Revolt: the 1936–39 Rebellion and the Struggle for a Palestinian National Past', Ph.D. thesis, University of Texas, Austin; S. Schleifer, 'The Life and Thought of 'Izz-id-Din al-Qassam', *Islamic Quarterly*, Vol. 23, No. 2, January/March 1979, pp. 61–81.

6. Most authors writing on the 1936–39 revolt have traced its origins to the same fighting groups involved in 1929; they also found a continuous link with the militant incidents around Haifa between the two dates. By 1936 three centres of underground militant activity had evolved, one in the Jerusalem-Ramallah area, another in the Tulkarem-Qalqilya area and the third in the Haifa-Galilee region. See Lachman, 'Arab Rebellion', p. 57; El-Nimr, 'The Arab Revolt', pp. 70–71; C. Tegart, undated report on al-Qassam movement, Box 1, File 3 (Private Papers, St Antony's College, Oxford).

7. His puritanical message was expressed by pressing for a reformed practice of Islam, shedding hateful innovations (Bid'a) which had filtered in because of slack observance and Christian influence. He opposed the rituals practised in Haifa during funerals and the Mar Elias (Khidr) grotto festivals. Schleifer, 'The Life', pp. 67–8; Hamouda, *Al-Wa'yi*, pp. 61–5.

8. Lachman, 'Arab Rebellion', p. 60; A. H. Ghunayyim, 'Thawrat al-Shaikh 'Izz al-Din al-Qassam' (The Revolt of Shaikh Izz al-Din al-Qassam), *Shu'un Falastiniyya* 6 (January 1972), p. 182. The CID reports on al-Qassam's activities showed that his recruitment was from among these strata, especially from Saffouriyya, the villages around Jenin as well as some of the *shabab* (youth) of Haifa. Tegart Private Papers, Box 1, File 3.

9. El-Nimr, 'The Arab Revolt', pp. 82–5; Schleifer, 'The Life', pp. 67–74; Hamouda, *Al-Wa'yi*, pp. 41–52.

10. B. N. Al-Hoot, *Al-Qiyadat wal-Mu'asasat al-Siyassiyya fi Filastin 1917–1948* (Leadership and Political Institutions in Palestine 1917–1948 (Beirut, 1981), p. 224.

11. Tegart Private Papers, Box 1, File 3.

12. This has been recorded by all biographers of al-Qassam, particularly Hamouda, *Al-Wa'yi*, pp. 121–7; Lachman, 'Arab Rebellion', pp. 69–70; Y. Porath, *The Palestinian Arab National Movement, 1929–1939* (London, 1977), pp. 137–9; A. M. Lesch, *Arab Politics in Palestine, 1917–1939* (London, 1979), p. 216; Yasin, *Al-Thawra*, p. 22.

13. Hamouda, *Al-Wa'yi*, pp. 57–8, 64.

14. Lachman, 'Arab Rebellion', p. 80. In an official CID report on Terrorism in Palestine, it was stated that the most ardent branches of the YMMA were those around Haifa, Nazareth and Jenin, which had a stronger religious bias than anywhere else. They were organized and their members were influenced

by 'fanatical' preachers such as the 'militant sheikh Izzedin Kassem' (Tegart Private Papers, Box 1, File 3(c), p. 6).

15. Rashid al-Hajj Ibrahim was director of the Arab Bank in Haifa, a landowner and a well-off businessman as well as a member of the Municipal Council in 1934. He was also deeply involved in Muslim community affairs, helped in the organization of the YMMA, and chaired it as well as al-Qassam at different times. In all the literature on al-Qassam his name is the one most often mentioned as a close contact, who had secret meetings with him, intimating a part in the rebel organization and planning. Along with al-Khadra and Madi he was among the original organizers of the Istiqlal Party in Palestine. Al-Khadra, originally from Safed, was the director of the Muslim *waqfs* of Haifa. His name has been closely associated with Hajj Ibrahim in the organization of Haifa youth groups, especially the YMMA, and with militant activities in the north committed by the Qassamite or pro-Qassamite activists since 1929. Mu'in al-Madi was a prominent Istiqlalist and lawyer in Haifa. He came from a well-off landowning family in Ijzim, in the northern district. See Porath, *The Palestinian Arab*, pp. 137–8; Hamouda, *Al-Wa'yi*, pp. 63, 84–90; Lachman, 'Arab Rebellion', pp. 60–61.

16. Lachman, 'Arab Rebellion', p. 73; Hamouda, *Al-Wa'yi*, p. 90.

17. Oral information by Christian residents of Haifa pertaining to the upper and lower middle classes, many of whom wished their names to be withheld. Noted oral information by: Wadi' Jabbur, Haifa, May 1975, Hanna 'Asfour, Beirut, May 1974, Elias Mobassaly, Washington, DC, June, 1993, Amin Abu Fadel, Detroit, August 1994.

18. Police Summaries for January 1936 (PRO FO 371 E19/19/31).

19. According to police reports, in Haifa Subhi Khazarran, a Shari'a court official, and Shaikh Mohammad Hashim al-Khatib were active supporters of al-Qassam (Tegart Private Papers, Box 1, File 3(b)). Shaikh Yousif Abu Dorra and Dr Sa'id Odeh helped al-Qassam rebels with financial and other support.

20. Special Report by Palestine Police, 14 December 1935 (PRO CO 733/297); Police Summaries, 6 March 1936 (PRO FO 371 E1293/19/31). Women, particularly those related to national figures, had played a contributory role in the nationalist struggle since the early 1920s. By 1929 a women's movement had developed in which women's congresses, demonstrations, cable and letter campaigns and other charitable activities were undertaken. From Haifa, women volunteers supported the strike of 1936 by contributing to various sub-committees. Names of Haifa women, mainly Muslim, who were active in supporting the nationalist struggle since the early 1930s are: Rabi'ah al-Salah, Su'ad al-Hajj Ibrahim, Ruqayya and Nada Murad, Faizah Haliq and Khairiyyah Biqa'i Houri (oral information, Khairiyyah Houri, Los Angeles/San Diego, July 1994). Some of these women became better-known because of their nationalist connections, such as the daughter of al-Qassam, Maymana, and the wife of Najib Nassar, Sathij. Both represented Haifa women at the Cairo Women's Congress of November 1938. Al-Hoot, *Qiyadat*, pp. 342, 385.

21. Lachman, 'Arab Rebellion', p. 79; al-Hoot, *Qiyadat*, p. 351.

22. Ibid., p. 340; A. Khalifa (trans.) *Al-Thawra al 'Arabiyya al-Kubra fi Filastin, 1936–1939: Al-Riwaya al-Israeliyya al-Rasmiyya* (The Great Arab Revolt in Palestine 1936–1939: An Official Israeli Account), From Books of the Haganah, Vol. 2, Books 5, 6 (Beirut, 1989), p. 14.

23. Ibid. El-Nimr, 'The Arab Revolt', pp. 100–101. Also see Chapter 9, note 55.

24. Lachman, 'Arab Rebellion', p. 78; Tegart Private Papers, Report on Shaikh Izzedin al-Qassam, Box 1, File 3, and List of Shari'a Court Officials in the same file.

25. Dr Sa'id Odeh, whose name is recorded repeatedly in CID reports, seems to have been one of the supporters residing in Damascus and active in organizing urban assassination plots and who had links with activist workers in the railways in Haifa and with prominent members of the Labour Federation in the city as well as some Arab communists (Tegart Private Papers, Box 1, File 3).

26. Oral information from Elias Mobassaly (Washington, DC/Los Angeles, August 1994) and other respondents who asked for their names to be withheld. CID records for the period indicated the existence of such networks and the intricate relationships between villagers and townspeople in the northern region. Tegart Private Papers Collection, Box 1, File 3: Statement of Faris Mohamad al-Ajjawi.

27. In Galilee the leading Qassamites were Farhan al-Sa'di, operating between Haifa and Jenin, Khalil Mohammad 'Issa (Abu Ibrahim al-Kabir), the commander in Galilee, and 'Attiyeh Ahmad 'Awad, who led his bands in the Carmel region. These militant leaders co-ordinated their activities as part of the active network between city leaders and the villagers. Lachman, 'Arab Rebellion', pp. 78–9; El-Nimr, 'The Arab Revolt', pp. 104–7; Hamouda, Al-Wa'yi, pp.101–4.

28. Tegart, 'Diaries', 22 December 1937; Yasin, Al-Thawra, pp. 55–7, and Ha'aretz, 17 August 1936.

29. Hajj Khalil Taha, who had suggested that orange growers should be taxed rather than striking, was assassinated in Haifa in September 1936 while he was still a member of the strike committee. He had a reputation of being soft on the Jews and having business contacts with them, and had been in opposition to the nationalist front since the 1920s. Other important Haifa people suffered the same fate, such as members of the al-Khalil family, and those who were attacked or threatened, such as Hasan Shukri and Hajj Taher Karaman. Sami Taha, the labour activist and nationalist, was also known to oppose the Jerusalem leadership, and helped to reinstate Arab workers in the Shemen quarries in late 1936. He too was assassinated, in the early 1940s. It was also recorded in Zionist reports on events that the entire strike committee, including Hajj Ibrahim, had second thoughts about the effectiveness of the strike. Tegart Private Papers, Box 1, File 3. Khalifa, Al-Thawra, pp. 14, 33, 101; D. HaCohen, Time to Tell (New York, London, 1984), pp. 90–91.

30. Private Papers of S. P. Emery. These were her personal views, expressed in private letters to her family in England. Her contacts in Haifa were mostly with the Christian community (Private Papers Collection, St Antony's College, Oxford). In fact, the Haifa Arab market was fined twice. This feeling of cohesion among the Arab inhabitants has been imparted in many interviews.

31. Davar, 2 September 1936; HaCohen, Time, p. 89; Khalifa, Al-Thawra, pp. 434–5.

32. Ibid. Ha'aretz, 19 July and 17 August 1936.

33. Memo by Arab senior officials to HC on the situation in Palestine, 30 June 1936; K. Sakakini, Kadha Ana Ya Dunya (Such I am, O World) (Jerusalem, 1955), entries for 30 May and 13 June 1936, pp. 284 and 286.

34. CID secret report to CS, 18 August 1936 (PRO FO 371 E12807/24/378). J. 'Asfour, Palestine: My Land, My Country, My Home (Beirut, 1967), pp. 83–5.

35. Khalifa, *Al-Thawra*, pp. 228–9.

36. Ibid., pp. 229–30. They were escorted to Hadar HaCarmel by British marines, who had arrived as part of reinforcements to combat the rebellion.

37. Khalifa, *Al-Thawra*, p. 51. The official position was that Haifa had ceased to be Arab both in theory and in practice and that force would not deter the Yishuf.

38. Pro-Zionist literature on the period has repeated the names and fate of those who were threatened, attacked and murdered by the rebels, labelling them as 'mild', 'supporters', 'friends of the Jewish people' and the like. See Khalifa, *Al-Thawra*, pp. 13, 101, 208, 229; HaCohen, *Time*, pp. 25, 79, 90, 91, 208; Lachman, 'Arab Rebellion', p. 80.

39. Khalifa, *Al-Thawra*, pp. 50–53.

40. Khalifa, *Al-Thawra*, p. 101; Lachman, 'Arab Rebellion', p. 80.

41. Oral information from many respondents who lived through the events in Haifa, such as Iskandar Majdalani and Wadi' Jabbur, Haifa, May 1975: Elias Mobassaly, Beirut, June 1977; Gabriel Seikaly, Amman, June 1975; Khalid al-Hasan, London, March 1982; Mohammad Houri, Los Angeles/San Diego, August 1994; and Amin Abu-Fadel, Los Angeles/Detroit, August 1994.

42. Arab Christians in Haifa were highly agitated during the deliberations of the Royal Commission and imparted their fears to the Protestant bishop who was visiting the city. They felt caught in a vice: on the one hand they were afraid of eventually being ruled by a Muslim majority and feared to strike out on a political line of their own and be attacked by the Muslims, and on the other hand they were opposed to the Zionists. This was the impression that S. P. Emery, who had long and close relations with the Christian middle class of Haifa, had of the situation. Emery Private Papers, St Antony's College, Oxford.

43. Khalifa, *Al-Thawra*, pp. 14, 230–35.

44. A. W. Kayyali, *Palestine: A Modern History* (London, 1978), p. 211.

45. A large number of the respondents in this study have concurred on this issue, and reported many cases of harassment by the police, when communal humiliation and fines were imposed on the civilian Arabs because of suspicion of support for the rebels. Christian and Muslim (male and female) stories tally and often repeat the same incidents of mistreatment and attacks. This is one angle that still needs to be properly investigated and documented from the collective memory of Palestinians who have survived from this period.

46. Khalifa, *Al-Thawra*, pp. 213–35; El-Nimr,'The Arab Revolt', pp. 126–8. Through interviews with villagers who had suffered such retaliatory operations by the 'special squads', El-Nimr provides important records of the period.

47. Lachman, 'Arab Rebellion', pp. 84–5; El-Nimr, 'The Arab Revolt', Chapter 4, pp. 213, 233, 525.

48. See CID Reports in 'CID News Bulletin' Tegart Private Papers, Box 1, for the years 1938–9. Also see: Khalifa, *Al-Thawra*, pp. 155, 162, 172.

49. Ibid., pp. 213, 233, 525.

50. This has been referred to by most authors on the period. It is interesting to note the social reaction to these peasant edicts from the various strata of Haifa. The Muslim population seemed to consider these measures socially repressive but politically important, while to the Christians they were alarming signs of social and religious repression, adding to their sense of panic and confusion. Oral information, especially from women, both Muslim and Christian. Also see: Emery Private Papers.

51. Economically the Jewish sector acquired great advantages as a result of the rebellion, especially within the government administrative structure. This did not limit the official British backing for contracts within Palestine during and after the Second World War, but it enabled some Zionist companies to perform British military contracts in other parts of the world, such as Solel Boneh's work in Syria, Lebanon, Egypt, Iraq, Iran, Bahrain and Cyprus. HaCohen, *Time*, p. 93.

Haifa's Prominent Arab Families 1918–39

In this list, family names having a commonly accepted English spelling are given in that spelling. Whenever possible, the names of one or more notable members are included, simply to give a sample. These names were collected from references in documents or interviews with members of those families and Haifa residents of the period under study. They were collected, adjusted and corrected up to the latest printing date. The country or town of origin, religion and occupation or occupations of that family are recorded in sequence. This list of Haifa's prominent families is not exhaustive; my apologies for those excluded from mention here because of lack of information and contact.

'Abbud, Ilyas: Haifa; Catholic; construction contractors

'Abdul-Hadi, Fakhri: 'Arraba; Muslim; landowners, merchants

'Abdul-Rahman, Kamel: Haifa rural background; Muslim; contractors, building industry

Abu Fadil, Salim, Mikha'il: 'Ain 'Anoub (Lebanon); Greek Orthodox; merchants

Abu Rahma, Ilyas, Joseph: Shefa 'Amr; Protestant; professionals

Abu Zaid, 'Abdallah, As'ad (Rayyis):   Haifa; Muslim; fishermen, stevedores

Abyad, Jamil: Lebanon; Greek Catholic; landowners, merchants, municipal councillor

'Asfour, Hanna (John):   Shefa 'Amr; Protestant; lawyer, merchants

'Assaf, –:   Lebanon; Maronite; merchants

'Attallah, Fu'ad, Wadi', Nasri: Jenin; Greek Orthodox; professionals, government employees

'Attallah, Nakhla, Mansur: Haifa; Greek Catholic; lawyer, government and railway employees

'Azzam, George, Jules, Habib: Nazareth; Greek Catholic; landowners, merchants

Baha'i, Musa: Iran; Bahai; land registry, government employment
Bahri, Jamil: Haifa; Greek Catholic; journalist, printer
Baidun, Rafiq: Beirut; Muslim; Assistant District Governor
Bajjali, Amin, Mitri: Acre; Greek Orthodox; merchants
(al)-Biqa'i, Khairi: Damascus; Muslim; merchants
Boutagy, Teofil, Emile: Haifa; Protestant; merchants, entrepreneurs
Bustani, Wadi':   Lebanon; Maronite; lawyer
Dallul, 'Ata (Abou 'Ali):   Haifa; Muslim; merchants, leadership (za'im)
Dik, Hasan: Haifa; Muslim; entrepreneur
Dumian, Ibrahim: Jaffa; Protestant; pharmacist, merchants
Dumit, 'Aziz: Lebanon; Protestant; professions related to arts and
    literature
Farsun, Philip: Haifa; Greek Catholic; merchants, entrepreneurs
Germaine, Victor: Haifa; Roman Catholic; French Embassy
    employees, merchants
Ghantus, Hanna, Tawfiq: Lebanon; Greek Orthodox; transport,
    railways employment
Habash, Najib: Jerusalem; Roman Catholic; government employees
Habayib, Ilyas, Hanna, Adib: Haifa; Greek Orthodox; landowners,
    railway employment
Habibi, Jamil, Wadi':   Shefa 'Amr; Protestant; attorney, railway
    employment
(al)-Hajj, 'Abdul-Rahman: Haifa; Muslim; merchants, civic
    employment
Hajj, Nayif: Haifa; Greek Orthodox; arak factory
Hakim, Najib: Nazareth; Greek Orthodox; lawyer, merchants
Hamza, Nayif: Haifa; Druze; medical profession
Houri, Anis: Haifa; Muslims; merchants, Municipality
Ibrahim, Mu'ayyid: Persian; Bahai; educator, Municipality
'Id, 'Id, Louis: Lebanon; Maronite; private employment
Imam, Ahmad: Haifa; Muslim; religious profession, journalist
'Issa, Raji: Haifa; Catholics; landowners
Itayyim, Ibrahim, Wadi':   Kufr Yasif; Protestant; medical doctors,
    pharmacists
Jabbur, Wadi':   Shefa 'Amr; Catholic; bookshop, business
Jada', Basila: Haifa; Greek Catholic; builders, merchants
Jad'un, –:   Haifa; Greek Catholic; landowners, employees
Kanafani, 'Uthman: Haifa; Muslim; merchants, civil servants,
    sweetmakers
Karaman, Tahir (Hajj):   Nablus; Muslim; entrepreneur
Karkabi, Farid: Shefa 'Amr; Roman Catholic; landowner, merchant
Kassab, Iskandar: Lebanon; Greek Orthodox; landowner
Khal, Raji: Lebanon (Marj 'Youn); Greek Orthodox; merchants,
    enterpreneurs

(al)-Khalil, Mustafa (Pasha), Ibrahim: Turkish; Muslim; notable
landowners

Khamra, 'Uthman: Haifa; Muslim; doctor, landowners

Khatib, Yunis: Haifa; Muslim; religious profession

Khayyat, 'Aziz: Tyre; Greek Catholic; landowner, entrepreneur

Khuri, Fu'ad: Kufr Yasif; Greek Catholic; professionals

Khuri, Jiryis: Jerusalem District; Protestant; Municipality

Khuri, Salim, Yusif, Qaisar, Nasrallah: Bkaisin (Lebanon); Maronite;
notable landowners

Madi, Mu'in, Mahmud: Ijzim; Muslim; landowners, lawyer

Majdalani, Tawfiq: Beirut; Greek Orthodox; merchants

Makhluf, Michel: Lebanon; Maronite; government employment

Malas, Khalil: Damascus; Muslim; wood merchants

Manassa, Iskandar: Haifa; Greek Orthodox; merchants

Mansur, Hanna, Jiryis: Haifa; Greek Catholic; merchants

Marshi, Jabra, Yusif: Haifa; Greek Orthodox; port contractors,
merchants

Mayyasi, –:   Haifa; Muslim; grain merchants

Mazzawi, Ilyas: Nazareth; Greek Catholic; government employment

Miqati, 'Aziz: Tripoli; Muslim; entrepreneur, merchant

Mirza, Jalal: Persian; Bahai; merchant

Mu'ammar, George: Nazareth; Greek Orthodox; landowner

Mudawwar, Qustandi: Acre; Greek Orthodox; merchants

Muhammadi, 'Abdul-Rahim (Hajj):   Haifa; Muslim; merchants

Mukhlis, 'Abdallah: Acre; Muslim; journalist, writer

Murad, Muhammad: Haifa; Muslim; religious profession

Nadar, Hanna: Haifa; Greek Orthodox; government employment

Nasif, Sulaiman: Lebanon; Protestant; entrepreneur

Nasr, Wadi', Michel, Amin: Shefa 'Amr; Greek Catholic;
professionals, landowners and merchants

Nassar, Najib, Rashid: 'Ain 'Anoub; Greek Orthodox, Protestant;
professions (journalist, pharmacist), hotel proprietor

Naqqara, Hanna: Acre; Greek Orthodox; lawyer

Nurallah, Amin: Haifa; Muslim; lawyer

Qanazi', Qustandi, Jad: Nazareth; Greek Orthodox; landowners,
merchants

Qa'war; Nasif, George: Nazareth; Greek Orthodox; merchants,
government employment, professionals

Qazaq, Subhi: Tireh; Muslim; merchants, landowners

Qutran, Sulaiman, Edward: Acre; Greek Orthodox; merchants,
government employment

Renno, Mahmud, Shafiq: Haifa; Muslim; fishermen, stevedores

Saba, Salih, Fu'ad: Haifa and Egypt; Protestant; religious profession,
private employment

Al-Sa'd, Farid, Fawwaz: Umm al-Fahm; Muslim; landowners, merchants

Sa'd, Fu'ad: Shefa 'Amr; Greek Catholic; landowner, merchant, entrepreneur

Sahyoun, Ibrahim: 'Iblin; Greek Catholic; landowner, merchant, entrepreneur

(al)-Salah, Rifa't, Sulaiman: Haifa; Muslim; merchants

Salama, Tannus: Lebanon; Maronite; government employment (railways)

Salti, Farah: Nazareth; Greek Orthodox; entrepreneur

Sanadiqi, Mohammad: Damascus; Muslim; merchants

Sanbar, Wadi', Habib: Haifa; Greek Catholic; government employees, merchants

Saraqibi, Shafiq: Damascus; Muslim; merchants, landowner

Seikaly, Sulaiman: Haifa; Greek Orthodox; merchants, government employees, landowners

Shabib, Salih: Damascus; Muslim; merchants, landowners

Shaikh Hasan, Muhammad: Haifa; Muslim; merchants, religious profession

Shalah, Shihadah: Haifa; Greek Catholic; builders, civic employment

Shhaibar, Khalil: Haifa; Greek Orthodox; police service

Shiblaq, –:   Nablus; Muslim; grain merchants

Shukri, Hasan: Haifa (Turkish); Muslim; Municipality

Sifri, 'Awad: Jaffa; Protestant; *Qa'im-maqam*

Swaidan, Jad: Lebanon; Greek Catholic; merchants

Taha, 'Umar (Hajj):   Haifa; Muslim; merchants, landowner

Tamimi, Rafiq: Nablus; Muslim; lawyer

Tawil, George, Jad: South Lebanon; Greek Orthodox; merchants

Tonb, Ilyas: Lebanon; Maronite; merchants

Tuma, Mikha'il: Haifa; Greek Orthodox; merchants, landowners, civic employment

Wardi, —:   Damascus; Muslim; merchants

(al)-Yaseen, 'Abbud: Haifa rural background; Muslim; fishermen, stevedores

Zahlan, Yusif, Jules: Haifa; Roman Catholic; merchants

Zaibaq, Tawfiq: Acre; Protestant; civic employment

Zain, Zain: Persian; Bahai; educator

Zakka, Iliya: Acre District; Greek Orthodox; journalists, printing

Zu'rub, Ibrahim, Tawfiq, Sami: Lebanon; Protestant; doctors, merchants

Bibliography

Unpublished sources

Archival records of government departments and international agencies

GREAT BRITAIN. PUBLIC RECORD OFFICE, LONDON (PRO)

Colonial Office, Original Correspondence (CO 733).
Foreign Office, General Correspondence, Political, Palestine (FO 371).

ISRAELI STATE ARCHIVES. JERUSALEM (ISA)

Government of Palestine, Chief Secretary's Office Papers, Record Group 2; Department of Migration Papers, Record Group 11; Listing of Arab Organizations, Record Group 61; Ministry of Labour Papers, Record Group 95; Department of Customs Papers, Record Group 128.
Miscellaneous Official and Other Papers 'Abandoned in 1948', including the Papers of the Higher Arab Committee (HAC), Record Group 65.

CENTRAL ZIONIST ARCHIVES, JERUSALEM (CZA)

The Zionist Organization/Town Planning, A/175 and J/15; Department of Trade and Industry, A/226 and 5/8; Development of Jewish Quarters, J/16; The Jewish Agency for Palestine, London Office, Z/4.

Private papers

Bowman, H. Private Papers Collection, Middle East Centre, St Antony's College, Oxford.
Brenin, Maj-Gen. Private Papers Collection, Middle East Centre, St Antony's College, Oxford. Thames TV Interviews – 1978.
Emery, S. P. Private Papers Collection, Middle East Centre, St Antony's College, Oxford.
Hackett, Sir J. Private Papers Collection, Middle East Centre, St Antony's College, Oxford. Thames TV Interviews – 1978.
Keith-Roach, E. Private Papers Collection, Middle East Centre, St Antony's College, Oxford.

Kirby, A. F. Private Papers Collection, Middle East Centre, St Antony's College, Oxford.

Kirkbride, Sir A. Private Papers Collection, Middle East Centre, St Antony's College, Oxford. Thames TV Interviews – 1978.

MacMichael, H. Private Papers Collection, Middle East Centre, St Antony's College, Oxford.

Moody, F. Private Papers Collection, Bodleian Library, Oxford.

Mukhlis, A. Palestine Research Centre, Beirut.

Samuel, H. Private Papers Collection, Middle East Centre, St Antony's College, Oxford.

Tegart, C. Private Papers Collection, Middle East Centre, St Antony's College, Oxford.

Tweedy, O. Private Papers Collection, Middle East Centre, St Antony's College, Oxford.

Manuscripts

THESES

Djaby, O. 'La Question Economique, La Syrie sous le Régime du Mandat' (University of Toulouse, Ph.D. thesis, 1934).

El-Nimr, S. F. 'The Arab Revolt in Palestine: A Study based on Oral Sources' (University of Exeter, Ph.D. thesis, 1990).

Al-Qaysi, S. A. 'Yasin al-Hashimi: A Study of his Role in Iraqi Politics between 1922 and 1936' (University of Basra, Iraq, M.A. thesis, 1976).

Seikaly, M. 'The Arab Community of Haifa 1918–1936: A Study in Transformation' (Oxford University, D.Phil. thesis, 1983).

Swedenberg, T. R. 'Memories of Revolt: the 1936–39 Rebellion and the Struggle for a Palestinian National Past' (University of Texas, Austin, Ph.D. thesis, 1988).

Taqqu, R. 'Arab Labor in Mandatory Palestine, 1920–1948' (Columbia University, Ph.D. thesis, 1977).

OTHER UNPUBLISHED SOURCES

Anonymous. 'Al-Hizb al-Arabi al-muwali li-Britania', unpublished document, n.d.

Boutagy, E. 'My Life Story', unpublished document, n.d.

Community Archives Marriage registers and other documents of the Greek Orthodox, Greek Catholic, Roman Catholic, Maronite and Protestant communities, Haifa.

Marriage register of the Muslim community, Istiqlal Mosque, Haifa.

Diretta delle Suore Carmelitane. 'Scuola Femminile Italiana Dell' ANMI', Haifa, 1975.

Washitz, Y., 'Jewish-Arab Relations in Haifa during the Mandate', unpublished manuscript, n.d.

Official publications

Parliamentary papers

Mandate for Palestine, Cmd. 1708, London, July 1922.
Palestine: Report on Immigration, Land Settlement and Development by Sir John Hope
   Simpson, Cmd. 3686, London, October 1930 (The Hope Simpson Report).
Palestine Royal Commission Report, Cmd. 5479, July 1937 (The Peel Report).

Government of Palestine

Annual Reports, Dept. of Health, 1928–1939; Dept. of Public Works, 1929–1940;
   Town Planning Advisor, 1936–1939.
Census of Palestine, 1922, Jerusalem, 1923.
Census of Palestine, 1931, Alexandria, 1933.
Great Britain and Palestine 1915–1945.
Palestine Blue Book 1926-1940.
Palestine Commercial Bulletin (fortnightly), Dept. of Commerce and Industry (1922–
   4) and Dept. of Customs, Excise and Trade (1924–37).
Palestine Economic Bulletin, 1932.
Principal Importers, Exporters and Manufacturers in Palestine, Dept. of Customs, Excise
   and Trade. Special Supplement to the *Palestine Commercial Bulletin*, November
   1933.
Statistical Abstract 1920–1925.
The Town Planning Handbook of Palestine, 1930.
Vital Statistics, 1922–1945, Dept. of Statistics, Jerusalem, 1947.
Wages Committee Report, Jerusalem, 1943.

Zionist publications

The Jewish Agency for Palestine, *Report and General Abstracts of the Censuses of Jewish
   Agriculture, Industry and Handicraft and Labour*, Jewish Agency's Dept. of Statistics,
   Jerusalem, 1931.

Newspapers

ARABIC

Haifa (Workers' Magazine), 1924–5; *Al-Karmil*, 1920–37; *Al-Nafir*, 1919; *Al-Yarmuk*,
   1924–30.

ENGLISH

The Palestine News, 1918–1919.
In the Public Record Office, London, there are many excerpts and translations
   from the contemporary press, both in Palestine and Britain, in the original
   correspondence files.

The Palestine Research Centre, Beirut, and the Beirut Municipal Museum both hold a large collection of original Arabic newspapers and some selected press cuttings.

In addition, the Oxford Centre for Post-Graduate Hebrew Studies, Yarnton, contains a collection of Hebrew press cuttings for some of the years covered by this book.

Books and articles

'Abboushi, W. F. 'The Road to Rebellion: Arab Palestine in the 1930's', *Journal of Palestine Studies* 6 (1977): 23–46.

'Abboushi, W. F. *Filastin qabla al-Dayaa'* (The Unmaking of Palestine), London: 1985.

Abcarius, M. F. 'The Fiscal System', in S. B. Himadeh (ed.), *Economic Organization of Palestine*, Beirut: 1938.

Abu-Lughod, I. 'The Pitfalls of Palestiniology', *Arab Studies Quarterly* 3 (Fall 1981): 403–10.

Abu-Lughod, J. L. 'The Demographic Transformation of Palestine', in I. Abu-Lughod (ed.), *The Transformation of Palestine*, Evanston, IL: 1971.

Adler (Cohen), Raya. 'The Tenants of Wadi Hawarith: Another View of the Land Question in Palestine', *International Journal of Middle East Studies* 20/22 (May 1988): 197–200.

Al-Agha, N. K. *Mada'in Filastin* (The Cities of Palestine), Amman: 1993.

'Allush, N. *Al-Muqawama al-'Arabiyya fi Filastin 1917–1948* (The Arab National Struggle in Palestine 1917-1948), Beirut: 1970.

Antonius, G. *The Arab Awakening*, London: 1955.

'Aqqad, A. K. *Tarikh al-Sahafa al-'Arabiyya fi Filastin* (History of the Arabic Press in Palestine), Damascus: 1967.

The Arab Bank. *Arab Bank Limited, 1930–1980*, Beirut: 1981.

'Asfour, J. *Palestine: My Land, My Country, My Home*, Beirut: 1967.

Badran, N. A. *Al-Ta'lim wal-Tahdith fil-Mujtama' al-'Arabi al-Filastini* (Education and Modernization in Arab Palestinian Society), Beirut: 1969.

Baedeker, K. *Palestine et Syrie*, Leipzig: 1912.

Bahri, J. *Tarikh Haifa* (History of Haifa), Haifa: 1922.

Barghouti, O. S. 'Local Self-Government Past and Present', in Viteles and Totah (eds), 'Palestine: A Decade of Development', *The Annals of the American Academy of Political and Social Science*, Vol. 164, November 1932.

Ben-Arieh, Y. 'The Population of the Large Towns of Palestine during the First Eighty Years of the Nineteenth Century According to Western Sources', in M. Ma'oz (ed.) *Studies on Palestine during the Ottoman Period*, Jerusalem: 1975.

Ben-Hilel, M. *Census of Jews in Palestine* (Hebrew), Jerusalem: 1917.

Ben-Zvi, I. 'Local Autonomy in Palestine', in Viteles and Totah (eds), 'Palestine: A Decade of Development', *The Annals of the American Academy of Political and Social Science*, Vol. 164, November 1932.

Bonné, A. 'The Concessions for the Mosul-Haifa Pipe Line', in Viteles and Totah (eds), 'Palestine: A Decade of Development', *The Annals of the American Academy of Political and Social Science*, Vol. 164, November 1932.

Brett, E. A. *Colonialism and Underdevelopment in East Africa*, Bungay, Suffolk: 1973.

'British Resident' [Thomas Hodgkin]. *Who is Prosperous in Palestine?*, London: 1936.

Brown, M. 'Agriculture', in S. B. Himadeh (ed.), *Economic Organization of Palestine*, Beirut: 1938.

Budeiri, M. *The Palestine Communist Party 1919–1948*, London: 1979.

Caplan, N. *Palestine Jewry and the Arab Question, 1917–1925*, London: 1978.

Carmel, A. 'The German Settlers in Palestine and Their Relations with the Local Arab Population and the Jewish Community, 1868–1918', in M. Ma'oz (ed.), *Studies on Palestine during the Ottoman Period*, Jerusalem: 1975.

Carmel, A. *Tarikh Haifa fi 'Ahd al-Atrak al-'Uthmaniyyin* (History of Haifa in the Ottoman Period), Haifa: 1979.

Chamber of Commerce and Industry (Jewish). *Haifa – City of the Future*, Haifa: 1932.

Chevalier, D. 'Western Development and Eastern Crisis in the Mid-Nineteenth Century: Syria Confronted with the European Economy', in Polk and Chambers (eds), *Beginnings of Modernization in the Middle East*, Chicago, IL: 1968.

Cohen, A. *Palestine in the 18th Century*, Jerusalem: 1973.

Cohen, M. 'Secret Diplomacy and Rebellion in Palestine, 1936–1939', *International Journal of Middle East Studies* 8, (1977): 379–404.

Conder, C. R., and H. H. Kitchener. *The Survey of Western Palestine* (4 volumes), London: 1881.

Cuinet, V. *Syrie et Palestine: géographie administrative, statistique, descriptive et raisonnée*, Paris: 1896.

Darwaza, M. I. *Nash'at al-Haraka al-'Arabiyya al-Haditha* (Development of the Modern Arab Movement), 2nd edition, Sidon: 1971.

Dawn, C. E. *From Ottomanism to Arabism*, London: 1973.

Durr, I. F. *Shefa 'Amr*, Beirut: 1988.

Dusterwald, D. 'The City in the Economic Life of Palestine', *Palnews*, Tel-Aviv: 1936.

Esco Foundation for Palestine. *Palestine: A Study of Jewish, Arab and British Policies* (2 vols.), New York, 1970.

Essaleh, S. *L'Etat actuel de l'économie syrienne*, Paris: 1944.

Esselmont, J. E. *Baha'ullah and the New Era*, London: 1923.

Fawaz, L. T. *Merchants and Migrants in Nineteenth Century Beirut*, Cambridge: 1983.

Ghunayyim, A. H. 'Thawrat al-Shaikh 'Izz al-Din al-Qassam' (The Revolt of Shaikh Izz al-Din al-Qassam), *Shu'un Falastiniyya* 6 (January 1972): 181–92.

Graham-Brown, S. 'The Political Economy of the Jabal Nablus 1920–48', in R. Owen (ed.), *Studies in the Economic and Social History of Palestine in the Nineteenth and Twentieth Centuries*, London and Basingstoke: 1982.

Granovsky, A. *The Fiscal System of Palestine*, Jerusalem: 1935.

Granovsky, A. *Land Policy in Palestine*, New York: 1940 (reprint, 1976).

Gross, N. *The Economic Policy of the Mandatory Government in Palestine*, Paper No. 816. Jerusalem: 1982.

Grunwald, K., and J. O. Ronall. *Industrialization in the Middle East*, New York: 1960.

HaCohen, D. *Time To Tell*, New York, London: 1984.

Haddad, Y. 'Al-Itijahat al-Wuhdawiyya fi Filastin fi 'Ahd al-Intidab al-Biritani' (Unity Orientations in Palestine during the British Mandate), *Shu'un Arabiyya* 8 (October 1981).

Hakim, G., and M. Y. El-Hussayni. 'Monetary and Banking System', in S. B. Himadeh (ed.), *Economic, Organization of Palestine*, Beirut: 1938.

Hamouda, S. *Al-Wa'yi wal-Thawra* (Awareness and Revolution), Jerusalem: 1985.

Hershlag, Z. Y. *Introduction to the Modern Economic History of the Middle East*, London: 1964.

Himadeh, S. B. 'Industry', in S. B. Himadeh (ed.), *Economic Organization of Palestine*, Beirut: 1938.

Al-Hoot, B. N. *Al-Qiyadat wal-Mu'asasat al-Siyassiyya fi Filastin 1917–1948* (Leadership and Political Institutions in Palestine 1917–1948), Beirut: 1981.

Hopkins, L. G. 'Population', in S. B. Himadeh (ed.), *Economic Organization of Palestine*, Beirut: 1938.

Hopwood, D. *The Russian Presence in Syria and Palestine 1843–1914*, Oxford: 1969.

Horowitz, D., and R. Hinden. *Economic Survey of Palestine*, Tel-Aviv: Economic Research Institute of the Jewish Agency for Palestine, 1938.

Hoskins, H. L. *British Routes to India*, London: 1966.

Hourani, A. H. *Minorities in the Arab World*, London: 1947.

Hourani, A. H. 'Ottoman Reform and the Politics of Notables', in his *The Emergence of the Modern Middle East*, London: 1981.

Hurewitz, J. C. *The Struggle for Palestine*, New York: 1968.

Al-Husri, S. *Yawm Maisalun* (The Day of Maisaloun), Beirut: n.d.

Hyamson, A. M. *Palestine Under the Mandate 1920–1948*, London: 1950.

Issawi, C. *An Economic History of the Middle East and North Africa*, New York: 1982.

Jacoby, F. J. (ed.). *The Anglo-Palestine Year-book 1946*, London: 1946.

Jadir, A. H. 'Siyasat Tawzi' Imtiyazat al-Mashari' al-kabira fi-Filastin Ayyam al-Intidab' (Policy of Distributing Large Concessions during the Mandate), *Shu'un Falastiniyya* 55 (March 1976): 184-205.

Jewish Community Council. *Kehilat Khaifa Beasar Hashanim, 1932–1941* (The Community of Haifa in the Ten Years 1932–1941), Haifa: 1942.

Kanafani, G. *Palestine: The 1936–1939 Revolt*, Tricontinental Society, London: n.d.

Kaufmann, R. 'Fundamental Problems of Haifa's Future Development', *Palestine and Near East Economic Magazine*, Vol. 3, No. 19 (October 1928): 433-6.

Kawtharani, W. *Watha'iq al-Mu'tamar al-'Arabi al-Awwal, 1913* (Documents of the First Arab Congress, 1913), Beirut: 1980.

Kayyali, A. W. (ed.). *Watha'iq al-Muqawama al-Filastiniyya al-'Arabiyya didd al-ihtilal al-Biritani wal Sahyuniyya* (Documents of the Arab-Palestinian Resistance to the British Mandate and Zionism), Beirut: 1968.

Kayyali, A. W. *Palestine: A Modern History*, London: 1978.

Kedourie, E. 'Religion and Politics: The Diaries of Khalil Sakakini', *Middle Eastern Affairs*, Number One (*St Antony's Papers* No. 4), London: 1958.

Khader, G. 'Arab Chambers of Commerce in Palestine', *Directory of Arab Trade, Industries, Crafts, Professions in Palestine and Trans-Jordan 1937–1938*, Chamber of Commerce, Jerusalem: 1937.

Khalidi, R. *British Policy Towards Syria and Palestine 1906-1914*, St Antony's Middle East Monograph No. 11, London: 1980.

Khalifa, A. (trans.). *Al-Thawra al-'Arabiyya al-Kubra fi Filastin, 1936–1939: Al-Riwaya al-Israeliyya al-Rasmiyya* (The Great Arab Revolt in Palestine 1936–1939: An Official Israeli Account), From Books of the Haganah, Vol. 2, Books 5, 6, Beirut: 1989.

Khuri, Q. *Al-Dhikrayyat* (Memories), Jerusalem: 1945.

Kisch, F. H. *Palestine Diary*, London: 1938.

Knightley P., and C. Simpson. *The Secret Lives of Lawrence of Arabia*, London: 1969.

Kupferschmidt, U. M. *The Supreme Muslim Council*, Leiden: 1978.

Lachman, S. 'Arab Rebellion and Terrorism in Palestine 1929-39: The Case of Sheikh Izz al-Din al-Qassam and his Movement', in Kedourie and Haim (eds), *Zionism and Arabism in Palestine and Israel*, London: 1982.

Lesch, A. M. *Arab Politics in Palestine, 1917–1939*, London: 1979.

Longrigg, S. H. *Oil in the Middle East*, London: 1954.

Mandel, N. 'Turks, Arabs and Jewish Immigration into Palestine, 1882–1914', in A. Hourani (ed.), *St Antony's Papers No. 17*, Oxford: 1965.

Mandel, N. *The Arabs and Zionism before World War I*, London: 1976.

Mansur, A. *Tarikh al-Nasira: Min Awwal 'Usuriha wa-hatta Ayyamina al-Hadira* (History of Nazareth from its Early Period until the Present), Cairo: 1924.

Mansur, G. *The Arab Worker under the Palestine Mandate*, Jerusalem: 1937.

Ma'oz, M. 'The Impact of Modernization on Syrian Politics and Society during the Early Tanzimat Period', in Polk and Chambers (eds) *Beginnings of Modernization in the Middle East*, Chicago, IL: 1968.

Marlowe, J. *Rebellion in Palestine*, London: 1946.

McCarthy, J. *The Population of Palestine: Population, History and Statistics of the Late Ottoman Period and the Mandate*, New York: 1990.

Meinertzhagen, R. *Middle East Diary, 1917–1956*, London: 1959.

Michaelis, A. 'The Industrial Development of Palestine', *Palnews*, Tel-Aviv: 1936.

Midland Bank. 'The Progress of Palestine', Midland Bank Review (November 1935).

Migdal, J. S. *Palestinian Society and Politics*, Princeton, NJ: 1980.

Miller, Y. N. *Government and Society in Rural Palestine, 1920–1948*, Austin, Texas: 1985.

Murad, A. R. *Safahat 'an Haifa wa Ma'rakatuha al-Akhira* (History of Haifa and its Final Battle), Damascus: 1991.

Nakhleh, K. and E. Zureik (eds). *The Sociology of the Palestinians*, London: 1980.

Nashif, T. 'Palestinian Arab and Jewish Leadership in the Mandate Period', *Journal of Palestine Studies*, Vol. 6 (iv) (1977): 113–21.

Nathan, R., O. Gass and D. Creamer. *Palestine: Problem and Promise*, Washington, DC: 1946.

Naval Intelligence Division (NID). *Palestine and Transjordan*, London: 1943.

Owen, R. *The Middle East in the World Economy 1800–1914*, London: 1981.

Peretz, D. 'Palestinian Social Stratification: The Political Implications', *Journal of Palestine Studies*, Vol. 7 (1978).

Playfair, I. S. O., G. M. S. Stitt, C. J. C. Molony and S. E. Toomer. *The Mediterranean and Middle East* (4 vols.), London: 1954.

Porath, Y. *The Emergence of the Palestinian Arab National Movement, 1918–1929*, London: 1974.

Porath, Y. *The Palestinian Arab National Movement, 1929–1939*, London: 1977.

Qasimiyyah, K. 'Mawaqif 'Arabiyya min al-Tafahum ma'al-Sahyuniyya 1913–1914' (Arab Approaches for Understanding Zionism 1913–1914), *Shu'un Falastiniyya*, Vol. 31 (March 1974): 127–49.

Qubʿain, N. Taqrir Tarikhi lil-taʾifa al-Injiliyya al-Usqufiyya al-ʿArabiyya bi-Haifa (Historical Report on the Arab Evangelical Episcopalian Community of Haifa), Haifa: 1940.

Rogers, M. E. Domestic Life in Palestine, London: 1863.

Rothschild, J. History of Haifa and Mount Carmel, Haifa: 1934.

Ruedy, J. 'Dynamics of Land Alienation', in I. Abu-Lughod (ed.), The Transformation of Palestine, Evanston, IL: 1971.

Ruppin, A. Syria: An Economic Survey, New York: 1918.

Ruppin, A. Three Decades in Palestine, Hartford, CT: 1936 (reprint, 1975).

St. Sauveur, A. Le Sanctuaire de Mont Carmel, Lille: 1897.

Said, E. W. The Question of Palestine, New York: 1979.

Sakakini, K. Kadha Ana Ya Dunya (Such I am, O World), Jerusalem: 1955.

Sawwaf, H. 'Foreign Trade' and 'Transportation and Communication', in S. B. Himadeh (ed.), Economic Organization of Palestine, Beirut: 1938.

Sayigh, R. Palestinians: from Peasants to Revolutionaries, London: 1988.

Schama, S. Two Rothschilds and the Land of Israel, London: 1978.

Schleifer, S. A. 'The Life and Thought of 'Izz-id-Din al-Qassam', Islamic Quarterly, Vol. 23, No. 2 (January/March 1979): 61–81.

Schölch, A. 'The Economic Development of Palestine', Journal of Palestine Studies, Vol. X, No. 3 (Spring 1981): 51–5.

Schölch, A. 'European Penetration and the Economic Development of Palestine, 1856–82', in R. Owen (ed.), Studies in the Economic and Social History of Palestine in the Nineteenth and Twentieth Centuries, Oxford: 1982; London, 1987.

Shamir, S. 'The Modernization of Syria: Problems and Solutions in the Early Period of 'Abdul-Hamid', in Polk and Chambers (eds), Beginnings of Modernization in the Middle East, Chicago, IL: 1968.

Al-Sharif, M. 'Muʾtamar al-ʿUmmal al-ʿArab al-Awwal' (The First Conference of Arab Workers), Shuʾun Falastiniyya, No. 50/51, October/November 1975: 293–302.

Shiffman, J. 'Building Activity in Palestine', Palnews, Tel-Aviv: 1935.

Shuqairi, A. Arbaʿun ʿAman fil-Hayat al-ʿArabiyya wal-Duwaliyya (Forty Years in the Arab and International World), Beirut: 1969.

Simon, H. J. British Rule in Palestine and the Arab Rebellion of 1936–1937, Chapel Hill, NC: 1977.

Smith, B. J. The Roots of Separatism in Palestine, Syracuse, NY: 1993.

Smith, C. D. Palestine and the Arab–Israeli Conflict, second edition, New York: 1992.

Smith, P. A. Palestine and the Palestinians 1876–1983, New York: 1984.

Stead, K. W. Report on the Economic and Financial Situation of Palestine, London: 1927.

Stein, K. W. The Land Question in Palestine, Chapel Hill, NC: 1984.

Stein, K. W. 'The Intifadah and the 1936–1939 Uprising', The Carter Center of Emory University, Occasional Paper Series, Vol. 1, No. 1 (March 1990).

Storrs, R. Orientations, London: 1943.

Szereszewski, R. Essays on the Structure of the Jewish Economy in Palestine and Israel, Jerusalem (The Maurice Falk Institute for Economic Research in Israel): 1968.

Tamimi, M. R., and M. B. Halabi. Wilayat Beirut, Beirut: 1335 H/1914.

Tannous, I. The Palestinians, New York: 1988.

Tibawi, A. L. Arab Education in Mandatory Palestine, London: 1956.

Tuma, E. *Sittun 'Aman 'ala al-Haraka al-Qawmiyya al-'Arabiyya al-Filastiniyya* (The Last Sixty Years of the Palestinian Arab National Movement), Beirut: 1978.

Vilnay, Z. *Khaifa Be'avar Ve Bahoveh* (Haifa in the Past and the Future), Tel-Aviv: 1936.

Wasserstein, B. *The British in Palestine: the Mandatory Government and the Arab–Jewish Conflict 1917–1929*, London: 1978.

Weinstock, N. *Zionism: False Messiah*, London: 1979.

Wilson, M. C. *King Abdullah, Britain and the Making of Jordan*, Cambridge: 1987.

Yacoub, M. H. *Nathra Jadida ila Tarikh al-Qadiyya al-Filastiniyya 1918–1948* (New Approaches to the History of the Palestinian Problem 1918–1948), Beirut: 1973.

Yasin, S. *Al-Thawra al-'Arabiyya al-Kubra fi-Filastin*, 1936–1939 (The Great Arab Revolt in Palestine 1936–1939), Cairo: 1959.

Yazbek, M. *Al-Hijra al-'Arabiyya ila Haifa* (Arab Migration into Haifa), Nazareth: 1988.

Zureik, E. 'Reflections on Twentieth-Century Palestinian Class Structure', in K. Nakhleh and E. Zureik (eds), *The Sociology of the Palestinians*, London: 1980.

Index

Abbas Effendi, 20, 43n47
'Abdul-Hadi family, 28, 31; Amin,
   165, 196, 201, 204
Abercrombie, Prof. P., 64
Abramson, Albert, 200
Abu Zaid family, 110, 120n46, 184
Abyad, 204
Acre, 15, 19, 20, 22, 27, 29, 33, 68, 74,
   106, 107
Advisory Council, 153, 154, 176, 183, 194
agreements, IPC concession, 75;
   Syria–Palestine customs (1921), 103
agriculture, 5, 23–4, 27, 34, 66, 81, 89,
   91, 98, 108, 155; *see also* cereals
'Ahduth Ha'avodah party, 220
Ahuza, 65, 124
'Ain Tura, 34
air base, 72
Alexandria, 30
Amery, L.S., 54–5
Andrews, L., 253
Anglo-Egyptian Bank, 56
Anglo-Palestine Bank, 99
'Anglophile Party', 165–7, 178n26, 28
Arab Agency, 154
Arab Bank, 100, 117n7
Arab Economic Development
   Association, 108
Arab Executive, 8, 86, 117, 152–4
   passim, 156, 172, 186–8, 190, 193,
   201, 208, 226–31 *passim*
Arabism, 37, 151, 161, 163, 165, 169;
   pan-, 32, 40, 42n22, 151–4 *passim*,
   162, 166, 217, 226, 229
Arabs, 6–10, 33–40, 85–6, 90–2,
   98–148, 151–261; *see also under*
   individual headings

Arab Youth Club (Nadi al-Shabab al-
   'Arab), 163
Ard al-Raml, 66, 129, 172; al-Yahud,
   250
Armenians, 17, 30
arms, 151, 155, 171, 173–4, 184, 218,
   219, 254
'Asfour, Hanna, 231, 234, 238n61, 244
Association of Brotherhood and
   Purity (Jam'iyyat al-Ikha' wa'l-
   'Afaf), 166
'Association of Muslim Youth', 188
Association for Produce of the
   Country (Haigud Letotseret
   Ha'aretz), 93
'Associations for Village Co-operation'
   (Jam'iyyat ta'awun al-qura), 187
Austria, 29, 37
awqaf, 31, 35, 152, 162, 191, 212n43

Bahai, 17, 20, 30, 33
al-Bahri, Jamil, 38, 227, 231
Baidas, Khalil, 33
Balfour Declaration, xi, 151, 154, 163,
   171, 186
Balfour, Lord, 174, 193
banking, 98–100, 110, 167; Ordinance
   (1921), 99
bankruptcies, 83, 111
Barclays Bank (DCO), 99, 106
Barghash, Iskandar, 196
Bat Galim, 65, 124, 172, 220
Bayside Land Corporation, 64, 70n6
Beirut, 7, 15, 16, 23, 30, 33–5 *passim*,
   37, 38, 40, 104, 185
Bek, 'Arfan, 39
'Black Hand' (al-Kaff al-Aswad), 163

276